China's Growth

China's Growth

The Making of an Economic Superpower

Linda Yueh

OXFORD
UNIVERSITY PRESS

OXFORD
UNIVERSITY PRESS

Great Clarendon Street, Oxford, OX2 6DP,
United Kingdom

Oxford University Press is a department of the University of Oxford.
It furthers the University's objective of excellence in research, scholarship,
and education by publishing worldwide. Oxford is a registered trade mark of
Oxford University Press in the UK and in certain other countries

First Edition published in 2013

Impression: 1

British Library Cataloguing in Publication Data

Data available

ISBN 978–0–19–920578–3

Printed in Great Britain by
Clays Ltd, St Ives plc

Preface

There is a book that every academic hopes to write that captures the arc of their work. For me, this is the one. *China's Growth* is the culmination of years of research into what drives the impressive improvement in the standard of living in the world's most populous nation that has propelled it to become the world's second largest economy. In other words, what makes an economic superpower.

Helping me along the way are too many to thank individually, but I would like to mention a few. My appreciation goes to the British Academy whose funds enabled me to collect key data that underpin the micro-level analysis that sheds light on the macroeconomic context for growth. I am also deeply grateful to the Shaw Foundation for their support of the China Growth Centre (CGC) that I direct at St Edmund Hall in the University of Oxford. The international conferences held at the CGC, including with the China Centre for Economic Research (CCER) at Beijing University, and seminars with leading scholars have generated thought-provoking discussions that have enriched this volume. My gratitude also goes to the retired former Oxford head of economics John Knight, Li Shi now at Beijing Normal University, previously at the Chinese Academy of Social Sciences (CASS), and Yang Yao of CCER for their long-standing collaboration with me to generate original data in China. Finally, I wish to acknowledge the superb research assistance provided by Xiao Mei Li, Ryan Manuel, among many others, over the years.

This book includes work started during my PhD to that completed in the research centre that I founded. It is the final of a trilogy of books on China's economy. The first was *The Economy of China*, which offered an overview of economic development. It was followed by another book published by Oxford University Press, *Enterprising China*, that showed how business, economics, and law evolved during reforms. This volume on growth completes the set and sets the stage for the next phase, with China poised as the next economic superpower.

Contents

List of Figures   xi
List of Tables   xiii
List of Abbreviations   xvi

1. Introduction   1
  1.1 Introduction to the Book   1
  1.2 Literature on China's Economic Growth   7
    1.2.1 *New Growth Theories: Institutions*   7
    1.2.2 *Neoclassical Growth Model: Factor Accumulation and TFP*   9
    1.2.3 *Endogenous Growth: Human Capital*   10
    1.2.4 *'Catch-up' Growth: Technology*   12
    1.2.5 *Summary of Growth Determinants*   16
  1.3 Structure of the Book   17

2. New Growth Theories: Transition and Institutional Change   19
  2.1 Introduction   19
  2.2 China's Approach to Economic Reform   23
  2.3 Creating Property Rights   25
    2.3.1 *Institutional Innovations*   25
    2.3.2 *Contractually Defined Rights*   27
    2.3.3 *Enforcement*   28
    2.3.4 *The Limits of the Informal System*   29
  2.4 Legal Reforms   30
  2.5 The China Paradox   32
    2.5.1 *Law and Markets*   34
    2.5.2 *An Evolutionary View of Legal and Economic
Development in China*   39
  2.6 A Comparative Perspective of Legal Development and Markets   40
    2.6.1 *Chinese Law*   40
    2.6.2 *Laws and Markets: China and the USA*   41
    Patent Laws and Economic Growth   45
    Corporate Law and Economic Necessity   47
    Regulatory Reform Supporting Markets: China's
CSRC and the US SEC   49
    Complementarities Between Law and Markets   51

Contents

2.7 Enforcement of Laws 52
2.8 China's Legal and Economic Reform in an Era of
Global Integration 53
2.8.1 *Expectations of Foreign Firms* 54
2.8.2 *WTO Law and Formal International Rules* 55
2.8.3 *Assessment of the Law and Economic Relationship* 56
2.9 Economic Growth, Laws, and Global Integration 57
2.10 Conclusion 58

3. Neoclassical Growth: Labour Productivity and Corporate
Restructuring 60
3.1 Introduction 60
3.2 Labour Productivity 60
3.3 Reforming Labour 64
3.4 Measuring Labour Productivity 69
3.5 Determining Labour Productivity 77
3.6 Allocative Versus Technical Efficiency 87
3.7 Corporate Restructuring 90
3.8 Incorporation and Ownership Reform 92
3.9 Data 95
3.9.1 *Panel Dataset* 95
3.9.2 *Ownership Forms* 96
3.10 Drivers of Firm Performance 98
3.11 Implications for Industrial Output 106
3.12 Conclusion 108

4. Endogenous Growth: Human Capital and Labour Market Reforms 110
4.1 Introduction 110
4.2 Labour Reforms 110
4.3 Wage Reforms 111
4.4 Human Capital Investment 113
4.5 Job Mobility 122
4.5.1 *Modelling Differential Mobility* 125
4.5.2 *Measuring Mobility* 127
4.5.3 *Impact of Reforms* 131
4.6 Migrants and Discrimination 142
4.7 Conclusion 152

5. 'Catch-up' Growth: Technology Transfers and Innovation 154
5.1 Introduction 154
5.2 Foreign Direct Investment Spillovers 155
5.3 Chinese–Foreign Joint Ventures 157
5.4 Estimating Technology Transfers 161

5.5 Economic Growth Implications 167
5.6 Innovation and Patents 169
5.7 Patents, Foreign Investment, and Growth 171
5.8 Effectiveness of Patent Laws 173
5.9 Determinants of Innovation 177
5.10 Conclusion 183

6. Informal Growth Determinants: Self-Employment and
Social Capital 184
  6.1 Introduction 184
  6.2 Social Capital and *Guanxi* 184
  6.3 Social Capital and Incomes 192
  6.4 Self-employment and Social Networks 204
    6.4.1 *Credit and Supply Networks* 206
    6.4.2 *Navigating an Uncertain Institutional Environment* 206
  6.5 Choosing Self-employment 207
    6.5.1 *Determinants of Self-employment* 216
    6.5.2 *Self-employed as Second Job* 225
    6.5.3 *Unemployment Impact* 225
  6.6 Conclusion 227

7. Financial and Legal Development: The Role of Private
Enterprises in Growth 231
  7.1 Introduction 231
  7.2 China's Private Enterprises 234
  7.3 Motivations of Entrepreneurs 236
  7.4 Legal Constraints and Financial Repression 248
  7.5 Private Firms and Provincial Legal Development 253

8. Global Integration and Growth: Rebalancing the Economy 256
  8.1 Introduction 256
    8.1.1 *Joining the World Economy* 257
    8.1.2 *The Exchange Rate* 260
  8.2 The China Effect 261
    8.2.1 *Becoming a Large, Open Economy* 263
    8.2.2 *China 'Going Global'* 265
  8.3 Global Imbalances 267
    8.3.1 *Changed Global Economy* 271
    8.3.2 *Genesis of a Crisis* 275
    8.3.3 *Global Reserve Currency* 279
    8.3.4 *Global Rebalancing* 280
  8.4 Rebalancing China 281
    8.4.1 *Structure of the Chinese Economy* 284

8.4.2 *The Salter-Swan Framework*   286
8.4.3 *Policy Reforms*   292
    Household Savings   293
    Corporate Savings   295
8.5 Conclusion   296
Appendix: Deriving the CCE Curve in the Salter-Swan Model   297

9. Conclusion: The Role of the State   301
    9.1 Introduction   301
    9.2 China's Visible Hand   303
    9.3 Reforming State-owned Enterprises   304
    9.4 The Non-level Playing Field   309
    9.5 High Savings and Labour Misallocation   312
    9.6 Costs of Distortions   314
    9.7 The Next Phase of Growth   315
    9.8 Optimal Size and Scope of the Chinese State   316
    9.9 Conclusion   318

Bibliography   321
Index   341

List of Figures

2.1	Real GDP growth in China, 1979–2011	20
2.2	China's nominal GDP as compared with G7 countries, 1980–2011	20
2.3	Economic growth and policy milestones	21
2.4	Patents in China	58
3.1	GDP per worker in manufacturing (1980 = 100), 1980–2005	62
3.2	Comparative labour productivity (USA = 100), 2005	62
3.3	Shares of employment by ownership sector	66
3.4	Industrial output shares of ownership types	68
3.5	Labour productivity levels for Chinese firms, 2000–5	72
3.6	Labour productivity levels for foreign-invested firms, 2000–5	72
3.7	Labour productivity by ownership type, 2000–5	83
3.8	Openness of province by year (% of GDP)	87
3.9	Shares of industrial output of foreign-invested enterprises	88
3.10	Simulated deflated industrial output assuming no incorporation of firms	107
5.1	Patents and real GDP per capita	174
6.1	Frequency distribution of the size of network	189
8.1	Real GDP growth, world and major economies, 1980–2011	271
8.2	Current account balances (% of GDP)	273
8.3	Current account balances (% of world GDP)	274
8.4	Global foreign exchange holdings, 1998–2008	274
8.5	Global reserve holdings of advanced and emerging economies, 1998–2008	276
8.6	US base interest rates, 2000–9	278
8.7	Yields on 10 Year Treasuries, 2000–9	278
8.8	China's macroeconomy	282
8.9	China's exports and imports	283
8.10	Exports as share of GDP	284
8.11	Savings in China (% of GDP)	285
8.12	Gross capital formation (% of GDP)	286

List of Figures

8.13 Salter-Swan framework   288

8.14 Long-run equilibrium in Salter-Swan   290

8.15 Sectoral composition of GDP   294

8.16 Return on assets on Chinese firms   295

9.1 Share of urban employment by enterprise type   307

List of Tables

2.1 Rule of law   36

2.2 Regulatory quality   37

2.3 Investor protection   38

2.4 Property rights and freedom from corruption   38

2.5 A comparative perspective of US and China economic and
legal development   43

3.1 Labour productivity in comparative perspective, 2005   63

3.2 Urban employment   67

3.3 Distribution of industrial sectors   70

3.4 Levels and growth rates of labour productivity   71

3.5 Average firm characteristics   74

3.6 Average firm characteristics per worker   75

3.7 Percentage of listed companies   76

3.8 Export share of output   76

3.9 Estimates of labour productivity   80

3.10 Estimates of labour productivity with heterogeneous
productivity growth   81

3.11 TFP growth by ownership   84

3.12 TFP by industrial sector   85

3.13 Openness and foreign presence in provinces   86

3.14 Labour sectoral shifts   89

3.15 Transformation into incorporated firms   97

3.16 Summary statistics   98

3.17 Mean differences in performance measures before and
after incorporation   99

3.18 First-stage propensity score matching   103

3.19 The impact of incorporation on firm performance   104

3.20 Estimations using Levinsohn-Petrin production function   105

3.21 The impact of incorporation on firm performance excluding listed firms   105

3.22 The impact of incorporation on firm performance controlling for privatization   106

4.1 Intra-household resource allocation model of expenditure on children's education   116

4.2 Determinants of income for working-aged individuals   119

4.3 Educational attainment of spouses in urban China   121

4.4 Predicted mean annual household income of children   122

4.5 Average and median tenure for select countries   123

4.6 Urban residents: determinants of mobility rates   130

4.7 Job separations for urban residents   132

4.8 Determinants of latent mobility for immobile individuals   134

4.9 Determinants of mobility for mobile and potentially mobile individuals   135

4.10 Determinants of earned income for employed individuals   137

4.11 Transition matrix for urban residents   140

4.12 Change in the urban labour market, 1994–2000   144

4.13 Managerial attitudes towards migrants   148

4.14 Urban worker attitudes towards migrants   149

4.15 Logit estimation of the determinants of urban worker's beliefs   150

5.1 Ownership types   158

5.2 Firm, provincial descriptive statistics   158

5.3 Total domestic and foreign direct investment in China, 1984–2007   163

5.4 Production functions (OLS)   164

5.5 Production functions (instrumental variables)   166

5.6 Patents and GDP per capita by province, 2002   175

5.7 Patent grant rate by province, selected years   176

5.8 Determinants of patents in China   179

5.9 Determinants of patents in China by region   182

6.1 Size of social networks and Communist Party membership for urban sample   188

6.2 First-stage instrumenting regressions: predicting social network and Communist Party membership   191

6.3 Income equations for working-aged employed individuals   195

6.4 Income equations for employed individuals, by age cohort   199

6.5   Income equations for employed individuals, by ownership
      sector of employer   201

6.6A Descriptive values: main sample   209

6.6B Descriptive values: sample with experience of unemployment   210

6.7   First-stage regression results for instrumental variable approach 215

6.8   Determinants of self-employment, urban sample, multinomial
      logit regression   217

6.9   Determinants of self-employment as a second job, urban sample,
      multinomial logit regression   220

6.10 Determinants of self-employment as a second job, urban sample,
      multinomial probit regression   222

6.11 Determinants of self-employment, unemployed sub-sample,
      multinomial probit regression   228

7.1   Conditional means of entrepreneurs   239

7.2   Socio-economic factors influencing urban entrepreneurship   244

7.3   Socio-economic factors influencing migrant entrepreneurship   247

7.4   Legal factors influencing entrepreneurship   249

7.5   Results of the 3SLS estimates   251

7.6   Determinants of provincial entrepreneurship   254

9.1   Share of total industrial output by enterprise type   306

9.2   Number of state-owned enterprises   306

9.3   Government expenditure as share of GDP, 2000–10   316

List of Abbreviations

2SLS	two-stage least squares
3SLS	three-stage least squares
ADR	alternative dispute resolution
BIS	Bank for International Settlements
BRS	Budgetary Responsibility System
BRW	bargained real wage curve
CASS	Chinese Academy of Social Sciences
CBRC	China Banking Regulatory Commission
CCE	competing claims equilibrium
CIETAC	China International Economic and Trade Arbitration Commission
CIRC	China Insurance Regulatory Commission
COE	collectively owned enterprises
COFER	Composition of Official Foreign Exchange Reserves
CPI	consumer price index
CRS	Contract Responsibility System
CSRC	China Securities and Regulatory Commission
DSU	dispute resolution mechanism
ETDZ	Economic and Technological Development Zones
FDI	foreign direct investment
FIE	foreign-invested enterprise
FSB	Financial Stability Board
FTZ	Free Trade Zones
GDP	gross domestic product
GLS	general least squares
GMM	generalized method of moments
HMT	Hong Kong, Macau, and Taiwan
HRS	Household Responsibility System
HTDZ	High-Technology Development Zone
ICT	information and communications technology

IFI	international financial institutions
IIA	independence of irrelevant alternatives
IPO	initial public offerings
IPR	intellectual property rights
IV	instrumental variables
JV	joint venture
JVTT	joint venture with technology transfer
LLC	limited liability company
LLP	limited liability partnership
LP	Levinsohn-Petrin
M&A	mergers and acquisitions
MFN	most favoured nation
MLE	maximum likelihood
MNC	multinational corporation
MOL	Ministry of Labour
MOST	Ministry of Science & Technology
NAIRU	non-accelerating inflation rate of unemployment
NBS	National Bureau of Statistics
NERI	National Economic Research Institute
NOCs	National Oil Companies
NYSE	New York Stock Exchange
OLS	ordinary least squares
OPC	Open Port Cities
PBOC	People's Bank of China
PPP	purchasing power parity
PQML	Poisson quasi maximum likelihood
PRW	price determined real wage
QFII	Qualified Foreign Institutional Investor
R&D	research and development
SASAC	State-owned Assets Supervision and Administration Commission
SCB	state-owned commercial bank
SEC	Securities and Exchange Commission (USA)
SEZ	Special Economic Zone
SIP	share issue privatization
SIPO	State Intellectual Property Office
SME	small- and medium-sized enterprises

List of Abbreviations

SOE	state-owned enterprise
SURE	seemingly unrelated regression estimation
SWF	sovereign wealth funds
TFP	total factor productivity
TRIPs	trade-related intellectual property
TVE	township and village enterprise
VA	value-added
WFOE	wholly foreign-owned enterprises
WTO	World Trade Organisation

1

Introduction

1.1 Introduction to the Book

China has accomplished a remarkable feat in transforming itself from one of the poorest countries in the world into the second largest economy in just thirty years. Growing at an average of an impressive 9.6 per cent per annum since market-oriented reforms began in 1979 which transformed the previously centrally planned economy, China has not only doubled its GDP and income every seven to eight years, it has also lifted 660 million people (or one-tenth of the world's population) out of abject poverty. With its 1.3 billion people accounting for one-fifth of the global population, China's economic growth has begun to shape the world and yet the determinants of its successful development are far from established or well-understood.

China, like other large countries, has fairly unique economic drivers. It is a transition economy that has dismantled most, but not all, of its state-owned enterprises and banks. It is also a developing country where half of its population is rural and in large parts agrarian; agriculture, even in decline as a share of GDP, accounted for 40 per cent of rural employment in 2010. China is also an open economy whose trade-to-GDP ratio was about 70 per cent in the 2000s, making it substantially more globally integrated than other comparable-sized open economies, such as the UK (37 per cent). It also does not fit well into the studies of institutions and growth, as China remains a Communist state dominated by the Chinese Communist Party. It is therefore unsurprising that the rule of law and other market-supporting institutions, such as private property protection, are weak, as there is no independent judiciary, giving rise to the so-called 'China paradox' where the country has grown well despite not having a well-developed set of institutions (see Yao and Yueh 2009). China's economic growth is therefore in many respects both impressive and puzzling. It is also, like any other rapidly growing economies, not assured of sustaining such economic growth.

The book examines the drivers of China's impressive development and rise as a potential economic superpower. The focus is on the microeconomic determinants that offer a more detailed picture behind the theory and evidence of China's economic growth. Data at the household and firm level are more reliable than the aggregate statistics, and can shed light on the details of the key growth drivers. A key theme of the book is that the structure of the economy is as important as the standard growth factors. And the best view of the structure is from the microeconomic perspective of firms and households.

Whether it has to do with reforming the state-owned enterprises or dismantling the allocated labour market or promoting exports, structural change modifies the traditional drivers of economic growth. An example is that China is not an industrializing country; it was already industrialized in the centrally planned period before 1979, thus was so since the start of the reform period. It is the re-industrialization process of upgrading obsolete machines and factories into more advanced ones that explains much of the continuing capital accumulation that has accounted for about half of its economic growth. In other words, China's growth can be explained by the standard economic models, but with additional features that are specific to its unusual institutional context. Another example is that neoclassical growth models emphasize factor accumulation of labour and capital as determinative of the steady state of the economy (the level of output given the people and savings of the country) whilst technology and productivity growth increase the rate of growth. In China's case, productivity is not only driven by technology but also by factor re-allocation; for example, the structural change of labour migrating from state-owned to private industries. The process of factor reallocation exists within the industrial sector, so it is not just captured by the urbanization and industrialization processes described by the Lewis model and others which explain how developing countries grow. It is but one feature of the complex background of China being both a transition and a developing economy. This is also why total factor productivity (or TFP) growth is often difficult to interpret because this measure covers both technologically driven as well as one-off productivity improvements, such as those related to privatization (moving capital from state-owned to private ownership), which are all counted as part of the residual in growth estimations that is considered TFP.

In terms of endogenous growth models including human capital, the Chinese experience is more straightforward, with the exception that the 'iron rice bowl' meant that the lifetime employment system prevented the relatively good levels of educational attainment and skills from being rewarded and also impeded labour mobility that reduced the matching of productive workers to the most appropriate jobs. Thus, human capital models which consider only the standard measures of educational levels will miss the allocative improvements from labour market reforms that finally rewarded human capital and contributed to China's impressive economic growth. Those improvements are captured in microeconomic studies of the returns to human capital and the changes occurring at the level of the changing labour market.

Moreover, China's context further confounds straightforward interpretations of the theories that link 'openness' to the global economy with economic growth. These explanations centre on the positive correlation between greater opening and faster development. The mechanisms include how the experience of exporting and accessing global markets can induce competitiveness improvements, as well as 'learning' from foreign investors with more advanced technology and know-how. It would enable a developing country like China to 'catch up' in its growth rate if it can imitate the existing technology embodied in foreign capital, the classical avenue through which countries achieve convergence in their growth rates according to the Solow model.

Again, the theories require adapting to China, as they do for many other countries. China is an open economy but exercises elements of control that prevents direct competition in its domestic economy and utilizes a policy toward foreign direct investment (FDI) that furthers its own active industrial policies to develop domestic companies. As such, the simple openness measure that underpins the models of openness and growth do not fully capture the nature of China's 'open-door' policy that introduced market-oriented reforms in the external sector first in 1978, which then accelerated from 1992.

Restrictions of its exchange rate and capital account while seeking technology transfers from FDI mean that several metrics are needed to calibrate the influence of opening on growth. For instance, FDI supplemented domestic investment, accounting for as much as one-third of all investment, at the start of the reform period when China was a poor country with a low rate of household saving of only 10 per cent of GDP. Foreign direct investment was also thought to be a source of productivity improvement, particularly via the Chinese–foreign joint venture policy that required transfers of technology to the Chinese partner as a condition of approval to produce in China. Furthermore, estimating those FDI spillovers requires firm-level data to estimate productivity. The joint ventures and other foreign-invested enterprises (FIEs) were also explicitly geared toward exports. They were initially located in Special Economic Zones (SEZs), which were created as export-processing zones that were similar to the export-oriented growth models of its East Asian neighbours.

China thus became integrated with East Asia, as it joined regional and global production chains, and eventually became the world's largest trader. The focus on exports and the fixed exchange rate plus the restrictions on the other side of the balance of payments for a high saving economy, though, contributed to large current account surpluses by the 2000s at a time when the United States became a large deficit country. By the late 2000s, China formed part of the global macroeconomic imbalances where the surplus countries (China, Asia, and the Middle East oil exporters) and the main deficit country (the United States) experienced growing and seemingly unsustainable imbalances. Therefore, analysing China as an export-led growth model would explain only part of its success and also misplace China amongst the theories which are geared towards small, open economies like those in East Asia. The global imbalances and other aspects of the 'China effect' (impact on global prices) point to the need to examine China as a large, open economy that affects the global terms of trade in order to understand the role of openness in its economic growth.

The other part of technological progress derives from innovation. Technology in endogenous growth models is generated by a knowledge production function and not treated as an exogenous shock in that innovation is created by research-ers within the model. This also applies to China particularly as it increased its focus on patents and investment in research and development (R&D) since the mid-1990s. Endogenous growth theories, including some variants of the human capital models, attempt to explain why some countries innovate and develop technologies that underpin a sustained rate of economic growth that is not subject to the usual diminishing returns. In other words, knowledge builds upon knowledge (the so-called 'standing on shoulders' effect) generating increasing returns, and unlike factor accumulation that is subject to decreasing returns per unit of investment. These models have been applied to the United States in particular which has been not only the world's largest economy but also the standard setter for the technological frontier. However, there has only been limited empirical support (see for example, Jones 1995, who finds that a larger number of US researchers does not increase innovation or growth). For China, where researchers and scientific personnel are numerous, this strand of theories can potentially help explain its sustained rate of growth, although being farther from the technology frontier means that it may be a phenomenon of the 2000s rather than earlier in the reform period.

The application of the institutions and growth theories to China is perhaps among the most complex. The predominant view is that market-supporting institutions (those which protect property rights and provide contracting secur-ity) and an effective rule of law support can thus drive strong economic growth (see for example, La Porta et al. 1997, 1998; Acemoglu, Johnson, and Robinson 2005). China is generally not included in the studies that argue for a causal relationship whereby good institutions lead to growth (see for example, Acemo-glu, Johnson, and Robinson 2005), as it does not have a colonial past with which to establish the exogeneity of its institutions. In this methodology, specific instruments related to colonial history are relied upon to address the reverse causality relationship whereby countries that grow well could develop good institutions rather than vice versa. Nevertheless, China has been measured against the rule of law and legal origins studies (see for example, Allen, Qian, and Qian 2005) and found to be a paradox in having a weak legal system but strong economic growth. This genre of models was proposed to try and explain why some countries grow faster than others, as existing growth theories did not seem able to account fully for the differential growth of countries in the post-Second World War period.

However, China as an 'outlier' requires a closer examination as to how markets were enabled given the poor formal legal system. Specifically, the informal institutional reforms of the various 'dual track' policies that created a market alongside an administered track were important when applied to agriculture and the state-owned enterprises (SOEs), but these 'institutional innovations' were seemingly sufficient to instil incentives short of formal law-based reforms. But even in terms of legal protection, China's adoption of laws in some key respects was not too dissimilar to that of the United States at a similar stage of economic development. The institutional theories of growth therefore apply to China, but its precepts again need to be modified to consider the effective role played by incremental legal and institutional improvements. This is particularly important when examining the development of the crucial private sector, which had been stymied by the preferential policies towards state-owned enterprises even after the mid-1990s reforms significantly reduced state ownership.

The role of informal institutions such as social capital also cannot be overlooked. Entrepreneurship relied on social networks or *guanxi* to overcome the lack of well-developed legal and financial systems. It is also the case that the cultural proclivity towards interpersonal relationships meant that social capital played a key part in understanding the development of self-employment and the impressive rise of the private sector. Measuring and quantifying social capital requires detailed individual and household-level surveys rather than aggregate-level studies.

Finally, to sustain a good rate of growth for another thirty years, which is a stated aim of China's, will require not only technological and human capital improvements, but also reform of its rule of law, the role of the state, and the rebalancing of its economy. Rebalancing the economy will involve boosting domestic demand (consumption, investment, government spending) to grow more quickly than exports, shifting toward services (including non-tradable areas) and away from agriculture, increasing urbanization to increase rural incomes, and permitting greater external sector liberalization, including the internationalization of the renminbi (RMB). To achieve these aims will also require examining the role of the state in China and the legal system. The retention of large SOEs and the increasingly perceived 'non-level playing field' for both foreign and domestic private firms raises doubts as to the efficiency of China's markets and thus its ability to overcome the 'middle-income country trap', whereby countries start to slow after reaching upper-middle income levels. For China to realize its potential as an economic superpower requires reforms of both the microeconomic drivers of productivity as well as significant transformation of the structure of its economy.

There are understandable concerns about the nature of China's macroeconomic statistics available to address these key questions. But its micro-level data are superior. Due to the decades of central planning that accounted for most households including in rural areas and the continuing close surveillance of its large and medium-sized enterprises (defined as those with 5 million RMB and above in revenue), household and firm-level data are closely checked and yield more satisfactory results than those generated by aggregate statistics alone. The need to understand the micro foundations of macroeconomics is prevalent in the economic discipline in any case. Where macro patterns are seen, it requires a finer analysis of household and firm behaviour to interpret aggregate trends, such as why labour reallocation has ceased to be as important as a productivity driver by the 2000s, or why the savings rate increased during the reform period, that are premised on analysing the behaviour of households and firms. It is the same for China as for other economies. As such, this book will draw on micro data to provide firm and household-level evidence to support the macroeconomic findings where possible. It is an approach that suits both the nature of Chinese data and the trend in the economic growth and macroeconomic literature.

This book will therefore aim to explain China's growth by examining the portions of growth that are explained by the various economic models and further identify and argue that there are specific aspects of China's transition and development which must be considered alongside the standard theories. China's growth does not fall outside of the standard growth drivers, but there are structural features to its transition and development which warrant a closer examination. Plus, micro-level estimations will provide further evidence; for example, earnings functions, production functions, measures of social capital, legal development, etc. A closer examination of the detailed findings based on those household and firm estimations as well as a qualitative view of structural factors can shed light on the most plausible interpretations. For instance, the productivity differentials generated by the corporatization policy that was used to transform the state-owned enterprises into shareholding companies can help explain the strong industrial output growth during the 2000s at a time when thirty years of industrialization would presumably have resulted in slower and not faster growth as compared to the earlier decades but for this structural change in the industrial sector.

The estimations will support the theme of the book that China's context, though unique, does not imply that economic growth models do not explain its success in the reform period. Rather, its being a transitioning and developing country that is following an export-oriented growth strategy whilst adopting rapid structural reforms must temper any direct application of the theories. Understanding these elements will identify the theories that can best explain China's growth since 1979. This book will review the best available evidence concerning growth and its drivers, as well as provide original, micro-level findings that can add further insight to the observed macro trends.

Next, this chapter will review the general literature on China's economic growth before subsequent chapters examine each key aspect in detail. The literature review covers the four main growth theories. First, new growth theories are assessed before turning to neoclassical growth models. This is followed by reviewing endogenous growth theories, particularly the importance of human capital. Technology as a growth driver is then reviewed both as a result of innovation and generated from imitation of existing know-how. The section concludes with breaking down the contributions of various growth drivers; for example, the role of capital accumulation, human capital/ education, technology, etc. The final part of the chapter will set out the structure of the book and reiterate its key themes of investigating China's productivity determinants and the role of structural transformation in its past and future economic growth.

1.2 Literature on China's Economic Growth

1.2.1 *New Growth Theories: Institutions*

The link between institutional development and economic growth has risen in prominence as a factor to explain the unexplained portions of growth (Acemoglu, Johnson, and Robinson 2005), although economists have long been interested in the role of institutions in explaining economic transition and growth (North 1990). The inability to explain long-run differences in growth has motivated a return to this subject, which was also revived by the instability of transition economies in the former Soviet Union when they underwent market-oriented reforms. China's underdeveloped institutions but relatively stable transition and remarkable growth rate make it an outlier in much of this literature, suggesting that analysis of China's growth has much to add to the understanding of how institutions interact with economic growth.

The late twentieth century witnessed the transformation of numerous centrally planned economies around the world into market-based systems. Many of these transitions were characterized by 'Big Bang' (Hoff and Stiglitz 2004) that combined economic liberalization with rapid privatization and democratization. The theory is that growth will accelerate with the removal of the inefficient and distortionary state and the introduction of market forces (Persson and Tabellini 2006). The result was a transformational recession whereby these nations underwent a decade-long period of contraction and stagnation in the immediate aftermath of shedding central planning.

By contrast, China followed a rather different path where economic reform and transition towards a market economy occurred without democratization. Liberalization proceeded only incrementally and privatization was delayed by almost two decades after the initiation of market-oriented reforms. China's gradual approach to reform has resulted in high and relatively stable growth rates for over three decades (Prasad and Rajan 2006). This remarkable growth performance was accompanied by a relatively undeveloped legal and financial system, which makes China a puzzle or paradox given the focus of economists on the importance of well-defined legal and formal institutions. La Porta et al. (1997, 1998, 2000) study the relationship between law and finance, and consequently economic development, and highlight the importance of legal institutions. According to Allen, Qian, and Qian (2005), China seems like 'a counterexample to the findings in law, institutions, finance and economic growth literature'. They document the poor legal protection of minority shareholder interests and outside investors as well as the dominant role of the state public sectors, and yet China managed to outperform other economies which score well on those measures.

Hasan, Wachtel, and Zhou (2009) examine the roles of legal institutions, financial deepening, and political pluralism on growth rates. The most important institutional developments for a transition economy are the emergence and legalization of the market economy, the establishment of secure property rights, the growth of a private sector, the development of financial sector institutions and markets, and the liberalization of political institutions. They develop measures of these phenomena, which are used as explanatory variables in regression models to explain provincial GDP growth rates. Their evidence suggests that the development of financial markets, legal environment, awareness of property rights, and political pluralism are associated with stronger growth. Based on a sample of thirty-one Chinese provinces for the period 1986–2003, their results indicate that those regions with better rule of law, more property rights awareness, and more political pluralism also have stronger growth. After controlling for the province-specific effects, endogeneity, and potential problems associated with weak instruments, the data suggest a strong, positive link between institutional development and economic growth in China, suggest that a one standard deviation increase in relative pluralism is associated with a 0.6 percentage point increase in the growth rate.

There are a large number of other studies that examine the disparities among provinces as a way of identifying the determinants of growth in China (see for example, Liu and Li 2001), but few include the role of institutions. However, there are a few studies that look at province-level data on financial sector development and the private sector. Chen and Feng (2000) find that growth of private and semi-private enterprises leads to an increase in economic growth, while the presence of SOEs reduces growth rates among the provinces based on their sample twenty-nine Chinese provinces from 1978 through 1989. Aziz and Duenwald (2002) and Boyreau-Debray (2003) find little influence of financial sector depth at the provincial level on growth primarily because little credit growth in the 1990s went to the private sector. In the latter part of the reform period, Liang (2005) and Hao (2006) find evidence that financial depth and the reduced role of government both positively influence provincial growth rates. In addition, Biggeri (2003), using provincial-level data for the period 1986 to 2001, finds that the level of aggregate output in each province is negatively influenced by the presence of state-owned enterprises, a proxy for the extent of the economy transforming into a market-oriented one. These studies of inter-provincial differences in growth indicate that the effort to measure institutional development is warranted. Allen, Qian, and Qian (2005) compare growth in the formal (state-owned and publicly traded firms) and the informal sector and find that the latter is the source of most economic growth even though it is associated with much poorer legal and financial mechanisms. They argue that there exist effective informal financing channels and governance mechanisms, such as those based on reputation and relationships (social networks), to support this growth.

An additional channel of financial sector influence on growth is through the capital markets, which also rely on institutions such as corporate governance and regulatory structures. Stock markets accelerate growth by facilitating the ability to trade ownership and by allowing owners to diversify portfolios easily. Rajan and Zingales (1998) argue that financial development facilitates economic growth by reducing the costs of external finance to firms; their empirical evidence from a cross-country study supports this rationale. Further, in terms of private sector development, Guiso, Sapienza, and Zingales (2004) find that differences in local financial development can explain the spread of entrepreneurship and economic growth. Zhang, Wan, and Jin (2007) provide evidence of financial depth effects on productivity growth at the provincial level in China. Rousseau and Xiao (2007) find that stock market liquidity and banking development are positively associated with growth for China (see also Rousseau and Wachtel 2000).

1.2.2 Neoclassical Growth Model: Factor Accumulation and TFP

China's rapid economic growth has stimulated a wide-ranging debate as to whether it is driven by productivity growth or by capital and labour factor accumulation. Some find evidence of a clear improvement of total factor productivity (TFP) in the reform period. Specifically, the increase in TFP contributes about 40 per cent to GDP growth, roughly the same as that contributed by fixed asset investment (Borensztein and Ostry 1996; Hu and Khan 1997; Jefferson, Rawski, and Zheng 1992; Yusuf 1994). Others conclude that economic growth in China is mostly driven by capital investment (Chow and Lin 2002; Wu 2003). For instance, Chow and Lin (2002) showed that the increase in TFP contributed 29 per cent of GDP growth during 1978 to 1998, compared to a 62 per cent contribution by capital (see also Chow 1993; Borensztein and Ostry 1996; Young 2003; Wang and Yao 2003; Islam, Dai, and Sakamoto 2006). Hu and Khan (1997) found that an average TFP growth of 3.9 per cent explained more than 40 per cent of China's growth during the early reform period. The studies, though, concur that capital accumulation contributes about half of GDP growth. The share of TFP is less clear.

There is one trend that most studies agree on; that is, the slowdown in TFP after the mid-1990s. For instance, the World Bank (1997) estimates that TFP growth accounted for 30 to 58 per cent of China's growth during 1978–95 but less after 1995 (see also Zheng, Bigsten, and Hu 2009). There are numerous explanations, but the slowdown after 1995 coincides with sluggish rural income growth and widespread industrial inefficiency. The OECD (2002) considers part of the reason to be that human capital, land, and other resources were misallocated, under-employed, and inefficiently used. Growth thus increasingly relied on capital accumulation since the growth of labour had also declined from 2.34 per cent from 1978–95 to 1.07 per cent for 1995–2005.

Zheng and Hu (2006) estimate that TFP growth fell dramatically during 1995–2001, accounting for as low as only 7.8 per cent of GDP growth. Whereas TFP had risen by 3.2 to 4.5 per cent per year before 1995, it rose by only 0.6 to 2.8 per cent per year afterwards. The OECD (2005) estimated that annual TFP growth averaged 3.7 per cent during 1978–2003, but slowing to 2.8 per cent by the end of that period. Young (2003), though, argues that on official figures it is 3 per cent but would adjust it downwards to 1.4 per cent from 1978–98.

Explanations for changes in TFP growth are often controversial, but the slowdown during 1995–2005 coincides with sluggish rural income growth and widespread inefficiency as well as the waning of one-off, reallocative effects. From the late 1970s to the early 1990s, China's growth depended more on productivity growth and less on increased capital than other East Asian countries at a comparable stage of their development. However, since then, growth in capital inputs has exceeded GDP growth often substantially. The issue is whether TFP has slowed down, or there were one-off productivity gains associated with reform. This measurement is also perhaps why there is such wide disagreement as to whether China's growth is based on true productivity improvements. To investigate it further, Zheng, Bigsten, and Hu (2009) examined reform measures and found that they often resulted in one-time level effects on TFP; for example, movement of capital from state-owned to private enterprises.

A similar trend affected labour productivity. Jefferson, Hu, and Su (2006) explore the sources of China's growth covering the period, 1995–2004, and conclude that there is evidence of improved allocative efficiency from labour moving out of agriculture and between industrial and ownership sectors resulting in productivity advances. Brandt and Zhu (2010) come to a similar conclusion, but find that the reallocation effect weakens in the 2000s. Yet, labour productivity accelerated in the 2000s. In my estimations, moving labour out of the state sector contributed 8.5 per cent of the total average labour productivity growth of 9.2 per cent in the 2000s (Yueh 2010c). The predominant factor (accounting for around 85–92 per cent) of labour productivity growth in the 2000s is due to improvements in technical efficiency, which are promising as a basis for sustained growth. It does, though, again suggest that the early measures of TFP include the one-off gains from sectoral reform. As that waned, TFP appeared to be slowing down but there was some mismeasurement in the earlier period since prior growth data included allocative gains from reform and not true productivity growth driven by increased efficiency and technological progress.

1.2.3 *Endogenous Growth: Human Capital*

Compared to capital investment and TFP, the increase in the supply of labour has generally been found as a less important growth factor for China. The one-child policy slowed down population growth and the high degree of labour force participation limited labour as a source of factor accumulation driving growth. Perhaps also as a result, there are fewer studies of the contribution of human capital to China's growth rate. This set of models internalize human capital as the source of productivity and technology advancements that implies that endogenous growth occurs when there are improvements in human capital. Technological progress is thus explained by the accumulation of education, skills, training, etc. and not left as the unexplained portion of growth as in the neoclassical models.

Although it has long been believed that human capital plays a fundamental role in economic growth, studies based on cross-country data have produced surprisingly mixed results (Barro 1991; Mankiw, Romer, and Weil 1992; Benhabib and Spiegel 1994; Islam 1995; Pritchett 2001; Temple 2001). For instance, Barro (1991), Benhabib and Spiegel (1994), Barro (2001), and Bils and Klenow (2000) find that the initial stock of human capital has a larger impact on the growth rate than the improvement in human capital. The exception is Gemmell (1996) who finds that both the stock and accumulation of human capital were significant determinants of growth. In addition, human capital had both a direct effect on growth and an indirect effect through physical capital investment. One reason for the mixed findings is that the impact of education has varied widely across countries because of very different institutions, labour markets, and education quality making it hard to identify an average effect (see Temple 1999; Pritchett 2001).

It is widely hypothesized that human capital has a direct role in production through the generation of workers' skills and also an indirect role through the facilitation of technology spillovers. The incorporation of a measure of human capital 'inside' the production function is based on micro-level evidence that better educated workers are more productive. Most studies use different measures of human capital such as secondary-school enrolment, student–teacher ratio, spending on education and science, and the number of science and technology workers.

China's economic growth is largely labour-intensive with high levels of fixed capital investment (Arayama and Miyoshi 2004; Chow 1993; Yusuf 1994). Differentiating the portion from human capital is essential as growth driven by education and skills improvements has the potential to be sustainable due to the associated increase in productivity, technological innovation and diffusion (Aghion and Howitt 1998; Lucas 1988; Romer 1990). During China's reform period, 10 to 20 per cent of GDP growth may be attributable to the growth of the labour force, a less important source of factor accumulation than capital which accounts for about half, as discussed earlier (Chow and Lin 2002; Hu and Khan 1997; Wu 2003).

In terms of separating out human capital, Wang and Yao (2003) find that capital, labour, human capital, and TFP each accounted for 48, 16, 11, and 25 per cent, respectively, of GDP growth during the period 1978–99 for China. Most studies rely on provincial data and compare cross-province growth determinants. In about the same period of 1978–98 using provincial data, Arayama and Miyoshi (2004) similarly find that human capital contributes about 15 per cent to China's growth. This is again confirmed by Qian and Smyth (2006); using provincial data for 1990–2000, they find that the contribution of human capital to GDP growth was 13 per cent while physical capital contributed 55 per cent and TFP growth accounted for 22 per cent. Comparing across twenty-eight provinces from 1978–2005, Li and Huang (2009) concur that education (quality measured as teacher–pupil ratio and educational attainment) and health both positively contribute to provincial growth rates. Démurger (2001) also finds evidence that education at the secondary or college level helps to explain differences in provincial growth rates.

However, these studies have not differentiated between the stock and accumulation of human capital (Krueger and Lindahl 2001). Chi (2007) distinguished between the stock and accumulation of human capital as well as the potential endogeneity of physical asset investment, and finds that the effect of human capital on China's economic growth may be indirect through physical capital investment, using provincial data from 1996 to 2004. He finds that investment in fixed assets is endogenous as 84 per cent of variation across provinces may be explained by the initial human capital stock and wealth levels. Moreover, the number of graduates who have college or above level education is a more important determinant of physical capital investment decisions than the number of workers with primary or secondary education.

Fleisher and Chen (1997) also specifically separate out the effect of the stock of human capital on TFP. They measure human capital as the percentage of university graduates in the population, and find that it had a significant effect on total factor productivity. Chen and Feng (2000) use a similar measure and find that human capital is a significant determinant of differential provincial growth rates. Fleisher, Li, and Zhao (2010) also show how regional growth patterns in China depend on regional differences in physical, human, and infrastructure capital as well as on differences in foreign direct investment flows. They find that human capital affects output and productivity growth positively across provinces. Moreover, they find both direct and indirect effects of human capital on TFP growth. The direct effect is hypothesized to come from domestic innovation activities, while the indirect impact is the spillover effect of human capital on TFP growth (see also Liu 2009a, 2009b, who finds an impact of human capital on productivity in both rural and urban China).

Using a less technical approach but one that is highly informative and suggestive, Sonobe, Hu, and Otsuka (2004) show that subtle and important changes in quality control, efficient production organization, and marketing of manufactured goods among emerging private enterprises have been more likely to occur in firms where managers have acquired relatively high levels of education. Using firm-level data to obtain a more precise gauge of this hard-to-measure but important aspect of how human capital can endogenously drive growth, Fleisher and Wang (2001, 2004) find evidence that highly educated workers have significantly higher marginal product than workers with lower levels of schooling incorporating these qualitative factors.

1.2.4 'Catch-up' Growth: Technology

There have also been a number of studies on the role of technology on innovation in China. The government during the latter part of the reform period recognized the importance of innovation and enacted a patent law in 1985 and a slew of associated copyright and trademark legislation subsequently. Since the imposition of tougher intellectual property rights (IPR) requirements with WTO

(World Trade Organisation) accession in 2001, Chinese firms have devoted more resources to innovative activities gradually and acted aggressively on patent applications (Hu and Jefferson 2009). But, in the early part of the reform period, China's policies were geared at attracting FDI and promoting trade in order to benefit from the positive spillovers of technology and know-how that characterizes the 'catch-up' phase of development, whereby a country learns and imitates rather than re-invents or innovates as it is far from the technology frontier.

There are several arguments as to the mechanism through which FDI and trade boost economic growth (Gylfason 1999). One of the widely recognized views is that FDI and trade are technology spillover channels for absorbing advanced knowledge. One of the benefits from FDI is that new technology is brought in by foreign firms. Technology transfer occurs through two channels— new technologies sold directly through licensing agreements or the transfer of new technology to exporters from their foreign purchasers. Alternatively, international trade also generates technology externalities through learning-by-exporting or imitating technologies embodied in the imported intermediate goods. There is also a productivity effect from facing greater competition at a global level. The argument that FDI and international trade serve as major driving forces contributing positively to China's faster growth during the late 1980s to mid-1990s is well recognized (Chen, Chang, and Zhang 1995; Harrold 1995; Liu, Burridge, and Sinclair 2002; Pomfret 1997; Shan 2002).

For China, FDI has facilitated the transformation of the state-owned and the collective sectors (Liu 2009c). The location of FDI is also encouraged by exogenous geographical and political factors such as proximity to major ports, policy decisions to create special economic zones and free trade areas, local institutional characteristics such as laws and regulations, contract enforcement, local expenditure on infrastructure, schools, etc., and by labour market conditions. Using city-level data, Wei (1993) arrives at the conclusion that FDI contributes to economic growth through technological and managerial spillovers between firms as opposed to simply providing new capital. This is supported by studies such as by Dees (1998), Sun and Parikh (2001), and Wei (1993) who conclude that inward FDI affects China's economic growth in ways beyond simple capital formation.

Indeed, FDI has played an important role in both China's TFP and its fast growth. The classic catch-up mechanism in neoclassical growth models is for capital to flow from developed to developing countries bringing with it technology and know-how. China has certainly been the recipient of a large amount of FDI since its 'open-door' policy took off in the early 1990s. And FDI appears to have had positive effects on its growth. Using econometric methods to regress GDP (or GDP growth) on FDI and other variables, a large number of studies find a positive and significant coefficient on FDI, concluding that foreign investment has played a notable part in China's GDP growth (Tseng and Zebregs 2002; Lemoine 2000; Berthelemy and Demurger 2000; Graham and Wada 2001; Chen, Chang, and Zhang 1995; Liu, Burridge and Sinclair 2002; Wei 1993; Dees 1998;

Sun and Parikh 2001; Wei et al. 1999; Borensztein, De Gregorio, and Lee 1998). Whalley and Xin (2010) further examine the role of foreign-invested enterprises. FIEs are often joint ventures between foreign companies and Chinese enterprises, and account for over 50 per cent of China's exports and 60 per cent of China's imports. Without FDI inflows in 2004, they estimate China's overall GDP growth rate would be lower by around 3.4 percentage points. Excluding investors from Hong Kong, Macao, and Taiwan, FIEs still account for around 30 per cent of China's GDP growth.

Fleisher, Li, and Zhao (2010) find that FDI had a much larger effect on TFP growth before 1994 than after, and they attribute this to the encouragement and increasing success of private firms. After 1994, they find a much smaller, even insignificant, economic impact of FDI. They conjecture that the drop in the impact of FDI after 1994 can be attributed in part to the encouragement of the non-state sector. Since then, private and 'red cap' enterprises (nominally rural collectives, but in fact privately owned) and the evolution of township and village enterprises (TVEs) from collectives to *de facto* private firms have become relatively more important sources of growth, while the relative importance of FDI-led growth has declined. Consistent with this conjecture, Wen (2007) reports that at least since the mid-1990s, FDI has tended to crowd out domestic investment, more so in the non-coastal regions. A similar finding is reported for the early 2000s by Ran, Voon, and Li (2007).

But there is likely to be a degree of endogeneity in these relationships between FDI and TFP growth if TFP growth encourages FDI (Li and Liu 2005). A number of studies conclude that technology transfers and the spillover effects are limited, and much if not most of the correlation between FDI and superior economic performance is driven by reverse causality (Young and Lan 1997; Woo 1995; Lemoine 2000). Woo (1995) argues that the role of FDI in spillover effects is overstated because foreign investment is located in liberalized regions. Rodrik (1999) also expresses doubts over spillover effects, arguing that greater productivity in domestic firms in producing for exports does not necessarily suggest efficiency spillovers from foreign firms, since more productive firms, domestic or foreign, tend to locate in export sectors.

Turning to R&D, studies of the roles of research and development, spillovers, and absorptive capacity on growth are limited in China. Using provincial data covering the period 1996–2002, Lai, Peng, and Bao (2006) find that domestic R&D has a positive and statistically significant impact on economic growth, although that study does not include the external effects of technology imports. Their estimates also indicate that international technology spillovers depend on the host province's absorptive ability as measured by human capital investment and degree of openness. Brun, Combes, and Renard (2002) attempt to test for the existence of provincial spillover effects, although their concept of regional spillover is of 'regional growth spillover effects' rather than 'regional technology spillovers'. Utilizing a panel dataset of twenty-eight provinces covering the period of 1981–98, they find that spillover effects have not been sufficient to reduce disparities across Chinese provinces in the short run. Kuo and Yang

(2008) also assess how and to what extent knowledge capital and technology spillover contribute to regional economic growth in China. Moreover, a region's absorptive ability is considered as they measure the critical capability to absorb external knowledge sources embodied in FDI and imports, which then contribute to the regional economic growth; for example, the absorptive capacity of human capital on using acquired advanced foreign technologies. They find that knowledge capital, both in terms of R&D capital and technology imports, contribute significantly, with similar magnitude, to regional economic growth. There are also suggestions of the existence of R&D spillovers as well as international knowledge spillovers. R&D has a positive impact on regional growth with an estimated magnitude of R&D elasticity of 0.043, indicating that a 1 per cent increase in R&D capital would raise regional GDP about 0.043 per cent, controlling for other variables.

Along these lines, Dobson and Safarian (2008), using the evolutionary approach to growth in which institutions support technical advance and enterprises develop capabilities to learn and innovate, examine China's transition from an economy in which growth is based on labour-intensive production and imported ideas and technology to one in which growth is driven by domestic innovation, and find the increasing competitive pressure on firms that encourage learning. Their survey of privately owned small and medium enterprises in five high-tech industries in Zhejiang province found a market-based innovation system and evidence of much process and some product innovations. These enterprises respond to growing product competition and demanding customers which intensive internal learning, investment in R&D, and a variety of international and research links. Zheng, Liu, and Bigsten (2003) find that TFP growth in China has been achieved more through technical progress than efficiency improvement.

Without question, the role of international knowledge spillovers in generating endogenous economic growth has been long-emphasized in theory; for example, Grossman and Helpman (1991). And a growing trend in empirical studies finds that international technology spillover is one of the major sources of productivity growth (see Coe and Helpman 1995; Eaton and Kortum 1996; Keller 2000). The mixed studies in China and elsewhere point to a measurement void. But this crucial and still underexplored issue could provide evidence for the possibility of more sustainable growth for China in the coming decades. In Van Reenen and Yueh (2012), we investigated the impact using a specially designed dataset with measures of technology spillovers at the Chinese firm level (see also Chapter 5).

Working on the premise that capital accumulation has accounted for about half of China's real GDP growth of 9.6 per cent per annum since 1979, Van Reenen and Yueh (2012) find that the contributions of Chinese–foreign joint ventures (JVs) of 9 per cent and FDI as a whole accounting for 15 per cent of investment translate into between 0.42 to 0.71 percentage point additions to growth. In other words, had China not attracted FDI, China would have grown by up to three-quarters of a per cent slower, bringing the average growth rate down to 8.9 to 9.2 per cent. Adding in the productivity boost of JVs, they are 23 per cent more productive as compared with other firms and JVs with technology transfer agreements hold a 73 per cent productivity advantage. As JVs comprise 15 per cent of all firms in the 2000s, China's GDP has been increased by between 3.45 per cent and 10.95 per cent, respectively. Translating this into growth terms (and assuming a cumulative process starting in 1979 for the increase in GDP by 2009) means that average growth would have been lower by 0.43 per cent per annum by 2009 if there had not been JVs.

Putting all this together, we calculate that had China not attracted FDI and JVs in particular with their potential to allow for 'catching up' via technology transfers and other indirect avenues of learning, then China's annual GDP growth could have been between one-half to over 1 percentage point slower, that is, as low as 8.5 per cent, over the past thirty years. As JVs were more important as a share of investment during the 1990s, accounting for around one-quarter of total investment, this is a conservative estimate. The contribution of joint ventures is therefore sizeable, as one percentage point in compound growth terms translates into large differences in income levels, as countries like India which has grown at 7–8 per cent instead of China's 9 to 10 per cent over the past few decades can attest. China has surpassed its Asian neighbour even though it was poorer in 1980.

1.2.5 Summary of Growth Determinants

Capital accumulation accounted for 3.2 percentage points of the 7.3 per cent growth in output per worker from 1979–2004 with TFP accounting for 3.6 percentage points (Bosworth and Collins 2008). From 1993–2004 since the take-off of the 'open-door' policy, capital accumulation has accounted for 4.2 percentage points of the higher 8.5 per cent growth in China, and interestingly outweighs the contribution of TFP (3.9 percentage points). Both estimates suggest that capital accumulation has contributed around half of China's economic growth, which is in line with other estimates that find that most of China's growth is accounted for mostly by capital accumulation rather than TFP growth during the reform period thus far.

Labour accumulation accounts for much less: 10 to 20 per cent of GDP growth may be attributable to the growth of the labour force. Human capital accounts for a similar, even slightly less, proportion of between 11 to 15 per cent of China's growth. Factor accumulation (capital and labour) thus accounts for about 60–70 per cent of GDP growth. Once human capital is accounted for, TFP contributes much less.

Within TFP, there is a need to separate the one-off productivity gains due to factor reallocation from the efficiency-driven improvements. By the 2000s, labour reallocation accounted for 8–15 per cent of TFP gains but with higher contributions in the decades before. It is similar for capital and could explain the decline by about one-third in TFP after the mid-1990s. Thus, these calculations imply that around 8 per cent of China's GDP growth is driven by factor reallocation, leaving about 7–21 per cent that is explained by efficiency gains driven not by one-off but sustained productivity improvements.

And of those efficiency improvements, Van Reenen and Yueh (2012) show that GDP growth would be lower by between 0.43 to 1 per cent per annum if not for joint ventures that allowed for transfers of knowledge and technology, the 'catch-up' mechanism as opposed to domestic innovation. Positive spillovers and imitation of existing know-how thus could account for between one-third to two-thirds of TFP. It implies that TFP driven by innovation and technological progress not traced to FDI accounts for about 5 to 14 per cent of GDP growth. Given the poverty of China when it started market-oriented reforms in 1978 and the apparent 'catch-up' potential, this is not surprising. It does mean, though, that after thirty years of development, China's promising reorientation towards R&D and innovation and will need to bear fruit to sustain a strong growth rate in the coming decades.

1.3 Structure of the Book

The book is structured to apply the above models and also introduce the micro-level evidence that goes beyond the standard theories to help explain China's strong economic growth. The second chapter focuses on the new growth theories. It starts with this latest set of models from the economic growth literature that places greater emphasis on institutions and transition. The following chapter covers neoclassical growth models, but emphasizes drivers that are specific to China; namely, the importance of factor (labour and capital) reallocation in generating productivity improvements. Chapter 3 thus covers both the reallocation of labour from state to non-state enterprises, and the effects of corporate restructuring as assets and firms shift from public ownership into private hands.

Chapter 4 turns to endogenous growth theories and focuses on human capital as a growth driver. It examines how significant labour market reforms in terms of wages, mobility, migrants versus urban residents, have generated beneficial returns to human capital that have in turn increased productivity in the economy. More is still left to do in terms of improving labour mobility and matching workers to jobs, but the incentives gained by moving away from the allocated employment system have been a key part of the growth path for China. The next chapter focuses on technology, both from 'catching up' via technology transfers and in terms of China's own domestic innovation that is evident in the rapid growth increase in patents during the latter half of the reform period. Both sets of drivers suggest that technological improvements are a key part as to why China has grown so well and may continue to do so as it shifts from the imitation phase to innovating its own technological developments that are essential to sustain growth.

The following two chapters examine the informal growth determinants and the imperfect legal institutional structures in China. Chapter 6 analyses self-employment and the role of social networks and capital in facilitating the all-important development of the non-state sector. Chapter 7 then adds in the financial and legal impediments against starting private firms. Entrepreneurs and small- and medium-sized enterprises (SMEs) are important drivers of growth for any economy. For China, the development of the private sector is all the more crucial as it is partly the reason why the reform of state-owned enterprises could be gradual and preserve stability during the transition. Nevertheless, the challenges faced by private businesses are considerable.

Chapter 8 investigates the role of opening to the global economy, including the consequences of contributing to global macroeconomic imbalances and the challenges of rebalancing the Chinese economy. With the global financial crisis of 2008 and the slow recovery of the West, the issue of rebalancing the Chinese economy away from excessive reliance on exports has certainly come to the forefront. This chapter examines the need for macroeconomic restructuring in China as it looks ahead to the next thirty years and sees the need to reform the economy to be more balanced towards its own burgeoning middle class and to develop multinational corporations. This is all in an effort to overcome the so-called 'middle-income country trap' whereby economies slow down considerably once they reach middle-income levels and fail to reach the ranks of rich countries.

The final chapter of the book examines the role of the state, a recurring issue that has changed considerably during the reform period. The state has exited many parts of the economy as the market has developed rapidly. But its reach continues to be wide although more opaque. And, in a number of respects, the state has created an non-level playing field for foreign and domestic private Chinese firms. The concluding chapter analyses the state in China and posits how it needs to reform to help the country achieve its aim of growing strongly for another thirty years. If China manages to do so, it has every opportunity to become the world's next economic superpower. This book details its making, its unparalleled transformation, and its remaining challenges.

2

New Growth Theories: Transition and Institutional Change

2.1 Introduction

China has been a remarkably successful economy since its adoption of market-oriented reforms at the end of 1978, some thirty years ago. Figure 2.1 shows that China's real GDP growth has averaged over 9.5 per cent per annum since then.

Figure 2.2 shows the rapidity with which China has propelled itself to become the world's second-largest economy. It is also the most populous nation, a leading destination for foreign direct investment (FDI), and the largest global exporter. Concomitantly, it is a developing country with a per capita GDP that only exceeded US$1,000 this past decade and has around 100 million people living in poverty. Despite its aggregate size, China's per capita GDP of just over US$4,000 or US$7,000 (when adjusted for purchasing power parity) suggests that it has substantial growth potential, since its average income is substantially below that of OECD countries of comparable size.

It is often observed that China's strong economic growth has taken place in the midst of uncertain property rights and arguably high transaction costs, which defies the usual depiction of efficient markets in the traditional (Coasian or Walrasian) economic sense (see for example, Jefferson and Rawski 2002) supported by the rule of law (see for example, Acemoglu, Johnson, and Robinson 2005). Its gradual approach to transition from central planning has resulted in a partially reformed economy within a communal property state. This particular path raises questions about the foundations of China's increasingly decentralized economy and its ultimate sustainability. By contrast, with rapid liberalization toward a private economy, property rights would have been established quickly and allowed for efficient exchange, in theory. China's incremental reform process has left it with poorly defined property rights and high transaction costs, and yet economic growth has been rapid.

Yet, the process of transition and the importance of institutional change can't be underestimated in terms of shaping China's growth trajectory. This chapter will detail the so-called 'institutional innovations' which allowed the state to

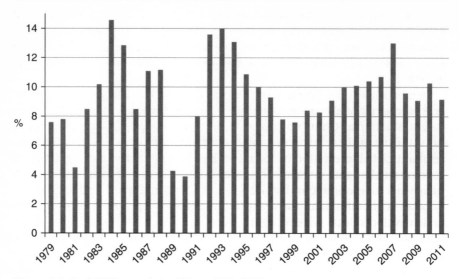

Figure 2.1 Real GDP growth in China, 1979–2011
Source: China Statistical Yearbook.

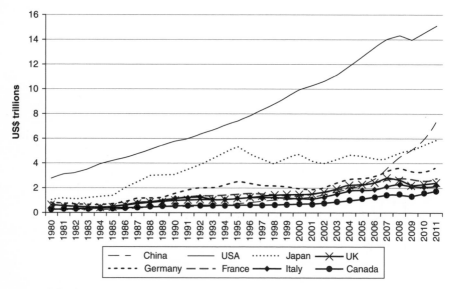

Figure 2.2 China's nominal GDP as compared with G7 countries, 1980–2011
Source: IMF.

create property rights without a change in ownership from public to private. But, as the economy became increasingly complex due to increased market-ization, legal reforms played a greater role in the decentralized market, such as through the creation of regulatory agencies which enabled capital market development. The underdeveloped legal system is itself part of the 'paradox' of China's growth, while a detailed examination will show that China's legal reforms have been somewhat underappreciated, although a great deal more in terms of reforming their effectiveness is needed for the second thirty years of growth.

Membership in the World Trade Organisation (WTO) also introduced elements of international economic law which sped up the legal reforms and further decentralization as China's accession terms included acceptance of global trade rules, including those governing intellectual property rights (IPRs). In turn, the resultant global integration increased the need for more laws and regulation to govern fast-changing markets. This process has culminated in an evolutionary framework for economic and legal reform in China that is not dissimilar to that of other economies at an early stage of market development with an initially underdeveloped legal system (see for example, Franks, Mayer, and Rossi 2009), but has distinct elements such as the eventual need to extend protection to the *de facto* private property created through decades of institutional innovations in a formal context of communal property ownership.

Figure 2.3 traces the major policy milestones which created first the informal institutional reforms that instilled incentives into China's economy without

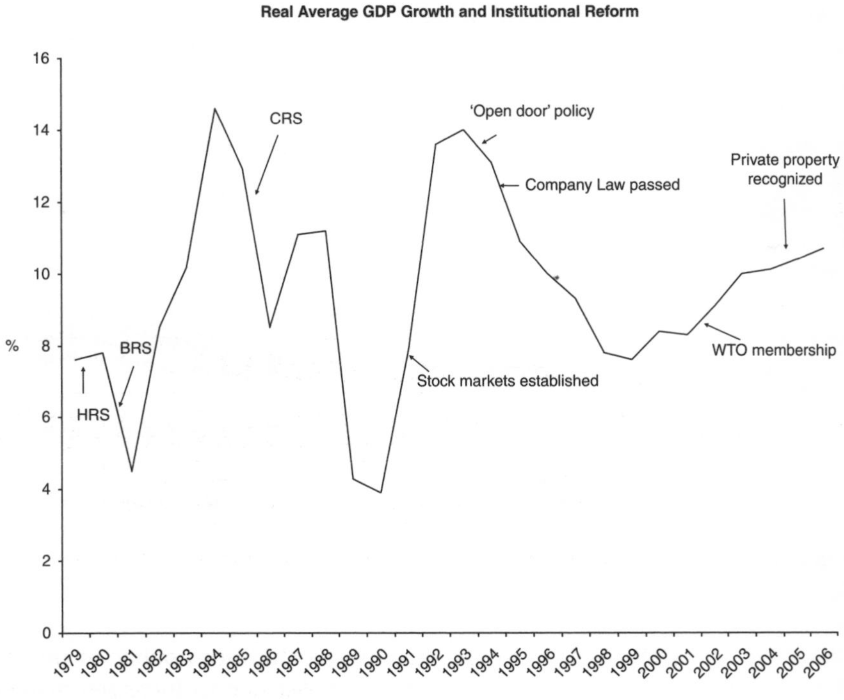

Figure 2.3 Economic growth and policy milestones

Source: *China Statistical Yearbook*, and author's research.

privatization, and highlights the eventual adoption of formal legal reforms. The 'institutional innovations', which were informal institutional arrangements that gave profit incentives to farmers, state-owned enterprises (SOEs), and even local governments, are highlighted as the Household Responsibility System (HRS) in 1979 which lasted until 1984, Budgetary Responsibility System (BRS) starting in 1980, the Contract Responsibility System (CRS) which began in 1981 and lasted until the late 1980s alongside direct lending by state-owned commercial banks (SCBs). The more formal institutional and legal reforms that China adopted to create incentives for economic activity included the 'open-door' policy that took off in 1992 which created for foreign investors the legal entities of Chinese, formal joint ventures (JVs) as vehicles for their investment; the creation of the two stock exchanges in Shanghai in 1990 and Shenzhen in 1991; the passage of the Company Law in 1993 that heralded the era of legally defined corporations, and eventually the restructuring of the state sector into shareholding companies; and membership of the World Trade Organisation in 2001 which introduced international economic laws into China and ushered in a period of rapid regulatory reform such as by creating agencies like the China Banking Regulatory Commission (CBRC) to govern increasingly globally integrated markets. Finally, China recognized private property in its constitution in 2004 and gave equal protection to private and public property in the Property Law of 2007, heralding an era of more formal, legal rights in its property ownership system although it is a long way still from being a system of private ownership with effective rather than just formal legal protection extended to such property rights.

This is a broadbrush overview of institutional reforms in China and there have been numerous other policy initiatives that have taken place. Some of the main legal/institutional and economic reforms will be discussed in this chapter, whose aim is to assess the interplay between these factors in explaining thirty years of strong growth in China. This is an attempt to address the notion that Chinese growth has been without institutional foundations.

This chapter sets out how institutionally and contractually defined rights were sufficient to support China's economic growth in its initial stages, particularly as this approach suited the gradualist transition path. As China becomes increasingly marketized, though, there are limits to using informally defined rights and a growing need for explicit legal reforms. These contractually and institutionally defined rights have the additional advantage of not relying on formal mechanisms for enforcement as they are not clearly rooted in the Chinese legal system, but can be enforced informally through social and business relationships or sometimes through contractually defined measures such as binding arbitration. In other words, villagers know the implicit ownership of farm land despite public ownership, while foreign investors are aware that their rights are defined in the contract and disputes are often settled outside of formal litigation. For instance, although subject to the Chinese legal system, Chinese–foreign joint ventures are often entered into with trusted parties and sometimes externally enforced through international arbitration procedures. It helps to explain the China 'paradox' of strong growth and a weak rule of law. A comparison, though, of China and the US at a comparable stage of development shows that not all legal development is lagging in China, but that China lacks an effective rule of law in crucial parts of the economy and further reforms are needed.

This chapter will proceed as follows. The first part is a review of China's economic reform strategy and why the institutional innovations appeared to have enabled China's rapid growth in the earlier part of the reform period, particularly in the 1980s. This is followed by an evaluation of China's creation of certain forms of property rights (such as corporatization via the Company Law of 1993) in the course of its transition in the 1990s. Then the chapter will turn to the legal reforms which have at times accompanied economic reforms and include an international dimension with China's WTO accession and greater opening to the world economy in the 2000s. The paradox between strong growth and weak laws will be explored. The chapter then assesses the implications of this approach for China's growth prospects and global integration, including the influence of international laws and rules.

2.2 China's Approach to Economic Reform

China's approach to economic growth must be viewed within the context of its status as a transition economy that is also a developing country. China has been in transition for more than thirty years from a centrally planned economy, which had followed Soviet-style heavy industrialization for a time, toward becoming a marketized economy. China adopted its reforms gradually or incrementally during this period. By so doing, it has phased in market forces into an administered economy but without a fundamental ownership transformation into a privately owned economy.

Economic reform in China is a partial reform strategy, which has been characterized by institutional innovations and regional experimentation (for example, Qian and Xu 1993; Fan 1994). Reform began in the countryside and the early successes were seen in the creation of township and village enterprises (TVEs) in rural areas, a classic development challenge of a lagging agrarian sector. TVEs injected industry and market orientation into the rural economy, which was endowed by abundant and surplus labour. Further, the Household Responsibility System gave residual ownership to farmers so that they could earn a return on their effort within a framework of communal ownership of land. These reforms reoriented national saving to households, injected incentives into an economy that did not recognize private property, and reallocated the essential factor of labour to more productive enterprises. Output grew rapidly in the early 1980s as seen in Figure 2.1, leading to the observation that China's growth began in the countryside (Riskin 1987).

When these measures were seen to be successful, China introduced further reform into urban areas in 1984. The 'experiments' with market processes in the countryside gave the authorities confidence to do so since overall stability was maintained while economic activity was incentivized. Managers in state-owned enterprises were granted more autonomy and allowed to retain a portion of profits by use of a further institutional innovation known as the Contract Responsibility System. Wage reform introduced a performance element into pay (Yueh 2004).

Stability is viewed as essential in maintaining a 'dual-track' transition. In allowing enterprises to sell part of their output at market prices, the authorities must be able to control the sale of goods to the administered part of the market in order to implement a partial liberalization strategy (Murphy, Shleifer, and Vishny 1992). At the same time, China sustained a degree of decentralization that permitted experiments to take place so that market-oriented reforms could be introduced without affecting the economy as a whole (Qian and Xu 1993). This approach further allowed the authorities to adapt practically to changing circumstances rather than follow a prescribed plan of reform.

The final prong of China's reform approach is the 'open-door' policy. China created Special Economic Zones (SEZs) initially in southern coastal provinces, which were essentially export-processing zones that were open to inter-national trade and foreign investment (Lardy 1998). The introduction of market forces into SEZs allowed the government to experiment with a limited degree of opening. These measures began in 1979, but did not take off until 1992 when Deng Xiaoping took a tour of the earliest SEZs in Fujian and Guangdong. Since then, China has created further forms of SEZs, such as Free Trade Zones and High-Technology Development Zones (HTDZs), which are geared at attracting foreign investment in technology sectors and promot-ing research and development (R&D). The SEZs gave foreign investors a degree of legal protection that was not enjoyed by Chinese enterprises, and was sufficient to induce significant amounts of inward FDI into China despite an otherwise poor legal system. China has been transformed from an economy with an export-to-GDP ratio of 15 per cent in 1990 to an impressively open 30 per cent by the year 2000. In the span of a decade, China reached the global market share of the East Asian 'tiger' economies at the peak of their export-led growth.

Therefore, China's gradual transition has been characterized by an ability to inject market-oriented incentives across a myriad of sectors in the economy without wholesale privatization and instead was achieved through numerous 'institutional innovations' that enabled economic growth but did not result in macroeconomic instability, for example, the rise in unemployment often seen in transition economies. China's 'dual-track' approach in which one part of the market was liberalized while another was kept under administrative control depended on the creation of rights to retain returns from the marketized part of the economy. The next section will trace those attempts to create sufficient property rights to enable market-based activity without a change in ownership from public to private.

2.3 Creating Property Rights

For rural residents, SOEs and multinational corporations, China's instillation of incentives took the form of 'institutional innovations' and contractually defined rights for the latter, such as those which created the JV vehicles for foreign investors. By gradually building institutions that were not an overhaul of the communal property system and therefore did not jeopardize the implicit social contract and stability of transition, these new economic entities did not herald a transformation of China's property rights system but were nevertheless sufficient to instil profit motives within an imperfect formal legal structure. However, the limits of these institutional innovations and contractually defined rights became apparent later on when the market became increasingly decentralized and more formal institutions were seemingly required.

2.3.1 Institutional Innovations

China does not have a system of formal property rights conventionally defined and only recognized the existence of private property in March 2004, when the concept was included in its constitution. Yet, China's phenomenal growth has taken place through the creation of residual claimant rights in its partially marketized economy, notably via the Household Responsibility System for farmers implemented to great success in the late 1970s, and the Contract Responsibility System instigated in the 1980s for SOEs.

In the rural economy at the start of reform in 1979, the Household Responsibility System created a system of effective residual claimants. Farmers were given incentives to share risk with the state by retaining some returns from their labour above what they were to remit to the state. Prior to this 'institutional innovation', collectivization meant that there was little incentive for farmers to produce output as their work points were allocated on the basis of a day's labour and not linked to effort. The creation of these implicit property rights can be likened to a sharecropping system where there is a residual ownership right to instil incentives while not granting private property to the farmers. Rural township and village enterprises which appeared at the same time were also subject to a two-tiered compensation structure whereby profits could accrue to the labourers in the rural industry so long as sufficient remittances or transfers went to the state. This system was subsequently extended in a qualitatively different manner in urban areas and to foreign investors.

The evidence of growth stemming from these incentives is notable, as China's real GDP growth in this period averaged over 9 per cent, agricultural output was high, and rural industrialization helped remove surplus labour from the farms (Riskin 1987). Whereas the HRS refined the incentives facing households and is often termed an 'institutional innovation', the creation of TVEs is a more striking example of how China created a new institutional form whose parameters were defined by policy and not by private ownership or outright transfer of the ownership to individuals. Yet, the reliance of the Chinese rural workers on this new institution was sufficient to instil market-driven incentives, and a significant part of China's growth in agricultural productivity and the rural economy can be traced to both the HRS and decollectivization (Lin 1992; Huang and Rozelle 1996).

Decentralization and institutional innovations within the state sector in urban areas were also important. Decentralization has occurred in almost all areas of decision making in production, pricing, investment, trade, expenditure, income distribution, taxation, and credit allocation with the exception of interest rates which remain largely under the control of the People's Bank of China. The main institutional innovations in urban areas were the Budgetary Contracting System (BCS), the Contract Responsibility System, and permitting direct borrowing (Riskin 1984). Since 1980, under the BCS, the central government shares revenues (taxes and profit remittances) with local governments. For local governments which incur budget deficits, the contract sets the subsidies to be transferred to the local governments. Fiscal decentralization further gave scope for regional experimentation, another key element to China's gradualist path as it permitted increased market-oriented activity while limiting the possibility of instability from arising given the nature of China's semi-federal structure (Qian and Xu 1993).

The CRS in 1981 permitted SOEs to pay a fixed amount of taxes and profits to the state and retain the remainder (Koo 1990). In principle, so long as the SOEs delivered the tax and profit remittances specified in the contracts, they were free to operate. This resulted in increased production of SOEs in the 1980s through the reorientation of incentives of managers (Groves et al. 1995). However, the decline of SOEs in the 1990s illustrated the limit of relying on institutional innovations as 'soft budget constraints' continued to plague the enterprises despite the positive incentive effects of the CRS (Choo and Yin 2000).

Since 1985, state grants for operating funds and fixed asset investments were replaced by bank loans, the final element of the main set of institutional innovations. Local governments and SOEs are allowed to borrow directly from banks. Six years later, local governments and SOEs were permitted to borrow from household and other institutions. By liberating one 'track' of the dual-track system, there was scope for these institutionally defined rights to foster a profit incentive to SOEs and state-owned banks which helped boost output again without creating private property rights in the ownership of these enterprises and banks.

This process of creating and defining some forms of rather informal property rights therefore helps to explain China's successful gradualist or incrementalist approach to marketization.

2.3.2 Contractually Defined Rights

This system of informal property rights was extended, though in a qualitatively different form, to multinational corporations investing in an economy otherwise characterized by communal property. Since the 'open door' policy was adopted and its take-off in the early 1990s, China has rapidly become one of the world's top destinations for foreign direct investment. For most of the reform period especially prior to WTO accession, the predominant form of FDI was Chinese–foreign joint ventures, where the Chinese and foreign partners set up either equity or cooperative joint ventures. Equity joint ventures partitioned returns on the basis of the invested capital in the joint venture while returns were contractually defined in cooperative joint ventures. Both forms of joint ventures, however, were vested in essentially a set of contractually defined rights. The uncertainty that might have been generated by the lack of recognition of private property such as those held by joint ventures, though, did not seem to serve as a deterrent to FDI. Because of the lack of private property rights in the rest of the Chinese economy, the joint venture laws in some ways provided more protection to foreign-invested enterprises than that accorded to non-state Chinese firms, such as *getihu* (sole proprietorships) (Huang 2006).

This system of contractually defining property rights was not limited to foreign investment as such an approach was eventually extended to the domestic market by the late 1990s. In 1998, for example, China undertook privatization of housing, whereby the formerly allocated housing through work units were sold off at preferential prices to urban residents (Li 2005). By 2001, the housing market was effectively privatized. However, the rights of the owners of the housing were limited to residing in the flat or house for a designated period of time, some seventy years. This contractually defined right is in effect in the form of a leasehold and thus not outright ownership. The expectation of housing owners is that they will have the right to renew their contract and the passage of the 2007 Property Law largely confirms this expectation that greater protections will be extended to property ownership. Investment, moreover, is high in the real estate market despite a lack of comprehensive protection of private property and uncertain land-use rights. These contracts also carry enforcement risk; however, the implicit social contract that arises means that should expectations not be fulfilled, there is the possibility of social instability as has been seen when housing and land have been confiscated by the state for development. The aim to prevent instability therefore remains as a policy driver.

Another example of these contractually defined rights is the corporatization and effective privatization of state-owned enterprises through a process of share issue privatization (SIP) following the lack of success of the CRS in sustaining the profitability of SOEs after a time (Sun and Tong 2003). Since the early 1990s, many SOEs have become shareholding companies where the ownership is in the hands of shareholders and a portion of the shares are traded on domestic and international stock exchanges. Corporatization was intended to effectively privatize SOEs by making them shareholding companies when the institutional innovation of the CRS failed to address the soft budget constraints that plagued the inefficient SOEs. Unlike immediate mass privatization of state-owned enterprises, stock ownership sets up the possibility of a gradual transformation into private ownership. By corporatizing its enterprises but retaining state control in many instances, China managed to instil profit incentives without a change in ownership for many SOEs. This was effective for a time, but it became clear that further reform was needed and a large-scale restructuring (*gaizhi*) programme was undertaken in the mid-1990s that paved the way for the later effective privatization of the small- and medium-sized SOEs. The larger ones, by contrast, remained in state hands or under state control. Thus, the corporatization reforms were premised on creating contractually defined shareholdings which could eventually, but not necessarily, lead to private ownership.

2.3.3 *Enforcement*

China has successfully established a system of contractually defined and institutionally structured rights encompassing the set of so-called 'institutional innovations'—the market-oriented institutional reforms governing households, firms, and even local governments—as well as with respect to foreign investors and the domestic non-state sector. This system of institutionally and contractually defined, but arguably informal, property rights stimulated China's impressive economic growth during the reform period despite the lack of recognition of private property per se and within an incomplete legal system particularly with respect to enforcement.

In a system of contractually or institutionally created rights, enforcement would seemingly be of considerable significance, yet China's legal and regulatory systems lagged, and still lag, behind the set of contractually defined obligations underpinning its economy. Clarke (2003a) emphasizes the security of property rather than enforcement as important in China, and informally defined, but still set by policy or denoted by contract, property would be consistent with this view. Indeed, the studies of social capital/networks in China and elsewhere reinforce the notion that socially acknowledged ownership rights are secure through informal enforcement rather than a formal process, reducing the importance of the formal legal system and the effectiveness of its enforcement procedures (see Greif 1993). For instance, Ho (2006) finds that collectively owned land is subject to periodic division within a village and that these rights to the land are well known, expected, and respected despite a lack of formal private ownership of land in villages. However, the recent reforms of the property laws in China will protect these informal rights through formal channels, which perhaps signals the limits to a purely informal institutional framework.

A further advantage of a system of contractually defined rights is that arbitration can be specified as an enforcement mechanism in an agreement. Although arbitration is not a possibility for all transactions, particularly those related to SOEs, it provides another avenue of specifying a manner of conflict resolution that does not rely on the courts but can utilize an agreed set of terms and laws. The China International Economic and Trade Arbitration Commission (CIETAC) is often used by international investors, for instance, and has a better reputation than the Chinese court system.

2.3.4 *The Limits of the Informal System*

In the rural economy, although agricultural productivity was stimulated by the Household Responsibility System (Lin 1992), longer-term investments required more certainty. Thus, by the late 1990s, China adopted a land tenure system whereby instead of regular reallocations of farm land, rural farmers owned leaseholds of fifty years and could plan and invest for the longer term.

Similarly for enterprises, the early success of the CRS was insufficient to stymie the accumulation of non-performing loans in the banking sector that grew throughout the 1980s and 1990s. The 'soft budget constraints' of SOEs in particular induced inefficient over-investment especially as output was stimulated by the CRS while inputs were still largely allocated or funded by the state and meant that further SOE reforms were needed. The corporatization policy coupled with the *gaizhi* or restructuring policy was enabled by the promulgation of the Company Law in 1994 and the creation of two stock exchanges in the early 1990s. These formal measures created shareholding structures in SOEs and thus legally defined ownership of these companies. However, as many SOEs were still majority owned by the state, the extent of private ownership was limited to a minority holding (Du and Xu 2009). Nevertheless, TVEs as well as private Chinese firms also took advantage of the greater certainty afforded to legally recognized corporate entities by incorporating in various forms such as limited liability companies (LLCs) and China's growth remained strong during the 1990s even as the efficiency of SOEs declined during this period.

Finally, the system of informal institutions never fully suited foreign investors who required more certain property rights. Thus, the first laws governing corporate forms were passed in the 1980s to create Chinese–foreign joint ventures and in rarer cases, wholly foreign-owned enterprises. The JV and foreign enterprise laws contractually defined the rights and obligations of these firms, which provided for a greater level of certainty than those governing other enterprises in China. Even though enforcement of the contractually defined rights and ensuing commercial contracts were imperfect, the rapid growth of FDI in China attests to the perceived relative security of contractually defined rights even within a markedly communal property system. However, as the market evolved and increased in complexity, the push for an ever-growing number of laws to protect both the rights of foreign and domestic firms grew. In the years leading up to, and certainly after, WTO accession in 2001, China passed a large number of laws to govern its markets, including mergers and aquisitions (M&A) and (revamped) bankruptcy laws in 2002 and 2006, respectively, as well as improved patent laws, to underpin the growing complexity of its economy. In this way, formal legal reforms began to support the predominantly informal institutions that had underpinned China's economy, and the interaction between formal/ informal institutions and economic development became increasingly evident.

2.4 Legal Reforms

These themes of stability and economic necessity pervade the tenor of legal reforms. While permitting reform as a vehicle for achieving growth, policy and law are used to maintain stability and offer the promise of predictability, with the new legal system providing a critical institutional basis for market behaviour, contract enforcement, and dispute resolution when necessary. For instance, township and village enterprises arose due to the need for light industrial goods after decades of heavy industry-biased central planning and as an avenue to absorb surplus labour in the agricultural sector, one of the key challenges for a developing country like China. Permitting the institutional form of TVEs and as initially articulated in law pursuant to regulations governing 'collectively owned' enterprises allowed the economy to sustain economic growth and stability since it also reallocated labour from agriculture to industry but without change in ownership. Similarly, the need for FDI and technology meant that China experimented with opening at the start of the reform period in 1979. Realizing that foreign investors needed investment vehicles, various joint venture laws were adopted to facilitate economic growth, all the while limiting the reach of FDI to SEZs and keeping the new institutional form out of the reach of private Chinese businesses.

The reform of the SOEs starting in the 1980s followed from the lack of competitiveness of these enterprises. Those policy reforms were only 'legalized' in 1988 with the promulgation of an SOE Law (Law on Industrial Enterprises Owned Wholly by the People), already somewhat out of date at the time of promulgation. Permitting corporatization under the rubric of 'share experimental' enterprises was meant to make Chinese firms more efficient and ameliorate the internal incentives determining governance. These policy initiatives were supported first by local level regulations governing local establishment of companies limited by shares, then national standards for the same legal form and only rather late in the day by the promulgation of the Company Law in 1994, which was completely amended in 2006 to reflect a very seriously altered environment with WTO accession. Indeed, the reform of the Contract Law preceding it in 1999 subsumed the various corporate laws that had governed foreign firms separately from domestic ones, so that one regime governed all firms by the 2000s. Similarly, the allowance for *getihu* or self-employment/sole proprietorships was necessary as a policy matter to ease the impact of the large-scale redundancies from SOEs and facilitate the emergence of a dual track of private economic activity in the mid-1990s. Yet, the form only existed in regulation and often less formally, and was lately subject to codification with the 'sole proprietorship form' in 1999. Finally, after WTO accession and the promised opening of the service sector as well as the need to stymie non-performing loans in a weak banking sector that is often a source of macro-economic instability in transition economies, China adopted a series of regulatory measures such as the agencies of the China Banking Regulatory Commission (CBRC), China Securities Regulatory Commission (CSRC), and China Insurance Regulatory Commission (CIRC), to provide an institutional base for, and governance of, the developing financial sector.

In each instance, economic necessity drove policy reform, while also requiring stability, so that the market could come into being and develop. In turn, legal reforms generally followed to provide further institutional support for already established market mechanisms under a partially reformed system. And yet, China has in recent years seen a change in this dynamic—with substantive and institutional (including regulatory) legal reforms begetting further economic reform. The laws bolstered the foundation of the market which enabled further marketization to take place, particularly where regulations were enacted following the legislation so that implementation resulted in better governed markets. Not only the Company Law, but the Mergers and Acquisitions Law of 2003, the Bankruptcy Law of 2006 (significantly revising the previous law of 1986), and the Anti-Monopoly Law passed in 2007, all established the basis for more complex market development to bolster economic reforms that relied increasingly on governing a decentralized economy. After the passage of the M&A Law, China's first overseas commercial investments and acquisitions occurred; for example, TCL bought the RCA brand from France's Thomson in 2004, and Lenovo purchased US IBM's brand and PC business in 2005. Similarly, the trio of regulatory establishments of the CSRC, CIRC, and CBRC led reform of financial markets by establishing supporting, and enabling regulation.

The interaction and reinforcing nature of economic (policy) and legal reforms serves as the premise for understanding marketization in China. Even though this approach may not be the most economically efficient or most rapid, this type of gradual transition accompanied by both economic and legal reforms allows the Chinese system to maintain a degree of stability. Stability, in turn, enables the partially reformed economy that results from a gradual approach to transition, and suits the policy aims of the Chinese government. Moreover, the adoption of laws hastens China toward a functioning market economy where the complexity of economic transactions requires an established legal system. In other words, laws and the legal institutional system are increasingly critical as China's economic reforms progress.

It is also evident that there has been a speeding up of substantive reform of laws needed to govern the increasingly decentralized and open market, particularly in the 2000s with greater global integration. With WTO membership, China subscribed to the rules-based international system governing trade which also required transparency in domestic laws and regulations. More potently in many ways, it was not the formal aspects of international economic law which led to Chinese legal reforms, but the norms-based, voluntary standards such as the Basel standards for capital adequacy that governed expectations in global markets which led China to revise and thus to adhere to better governance requirements in its banks and financial firms. In other words, although the WTO did compel China to revise its intellectual property laws to become harmonized with the international law governing intellectual property rights, much of the legal and regulatory reforms were associated with China's greater integration with global markets where multinational firms had expectations as to how markets were to operate such that China's capital market reforms proceeded quickly to offer foreign (and also domestic) firms the regulatory guidelines to invest in China, such as the 2002 Qualified Foreign Institutional Investors (QFII) regulations that allowed foreign investment in China's stock markets, and better corporate governance such as via regulations concerning disclosure requirements passed in 2004. It is possible that WTO and global demands hastened and perhaps even overcame domestic resistance to greater law-based marketization and offered an additional impetus to hasten the development of the market economy, and move it toward sound institutional foundations. By doing so, China's economic growth stands a better chance of being sustained.

2.5 The China Paradox

Focusing in detail on those legal reforms, one of the enduring paradoxes in China's remarkable economic growth experience over the three decades since 1978 is the lack of a well-established legal system supporting the increasingly decentralized marketizing economy (see, for example, Allen, Qian, and Qian 2005; Cull and Xu 2005). It is a notable puzzle in that robust institutions are thought to be required both in theory and in practice to support markets (see for example, Acemoglu and Johnson 2005). For instance, in a Coasian or Walrasian sense, a market economy is predicated on well-defined property rights and low transaction costs that permit efficient exchange to take place (Coase 1937). The rapid transition experience of many other economies such as the former Soviet Union was in part predicated on the establishment of private property rights and removal of the inefficient state in the burgeoning market economy. In China's case, however, many of its reforms have been undertaken without an established rule of law and in the absence of a change in ownership from state to private. It raises the questions as to how China was able to instil economic incentives in the absence of private property rights and how an imperfect legal system could protect against expropriation that would normally limit investment and other private economic activities, particularly foreign direct investment (FDI).

The gradual and evolutionary nature of both economic and legal reform provides a basis for understanding the relationship between law and growth in China. The Chinese legal tradition is distinct from that of common law (UK, USA) and civil law (Continental Europe) countries; although that does not negate the incremental nature of legal reforms which can exist in all legal systems (see Jones, 2003, for the modern day influences of China's dynastic legal system). Perhaps most evident in common law countries, law develops from case law—judicial pronouncements which give meaning to, and shape, the interpretation of the statutory laws. Common law itself is premised on cases furthering common laws. *Stare decisis* and precedent naturally carry significant weight in judicial rulings and in shaping the development of the rule of law. Law, therefore, develops over time rather than appearing as a pre-existing and wholly formed system of a 'rule of law'. Even in countries with a civil law tradition, laws are evolutionary as comprehensive codification is not feasible and the state, including its administrative organs, largely takes on the interpretative role.

In the law and finance literature, this debate has started to take shape for China. Chen (2003) argues that China's financial development follows a 'crash then law' path proposed by Coffee (2001). From a legal perspective, Coffee (2001) argues that capital market developments precede—rather than follow—legal protection for shareholders. This runs contrary to the view of economists, namely, La Porta et al. (1997, 1998) who posit that the rule of law causes financial markets to develop (see also Acemoglu, Johnson, and Robinson 2005 for a similar argument regarding institutions and economic growth). Coffee (2001) offers evidence from the historical development of the USA and UK, where dispersed ownership by shareholders arose with the establishment of their bourses in the nineteenth century and legal protection for minority shareholders came afterward, largely in the early twentieth century. His argument is premised on the creation of interested parties: legal reforms are enacted due to the agitations of a motivated constituency that believes that it will be protected by the proposed reforms. Therefore, he argues that the constituency must arise before it can become an instrument for legal change. Chen (2003) applies this approach to China's capital markets and shows that an interested constituency arose after the creation of the two stock exchanges in Shanghai and Shenzhen in the early 1990s which led to the Securities Law of 1999. La Porta et al. (1997, 1998), by contrast, draw a distinction between common law and civil law countries and show that common law countries provide better shareholder protection which fosters the development of financial markets. Their argument is that legal protection allows markets to develop through providing protection against expropriation and improved contracting security; therefore, law creates markets. Allen, Qian, and Qian (2005) compare China against the La Porta group of countries and conclude that informal institutional arrangements, such as trust-based contracting, supplanted the role of law in fostering capital markets.

Aside from the question of the sequence of law and market development, there remains a further mystery as to how markets developed in China in the absence of private property rights, which are typically established in law. Unlike the US or UK and even other transition economies which adopted private ownership early in their transition, China's lingering communal property system should have impeded market development. Without property rights allocations, transactions should have been hampered and the market stifled.

Therefore, this chapter proposes that legal and economic reforms—extending beyond financial development—give rise to, and reinforce, each other in China. Also, institutional reform through administrative dictates, such as the Contract Responsibility System that injected market forces into state-owned enterprises (SOEs), was sufficient to instil incentives to create markets in the absence of strong legal protection. Then, once a market is created by law or institutional reform (for example, administrative dictate or absence of notable prohibition), then interested constituencies and stakeholders will push for more formal and explicit legal reforms to protect their interests. Better legal protection in turn promotes market development by providing greater security of economic transactions. Informal, trust-based relationships supplant the incomplete legal system, particularly in terms of enforcement. In this way, the complementary processes of legal, institutional, and economic reform in China can explain the paradox of remarkable growth within an underdeveloped system of law.

2.5.1 *Law and Markets*

There are both theoretical and empirical perspectives on the relationship between law and markets that drives economic growth. At first glance, it may appear that some laws are less relevant to economic growth, such as the workings of the criminal law system. However, crime may well deter investment and social stability can be a determinant of location for risk-averse firms (see for example, Brock 1998). Thus, the functioning of the legal system across its various dimensions may well be relevant for economic growth, although the focus would presumably be on civil and commercial legal developments.

From the theoretical perspective, the 'invisible hand' of the market works efficiently when there exist optimizing agents transacting in a framework of well-defined property rights and sufficiently low or zero transaction costs (see Coase 1937). Law establishes those conditions. A legal system defines the property rights and the costs of transacting and exchange. For instance, ownership recognized by law establishes the security of the private property to be exchanged. A well-functioning legal and regulatory system can ensure that transactions involving those properties take place; that is, it provides contracting security. For China, one element of the paradox is the lack of legally protected private property rights (see for example, Jefferson and Rawski 2002). It was not until the Property Law of 2007 that equal protection was granted to both private and public property. Indeed, much of China's growth and reform has taken place with the state retaining ownership of enterprises, land, and housing. Privatization of SOEs only occurred gradually over the three decades of market-oriented reforms. The private housing market was only recently established, perhaps measured by the conclusion of the housing privatization reforms in 2001, and the creation of long-term rights of use rather than freehold ownership resulted since land remained largely in state hands (see, for example, Ho 2006).

From an empirical standpoint, these theoretical insights have been incorporated into the literature advocating the importance of laws and institutions in explaining persistent economic growth (see, for example, Rodrik, Subramanian, and Trebbi 2004; Acemoglu and Johnson 2005; Acemoglu, Johnson, and Robinson 2005; Dam 2006). La Porta et al. (1997, 1998) emphasize the importance of legal origin, for instance, whether a country had a common or civil law system, in influencing financial sector development and consequently economic development. China did not fit well within this framework, particularly because legal origin was based on the externally imposed legal system of the colonial powers on developing countries. But, for countries such as China which did not adopt a legal system from a particular colonial power, the legal formalism hypothesis would seem to have minimal explanatory power. Studies of other transition economies conclude that the effectiveness of laws is more important than the completeness of the written formal law for economic growth, further reducing the force of the legal origins school. One significant conclusion is that a 'transplanted' legal system into a neophyte transition economy—whereby the wholly formed laws of developed countries which would presumably encompass the necessary elements for a 'rule of law'—did not work (Pistor, Martin, and Gelfer 2000). Glaeser et al. (2004) also emphasize the functional rule of law as relevant for growth. Therefore, the elements of a well-functioning legal system would include an independent judiciary, freedom of executive branch interference, and low risk of expropriation (Pistor and Xu 2005; Fan et al. 2009)

Institutional development was therefore considered to be important and the focus has shifted away from legal formalism and legal origin to some extent (see for example, Rodrik, Subramanian, and Trebbi 2004). For instance, Acemoglu and Johnson (2005) emphasize two types of market-supporting institutions which are important for economic growth: property rights institutions which protect against expropriation by government, and contracting institutions which ease contract enforcement. For China, these empirical measures also do not measure up well as compared against its impressive growth rate, giving rise to the 'China paradox' (see Cull and Xu 2005; Lu and Yao 2009).

Various measures of the rule of law and institutional development in China all suggest that its formal legal system is underdeveloped (see for example, Allen, Qian, and Qian 2005; Cull and Xu 2005, for a range of indicators). Using the World Bank's *Worldwide Governance Indicators* for 2006, Table 2.1 shows that China ranked in the bottom 25th to 50th percentile of all countries surveyed for rule of law. It is also evident from Table 2.1 that China grew more rapidly than comparable sized economies (largest ten economies in the world) in the top half of the table and outpaced the growth of other transition economies from 1990–2003. Its growth in per capita GDP exceeded 7.6 per cent over this period, which was substantially higher than Brazil, which ranked close to China in the rule-of-law indicator, and also Estonia, which had a rule-of-law indicator that was higher than that of the USA. No proxy for rule of law will be perfect, although nearly all studies conclude that China has an underdeveloped legal system (see, for example, Yao and Yueh 2009). When measured in terms of regulatory

Table 2.1 Rule of law

Country	Percentile rank (0–100)	Rule-of-Law score (−2.5 to +2.5)	Average annual growth rate of real per capita GDP, 1990–2003
China	45.2	−0.40	7.61%
Brazil	41.4	−0.48	0.96%
India	57.1	0.17	3.95%
Russia	19.0	−0.91	−1.27%
Italy	60.0	0.37	1.25%
France	89.5	1.31	1.47%
Germany	94.3	1.77	1.43%
Japan	90.0	1.40	0.95%
United Kingdom	93.3	1.73	2.03%
United States	91.9	1.57	1.75%
Select Eastern Europe and former Soviet bloc countries			
Albania	48.8	−0.14	2.58%
Bulgaria	66.3	0.54	1.03%
Croatia	61.5	0.35	0.25%
Czech Republic	79.5	0.95	0.92%
Estonia	92.2	1.42	2.45%
Hungary	85.9	1.10	1.72%
Poland	69.3	0.64	3.23%
Romania	62.0	0.37	0.19%
Slovakia	83.4	1.08	1.65%

Source: World Bank Worldwide Governance Indicators, 2006.

Note: Rule of law measures the extent to which agents perceive that the rules of society, in particular the quality of contract enforcement, the police, and the courts, as well as the likelihood of crime and violence, are enforced. The percentile rank places the country on a scale of 0–100 where 100 indicates a country that scored the highest possible value on the rule-of-law indicator. The governance score is normally distributed with a mean of zero and a standard deviation of one. Governance is better as the value increases. See Kaufmann et al. (2007) for a complete definition and discussion. The growth rate of per capita GDP is in 1990 US dollars and calculated from Maddison (2001).

quality, a counterpart to an effective legal system, China fares even worse. Table 2.2 ranks the countries in terms of their regulatory quality, measuring the ability of the government to formulate and implement sound policies and regulations that permit and promote private sector development. Whereas it ranked better than Russia and Brazil on rule of law, it ranked only better than Russia on the composite index for regulatory quality.

Table 2.3–2.5 provide more disaggregated measures of different dimensions of the rule of law in China, as compared with other countries; namely, investor protection, contract enforcement, security of property rights, and freedom from corruption. Table 2.3 measures the extent of investor protection as measured by the World Bank *Doing Business* survey from 2008, where China's rank out of 175 measured countries is eighty-sixth or in the bottom half. In particular, it obtained the poorest rating on the transparency of related-party transactions (extent of disclosure index), which reflects the lack of arms' length dealing and opacity in its enterprises. A comparable measure by the Heritage Foundation is that of enforcing property rights, and China fares among the worst of selected countries, as seen in Table 2.4.

Table 2.2 Regulatory quality

Country	Percentile rank (0–100)	Regulatory quality score (−2.5 to + 2.5)	Standard error
Russia	35.0	−0.44	0.17
China	45.6	−0.24	0.17
India	46.1	−0.22	0.17
Brazil	53.4	−0.04	0.17
Albania	55.8	0.09	0.18
Croatia	64.1	0.43	0.17
Romania	66.0	0.48	0.17
Bulgaria	69.9	0.61	0.17
Poland	72.3	0.71	0.17
Italy	74.3	0.81	0.21
Czech Republic	80.1	0.96	0.17
Slovakia	81.1	0.99	0.17
Japan	83.5	1.05	0.21
France	85.9	1.15	0.21
Hungary	86.4	1.15	0.17
United States	90.8	1.45	0.21
Estonia	92.2	1.50	0.17
Germany	92.7	1.50	0.21
United Kingdom	98.1	1.86	0.21

Source: *World Bank Worldwide Governance Indicators,* 2008.

Note: Regulatory quality measures the ability of the government to formulate and implement sound policies and regulations that permit and promote private sector development.
The percentile rank places the country on a scale of 0–100 where 100 indicates a country
that scored the highest possible value on the indicator. The indicator score is normally
distributed with a mean of zero and a standard deviation of one. Quality improves as the
value increases. See Kaufmann, Kraay, and Mastruzzi (2007) for a complete definition and
discussion.

Table 2.4 measures the security of property rights, with regard both to
obtaining and to enforcing them. China has one of the least secure systems of
property rights, most likely due to its underdeveloped private property system
that only ostensibly existed since the notion was recognized in the Constitution
in 2006, and with the passage of the Property Law in 2007, extending equal
protection to private and public property. China performs better in Table 2.4
measuring the extent of corruption. China's degree of corruption is comparable
to India and Brazil, while it fares better than Russia and the Ukraine. Overall,
China ranked 126th out of 157 countries based on these and other indicators
produced by the Heritage Foundation's 2008 *Index of Economic Freedoms*.

In summary, although no indicators are perfect, across measures of legal/
institutional development, China ranks in the bottom half of the ranked countries despite being the fastest growing major economy in the world. The accumulated evidence suggests that the paradox of fast growth and a poor legal
system remains after three decades of reform.

Table 2.3 Investor protection

	Rank	Investor protection index	Disclosure index	Director liability index	Shareholder suits index
Brazil	64	5.3	6	7	3
Canada	5	8.3	8	9	8
China	83	5	10	1	4
France	64	5.3	10	1	5
Germany	83	5	5	5	5
India	33	6	7	4	7
Italy	51	5.7	7	4	6
Japan	12	7	7	6	8
Poland	33	6	7	2	9
Romania	33	6	9	5	4
Russia	83	5	6	2	7
Slovakia	98	4.7	3	4	7
South Africa	9	8	8	8	8
Ukraine	141	3.7	1	3	7
United Kingdom	9	8	10	7	7
United States	5	8.3	7	9	9

Source: World Bank Doing Business Database, 2008 (http://www.doingbusiness.org).

Notes: The investor protection index (measured from 1–10) calibrates the strength of minority shareholder protection against directors' misuse of corporate assets for personal gain. The indicators, also out of 10, distinguish three dimensions of investor protection: transparency of related-party transactions (extent of disclosure index), liability for self-dealing (extent of director liability index) and shareholders' ability to sue officers and directors for misconduct (ease of shareholder suits index). Countries are ranked out of 175.

Table 2.4 Property rights and freedom from corruption

Protection of property rights		Freedom from corruption	
United States	90	United Kingdom	86
Canada	90	Canada	85
United Kingdom	90	Germany	80
Germany	90	Japan	76
Japan	70	France	74
France	70	United States	73
Slovak Republic	50	Italy	49
South Africa	50	Slovak Republic	47
Italy	50	South Africa	46
Poland	50	Poland	37
Brazil	50	Brazil	33
India	50	India	33
Romania	30	China	33
Ukraine	30	Romania	31
Russia	30	Ukraine	28
China	20	Russia	25

Source: Heritage Foundation Index of Economic Freedom, 2008.

Notes: Property rights are an assessment of the ability of individuals to accumulate private property, secured by clear laws that are fully enforced by the state. The index is from 1–100. Freedom from corruption is based on quantitative data that assess the perception of corruption in the business environment, including levels of governmental legal, judicial, and administrative corruption. The index is from 1–100.

2.5.2 *An Evolutionary View of Legal and Economic Development in China*

The next section will review the literature on the experience of other countries in fashioning a corporate law framework. Specifically, a comparative view of market development and legal reform will be taken of China and the US. The comparison will aim to shed light on the extent to which it is feasible to establish a comprehensive legal system at an early stage of economic development. The focus is on China's particular sequence of legal, institutional and economic reform. In the case of the early reforms of the late 1970s and early 1980s, the particular context of Chinese gradualist transition meant that institutional reform—through creating an expectation of property rights—was sufficient to instil the necessary incentives for the development of markets. However, as markets developed, more formal and explicit legal reforms were needed and thus China began to rapidly adopt laws during the 1990s and 2000s, particularly with the additional pressures of international economic laws with WTO accession in 2001. Enforcement will be examined as well, particularly in respect of foreign-invested enterprises (FIEs) and the reliance on informal relational contracting where official enforcement is weak. This section will conclude with an assessment of the relationship between law and economic growth in China, and posit that China's experience is unusual in the post-war period where the transition and development models are heavily tilted toward formal legal rules, but is not atypical of the experience of developed countries' legal and economic development during their industrialization at the turn of the last century. The conclusion will also assess the influence of international laws and rules, particularly in shaping the enforcement of laws in China.

This chapter argues that legal development in China should be viewed as an evolutionary process alongside incremental economic reforms undertaken during its transition from central planning. This is not dissimilar to the experience of rich countries at a similar stage of development when their legal systems developed alongside their markets. What makes China unusual is a confluence of factors. First, it was able to establish markets within a communal property system, which highlights the importance of administrative measures and institutional reforms. Second, its transition and therefore its marketization were gradual, such that markets were not always established by laws at the outset but developed over time with experimentation of various market mechanisms, such as the 'dual-track' pricing system and the export-oriented Special Economic Zones (SEZs). Third, it is undertaking reform and global integration at a time when international economic laws and rules extend beyond trade and into financial regulation and intellectual property rights. The external influence of laws and rules will affect expectations within and beyond China, particularly in emphasizing regulatory transparency and the enforcement of laws.

2.6 A Comparative Perspective of Legal Development and Markets

2.6.1 *Chinese Law*

The legal system in China is modelled after the Japanese civil law system (Jones 2003). The Japanese legal system was itself fashioned after the German civil law tradition during the nineteenth century period of the Meiji Restoration. However, strong elements of China's own legal tradition persist, particularly in terms of the emphasis on administrative law and the lack of separation between the legal and administrative systems. Adjudication was undertaken by administrative officials who acted on behalf of the emperor in all matters of state, including deciding lawsuits. The judicial system in China today is still part of the administrative system and hence there is no effective independent judiciary (Alford 2000). As a result, procedural laws are comparatively underdeveloped, whilst administrative law is at the core of the Chinese legal tradition with criminal and administrative sanctions preferred for enforcement. Jones (2003) argues that this stands in contrast to the tradition of Roman law from which many Western legal systems are derived. As Roman law was developed primarily to resolve civil disputes amongst individuals and groups in a largely agricultural society, civil matters are central to Western laws.

This mixed legal tradition renders it difficult to situate China in the comparative law and finance literature, which emphasizes the distinction between common law (US, UK) and civil law (Continental Europe) countries. In particular, the La Porta et al. (1997, 1998) perspective views civil law countries as less effective in promoting financial sector development than common law countries due to common law providing better protection for investors. La Porta et al. (1998) draw the further distinction that civil law countries such as Germany and Scandinavian nations provide better protection than France and other civil law countries, although not as much as common law countries in a survey of forty-nine countries. Strong protection of shareholders and security holders is associated with more liquid capital markets and more dispersed share ownership. This seminal work has led to the 'law matter' thesis whereby effective legal protection is assumed to cause financial sector development (see also Levine 1997, 1998). This thesis has been challenged by Coffee (2001). Coffee (2001) disputes the significance of the difference between the two sets of legal traditions and goes further in arguing that market development leads to better legal protection as evidenced by the historical pattern of laws following security market developments in the US, UK, and Continental Europe. He argues that the chief difference between the two legal systems is the extent of state involvement in the market. In the US and UK, in contrast to Continental Europe, the state did not actively intervene in capital markets and instead relied on private stock exchanges to self-regulate in their own self-interest. In France, and to some extent in Germany, the state intervened frequently in the market which left no room for what he calls 'enlightened self-regulation' (Coffee 2001, p. 9).

More generally, Coffee (2001) reiterates the pattern observed by legal scholars that laws tend to follow from market developments historically (see also Banner 1997, who surveys 300 years of legal developments to conclude that securities regulations are consistent with this pattern). Pistor (2002) comes to a similar assessment after surveying shareholder rights in twenty-four transition economies during the 1990s. She concludes that legal reforms tend to be responsive to economic changes rather than precede them.

China does not fit into the paradigm of common versus civil law countries, particularly as these cover only roughly forty-nine or less than a third of the countries in the world, virtually all of which are former European colonies (see Acemoglu, Johnson, and Robinson 2005). China's case is much closer to other transition economies as they had to re-initiate the market during the 1990s after decades of central planning (see for example, Pistor and Xu 2005). However, unlike these countries, China did not adopt a legal system transplanted from developed economies (see for example, Pistor, Martin, and Gelfer 2000; Berkowitz, Pistor, and Richard 2003). Instead, it developed its own legal system, which has been influenced by the legal codes of other countries; for example, Chinese civil law has elements of German law. Nevertheless, the sequence of law and markets would remain relevant. The paradox casts doubt on the 'law matters' thesis and has implications for the progress of reform in China some three decades into marketization.

There has been a definite push for legal reform in China. This has derived from its global integration and membership in the multilateral rules-based trading system (WTO) as well as in response to domestic pressures, which led to the recognition of the existence of a 'rule of law' in the Constitution in 1999. Although on the face of it, the amendment appears symbolic, Clarke (2007) argues that it formally incorporates the legal system into China's system of governance. Legal reform, therefore, became prominent at the same time that the private sector was also recognized as part of the socialist market economy in the amended Constitution. The latter shift culminated in the 2001 embrace of entrepreneurs in the Chinese Communist Party. This symbolic move also occurred in the midst of ongoing legal and economic reforms which had taken place since 1978 (such as establishing a Company Law in 1993 that accompanied the transformation of SOEs into corporations), adding more credence to the view that legal and economic reforms did not progress in a particular sequence but developed alongside the other.

2.6.2 Laws and Markets: China and the USA

Although there are pitfalls with a comparative perspective, an examination of whether markets precede or follow laws in China and the US can inform the debate over whether the rule of law is necessary before markets develop. Examining the respective legal developments at similar stages of economic development for these two countries would be informative.

Although Table 2.5 outlines the key pieces of commercial law for the US and China as compared against the level of economic development, there are notable differences between the two countries to consider. The first is that the US common law tradition means that cases rather than legislation shape the law, although laws can certainly be amended, such as the Bankruptcy Act of 1898 which was entirely superseded by the Bankruptcy Code of 1978 which governs corporations today. This can take place in federal or state courts, and much of US corporate law is state law with notable exceptions such as bankruptcy and patents which remain under federal jurisdiction. The corporation law identified in the table refers to the State of Delaware, which accounts for some half of all US corporations due to its favourable climate for corporate governance.

China, by contrast, has elements of civil law and a strong administrative component, as compared with the common law and judicial review emphasis of the US. Its laws, moreover, have to contend with the transition of its economy from the dominance of SOEs to one with private domestic and foreign enterprises, of which the latter was gradually managed through specific legislation. For instance, the United States was confronted with the 'robber barons' of US Steel and other monopolists at the conclusion of the Industrial Revolution, which raised concern about anti-competitive practices. The 'trust busters' of the late nineteenth century, therefore, enacted the Sherman Act of 1890 which was geared at dismantling monopolies. China, however, did not pass an anti-monopoly law until 2007, quite late in its market transition, due to the unique dominance by SOEs which accounted for over 90 per cent of GDP in 1978, and gradually declined in importance throughout the next three decades. With the creation of a more competitive market after the large-scale SOE reform of the late 1990s as well as the incursion of foreign firms after WTO accession in 2001, there was a need to ensure that monopolies did not distort the market. In China, moreover, there were numerous laws geared at managing foreign investors to control their presence in the domestic market; for example, the Chinese–foreign Equity Joint Venture law of 1979, as well as those which governed the gradual emergence of domestic private firms, for example, the Law on Individual Wholly Owned Enterprises in 1999. Parallel laws for foreign and domestic firms resulted. Therefore, there was subsequent unification of various pieces of law governing the same issue, such as the Contract Law of 1999 which unified the three forms of contract law that had governed domestic and foreign enterprises separately.

Examining the periods of adoption of key commercial laws harkens back to the age of industrialization. At the start of the Industrial Revolution in 1820, the US had a purchasing power parity (PPP)-adjusted per capita GDP of US$1,257, which had doubled by the end of the period in 1870 (see Maddison 2001, for the historical GDP per capita measures reported in 1990 US dollars). If China's industrialization is considered to have taken place between 1950 and 1978 under the command economy when it was transformed from an agrarian to an economy whose GDP is generated largely by industry, then both countries experienced a doubling of incomes during the industrialization process

Table 2.5 A comparative perspective of US and China economic and legal development

	US		China	
	Year	GDP per capita[a]	Year	GDP per capita[a]
Start of industrialization period	Industrial Revolution of 1820	$1,257	Start of industrialization under central planning in 1950	$448
End of industrialization period	Industrial Revolution concluded in 1870	$2,445	End of planned economy in 1978	$978
Anti-trust legislation	Sherman Act of 1890	$3,392	Anti-Monopoly Law of 2007	$5,564[b]
Bankruptcy law	Bankruptcy Act of 1898[d]	$3,780	Enterprise Bankruptcy Law of 1986[e]	$1,597
Corporate law	Delaware General Corporation Law of 1899	$4,051	Company Law of 1994	$2,515
Securities regulator	US Securities and Exchange Commission (SEC) of 1934	$5,114	China Securities and Regulatory Commission (CSRC) of 1992	$2,132
Patent law	Patent Act of 1790	$1,257[c]	Patent Law of 1985	$1,519

Notes: (a) Per capita GDP is adjusted for PPP and in 1990 US dollars (Maddison 2001).
(b) This figure is from the World Bank.
(c) The figure pertains to 1820 (Maddison 2001).
(d) The Nelson Act was superseded by the Bankruptcy Code of 1978.
(e) Substantially revised in 2006.

(see Table 2.5 for US incomes doubling between 1820 and 1870, and China's incomes doubling between 1950 and 1978). However, China's GDP per capita was half of that of the US at the start as well as at the end of the industrialization period.

The US had a per capita GDP of around US$3,000–4,000 at the time of the adoption of a key body of corporate laws at the turn of the twentieth century, such as anti-trust legislation, bankruptcy law, and the Delaware General Corporation Law, which were all passed between 1890 and 1900 (see Table 2.5). The comparable set of laws for China was adopted when market-oriented reforms were implemented in the mid-1980s to mid-1990s, when its per capita income was around US$1,500–2,500. Focusing on the main pieces of corporate law for these countries, the Delaware General Corporation Law of 1899 was adopted when US per capita GDP was US$4,051, while China's Company Law was promulgated in 1994 when its GDP per capita was US$2,515. The adoption of commercial laws at an earlier stage of economic development by China is also evident when comparing the establishment of the securities regulator in both countries. The US Securities and Exchange Commission (SEC) was founded in 1934 when US mean income was US$5,114, while the China Securities and Regulatory Commission (CSRC) was created in 1992 when Chinese average income was US$2,132. China's commercial laws came into existence at an earlier point of its economic development than the US.

A number of reasons for this earlier adoption include the imperfect parallel of industrialization which in the US was founded on technological breakthroughs which transformed industry, while China undertook industrialization under quite different circumstances within a centrally planned economy. Second, China under Communism and the command economy was poorer at the start and end of the process than the US (China's per capita GDP in 1950 was less than US$500, while US income in 1820 was US$1,257). Third, China's laws are adopted in a context of global trade and financial rules stemming from the WTO and the international financial institutions (IFI) such as the Financial Stability Board (FSB) of the Bank for International Settlements (BIS); for example, the TRIPs or trade-related aspects of intellectual property rights agreement of the WTO which harmonizes intellectual property regimes across countries, and the Basel standards of banking regulation from the BIS. Due to this trend of harmonization of international laws, there are proponents of a view that there is convergence of corporate governance systems worldwide (see Hansmann and Kraakman 2001). Therefore, the expectations of the actors in the global economy include rapid implementation of commercial laws and rules to facilitate cross-border transactions, which form an external impetus for China and other developing countries to have a legal framework at an earlier stage of development.

Where China lags behind, for example, anti-monopoly and bankruptcy laws, reflects a lack of market need because of SOEs making it irrelevant to be concerned with competition policy or bankruptcies. Overall, China appears to have adopted legal reforms at earlier stages of economic development than the US, making the Chinese paradox—growth without legal development—less of one.

A comparison of the key laws—patent law designed to foster innovation, corporate law to enable commercial activity, and financial regulation to safeguard capital markets—will highlight the complex interaction, rather than present a clear sequence, of how law and markets evolved in both the US and China. A distinction that appears is between the *de jure* promulgation of the law on the books and the *de facto* effectiveness of the law. The relationship of the latter to markets is where the disagreement between the two schools of thought lies. Lawyers such as Coffee (2001) as well as economists such as Chen (2003) would argue that the laws follow markets, while economists like La Porta et al. (1997, 1998) believe that effective laws (such as providing better shareholder protection) precede market development. In the comparative analysis that follows, laws appear to largely follow economic developments and thus play a market-supporting role, although overall, the pattern is that of a complementary process whereby laws create markets, markets foster a need for more and better laws, which in turn leads to more robust market development.

PATENT LAWS AND ECONOMIC GROWTH

Where there is some correspondence between the levels of income and legal reform between the US and China is in the area of patent law and the protection of intellectual property rights (IPRs). As seen in Table 2.5, the US Patent Act of 1790 was adopted when US per capita GDP was US$1,257, and China's Patent Law was first promulgated in 1985 when its GDP per capita was US$1,519. It is often thought that international pressures persuaded the Chinese to improve protectection of intellectual property within their borders against the risk of expropriation and thus safeguard the incentive to invent (and invest in China). Interestingly, both the US and China adopted their own laws preceding the existence of the relevant international laws; however, the US was a leader in international norms, whereas China revised its IPRs to comply with international laws.

US patent law preceded the Paris and Berne Conventions of 1867 and 1871, respectively. By that time, the US had completed its industrial revolution, incomes had doubled and technological progress, such as the invention of the steam engine, had occurred. The breakthroughs of the two industrial revolutions of the UK during the late 1700s to early 1800s, and the US and Germany during the slighter late period from 1820–70 provided a strong motivation for protecting inventions. The steam engine, spinning and weaving machines, cast iron, and electric battery were among the key inventions of the nineteenth-century industrial revolutions. By the twentieth century, the international conventions on patents occurred during a time of inventions such as the telegraph, telephone, and electricity, which saw a fivefold increase in per capita incomes in Western Europe as compared with the threefold increase between 1700–1800 (Maddison 2001). This, of course, continued in the twentieth century with the promulgation of TRIPs and harmonization of IPR laws.

China's patent law also preceded the adoption of the global IPR regime but under a very different context. IPRs are governed by the WTO TRIPs agreement (trade-related intellectual property rights) which was passed in 1995 and bound China upon accession to the global trade organization in 2001. TRIPs governed IPRs on the dual premises of sovereignty and independence, whereby recognition and enforcement of such rights was within a country's control (Yueh 2007). TRIPs increases both the scope of the protection of IPRs and harmonizes such protection worldwide among WTO members, which runs contrary to the previous legal regime and led to several revisions of Chinese laws. As such, enforcement at the level of that of the developed countries is expected of China.

Interestingly, China grew faster than the US after the passage of the IPR regime, despite complaints of weak enforcement in China as compared with the strong protection in the US. In the decade or so after passage of the law, US per capita income grew at an average of 0.9 per cent per annum from 1820–30, while China's grew at 6.6 per cent from 1985–95. The relatively lower American growth rates may be simply because the Industrial Revolution was yet to occur, or the different context of these laws could also play a role. The common law tradition of the US would result in the effective development of the law only over time. Therefore, the patent law not generating as strong growth in the US could be due to the lack of case law affording the magnitude of protection that is evident today. By contrast, China's patent law was promulgated after it industrialized and during a period of initial transition from central planning when China undertook 'catch-up' growth. Inventions require time. Unlike the US, China is growing during a period when there already exists a number of innovations from more developed countries and thus can manage a faster process of technological adoption through imitation and incremental improvements on existing inventions.

The initial adoption of IPR protection at a similar level of economic development, though under very different contexts, could reflect a number of factors. The first is that when a society undergoes industrialization, there is a push for protection of commercial interests such as being able to profit from invention. It could also reflect the belief of government that innovation needs to be fostered in order to promote the commercialization of invention to create markets, or to generate the technological progress needed to fuel economic growth.

The adoption at a similar period of economic development could reflect the same impetus for promoting growth, although the contexts were rather different, as were arguably the outcomes as a result. IPRs indeed create a market for invention, which fuels clamours for better protection within a country and across borders as global integration progresses. The process is therefore one in which property rights are created by laws, but the market itself generates the constituency to agitate for more legal protection that meets the needs of that market which in turn fuels the development of that market. The early government focus is undoubtedly due to the importance of innovation in fuelling long-run economic growth, which is evident in the US and China which turned to

IPRs at roughly the same level of economic development, albeit with rather different forces driving their varied aims in this area.

CORPORATE LAW AND ECONOMIC NECESSITY

Corporate law in the US and China both developed in response to their respective economic needs (see for example, Horwitz 1992, on the evolution of US contract law during the late nineteenth and twentieth centuries in response to the economic and social conflicts of the time). In the US, corporation law was left to the states after the US federal constitution adopted in 1789 did not explicitly govern incorporation, thus paving the way for states to adopt their own laws during the early nineteenth century. The presumption of the US federal system is that unless explicitly claimed in the Constitution or Act of Congress, an area of law was to be governed by state law. The 'state's rights' doctrine is embodied in the Tenth Amendment concluding the Bill of Rights to the US Constitution, which states: 'The powers not delegated to the United States by the Constitution, nor prohibited by it to the States, are reserved to the States respectively, or to the people.' New York was the first in 1811, followed by New Jersey, both of which pre-dated the US Industrial Revolution. The Industrial Revolution, however, led states such as Delaware, which has come to dominate corporate law in the US, to pass its general corporation law in 1899 to govern and attract the growing number of companies with the resultant fiscal benefits to the state (see Hamermesh 2006).

In China, the corporatization process began in the early 1990s when SOEs were in need of reform. By 1992, an estimated two-thirds of all SOEs were thought to be loss-making (Fan 1994). By creating shareholding companies out of SOEs, the corporatization process transformed these enterprises into joint stock companies owned by shareholders and therefore began the gradual process of privatization, as many SOEs retained the state as their majority shareholder even as it reformed (see Clarke 2003c). The passage of the Company Law in 1993 and promulgation in 1994 provided a basis in law for defining the rights and obligations of shareholders. Subsequent laws created other corporate forms, such as partnerships through the Law on Partnership Enterprises in 1997 and the Law on Individual Wholly Owned Enterprises in 1999. The coincidence of laws with economic necessity is expected insofar as laws arise to address a specific development in the market, whether it is the growth of firms in the Industrial Revolution or the creation of companies defined by shares to reform the inefficient state-owned sector.

A common perception is that the US has and has had a well-defined and highly functional rule of law. However difficult that is to measure during the late nineteenth century, the US common law system is developed through case law which occurs over time and is unlikely to have existed as a fully fledged and effective 'rule of law' at the start of the era of the corporation. In examining ten countries of different legal origins (common law, civil law, and 'transplanted' countries such as Malaysia and Spain), Pistor et al. (2003) argue that the corporate laws at the time of adoption tend to be simple and concerned with establishing the corporation, but do not address more complex issues concerning corporate governance that demarcates an effective legal system, such as shareholder suits. They find that countries, even after adopting similar corporate laws, will diverge and follow their own paths. Therefore, they conclude that the indicators of effective corporate governance, which is typically relied upon as indicative of a well-functioning legal system, tend not to exist at the outset, including in the United States.

The evolution of corporate law is further complicated in China by its distinct legal tradition which does not rely on courts as the main institutional source of developing the legal system. Instead, legislative enactments will play a larger role, in line with civil law countries such as Germany, although the administrative law tradition in China will also play a part. Nevertheless, its company law has been in existence for less than two decades and the poor scores on the corporate governance indicators which are seen as representing the effectiveness of a legal regime most likely reflect the nascent stages of its legal development.

However, China's economic development has sped up, particularly with global integration after the 'open-door' policy accelerated in 1992. The rapid passage of laws and regulations during the 1990s following the 1993 Company Law, such as the unified Contract Law of 1999, M&A Law, and Securities Investment Fund Law, both of 2003, reflect the push to legislate and thus improve the effectiveness of the commercial laws to govern the fast-growing market economy. In a country with some civil law tradition, laws are developed through legislative action which in turn reflects the needs of the market, much as in a common law system where case laws arise from litigants seeking adjudication of disputes arising from market transactions. For instance, WTO-mandated liberalization of capital markets led to the passage of the Securities Investment Fund Law to govern the foreign and domestic firms expected to operate in this opened sector. Similarly, the 'going out' strategy of Chinese firms since the mid-1990s culminated in permission being granted to private firms investing overseas, as witnessed by TCL's purchase of the Thomson brand in 2003 and which was followed by Lenovo's purchase of IBM's personal computer business two years later. The acquisition and mergers associated with commercial transactions led to a need for an M&A law. Since the first transactions were dated in the same year as the passage of the law, it is unlikely that the law provided a strong basis for M&A transactions as its scope would not have been immediately evident, although it is plausible that the same forces pushing for permission to operate in international financial markets are the same firms and government officials who viewed the 'going out' strategy as sufficiently mature to take this step (see for example, Sun and Tobin 2009, for the argument that innovative Chinese firms can enter and learn from international capital markets, which in turn can induce market-level improvements through regulatory competition and demands for a more standardized system of economic regulation).

REGULATORY REFORM SUPPORTING MARKETS:
CHINA'S CSRC AND THE US SEC

Regulation plays a role in a legal system through providing the measures often necessary to implement laws and the apparatus with which to enforce the same. Regulatory agencies, therefore, oversee markets and are the source of regulations governing markets under their remit. Regulatory systems differ significantly across countries, with one key difference as between rules-based and principle-based systems which is evident in the US and UK respectively, although both are common law countries. In a rules-based system, the adherence to the letter of the law takes precedence whereas a principle-based system relies more on self-regulation to fulfil the spirit of the law. In both systems, however, there is a strong contrast with civil law countries where the latter are characterized by much greater state interference in markets. Coffee (2001) describes the late development of regulatory agencies in the US and UK after the establishment of the market as the reason that such markets governed in their self-interest due to a lack of government involvement. He describes it as 'enlightened self-interest'. In terms of the sequence of law and capital markets for China, this ground has been well covered by Chen (2003) for China who argues that capital markets are the most evident place for the 'crash-then-law' hypothesis because they generate a political powerful constituency to lobby for legal change given the high degree of commonality of interest among the interested parties and the ability to obtain immediately measurable benefits. Chen (2003) details the scandals and shortcomings in the Chinese stock market which led to better regulation and protection of shareholders.

Examining capital market development in a comparative perspective, there is evidence of regulatory reform adopted to better govern markets. The stock markets in Shanghai and Shenzhen were established prior to the regulatory agency, the CSRC in 1992, which is a pattern that is evident in the US as well. The US Securities and Exchange Commission (SEC) was established in 1934 in the aftermath of the 1929 stock market crash and subsequent Great Depression of 1929 lasting until the early 1930s. The bourse, however, pre-dates the regulator. The New York Stock Exchange (NYSE) was created in 1792 when a group of stockbrokers gathered together to trade securities on Wall Street in New York City. For the next 142 years, the NYSE operated without a central regulator until the stock market crash of October 1929. It triggered the Great Depression which was characterized by real output falls, deflation, and widespread banking failure when half of all US banks failed or merged between December 1930 and March 1933 when President Roosevelt was forced to shut down the entire US banking system (Bernanke 2004). Prior to the SEC which was created by the Securities and Exchange Act of 1934, securities trading was governed by states with decentralized supervisory authority that did not extend beyond their boundaries. Following the stock market crash in 29 October 1929 (known as 'Black Tuesday'), a plethora of laws as well as the SEC came into existence in order to safeguard markets. The plight of consumers, who had lost money in the stock market and their bank deposits due to widespread banking failure without deposit insurance for savers, heralded the need for a regulator to govern and restore confidence in the financial system. The SEC, therefore, was established in response to a crash in the market and charged with implementing laws to safeguard the financial sector, such as corporate governance reforms lately seen in the Sarbanes-Oxley Act of 2002.

China's CSRC was established just a year after the creation of the two exchanges, though the country did not have a banking regulator until 2003. Both were established to regulate the financial sector, alongside the insurance regulator (CIRC), following the establishment of the capital, banking, and insurance markets largely in the 1990s. As discussed earlier, China scores poorly on corporate governance indicators reflecting the lack of effectiveness of the law and the imperfect oversight of China's trio of regulators. The late establishment of the CBRC in particular suggests that the banking sector had developed in the absence of regulation, which would be paradoxical except for the dominance of state ownership and therefore state control in bank lending. As the banking sector became increasingly liberalized and the dominance of the state banks receded, there was a push—particularly with WTO-mandated opening to foreign banks—for a regulator and improved governance. The insurance market was also lately developed since before the late 1990s, insurance was provided by the *danwei* or work unit so a market hardly existed. With reform, the market developed and the CIRC undertook a corresponding governance role.

Regarding the CSRC, Chen (2003) documents the ways in which securities regulations were passed in response to the demands of interested constituents in the capital market (see also, Sun and Tobin 2009). Despite the relatively early establishment of the CSRC soon after the bourses and comparatively in relation to the United States, there were no significant securities laws for six years until the Securities Law was passed in 1998. Prior to its enactment, the stock markets still operated under administrative direction. Provincial governments selected firms to become listed firms and these governments in turn were allocated a certain quota to do so (Du and Xu 2009). As a result of the incentives of the quota system, provincial authorities selected the better performing firms for initial public offerings (IPOs) so that the stock market grew throughout the 1990s despite the Securities Law not coming into effect until 1999 (Du and Xu 2009). In this way, China's capital markets functioned prior to the establishment of the relevant laws and in the presence of a passive regulator. However, WTO accession changed the picture. As part of its WTO terms, China agreed to open its financial sector to foreign firms. The anticipated opening led to a series of securities laws passed since 2002, which rapidly reformed China's financial sector. Foreign firms and governments interested in accessing China's market as well as the *de novo* private sector would be among those clamouring for better defined rights. The Chinese government's desire to foster its own state-owned enterprises as well as safeguard the market from foreign dominance would be among other drivers; for example, the State-owened Asset Supervision and Administration Commission

(SASAC) was established in 2003 to oversee state-owned assets when SOEs continued to account for nearly half of China's GDP, while a 25 per cent ceiling on foreign equity ownership is maintained in SOEs. The result was a large number of regulations passed since 2002 that are geared at improving transparency, increasing disclosure requirements, reforming the non-tradable shares in the stock markets, extending protection to minority shareholders, forbidding insider trading, and monitoring mergers and acquisition activity, all of which address the needs of shareholders, investors, debtors, and firms in the market (see Chen 2003). In turn, the growth of the market leads to the need for regulation and regulators who, if effective, lead to the further development of the market. After the establishment of the SEC in 1934, the NYSE experienced its longest bull market of eight years from 1949. Although the same cannot be said of the CSRC in its first fifteen years, the numerous securities laws passed since greater market opening after WTO accession herald significant reform of the stock market in China.

In China's financial sector, the sequence seems to be one of markets preceding laws. Laws appear to develop alongside, and in response, to market needs. As in the United States, laws and regulations were not established in a vacuum to predate markets. Instead, some laws (and administrative dictates in China such as the provincial quota system for IPOs) create markets, which gives rise to further laws and regulatory bodies which in turn govern and establish new segments of the market. Therefore, it seems that whether it is 'crash and pass' like the US SEC and the post-2002 reforms of capital markets in China, or a more evolutionary process to accompany economic reform such as the Company Law and corporatization movement in China and the Delaware Corporation Law after the US industrial revolution, or the passage of IPRs to promote technological advancement, the process is better characterized as complementary rather than sequential or cause and effect.

COMPLEMENTARITIES BETWEEN LAW AND MARKETS

There appears to be a complementary process between law and markets, where law neither entirely precedes market or vice versa. Formal written law creates property rights in intellectual property, legitimizes corporate forms, and establishes capital markets. Informal markets can often also arise through barter or small-scale transactions or in response to market liberalization; for example, privatization of previously state-owned housing. Once the markets are established, then in both common law and civil law traditions, there is a process of interpreting and revising the laws respectively through a judicial or legislative process. This process is driven by interested constituents vested in the markets, which can include holders of IPRs, owners of private firms, and shareholders (see Coffee 2001; see also, Sun and Tobin 2009), as well as governments wishing to reform their state-owned enterprises (for example, China in the 1990s), or restore confidence in markets (for example, US SEC). Countries which produce more effective laws and regulations will have better functioning markets, which in both the common and civil law traditions occur over time (see La Porta et al. 1997, for the finding that better share-holder protection is associated with higher growth rates; see Cull and Xu 2005, for the finding that provinces in China with better legal protection are associated with improved firm performance). Evaluating the US at the time of the adoption of its corporate laws, the indicators of effectiveness of laws are unlikely to be as strong as they are at present since key protections are not specified in the statute when passed, but develop over time with judicial and legislative review. (See Pistor et al. 2003, for a historical review of common and civil law countries that finds that the countries do not have strong rule of law at the inception of the laws but effectiveness as measured by shareholder protection develops over time; see a contrary argument by Acemoglu, Johnson, and Robinson 2005, that countries which inherited better institutions, that is, those that protected against risk of expropriation, from colonial powers resulted in subsequently higher growth rates.)

For the US and China, key commercial laws were adopted at comparable levels of development, with China having done so at an earlier stage and with seemingly more impressive economic growth rates. However, the speed of setting up a market or adoption of laws does not equate to effectiveness of the legal system. Undoubtedly, the transition and globalization context increases the complication of this comparison.

2.7 Enforcement of Laws

The issue of enforcement further points to the continued presence of informal institutions, such as reliance on relational contracting or trust-based relationships in China. There is undoubtedly a cultural element in that interpersonal relationships, such as *guanxi*, play a notable role in economic transactions within and without China, even among the overseas diasporas. Within China itself, this was also perhaps enabled by the reliance on administrative dictates—a legacy of China's administrative law tradition.

Due to the absence of a well-established legal system, developing countries tend to rely on informal institutional arrangements, such as utilization of social capital or relational-based contracting whereby contracting is undertaken on the basis of trust. Even developed countries at the start of their marketization relied on such relationships (see for example, Franks, Mayer, and Rossi 2009, who studied the development of the UK capital market and found that ownership dispersion relied more on informal relations of trust than on formal systems of regulation). Enforcement, which is often a challenge in an underdeveloped legal system, can be by means of social capital instead of courts. For instance, social sanctions and norms account for the success of micro-finance institutions such as the Grameen Bank in Bangladesh. The high repayment rate of loans is not due to threatened legal action, but on account of social capital in the community which acts to enforce the terms of the loan. By overlooking informal institutional arrangements which support the rule of law and other formal institutions, the extent of legal and institutional reform can be misjudged and developing countries' could suffer from poorly fashioned policies as a result. In other words, as countries are increasingly judged on the quality of their institutions, poor legal systems are a common area of criticism of developing countries, and aid or technical assistance can hinge on legal reform so leading to adoption of laws that may not suit the country. At the extreme, 'transplanting' legal systems into less-developed countries has not been successful (see Pistor, Martin, and Gelfer 2000, for the conclusion that legal systems transplanted into newly transitioning economies were not successful in fostering economic growth).

Enforcement is easier in a community; thus, the judicial system needs improvement as the number of arms' length agreements increase which makes informal enforcement less feasible. The development of legal reforms in the West followed a similar pattern, suggesting that greater marketization will require more legal reform to govern relationships that can no longer rely on trust alone. However, relational contracting, that is, dealing with trusted parties, is much cheaper than litigation if a relationship goes sour, which also explains the continued reliance on social capital by small businesses even in developed economies with more complete but expensive legal systems. China is at a stage where its small businesses and entrepreneurs can still effectively utilize informal institutional arrangements for enforcement alongside the reforming formal legal ones.

Given the necessarily slow pace when creating an independent judiciary, it is likely that informal arrangements, as well as arbitration when the transactions are more at arm's length, will remain in place for some time to come. But, this can also help explain how China has been able to grow and become marketized with a legal system that suffers from weak enforcement and thus lacks effectiveness.

2.8 China's Legal and Economic Reform in an Era of Global Integration

China's experience over the past thirty years has been the envy of many developing and transition economies, as well as being an 'outlier' with its poor legal system and rapid growth. A final aspect of China's reform is the influence of the international economic system. Whilst China has gradually integrated itself into the global economy during the 1990s, the world economy also underwent a transformation with the emergence of a growing body of international economic laws and rules.

2.8.1 *Expectations of Foreign Firms*

China's treatment of foreign firms, in contrast with domestic enterprises, was governed by formal laws which nevertheless suffered from imperfect enforcement. Gauging their response sheds some light on how China's imperfect enforcement of laws, which is as important as the written law itself, has not impeded its marketization process.

Since the 'open-door' policy reforms of China's external sector were adopted in the late 1970s and sped up in the early 1990s, China has rapidly become one of the world's top destinations for foreign direct investment (FDI). The first significant commercial law passed in China is the Chinese–foreign Equity Joint Venture Law of 1979. This, and its counterpart laws establishing cooperative JVs and WFOEs passed in 1986 and 1988 respectively, pre-date laws establishing the legal forms for Chinese domestic firms which were passed a decade or so later. The better delineated rights of foreign investors has been a source of contention amongst even Chinese private firms whose rights were less clearly protected for much of the reform period (see for example, Huang 2006).

For most of the reform period especially prior to WTO accession in 2001 after which legal reforms were targeted for improvement, the predominant form of FDI was Chinese–foreign joint ventures (JVs), where the Chinese and foreign partners set up either equity or cooperative joint ventures. Both forms of joint ventures were vested in contracts that legally specified the rights and obligations of both parties and subject to judicial enforcement. The same could be said of the law governing wholly foreign-owned enterprises (WFOEs). The uncertainty that might have been generated by the lack of adequate protection of private property due to a weak legal system, though, did not seem to serve as a deterrent to FDI, which is another puzzle in China's growth narrative. Indeed, China is a competitive destination for foreign direct investment even measured against developed economies, such as the US and UK, despite its underdeveloped legal and institutional system (see for example, UNCTAD 2006).

Therefore, China recognized early on that foreign firms operating in a global context and from developed economies needed laws to govern their rights even if the enforcement of those rights was imperfect. Unsurprisingly, it generated an interested constituent of private Chinese firms who sought a similar level of legal protection of their property and transactional security, which led to the passage of laws on partnerships and sole proprietorships in the 1990s. Whereas Chinese firms can accept administrative rule in lieu of judicial enforcement or an open legislative process to effect change, the puzzle is that the lack of effectiveness of laws, particularly in the area of enforcement, did not deter foreign investors (see Clarke 2003a for the argument that rights in China are interpreted differently than property rights in developed countries). However, since WTO accession, the clamour for better protection in particular of IPRs from foreign firms and governments has increased.

One potential explanation has to do with the rise in alternative dispute resolution (ADR), notably arbitration, in China, which sought to supplant an incomplete legal system. The China International Economic and Trade Arbitration Commission (CIETAC) is relied upon by international investors, for instance, as is resort to international arbitration based in Europe or elsewhere (see Bosworth and Yang 2000, for the importance of CIETAC and arbitration in resolving commercial disputes in China). Alternative dispute resolution has become more popular even in countries with well-developed legal systems such as the United States due to its being cheaper. Another reason is that the well-known Chinese reliance on relational contracting, that is, transacting on the basis of trust and known relations, is in part cultural, as it is evident even in overseas Chinese diasporas. Finally, there is a degree of risk in investing in any developing country so foreign firms have a greater appetite for uncertainty when dealing in China or other emerging markets such as Russia than in the United States. In their initial calculus, they would have measured the risks of expropriation and lesser contracting security against the rewards of efficiency, cost saving, and market access.

2.8.2 *WTO Law and Formal International Rules*

The context of more international rules also affected expectations of China's development of laws to support the market. Although global trade rules in particular have existed previously, the creation of the WTO in 1995 brought into prominence a number of laws, rules such as those governing intellectual property, as well as a dispute resolution mechanism (DSU) with influences on China's legal reforms with accession in December 2001. Clarke (2003b) asserts that the main effect of WTO-related changes is to increase the transparency of laws in China. Other rules that China accepted, such as the TRIPs provision, further led to revisions of its intellectual property rights regime in order to comply with the harmonized global laws governing IPRs. Moreover, the DSU provides a forum for countries to bring actions against other WTO members who are thought to have violated a precept of the WTO rules. For instance, China was the largest target of anti-dumping actions before the DSU in the 2000s. Threatened action alone can at times discourage the behaviour, such as the US rescinding tariffs on steel imports under the prospect of a WTO action. Moreover, legal protection and enforcement of IPRs as provided for under the TRIPs agreement can also be actioned before the DSU, such as the US case brought against China.

Aside from trade rules, the past decade has also witnessed the development of greater integration among financial markets, which led to the creation of financial codes such as the Basel accords governing capital adequacy ratios of banks, among others, promulgated by the Financial Stability Board of the Bank of International Settlements. In particular, the Asian financial crisis of the late 1990s highlighted the links among banking and financial systems, which prompted the need for coordination of financial regulation and commonly understood standards. Unlike the WTO-related rules, countries voluntarily adopt the standards to signal their management of risk and financial soundness to global capital markets. Sun and Tobin (2009) argue that Chinese firms which list overseas and operate in international financial markets do so as a signal when capital could be otherwise raised in China's high savings economy. However, the more rigorous standards of overseas listings are borne as a sign of a robust enterprise that a Chinese domestic listing could not provide. Other examples include the voluntary code of conduct adopted by Sovereign Wealth Funds (SWF), that is, state-owned funds investing foreign exchange surplus overseas. Although there are no rules which compel a SWF to do so, those owned by countries such as Singapore declare their activities and their intent to invest as passive, minority shareholders in the companies of other countries. By so doing, they seek to avoid political interference in their investments, but operate in a lacuna where international economic law is concerned. All of these factors suggest that China's legal reforms will not be advanced in a vacuum, particularly given its prominence in the global economy.

2.8.3 Assessment of the Law and Economic Relationship

This chapter has examined several aspects of the relationship between law and economic growth in China. It assessed the theoretical and empirical relationship between laws and the development of markets across countries, spanning currently developed, developing, and recently transitioned economies. The relationship between law and markets appears asynchronous for China. The argument that laws and economic development reinforce each other was made through an examination of the experience of the United States at a similar stage of economic development. By comparing three facets of Chinese and American legal reforms—intellectual property protection, corporate law, and securities regulation—the pattern was largely evolutionary in that laws may have created a market in the case of IPRs and enabled corporations, but regulations which gave substance to the law and therefore its effectiveness generally were passed after there was an evident economic necessity, such as abuse of monopoly power or financial sector scandals. Therefore, although a law or administrative dictate (or absence of strict prohibition) may create a market (or an informal one), this factor is insufficient to argue that the sequence must be laws preceding markets. Even innovation can happen without IPRs. By the yardstick of whether an effective rule of law exists, which goes beyond just the provisions that create an IPR or a corporate form, laws appear to develop in response to market demands and needs, which in turn leads to more marketization and economic development.

This perspective reconciles the existing views in the literature by arguing that it is the case that laws both precede and follow markets. Thus, this chapter posits that the literature is describing different facets of an evolving picture (see for example, Chen 2003 who subscribes to the 'crash-then-law' hypothesis versus La Porta et al. 1997, 1998, and Acemoglu, Johnson, and Robinson 2005 who argue that the existence of market-supporting institutions is the cause of subsequent robust growth).

It is difficult, if not impossible, to fit China into the paradigm given its history and context. However, China's experience suggests that there are more parallels than would at first appear between its legal and economic development with the United States. Specifically, China's legal development is similar to the US, and even at a comparable time in their economic development.

A further paradox in China's growth model was explored, which is the development of a market within a state-controlled communal property system. Administrative measures and ensuing institutional reform complete the picture for China, whereby its several decades-long economic transition has been driven by a series of experiments, trials, and 'no encouragement, no ban' policies. Given the context, the lack of laws establishing clearly defined property rights appears not to be as pertinent as in other countries.

2.9 Economic Growth, Laws, and Global Integration

In analysing China's growth model and evidence, the direction of reform points to the need for more formal legal protection as the economy aims to sustain its growth rate and stabilize its integration with the global economy. Since joining the World Trade Organisation in 2001, China has become part of a rules-based trading system that exposes it to the best-practice standards of international economic law, perhaps allowing China to leapfrog legal developments as well as technological ones if international norms can aid in the formulation of China's evolving legal reforms to supports its increasingly decentralized economy.

In return, China's adoption of international rules and standards serves to ease frictions with its trading partners over the extent of protection of the assets and proprietary information of their multinational corporations. As China adopts more rules granting market access and guarantees of protection to foreign investors in areas such as portfolio investments for the first time as part of its WTO commitments, including the QFII system adopted in 2002 and further intellectual property rights (IPRs) protection with the adoption of the TRIPs (trade-related aspects of intellectual property rights) agreement that is part of the WTO articles, these rules provide benchmarks for foreign investors seeking more certain protection while operating in China's underdeveloped legal system. For its part, China can gain know-how from investments as well as access to more advanced intellectual property which will benefit its economic growth. In other words, China can adopt legal measures commiserate with international best practice to induce more innovation and learning in its economy even whilst its own legal system is developing and improving to keep pace with its remarkable economic transformation.

As an example, Figure 2.4 indicates a nearly tenfold increase from 1990 to 2005 in patents, a legally protected innovation, since China's 2001 accession to the WTO and adoption of international rules governing intellectual property rights. Despite the furore over the incomplete protection offered to IPRs, China's remarkably fast development of intellectual property is consistent with an

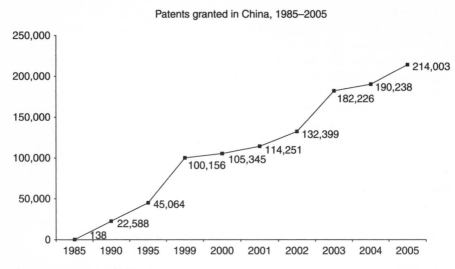

Figure 2.4 Patents in China

Source: *China Science and Technology Yearbook.*

economy that is integrating into a global standard for such protection. Knowing the global standards aids China in developing its IPR regime in a manner which is consistent with international expectations and facilitates the development of intellectual property which is essential to sustain economic growth.

2.10 Conclusion

China has performed admirably well since market-oriented reforms were introduced nearly three decades ago. This chapter has analysed the nature of its transition and resultant growth model, which has highlighted the importance of informal institutions in fuelling reform. The limits of such an approach began to be felt in the 1990s (and in the 1980s for foreign investors), which led to more formal, legal reforms taking place. This was evident in terms of treatment of foreign-invested enterprises and also private firms later on in the reform process.

Foremost among its ensuing challenges is to transform a growth model from one that has grown via productivity advances from factor reallocation to one which is fuelled by technological advancement and innovation. This in turn calls for more legal protection and clearly defined property rights in an economy increasingly open to global factors in the 2000s, including adherence to international economic law, among others.

For its part, the effects of China's rise have been widely felt in the global economy. Its global integration, therefore, further demands that its institutional structures quickly improve to become aligned with the expectations of the world economy despite its underdeveloped legal system that is not uncommon for a developing country. Nevertheless, the adoption of internationally recognized rules grants more certainty to investors and would help to underpin China's fast-growing economy.

There is also the influence of the global rules-based system that is gradually emerging and gained prominence around the same time as China's integration into the international system after years of inward-focused development. There are numerous limitations in the reach of the fledging international legal system, but certain rules such as IPR protection will influence the course of China's domestic reforms. The system, though, is two-way. Particularly in the area of voluntary adherence to rules and norms, China and its firms will seek those which advantage them while at the same time operate in the evolving global financial system. The picture may be more complex, but looks ever more evolutionary as countries gather at various international forums to negotiate and agree everything from liberalization of trade to rules governing risk assessment of banks.

China may continue to be viewed as a paradox, but its path will be enticing for many developing countries for which it is not unusual to have a nascent legal system that will not rate well in terms of effectiveness or enforcement. The success of China, and the prospect of it strengthening laws alongside robust economic growth, has the possibility of being a model to emulate.

This chapter has analysed China's reform approach in the last thirty years and focused on the importance placed on informal institutions that created incentives for economic activity in the absence of a transformation of communal into private ownership. However, as reforms progressed, legal and other formal reforms were needed to sustain growth, such that China has developed a corporate law system to support markets, and increasingly adopted international rules such as those pertaining to IPRs to safeguard innovation. As China's transition proceeds and its growth model moves more towards one that needs to achieve technological progress, legal reforms will become more pertinent, while in turn, such more formal reforms should support an increasingly decentralized, market-focused economy. Therefore, although China is often touted as an economy that has grown without having a strong rule of law, it had its own systems of informal institutional innovations and formal contractual rights which served to create the necessary property rights to stimulate market exchange. China's institutional development and evolving legal system may shed some light on how it has managed remarkable growth with an underdeveloped institutional structure—an issue of concern for many developing countries.

3

Neoclassical Growth: Labour Productivity and Corporate Restructuring

3.1 Introduction

Factor reallocation has been a significant driver of productivity gains in China. These have often been conflated with total factor productivity (TFP) growth as both show gains in output from the same quantity of inputs of labour and capital. However, there is an important difference between productivity gains from one-off structural reforms, such as the movement of factors from the state-owned sector to private firms, and the sustained productivity improvements from improving human capital and innovation. This chapter will show that the slowdown in TFP from the mid-1990s is associated with the slowing of one-off productivity gains from factor reallocation. By the end of the 1990s and 2000s, much of the shift from state-owned enterprises (SOEs) to private firms had taken place, including moving workers as well as corporate restructuring of former SOEs into shareholding firms and granting legal recognition to private firms. These reforms, though, hold the key for sustained productivity gains as more of China's economic growth will depend on increasing labour and firm productivity through rewarding output and better legal protection of commercial activities. The chapter will first examine what drives labour productivity and then analyse the impact of corporate restructuring on capital productivity.

3.2 Labour Productivity

Productivity advances drive long-run economic growth, and a crucial factor is labour productivity. The productivity of labour in China was marginally relevant in the pre-1978 period when the labour market was administered centrally, wages were centrally determined, and the 'iron rice bowl' of lifetime employment plus benefits reigned. However, the picture has changed dramatically in the post-1978 reform period due to numerous labour market reforms as well as radical changes in ownership structure, whereby the dominance of state-owned enterprises (SOEs) has given way to private sector firms and globalization, all of which introduce competition into the previously planned economy and promote reallocation of resources of capital and labour from less to more productive uses.

Labour market reforms have included liberalizing wages to improve the reward of productive characteristics such as education, as well as increasing job mobility to permit better matching between worker and employer characteristics, leading to a more competitive labour market (see for example, Knight and Yueh 2004). Ownership reform has also progressed significantly throughout the reform period (Dougherty, Herd, and He 2007). From state-owned enterprises dominating GDP to accounting for less than half of China's output by the 2000s, China's economy is increasingly characterized by private sector competition and greater market orientation (Jefferson, Hu, and Su 2006). Moreover, the 'open door' policy, culminating in membership of the World Trade Organisation (WTO) in 2001, heralded a period of global integration and market opening, which again results in greater competitive pressures and the prospect for learning from more technologically advanced firms and countries induced to invest in China given its cheap, abundant, and reasonably skilled labour force.

In most assessments of China's economic growth, (see for example, Borensztein and Ostry 1996), factor reallocation, particularly in terms of using labour more efficiently, is a strong component. Labour is also the source of China's comparative advantage in global trade. However, there are limits to factor reallocation; for example, state to private sector enabled by wage and other labour market reforms as well as from agriculture to industry. Productivity derived from more efficient use of capital as well as labour, though, cannot sustain long-run economic growth indefinitely. Instead, economic growth requires using existing factors more efficiently by increasing total factor productivity or TFP. Technology, therefore, holds the key to sustaining productivity that can fuel economic growth. Often difficult to distinguish in macro-level studies, factor inputs can be measured, but the differentiation between productivity improvements from factor reallocation versus more sustainable technical gains is more difficult. For instance, even where factor reallocation is measured as the movement of labour between sectors of the economy (for example, agriculture to industry or between ownership types such as from state to non-state firms), the measurements underestimate the within-sector TFP improvements.

Figures 3.1 and 3.2 show China's labour productivity in comparative perspective and over time relative to a starting point in 1980 when it began its market-oriented reforms. Figure 3.1 in particular shows the extraordinary gains in labour productivity in China since then. Increases in GDP per worker in manufacturing were steady and comparable to international increases until the early 1990s when China's 'open door' policy took off, after which, while other major economies experienced a nearly tripling of productivity and India improved more modestly, China's productivity levels increased nearly sevenfold. The productivity leader nevertheless remains the USA, which is evident in Figure 3.2. China is around one-eighth as productive as the leader, although its

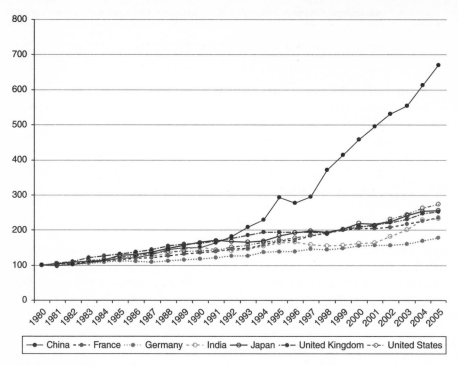

Figure 3.1 GDP per worker in manufacturing (1980 = 100), 1980–2005
Source: ILO.

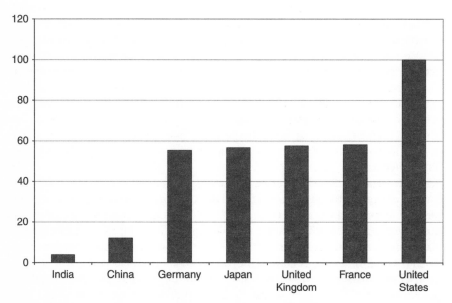

Figure 3.2 Comparative labour productivity (USA = 100), 2005
Source: ILO.

Table 3.1 Labour productivity in comparative perspective, 2005

Country	GDP per worker (1990 US$ at PPP)	GDP per worker in manufacturing (1997 US$ at PPP)
India	2,421	4,089
China	5,772	12,642
Germany	19,477	57,849
Japan	21,979	59,281
France	22,099	60,835
United Kingdom	22,412	60,235
United States	30,519	104,606

Source: ILO.

gains are much faster than the richer country. By 2005, as seen in Table 3.1, China's GDP per worker in the broader economy as well as in manufacturing was still modest relative to other comparable sized economies due to its low level of economic development, which contributes to its cost advantage. However, it has had faster labour productivity growth even against a similarly poor country such as India, which contributes to China's faster overall GDP growth.

China's labour productivity has indeed accelerated in the 2000s. Over the period 1952 to 1997, Wu (2001) concludes that China's comparative labour productivity increased from about 3.0 in 1952 to 7.6 in 1997 (USA=100), showing a significant gap with the US even after three decades of reform. But in less than a decade since 1997, China's productivity has nearly doubled to 12.1 as compared to 7.6, measured against the USA as 100. Jefferson, Hu, and Su (2006) likewise estimate that China's labour productivity must increase by some sixfold before it achieves a GDP per capita that is one-quarter that of the US, but find evidence that industries in the coastal regions are already nearly one-quarter of that of the US by the early 2000s.

Few studies have focused exclusively on the determinants of labour productivity in China, though a large number have examined the factors influencing TFP (see for example, Jefferson and Su 2006). Kraay (2006), using a panel of firms from 1988–92, finds a positive effect of exports on increasing labour productivity. Jefferson et al. (2000), using a dataset covering 1980–6, similarly find large increases in labour productivity, particularly in the 1990s, and notably for SOEs during this period attributed to the large-scale layoff policy (*xiagang*) over the latter period. Jefferson, Hu, and Su (2006) explore the sources of China's growth covering the period, 1995–2004. They conclude that there is evidence of improved allocative efficiency from labour moving out of agriculture and between industrial and ownership sectors resulting in productivity advances. Brandt and Zhu (2010) come to a similar conclusion, but find that the reallocation effect weakens in the 2000s. Yet labour productivity accelerated in the 2000s.

Labour productivity rose in the 1980s, 1990s, and 2000s due to sectoral shifts (state to private, agriculture to industry) as well as opening (exporting starting in early 1990s), both of which are linked to introducing competition in factor and product markets. In fact, these reforms of factor and product markets in the 1980s and 1990s largely concluded by 2001 at the end of the 9th Five Year Plan which had radically reformed Chinese markets. The studies of productivity generally find that the allocative effects of moving labour into more productive sectors exist, but lessen, during the 2000s when most of China's reforms had taken place in the labour and product markets. The growth of labour productivity, therefore, seems to point to technical rather than allocative efficiency; that is, more sustained improvements due to technology rather than factor reallocation.

Using a national firm-level panel data set from 2000 to 2005, this chapter seeks to explain the rapid increase in labour productivity in China in the 2000s. The acceleration in productivity in the 2000s is greater than in the previous decades, which suggests that there are improvements in technical rather than allocative efficiency associated with structural transformation. In the 2000s, when China joined the world trade system as a member of the WTO, its significant reforms in the previous two decades laid the foundation for 'catching up' by enabling it to utilize more advanced technology. There may well still be allocative effects, but this chapter will investigate whether technical improvements such as those obtained from technology transfers and R&D can explain the larger labour productivity of the 2000s.

The extent of labour productivity advances would inform China's growth prospects and gauge the effectiveness of the policies geared to increasing the market-driven elements of the Chinese economy and sustained economic growth (see Kokko 1996 who argues that labour productivity essentially reflects the technological ability of firms which constitutes the long-run driver of economic growth of a country). The conclusion across these studies emphasizes the importance of labour productivity in driving China's economic growth.

The chapter will test the hypothesis that the acceleration of labour productivity gains in China's third decade of reforms is a result of technical efficiency gains more than one-off allocative effects. Is there evidence that labour productivity driven *to a greater extent* by technical rather than allocative efficiency or is it still largely a process of structural transformation?

3.3 Reforming Labour

In the 1980s, waves of reforms were undertaken that dismantled the administrative wage structure. By the 1990s, labour market reforms created a fixed plus bonus wage structure that granted higher returns to productive characteristics, although it also permitted some discrimination, as the 'iron rice bowl' was dismantled (see Yueh 2004). The late 1990s (1996–2000) restructuring led to greater labour market flexibility, including job mobility, which resulted in a more competitive labour market by the 2000s.

In the 1980s and 1990s, domestic reforms in the labour and product markets increased marketization and meant that labour productivity was driven by structural reforms that increased allocative efficiency. The large-scale restructuring of the state sector in the 1990s coupled with significant reform of the labour market led to the notable structural transformation of the late 1990s. The *xiagang* policy which introduced the first layoffs from SOEs took place between 1997 and 2000 during the 9th Five Year Plan.

The large-scale layoff policy was undertaken during the *gaizhi* or restructuring policy of SOEs. In the mid-1990s, loss-making SOEs were restructured. The 'save the large, let go of the small' policy saw the effective privatization of SOEs. Their numbers fell from 10 million in 1994 to 162,000 in 2000. By 2000, the large-scale restructuring of SOEs had taken place with significant sectoral shifts in employment. This trend continued in the 2000s as SOE share of employment steadily fell to around one-fifth in urban areas while the non-state sector rapidly grew. The extent of the inefficiency can be seen in how little it affected the share of SOEs in producing total industrial output, which was 37 per cent in 1994 and 38 per cent in 2000, suggesting that the restructuring policy has increased the efficiency of the remaining SOEs, similar to the findings of Jefferson, Hu, and Su (2006).

Figure 3.3 shows the dramatic decline of SOE employment by 2000. Table 3.2 displays the figures for urban employment and reveals a staggering reduction of some 40 million workers from SOEs between the mid to the end of the 1990s, such that SOEs accounted for less than one-quarter of all urban employment by the mid-2000s. Correspondingly, the non-state sector has risen dramatically to become the largest employment sector, which includes not only private firms but also privatized SOEs and collectives. In the 2000s, therefore, the large-scale layoff policy that accompanied the restructuring of SOEs meant that significant reallocation from the state-owned to the non-state-owned sector had taken place.

Over the course of China's reform period, a system of allocated labour whereby workers were allocated jobs for life was replaced by an increasingly competitive labour market. The result was greater returns to human capital in the form of wages, and compensation was linked to performance rather than an administered pay scale (Yueh 2004). Also, reforms to increase the flexibility of labour markets during the 1990s allowed workers to move to firms which suited their skills better and thus had the potential to improve productivity. This stands in stark contrast to the lifetime employment system that resulted in over-manning and surplus labour, which reduced productivity as labour, like other factor inputs, is subject to decreasing returns. Reforms geared toward a more competitive labour market should thus increase labour productivity. This reallocation from less to more productive sectors, though, has limits, particularly by the 2000s when the share of SOE employment roughly matched its share of output, in contrast to the 1980s and early 1990s when inefficient SOEs maintained their employment despite rapidly declining output, as shown in Figure 3.4. Indeed, SOE share of urban employment did not fall below 30 per

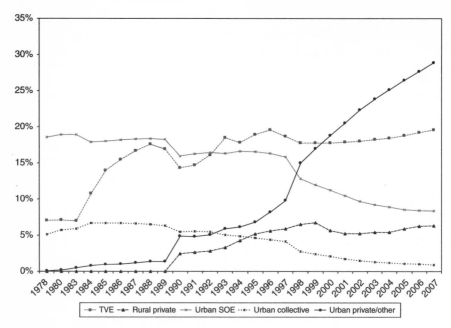

Figure 3.3 Shares of employment by ownership sector

Source: *China Statistical Yearbook*.

Note: The figures do not total 100% because employment in the non-industrial sector is not shown.

cent until 2000. Up until then, it accounted for 70 per cent in the 1980s and 60 per cent in the 1990s until 1994 when the *gaizhi* policy was implemented.

On the product market side, there has also been increasing marketization. Market liberalization in the wholesale and retail sector took place in the late 1980s/early 1990s, and the anticipation of greater competition from opening fuelled further market development, which resulted in improved conditions for private firms in the 2000s when they were afforded better access to credit and legal rights, although there is still considerable financial repression in the economy. Nevertheless, Figures 3.2 and 3.3 and Table 3.2 show the dramatic increase in the non-state sector in employment and output, albeit with privatized SOEs counted within the statistics.

One of the main conclusions from studies of other transition economies undergoing transformation from centrally planned to market economies is the importance of competition from the private sector (see Estrin 2002). For instance, Earl and Estrin (2003) found that labour productivity increased in Russia due to increased product market competition. Labour productivity is also influenced by the reform of the market for the other factors of production; notably, capital. With overinvestment common in SOEs that seek their funding from the state or state-owned banks and the continued presence of the state-owned sector, the capital-to-labour ratio is inefficiently high in China (see for

Table 3.2 Urban employment

Year	Total urban employment (million)	Urban SOEs (million)	Urban collectives (million)	Urban private/ other (million)
1983	117	86	32	2
1984	122	90	33	4
1985	128	93	34	5
1986	133	97	35	5
1987	138	100	35	6
1988	143	101	35	8
1989	144	103	35	8
1990	170	107	36	31
1991	175	109	36	32
1992	179	109	34	34
1993	183	112	33	39
1994	187	113	31	42
1995	190	112	30	46
1996	199	110	29	57
1997	208	91	20	69
1998	216	86	17	106
1999	224	81	15	121
2000	232	76	13	136
2001	239	72	11	150
2002	248	69	10	165
2003	256	67	9	178
2004	265	65	8	189
2005	273	64	8	200
2006	283	64	7	211

Source: China Statistical Yearbook.

example, Naughton 1995). By reforming the industrial sector and reducing obsolete capital, labour becomes more productive as the capital-to-labour ratio falls (see for example, Jefferson, Hu, and Su 2006).

Fundamentally, labour productivity is further determined by not only the factor inputs but also by technology and the efficiency of the use of its workers and capital. Market development that includes private-sector development could be associated with greater efficiency and induce higher labour productivity. A firm with lagging technology would be less efficient than one with more advanced production capabilities, affecting its cost curves and therefore the productivity of its workers. R&D, therefore, would be an important factor.

Chinese and firms from developing countries which lag behind the know-how of competitors from more advanced economies, would have lower labour productivity than otherwise comparable firms (see for example, Blomström and Sjöholm 1999, for the finding that firms with foreign equity in Indonesia had higher labour productivity). Opening, though, is also associated with greater competitiveness pressures; which is a reason why countries like China selectively managed the process. Globalization and the incursion of foreign firms directly into the domestic market as well as competition in the global economy would expose these differences, while at the same offering an opportunity for Chinese companies to become exposed to, learn from, and even obtain the

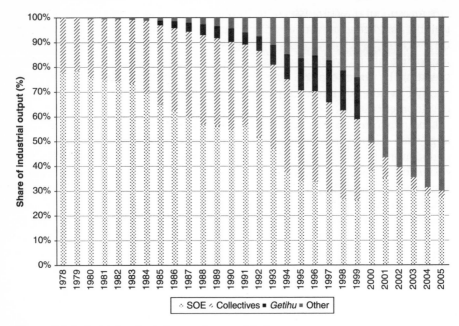

Figure 3.4 Industrial output shares of ownership types

Source: China Statistical Yearbook, various years.

Note: Collectives refer to both urban and rural collectively owned organizations and *getihu* disappears as a classification in 2000 when it is counted in the 'other' ownership type.

technological know-how of those firms. This mechanism of learning from technology embodied in foreign capital is well-known and forms the basis for the theory of 'catching up' often discussed in economic growth models (see for example, Solow 1956).

Therefore, accompanying opening is an impressive influx of foreign direct investment (FDI), which averaged some US$60 billion per year in the 2000s, growing at a faster pace than the previous decade. Although China received FDI steadily throughout the 1990s, the rapid growth of FDI in the 2000s could reflect the greater extent of marketization of Chinese firms, which positioned them better after the structural reforms of the late 1990s to utilize the technology embodied in FDI and to work with foreign investors.

For some years, China's foreign direct investment policy was geared towards attracting foreign capital which had more advanced technology. As such, China exerted considerable control over FDI through soliciting and approving investments that could help its firms upgrade and move up the value chain. Therefore, although it became less common after WTO accession when FDI controls loosened, some Chinese–foreign joint ventures (JVs) included technology transfer agreements signed whereby the foreign partner transferred technological know-how to the Chinese–foreign entity as part of the JV agreement. This is a rare measure of direct transfer of technology often assumed to be embodied in FDI that could generate productivity gains in developing countries. By including this variable, whether such technology transfer agreements are valuable in improving labour productivity in China can be investigated. Certainly, R&D spending by firms can also increase their technical capabilities and offers another avenue for improving labour productivity, especially once a level of development has been reached.

Labour reforms, conducted in tandem with SOE reforms, have resulted in large-scale sectoral shifts between the state and non-state sector in the reform period; none more significant than the mid to late 1990s reforms enacted by the *gaizhi* and *xiagang* policies. By the 2000s, the sectoral shifts continued but at a slower pace, suggesting that the burst in labour productivity recorded is not readily attributed to the reallocation of labour from the inefficient state to the non-state sector. Instead, greater global integration and more extensive market-ization associated with the rise of the non-state sector point to technical improvements that can significantly improve labour productivity. Greater global integration and marketization herald the potential for technical improve-ment, thus suggesting that technology and TFP growth should be explored, both domestically derived such as through R&D, and also through transfers from more advanced foreign firms as well as potential interactive effects between innovative activities.

3.4 Measuring Labour Productivity

The primary dataset used in this chapter comprises a national firm-level panel. The National Bureau of Statistics of China (NBS) annual enterprise survey is supplemented by an original survey. The questionnaire was designed by an international research team, and carried out by NBS with support from the World Bank. The survey was conducted in the summer of 2006 in twelve cities (province in parenthesis): Beijing (municipality), Changchun (Jilin), Chifeng (Inner Mongolia), Dandong (Liaoning), Hangzhou (Zhejiang), Shijiazhuang (Hebei), Shiyan (Hubei), Shunde (Guangdong), Wujiang (Jiangsu), Xian (Shaanxi), Zibo (Shandong), Chongqing (municipality). The NBS takes consider-able care with their annual enterprise survey such that the figures match data obtained independently by the Chinese tax authorities.

The unbalanced panel data consists of 1,201 industrial firms for the years 2000–5 for which 2005 provides survey information as well as the NBS data. The information was also checked against the provincial-level data, which revealed that the sub-sample is broadly in line with the provincial averages. Comparison with the averages for other studies using the large NBS firm-level dataset (Dougherty, Herd, and He 2007) yielded similar results. Also in line with most enterprise firm studies, the survey only covered firms with an annual sales volume larger than 5 million RMB following the NBS practice (see for example, Jefferson and Su 2006). The NBS dataset only includes industrial firms and does

Table 3.3 Distribution of industrial sectors

Sector	Share of total industry (%)	FIE share of industrial sector output (%)
Mining	1.06	0.05
Food, beverages, and tobacco	13.17	36.41
Textiles, apparel, and leather products	11.63	33.84
Wood, furniture, and paper products	6.54	32.97
Crafts, other manufacturing, and non-specified	1.15	33.59
Oil processing, coking, and nuclear fuel processing	1.54	6.86
Chemicals and chemical products	13.75	35.14
Rubber and plastic products	3.75	49.66
Non-metallic mineral products	6.25	30.08
Metal processing and products	8.94	27.41
Machinery, equipment, and instruments	7.02	37.87
Transportation equipment	11.73	36.89
Electrical machinery and equipment	7.12	30.30
Electric power and utilities	6.35	13.85

Note: The proportion of firms in each of the industrial sectors is reported. The total shares of industry sums to 100%. The two-digit industrial codes have been grouped into fourteen industrial sectors as follows: (1) Mining includes: coal mining and cleaning, black metal mining, non-ferrous metal mining, non-metallic mining; (2) Food, beverages and tobacco includes: food processing, food manufacturing, beverages, tobacco; (3) Textiles, apparel, and leather products include: textiles, textiles and garments, shoes, hats manufacturing, leather, fur, feathers, cashmere and its products; (4) Wood, furniture, and paper products includes: wood processing and timber, bamboo, rattan, brown grass products, furniture manufacturers, paper, and paper products; (5) Crafts, other manufacturing and non-specified includes: printing and recording media, cultural sporting goods manufacturing, crafts and other manufacturing industries; (6) Oil processing, coking, and nuclear fuel processing; (7) Chemicals and chemical products includes: chemicals and chemical products, chemical fibre manufacturing; (8) Rubber and plastic products includes: rubber products, plastic products; (9) Non-metallic mineral products; (10) Metal processing and products includes: black metal smelting and pressing, non-ferrous metal smelting and pressing, fabricated metal products; (11) Machinery, equipment, and instruments includes: general equipment, special equipment; (12) Transportation equipment; (13) Electrical machinery and equipment includes: electrical machinery and equipment, communication equipment, computer and other electronic equipment, instrumentation and culture, office machinery; (14) Electric power and utilities includes: waste resources and recycling waste materials processing, electricity, heat production and supply, gas production and supply, water production and supply.

not include construction and transportation companies. Thus, the majority of firms operate in the manufacturing sector, with a small number of firms in mining or utilities, as seen in Table 3.3.

To avoid influential observations due to reporting error, the data is cleaned using standard procedures of 'windsorizing': for the pooled data on firm-level value-added, capital stock and labour, the values at the first and ninety-ninth quantile of the distribution are first determined. Then, all observed values below the former cut-off are replaced with that of the first quantile and all observed values above the latter cut-off with that of the ninety-ninth quantile. Additional information available allows for identification of firms which are multi-plant groups. Data for multi-plant enterprises may lead to bias in the estimates, and are controlled for with a separate dummy variable in the estimations, as is the age of the firm. The year of entry into the dataset is also controlled for with a dummy variable to control for any bias resulting from the date of appearance in the dataset.

Other sources of data used in the chapter include China's national and provincial statistical yearbooks. These sources of data are used to provide additional measures of the variables of interest, such as openness.

Table 3.4 Levels and growth rates of labour productivity

Average value-added per worker (RMB)	50,249
Average annual growth rate of VA per worker	4.77%
Average sales per worker (RMB)	373,768
Average annual growth rate of sales per worker	13.54%
Average profit per worker (RMB)	2,032
Average annual growth rate of profit per worker	6.33%

Note: Values are only reported for those firms with four years or more of data.

Table 3.4 provides measures of both the levels and growth rates of labour productivity. Per the standard computation, value-added is the sum of profits, profit taxes, wages, and additional labour compensation (insurance and welfare payments). The value-added measure was deflated by the Ex-Factory Price Index of Industrial Products, while the capital stock was deflated by the National Price Index for Investment in Fixed Assets.

Table 3.4 shows that average annual real value-added per worker was 50,259 RMB during 2000–5 with an annual average growth rate of 4.77 per cent. This is in line with other raw estimates of labour productivity growth during the reform period, which are around 4–6 per cent (see Jefferson and Rawski 1994; Dougherty, Herd, and He 2007). This rate is echoed in the average profit per worker, growth of which was around 6 per cent for the period. Measured in terms of sales per worker, the real annual average growth rate is an impressive 13.5 per cent for the sample time frame. Although less precise as a measure of labour productivity, the sales measure indicates that real output per worker has grown rapidly over the period 2000–5, while growth in profits and value-added had slowed. It suggests that margins are becoming tighter.

The next figures show raw labour productivity measures from the data, differentiating between the various ownership sectors, measuring the extent to which the state and non-state sectors differ, as well as between Chinese and foreign-invested enterprises (FIEs). The non-state sector comprises privatized SOEs, private Chinese firms, and foreign-invested enterprises, such as Chinese–foreign joint ventures and wholly foreign-owned enterprises (WFOE). FIEs can be further disaggregated into those from Greater China (Hong Kong, Macau, and Taiwan, or HMT) and other countries, namely, the United States, Japan, and Europe. Since the establishment of the two stock exchanges in Shanghai and Shenzhen in the early 1990s and the more recently permitted overseas listings, a number of firms have also become publicly listed (*gufen*) companies. As these firms are different in a number of respects, listed firms are excluded from the comparative statics and listed status is also controlled for in the estimations.

Figures 3.5 and 3.6 provide a comparison of value-added per worker for Chinese firms versus FIEs. The graphs confirm the need to separate FIEs from Hong Kong, Macau, and Taiwan and other countries. Greater China FIEs are more productive than Chinese domestic firms, but the productivity differential with domestic firms is greater between FIEs from other countries. Comparing

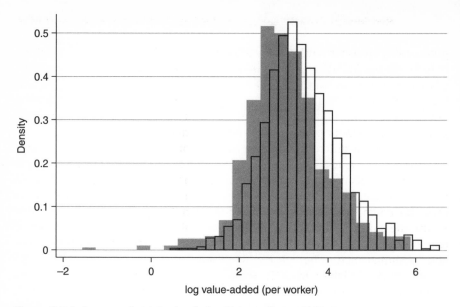

Figure 3.5 Labour productivity levels for Chinese firms, 2000–5

Note: Shaded bars refer to 2000–1 and the clear bars are 2004–5. Values are only reported for those firms with four years or more of data.

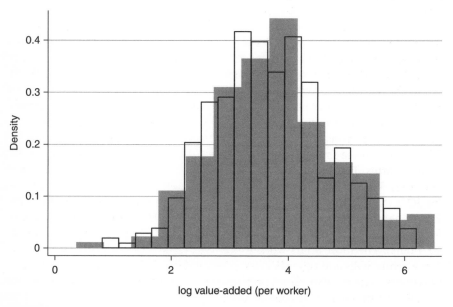

Figure 3.6 Labour productivity levels for foreign-invested firms, 2000–5

Note: Shaded bars refer to 2000–1 and the clear bars are 2004–5. Values are only reported for those firms with four years or more of data.

productivity levels for 2000–1 with 2004–5, Chinese firms have higher productivity levels by 2005 than in 2000, whereas foreign firms have shown little change. In other words, the level of labour productivity in Chinese firms was higher over the five year period while foreign firms look on the raw figures to be largely static. The implication being that it is Chinese domestic firms with greater gains in labour productivity over the period.

Focusing on the differences in ownership sectors, Table 3.5 provides firm-level information on value-added, employees, capital stock, and the wage bill for the different types of enterprises. It shows that mean value-added per firm is highest for JVs from countries other than Greater China and lowest for private Chinese firms, although WFOEs from other countries have the highest median value whilst the lowest remains that of private Chinese firms. Mean number of employees is highest in SOEs and lowest for private firms, while the median gives a similar picture but tie for being largest with Greater China WFOEs. Capital stock is highest in SOEs measured in means, but greatest for other WFOEs when measured in medians which are less prone to skewness in the data. It also suggests that there are large SOEs in capital-intensive sectors. Private Chinese firms continue to have the lowest value of the different ownership types measured in both mean and median. Finally, the average wage bill is highest in SOEs and lowest in private firms. But, when measured in medians, the highest wage bill belongs to Greater China WFOEs and the lowest still for Chinese firms. The firm characteristics indicate that private Chinese firms tend to be the smallest in terms of labour and capital, as well as value-added, while the privatized SOEs are only slightly larger.

Table 3.6 provides information on average firm characteristics per worker: value-added per worker, capital stock per worker, or the capital/labour ratio, wage bill per worker, hourly wage, and the average number of hours worked per week. Value-added per worker is highest in other JVs by both average measures, while the lowest is privatized SOEs, again measured in terms of mean and median. The raw descriptive information indicates that FIEs all have higher labour productivity than Chinese firms with SOEs at about the same level as private Chinese firms on average. Capital per worker is also uniformly higher for FIEs than Chinese firms, while SOEs have more capital per worker than other Chinese firms. The largest capital to labour ratio is found in WFOEs from other countries. Wage bill per worker is also higher for FIEs, although the hourly wage for SOEs exceeds that of WFOEs from Greater China and is broadly in line with FIEs rather than domestic firms. Of the FIEs, WFOEs from Greater China pay the lowest hourly wage and have the second longest hours in a working week (forty-six hours). The most hours worked per week on average is in private Chinese firms, while SOEs and other JVs have the shortest working week (around forty-two hours). The median values provide a similar picture with the longest hours worked in Chinese firm as compared with FIEs.

Table 3.7 shows the percentage of firms which are listed on domestic or international stock exchanges. The average is just under 5 per cent of all firms, with SOEs having the highest proportion at over 12 per cent. The lowest share of

Table 3.5 Average firm characteristics

Firms		Value-added (in RMB)			Employees (number)			Capital stock (in 100 RMB)			Wage bill (in 100 RMB)		
Ownership type	N	Mean	Standard deviation	Median	Mean	Standard deviation	Median	Mean	Standard deviation	Median	Mean	Standard deviation	Median
SOE	470	47,078	118,475	8,773	1,071	2,189	320	117,606	316,789	16,955	23,134	108,439	3,472
Privatized SOE	175	11,081	24,127	4,268	266	335	172	20,421	62,664	6,497	3,047	5,124	1,200
Private firm	370	6,702	11,510	3,203	184	214	117	12,665	25,808	4,745	2,076	2,930	1,115
Greater China JV	64	22,975	54,190	9,753	519	1,198	269	40,569	59,081	13,486	8,285	19,436	3,717
Other JV	99	55,335	137,210	14,448	825	1,910	283	105,412	287,332	23,476	21,089	77,185	5,351
Greater China WFOE	41	28,657	46,897	12,344	888	1,362	320	64,765	93,148	22,170	15,081	26,207	5,606
Other WFOE	41	37,007	75,847	109,863	707	1,310	280	91,480	195,711	297,780	11,693	21,244	5,137

Notes: Eight firms did not indicate their ownership type and are omitted.

Table 3.6 Average firm characteristics per worker

Firms		Value-added per worker (in RMB)			Capital per worker (in RMB)			Annual wage bill per worker (in RMB)			Hourly wage per worker (in RMB)			Average working week (in hours)		
Ownership type	N	Mean	Standard deviation	Median	Mean	Standard deviation	Median	Mean	Standard deviation	Median	Mean	Standard deviation	Median	Mean	Standard deviation	Median
SOE	470	44,844	61,245	26,378	94,490	256,425	56,741	13,637	10,215	11,246	6.10	3.18	5.28	42.9	5.9	40
Privatized SOE	175	41,816	51,648	24,561	71,031	123,777	36,503	11,089	6,537	9,688	4.41	1.50	4.17	46.1	6.5	48
Private firm	370	42,363	47,728	26,419	72,327	89,465	44,060	11,315	8,113	9,800	4.61	2.44	4.40	47.1	7.3	48
Greater China JV	64	54,990	65,591	34,669	115,044	190,531	53,107	17,819	14,019	14,131	6.16	3.02	5.26	45.4	7.1	44
Other JV	99	87,603	112,056	57,525	155,933	241,601	81,624	22,313	20,389	16,670	6.60	3.33	5.56	42.8	5.6	40
Greater China WFOE	41	56,533	108,963	27,201	116,560	268,357	59,824	17,019	8,859	14,476	5.22	2.06	4.72	46.1	8.0	44
Other WFOE	41	44,844	61,245	26,378	160,755	184,121	109,149	18,794	10,570	16,522	6.22	4.75	5.56	44.2	7.9	40

Note: Eight firms did not indicate their ownership type and are omitted.

Table 3.7 Percentage of listed companies

	Percentage of publicly listed firms (%)
SOE	12.2
Privatized SOE	1.6
Private firm	1.3
Greater China JV	2.9
Other JV	2.7
Greater China WFOE	1.7
Other WFOE	8.8
Average across firms	**5.8**

Table 3.8 Export share of output

Percentage:	0–1	1–3	3–5	5–10	10–20	> 20	**Average export share (%)**
SOE	33.8	16.5	10.4	12.1	9.2	18.1	**13.2**
Privatized SOE	41.1	15.2	14.4	11.5	5.3	12.6	**9.9**
Private firm	47.4	15.9	9.5	8.4	9.3	9.6	**7.9**
Greater China JV	29.0	11.6	5.6	15.5	12.5	25.7	**18.6**
Other JV	24.3	19.5	6.8	11.3	13.2	24.9	**16.3**
Greater China WFOE	47.3	16.1	2.7	14.3	8.0	11.6	**7.7**
Other WFOE	21.5	15.4	0.7	13.4	18.1	30.9	**19.4**
Average across firms	**36.7**	**16.1**	**9.5**	**11.3**	**9.6**	**16.7**	**11.5**

Note: The total for each ownership type does not sum up to 100% due to missing values. The average export share is computed taking average of the mid-point of the bands of the reported export shares; for example, 10–20% is computed as 15%. As the maximum value is 0.6 or 60%, this is an underestimate. This is counterbalanced by the lower band for which 0.05% is estimated from the band of 0–1%.

listings is found in private Chinese firms, privatized SOEs, and Greater China WFOEs.

Table 3.8 provides information on the proportion of output that is exported to global markets. Most firms either do not export or export less than 1 per cent of their output. Across firms, the average export share is only 11.5 per cent with other WFOEs exporting more than other types of FIEs and SOEs exporting a greater proportion of their output than other domestic firms. Greater China WFOEs have the smallest share of exports in their total output, while private Chinese firms also export just a fraction more of their output. Both types of firms appear to be producing for the domestic Chinese market, while other WFOEs, SOEs, and both types of JVs export a greater share of their products, but it is less than 20 per cent in all cases.

Turning to the measures of technology transfers, some one-eighth of the joint ventures signed a technology transfer agreement. These agreements are signed at the time of the formation of the JV, so they should not be endogenous with respect to current firm performance as the firm did not exist until the year of the agreement. It is possible that the more productive firms were the ones which entered into Chinese–foreign joint ventures. As nearly all JVs are formed with SOEs as a matter of regulatory approval, it was the case that the Chinese government mandated the JV as a result of FDI policy and firms did not self-select. The government could wish to either bolster loss-making firms (which was common in the 1990s) with productive partners to save jobs, or choose better performing SOEs to produce with foreign firms. As most of the productive SOEs were privatized or remained solely in national hands, the likely candidates for JVs were those which could not be sold off and were small enough to not warrant rescue as a 'key industry'. In any case, there was not self-selection to become a JV by more productive domestic firms that would generate the usual concerns regarding causality. Most importantly, these JV firms did not exist or operate until the agreement, including the transfer of technology, was enacted.

The average age of such JVs is around 8.7 years, indicating establishment in 1996/7, which is the same mean age as JVs which did not sign technology transfer agreements. The oldest JVs were formed in 1979 at the start of market-oriented reforms. As Guangdong is included in the survey and it was one of the earliest provinces to open right at the start of reform, the data captures the earliest to the latest JVs which received technology transfers which were in 2005.

The mean value of the agreements was 14.39 million RMB with the largest contract worth 400 million RMB. The Chinese side often insisted on these transfers as they would be less costly than presumably licensing the same technology given the monopoly pricing of intellectual property. Thus, around 43 per cent of such agreements were bundled as part of the capital investment in the JV without payment of additional consideration, supporting the favourable position of obtaining technology via this route instead of via the open market. Around one-fifth (21.1 per cent) of firms reported producing new products with the technology obtained in these transfer agreements.

3.5 Determining Labour Productivity

In a standard firm production function, y_{it} is determined by the following equation:

$$y_{ij} = \beta_k k_{it} + \beta_l l_{it} + \varepsilon_{it}, \tag{1}$$

where y_{it} represents the log form of output such as value-added (y) for firm i at time t produced by inputs of capital (k_{it} is the log of capital) and labour (l_{it} is the log of labour) and an error term (ε_{it}) which could represent technology, managerial ability, etc. The error term has the usual form of:

$$\varepsilon_{it} = \eta_i + v_{it} + \mu_t, \tag{2}$$

where η_i is the time-invariant fixed effect, μ_t are time dummies, and v_{it} is an AR(1) error term:

$$v_{it} = \rho v_{it-1} + \varepsilon_{it}. \qquad (3)$$

If there are unobservable firm-specific effects (such as managerial quality) which are correlated with both the dependent and the explanatory variables in the ordindary least squares (OLS) estimation, then a fixed-effects estimator can be used to sweep out unobserved firm-specific differences. Also, the inputs can be endogenous with respect to ε_{it}, which will cause biased results in OLS. To control for the time-invariant factors, first differences of equation (1) can be taken so that the η_i terms are eliminated. However, in first differences, there will not be any instruments for the factor inputs because lags of y_{it} and the factor inputs are correlated with past ε_{it} shocks and the autoregressive error term. Instead, the model can be transformed into a dynamic model with serially uncorrelated shocks that can be estimated using levels and differenced equations using a difference GMM estimator (Hansen 1982; Arellano and Bond 1991). But, the capital terms are likely to be highly autocorrelated, so using just the difference equations will be problematic due to the potential bias from weak instruments in finite samples. Thus, Blundell and Bond (2000) propose using the extra moment conditions (see also Blundell and Bond 1998). This means that lagged differences are used as instruments for the levels equations, in addition to the lagged levels as instruments for the differenced equations in the system GMM. The overall validity of the moment conditions is tested through the Sargan test with the null hypothesis that the instruments are valid or exogenous. Where the number of over-identifying restrictions is large, the Sargan test may have low power to reject the null hypothesis. Therefore, the Difference-in-Hansen tests for the validity of the additional lagged differences instruments in the levels equation are also both used as diagnostics in the system GMM procedure.

To estimate labour productivity using system GMM, equation (1) is rewritten as follows:

$$VA_{it} = \beta_1 k_{it} + \beta_2 l_{it} + \omega_i + \chi_t + \varepsilon_{it}, \qquad (4)$$

where VA_{it} is value-added per worker (in logs), capital per worker is k_{it}, employees is l_{it}, ω_i represents time-invariant characteristics which affect firm performance such as the ownership sector of the firm, whether it is listed and publicly traded on a stock exchange, the industrial sector, location (city/province), and also other control variables such as age of firm and if it is part of a multi-plant firm as well as the year of entry into the dataset, χ_t is the change in the macroeconomic conditions from year to year, and ε_{it} is the error term. Measures of R&D and information and communications technology (ICT) spending are also entered as instrumented inputs like capital and labour, whilst technology transfer agreements are treated as time-invariant. The panel element means that system GMM can be used to address endogeneity by using lagged differences as instruments for the levels equations and the lagged levels as instruments for the differenced equations. The province-level measures of openness and marketization are also time-varying for each province.

Tables 3.9 and 3.10 show the estimates from the system GMM regressions. First, the Sargan test does not reject the validity of the instruments even when the Windmeijer (2005) finite-sample correction is implemented, which addresses the severe downward bias of the standard errors that can cause the Sargan test to under-reject. Also, the Difference-in-Sargan test of the validity of the additional lagged differences instruments in the level equations also does not reject the null hypothesis that those instruments are exogenous.

Table 3.9 shows that there are significant differences in labour productivity among different ownership sectors with privatized SOEs and Chinese–foreign joint ventures which signed technology transfer agreements, particularly the latter, registering significantly higher levels of labour productivity than unreformed SOEs. Interpreting the coefficients in column (4), which includes the additional input measures of R&D and ICT spending as well as provincial-level measures of openness and marketization, the magnitude of the difference is 0.182 percentage points for privatized SOEs and 0.867 percentage points for those JVs, translating into a 18.2 log points differential for the former, and a large 86.7 log points differential for the latter. Across all specifications, these two ownership types registered significantly higher productivity of labour, with the coefficient falling for privatized SOEs from 0.280 to 0.182 with additional control variables included. Conversely, the coefficient on joint ventures with technology transfer agreements increased from 0.707 in column (1) to 0.867 in column (4), suggesting that the baseline specification may underestimate the productivity differential.

One of the ways in which technical efficiency gains can be obtained is through technologies transferred from the foreign partner, which is evident in the significance of the joint ventures which signed technology transfer agreements. Another avenue is through R&D spending to produce innovation that enhances the productivity of a firm's workers, which can have interactive effects. Indeed, when R&D and ICT spending are accounted for—separately in columns (2) and (3)—they are found not to affect labour productivity. However, the interaction term between R&D spending by a firm and technology transfer is positive and increases labour productivity by 18.5 log points (column 4). This is in addition to the 86.7 log point productivity differential by just having a technology transfer agreement in a joint venture. Therefore, joint ventures with technology transfers appear to increase labour productivity via the transfers of technology which have the additional effect of positively interacting with R&D spending, further suggesting that the mechanism for the productivity differential is technical efficiency improvements in the utilization of labour through increasing the technological capacity of the firm.

Turning to Table 3.10, the final specification from Table 3.9 is reported again in column (1) with the time trends which shows that the average annual growth rate of labour productivity is 8.7 per cent. Column (2) then reports the ownership-specific productivity trends, which shows that the trend growth rate is the same for the different types of firms, but for Greater China JVs and JVs with technology transfers demonstrating a slower pace of trend growth. Given the

Table 3.9 Estimates of labour productivity

Dependent variable: ln VA/L	(1)	(2)	(3)	(4)
ln L	0.534**	0.593***	0.377*	0.328*
	(0.228)	(0.204)	(0.218)	(0.181)
ln K	0.457***	0.497***	0.403**	0.362**
	(0.162)	(0.156)	(0.177)	(0.150)
ln R&D spending		0.052		0.271
		(0.209)		(0.193)
Interaction between R&D and technology transfers				0.185**
				(0.087)
ln ICT spending			−0.168	
			(0.177)	
Ownership type				
Privatized SOEs	0.280***	0.272***	0.201**	0.182**
	(0.107)	(0.099)	(0.087)	(0.080)
Private firms	0.325	0.231	0.274	0.280
	(0.221)	(0.225)	(0.208)	(0.200)
Greater China JVs	0.103	0.029	0.146	0.169
	(0.159)	(0.152)	(0.161)	(0.147)
Other JVs	0.083	−0.026	0.236	0.294
	(0.217)	(0.206)	(0.203)	(0.192)
JVs with technology transfers	0.707**	0.614*	0.807**	0.867***
	(0.324)	(0.327)	(0.325)	(0.328)
Greater China WFOEs	−0.449*	−0.563**	−0.329	−0.256
	(0.253)	(0.251)	(0.274)	(0.254)
Other WFOEs	−0.168	−0.254	−0.001	0.018
	(0.237)	(0.240)	(0.218)	(0.201)
Listed firm	0.112	−0.115	0.291	0.302
	(0.349)	(0.281)	(0.398)	(0.308)
Year dummies	Yes	Yes	Yes	Yes
City dummies	Yes	Yes	Yes	Yes
Industry dummies	Yes	Yes	Yes	Yes
Constant	−17.815	−4.787	−18.729	−15.581
	(23.752)	(21.361)	(23.424)	(19.532)
Observations	4253	4253	4253	4253
Number of firms	1169	1169	1169	1169
Wald χ^2 (68)	921.50***			
Wald χ^2 (70)		229.27***		
Wald χ^2 (72)			1015.37***	
Wald χ^2 (75)				681.79***
AR1	0.000	0.000	0.000	0.000
AR2	0.018	0.018	0.072	0.321
AR3	0.356	0.392	0.336	0.217
Sargan p-value	0.002	0.011	0.005	0.035
Difference-in-Sargan p-value	0.311	0.282	0.288	0.401

Note: Omitted variables are Shiyan in Hubei, the first year of the data, and the industrial sector of coal mining and cleaning, and the standard errors are adjusted for clustering at the firm level. Controls include year dummies, firm age, multi-plant firm, ownership type, listed company, city dummies, industrial sector, year of appearance in dataset, and being an outlier. Provincial-level measures of openness and the National Economic Research Institute (NERI) Marketization Index are also included in column (4). The Sargan tests suggest the exogeneity of the instruments, while the autocorrelation test for serial correlation in the structure of the error terms cannot reject AR2, so the lags are taken from t-2 for the endogenous factor inputs. Significance is denoted as: *** $p < 0.01$, ** $p < 0.05$, * $p < 0.1$.

Table 3.10 Estimates of labour productivity with heterogeneous productivity growth

Dependent variable: ln VA/L	(1)	(2)	(3)	(4)
ln L	0.328*	0.208	0.585*	0.410
	(0.181)	(0.187)	(0.324)	(0.323)
ln K	0.362**	0.268*	0.402*	0.344
	(0.150)	(0.142)	(0.241)	(0.235)
ln R&D spending	0.271	0.339*	0.225	0.253
	(0.193)	(0.177)	(0.203)	(0.190)
ln ICT spending	−0.211*	−0.136	−0.195	−0.141
	(0.117)	(0.111)	(0.121)	(0.113)
Ownership type				
Privatized SOEs	0.182**	0.005	2.968***	2.221**
	(0.080)	(0.173)	(1.145)	(1.128)
Private firms	0.280	0.176	3.988***	3.060**
	(0.200)	(0.238)	(1.497)	(1.541)
Greater China JVs	0.169	0.598**	4.026**	3.516**
	(0.147)	(0.264)	(1.610)	(1.615)
Other JVs	0.294	0.626**	2.288	1.832
	(0.192)	(0.314)	(1.413)	(1.348)
JVs with technology transfers	0.867***	1.451***	4.859**	4.776**
	(0.328)	(0.536)	(2.075)	(2.047)
Greater China WFOEs	−0.256	0.376	3.504*	2.955*
	(0.254)	(0.444)	(1.832)	(1.746)
Other WFOEs	0.018	0.149	3.398**	2.855**
	(0.201)	(0.343)	(1.343)	(1.386)
Listed firm	0.302	0.469*	0.240	0.339
	(0.308)	(0.260)	(0.339)	(0.306)
Provincial measures				
ln exports/GDP	−0.426**	−0.457***	−0.377*	−0.368**
	(0.185)	(0.160)	(0.210)	(0.185)
NERI index	0.760**	0.760**	0.757*	0.718*
	(0.377)	(0.341)	(0.426)	(0.387)
Year dummies				
2001	0.247***	0.224***	0.237***	0.217***
	(0.067)	(0.066)	(0.076)	(0.075)
2002	0.297***	0.277***	0.312***	0.298***
	(0.085)	(0.078)	(0.097)	(0.096)
2003	0.345***	0.332***	0.357***	0.347***
	(0.099)	(0.095)	(0.114)	(0.119)
2004	0.362**	0.336**	0.391**	0.370**
	(0.143)	(0.135)	(0.156)	(0.155)
2005	0.435***	0.413***	0.479***	0.458***
	(0.160)	(0.153)	(0.173)	(0.176)
Ownership-specific productivity growth				
Privatized SOEs		0.034		0.031
		(0.030)		(0.031)
Private firms		0.028		0.039
		(0.029)		(0.030)
Greater China JVs		−0.096**		−0.088*
		(0.043)		(0.050)
Other JVs		−0.061		−0.054
		(0.042)		(0.049)
JVs with technology transfers		−0.118*		−0.125*
		(0.069)		(0.070)

(*Continued*)

81

Table 3.10 Continued

Dependent variable: ln VA/L	(1)	(2)	(3)	(4)
Greater China WFOEs		−0.109		−0.090
		(0.069)		(0.067)
Other WFOEs		−0.010		−0.010
		(0.061)		(0.062)
Heterogeneous K,L	No	No	Yes	Yes
Year dummies	Yes	Yes	Yes	Yes
City dummies	Yes	Yes	Yes	Yes
Industry dummies	Yes	Yes	Yes	Yes
Constant	−15.581	−22.764	−15.483	−16.765
	(19.532)	(18.565)	(21.019)	(20.337)
Observations	4253	4253	4253	4253
Number of firms	1169	1169	1169	1169
Wald χ^2 (75)	681.79***			
Wald χ^2 (82)		548.36***		
Wald χ^2 (89)			5431.87***	
Wald χ^2 (96)				856.22***
AR1	0.000	0.000	0.000	0.000
AR2	0.321	0.387	0.206	0.196
AR3	0.217	0.175	0.378	0.353
Sargan p-value	0.035	0.060	0.045	0.065
Difference-in-Sargan p-value	0.401	0.455	0.291	0.311

Note: Omitted variables are Shiyan in Hubei, the first year of the data, and the industrial sector of coal mining and cleaning, and the standard errors are adjusted for clustering at the firm level. Controls include firm age, multi-plant firm, ownership type, listed company, city dummies, industrial sector, year of appearance in dataset, and being an outlier. In the specifications with provincial-level measures, additional controls include provincial GDP and industrial output. The NERI Marketization Index is compiled by the National Economic Research Institute of China (<http://www.neri.org.cn/>). The index is scaled between 1–10 based on aggregating and weighting five measures: (1) role of government, (2) economic structure, (3) interregional trade, (4) factor market development, and (5) legal framework. The Sargan tests suggest the exogeneity of the instruments, while the autocorrelation test for serial correlation in the structure of the error terms cannot reject AR2, so the lags are taken from *t-2* for the endogenous factor inputs. Significance is denoted as: *** $p < 0.01$, ** $p < 0.05$, * $p < 0.1$.

higher levels of labour productivity in these firms as seen in Figure 3.7, it suggests that there is some convergence towards the other ownership types. Columns (3) and (4) repeat the exercise by introducing heterogeneous production technologies such that the input shares of capital and labour are permitted to vary among ownership sectors. The findings are broadly in line with the homogeneous production functions in columns (1) and (2).

Notably, the productivity differentials noted in Table 3.10 remain for different types of firms. Privatized SOEs and JVs with technology transfers are more productive than SOEs, with the largest productivity differential across all of the eight types of ownership continuing to exist in those Chinese–foreign joint ventures that formed with technologies transferred from the foreign partner. Once ownership-specific productivity growth and heterogeneous production technologies are permitted, private Chinese firms, Greater China JVs, and

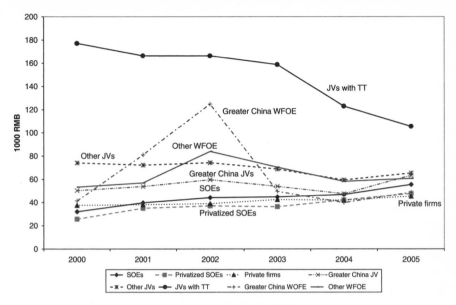

Figure 3.7 Labour productivity by ownership type, 2000–5

Note: Values are only reported for those firms with four years or more of data.

all WFOEs are also found to be more productive than SOEs. Production technologies in terms of shares of capital and labour, therefore, appear to differ notably across ownership types, pointing to differences in uses of inputs. But, Table 3.12 shows that TFP growth is not as different, such that the differences are found in input usage generating productivity differentials for value-added per worker and not overall TFP differences. Thus, examining TFP differences could obscure the productivity drivers for labour.

Table 3.11 shows that TFP growth of output was 3.4 per cent per annum on average during the sample period, but that the rate differed across ownership types. Using common factor shares of capital and labour, column (1) of Table 3.11 shows that SOEs had the lowest TFP growth while foreign firms congregated around the sample mean. Private firms and privatized SOEs had the highest TFP growth, particularly the latter. When factor shares are permitted to vary by ownership type, the differences remain although they are less stark once the different production technologies are permitted. Column (1) of Table 3.12 estimates TFP by holding factor shares constant across ownership sectors, while column (2) allows them to vary between sectors. It is evident that factor shares are consistent across FIEs but not SOEs, privatized SOEs, and private Chinese firms. Privatized SOEs continue to display the strongest TFP growth, while SOEs are just under the same mean TFP growth. It suggests that there is scope for reallocation from low to high TFP sectors; that is, state to non-state firms.

Table 3.11 TFP growth by ownership

TFP growth pa: 3.4%	Common L, K	L, K vary by ownership sector
SOEs	0.028***	0.032***
Privatized SOEs	0.051***	0.048***
Private firms	0.045***	0.040***
Greater China JVs	0.033***	0.034***
Other JVs	0.033***	0.033***
Greater China WFOEs	0.032**	0.030**
Other WFOEs	0.033**	0.034**

Note: Factor shares are 0.6 for capital and 0.4 for labour in column 1, while they are permitted to vary by ownership sector in column 2.

Although production sectors are controlled for in the estimations, Table 3.12 estimates the factor intensities and TFP for different industries as a further check. There are no significant TFP differentials between industrial sectors, which registered a 3.3 per cent TFP growth, consistent with the estimations in Table 3.11. There are, though, different input intensities. Oil processing and machinery were less labour-intensive, while the latter plus transportation and utilities were capital-intensive sectors. The lack of differences in TFP, though, suggests that ownership rather than industrial sectors account for the differences in labour productivity.

Table 3.13 reports the coefficients on the provincial-level measures of openness and marketization. By entering these, the ownership sector differentials remain robust and even grow in size. Openness is assessed as exports to GDP and marketization is proxied by the NERI (National Economic Research Institute) Marketization Index. The Index is compiled by the National Economic Research Institute of China. The index is based on aggregating and weighting five measures: (1) role of government, (2) economic structure, (3) interregional trade, (4) factor market development, and (5) legal framework.

Openness can imply greater competition and thus the negative coefficient on the extent of exports in a province. Figures 3.8 and 3.9 show the openness of the sample provinces by year and the share of foreign-invested enterprises in industrial output also by province and year. Some provinces such as Guangdong are very open (export share is over 70 per cent of GDP) while others are less so (exports are less than 5 per cent of GDP). Nevertheless, across all of the open and relatively closed provinces, the average share of FIEs in industrial output is around one-third (and rising), suggesting greater competition from foreign firms in provincial output as this is not correlated with the proportion of exports in provincial GDP. Table 3.8 shows that the average share of exports in firm output in 2005 was only 11 per cent, while Table 3.13 shows that FIE share of total provincial output was 34 per cent, such that their output accounts for a larger part of domestic and not export markets, contrary to the earlier impression of FIEs producing primarily for export which had been the case during the 1990s before the significant post-WTO opening of the Chinese market associated with greater market entry by FIEs.

Table 3.12 TFP by industrial sector

Dependent variable: ln VA/L	System GMM		
Sector	ln L	ln K	TFP
Mining	−0.0098	0.7920	−3.3984
	(1.0355)	(0.5982)	(8.3198)
Food, beverages, and tobacco	−0.3680	−0.4957	3.5671
	(0.4164)	(0.3419)	(3.1411)
Textiles, apparel, and leather products	−0.3375	−0.0750	1.3714
	(0.2292)	(0.2579)	(2.5155)
Wood, furniture, and paper products	0.7067	0.0855	−4.9246
	(1.4110)	(0.3052)	(7.2116)
Crafts, other manufacturing, and non-specified	−0.3119	−0.3663	2.8020
	(0.2732)	(0.3066)	(2.6545)
Oil processing, coking, and	−0.3128*	−1.0452	5.6573
nuclear fuel processing	(0.1686)	(0.9290)	(4.4906)
Chemicals and chemical products	0.1683	0.2749	−2.3685
	(0.3015)	(0.2468)	(2.4159)
Rubber and plastic products	0.2491	0.4503	−3.5020
	(0.2855)	(0.4037)	(2.3927)
Non-metallic mineral products	−0.0668	0.2267	−1.1796
	(0.3466)	(0.3592)	(3.0707)
Metal processing and products	−0.1010	0.0288	0.0717
	(0.2427)	(0.2656)	(2.4727)
Machinery, equipment, and instruments	−0.3772**	0.4713*	
	(0.1689)	(0.2849)	
Transportation equipment	−0.0128	0.3661**	−1.8632
	(0.2176)	(0.1589)	(2.3527)
Electrical machinery and equipment	0.2587	0.2423	−2.8772
	(0.3214)	(0.3308)	(2.1765)
Electric power and utilities	−1.0783	0.9512*	1.5589
	(0.7032)	(0.5386)	(4.9624)
Intercept			3.3194**
(omitted category TFP)			(1.4181)
Observations		4346	
AR1	0.000		
AR2	0.014		
AR3	0.685		
Sargan p-value	0.218		
Difference-in-Sargan p-value	0.228		

Note: t-1 year and city dummies are also included with Shiyan as the omitted city. The omitted category is 'machinery, equipment, and instruments', such that the intercept is the TFP of the omitted category, and the TFP measure for the various industrial sectors indicates whether it is significantly different from the omitted sector. The lags of the endogenous factor inputs are taken from t-2. Significance is denoted as: *** p < 0.01, ** p < 0.05, * p < 0.1.

Although greater openness is significant, the share of FIE in industrial output is not when entered alongside the provincial-level variables in the regressions. FIEs' share of industrial output had an insignificant coefficient of −0.009 (with a standard error of 0.164) when included in the specification in column (4) of

Table 3.13 Openness and foreign presence in provinces

Province	Export-to-GDP ratio (%)	FIE share of industrial output (%)
Beijing	31.38	37.23
Jilin	4.77	38.39
Inner Mongolia	3.19	24.09
Liaoning	20.49	31.54
Zhejiang	40.01	32.57
Hebei	7.57	34.64
Hubei	4.75	34.02
Guangdong	74.54	38.24
Jiangsu	47.02	40.88
Shaanxi	5.86	33.99
Shandong	17.44	29.36
Chongqing	5.75	35.97

Source: China Statistical Yearbook and author's calculations.

Table 3.10. The interaction term between the FIE share of output and joint ventures with technology transfers was also insignificant at 0.120 (with a standard error of 0.853). The presence of foreign-invested enterprises in industrial output is often used as a proxy for FDI spillover, which can be positive if there is technology transfer, or negative when foreign firms exert competitive pressures that overwhelm domestic firms (see for example, Blomström and Sjöholm 1999). In this instance, labour productivity is unaffected by this aggregate measure when precise measures of technology transfers are measured and taken into account. Finally, the NERI Marketization Index exerts a positive and significant effect on labour productivity, suggesting that institutional reforms of markets improve the productivity of workers.

Therefore, a number of factors influence labour productivity; namely, ownership sector as well as the characteristics of provinces. The trend growth rates in labour productivity do not differ significantly across ownership types. In fact, the JVs with technology transfers have the highest level of labour productivity but its trend rate is slower than the mean. Nevertheless, the JVs with technology transfer and the privatized SOEs, as well as other FIEs and non-state firms, are found to have higher levels of labour productivity than SOEs. As these private firms have become more important in the economy during the 2000s, the large gains in relative labour productivity in China can most likely be attributed to more of these firms gaining workers and output relative to SOEs. And, as labour shifts out of the state sector, labour productivity in SOEs could improve. Although such sectoral shifts had slowed in the 2000s relative to the large-scale layoffs of the late 1990s, there are still movements of labour between the state and non-state sectors. To account for the high labour productivity growth of the 2000s, therefore, the next section decomposes the relative contributions of allocative versus technical efficiency gains.

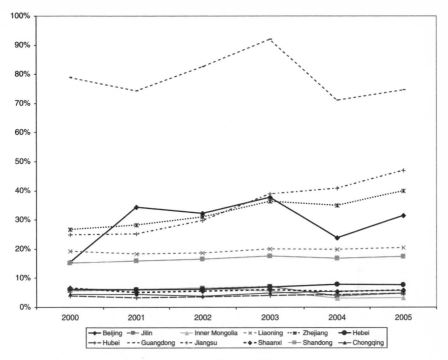

Figure 3.8 Openness of province by year (% of GDP)

3.6 Allocative versus Technical Efficiency

This section decomposes labour productivity growth into allocative versus technical efficiency changes to try and explain the reasons for the higher levels of value-added per worker in the 2000s. Aggregate labour productivity can be expressed as the weighted average of the productivity of the different ownership sectors. Aggregate labour productivity growth can be decomposed into two sources, allocative and technical gains. In other words, the overall growth of labour productivity can be divided into the labour productivity growth in the ownership sector (technical) and reallocation of labour across sectors (allocative).

If there were no labour reallocation, then aggregate labour productivity would be a weighted average (by industrial output) of the average growth rates of labour productivity in the different sectors. Any productivity growth above that would be attributed to labour reallocation. However, if the reallocation is due to TFP growth in the sector, then the decomposition would underestimate the role of labour productivity within the sector. Labour productivity itself is also dependent on the allocation of labour. This is particularly the case if there are diminishing returns to labour, such that the productivity gap will narrow with labour reallocation. This leads to the conclusion that it is likely that the reallocation effect will be overstated while labour productivity growth will be underestimated in this type of decomposition.

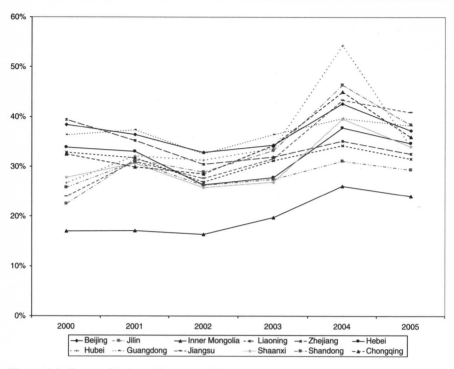

Figure 3.9 Shares of industrial output of foreign-invested enterprises

A further complication is that this decomposition presumes that each sector has the same average and marginal productivities of labour, which is only the case if the underlying production function had the same factor shares for different sectors. Looking again at Table 3.11, there looks to be heterogeneity. Thus, the decomposition analysis will account for different underlying technologies, but it does not resolve the bias that labour reallocation should depend on marginal and not average labour productivity differences. For instance, if private Chinese firms have lower marginal but higher average productivity than SOEs because they have less capital stock, then the decomposition will overstate the contribution of reallocation because labour should be less attracted by the gap between marginal products of labour between the two sectors; yet, the decomposition will attribute the higher average productivity growth to reallocation which underestimates the sectoral growth in labour productivity. Nevertheless, this is the standard methodology (see for example, Dougherty, Herd, and He 2007; Brandt and Zhu 2010), which sets the upper limit of the contribution of labour reallocative effects.

Table 3.14 shows the sectoral shifts. Over the sample period, some 10.22 per cent of labour moved out of SOEs and into the non-state sector in which all ownership types gained employment. Taking their share of industrial output as the weighting along with the labour productivity estimates from Table 3.10, the

Table 3.14 Labour sectoral shifts

	Total labour	SOEs		Privatized SOEs		Private firms		Greater China JVs		Other JVs		JV with TT		Greater China WFOEs		Other WFOEs	
		N	%	N	%	N	%	N	%	N	%	N	%	N	%	N	%
2000	199,857	159,954	80.03%	1,800	0.90%	3,359	1.68%	4,725	2.36%	19,175	9.59%	4,469	2.24%	1,887	0.94%	4,488	2.25%
2001	221,926	171,546	77.30%	2,779	1.25%	5,748	2.59%	5,956	2.68%	22,468	10.12%	5,764	2.60%	3,093	1.39%	4,572	2.06%
2002	235,298	174,309	74.08%	4,843	2.06%	11,528	4.90%	6,237	2.65%	21,698	9.22%	5,858	2.49%	3,071	1.31%	7,754	3.30%
2003	254,817	181,922	71.39%	7,023	2.76%	14,234	5.59%	8,346	3.28%	25,115	9.86%	5,187	2.04%	3,843	1.51%	9,147	3.59%
2004	296,108	177,886	60.07%	16,361	5.53%	23,983	8.10%	11,691	3.95%	32,555	10.99%	6,482	2.19%	13,653	4.61%	13,497	4.56%
2005	333,600	194,048	58.17%	19,988	5.99%	31,505	9.44%	14,225	4.26%	35,181	10.55%	6,237	1.87%	15,227	4.56%	17,189	5.15%

results are that labour reallocation accounted for 1.27 percentage points of total labour productivity growth of 8.25 percentage points utilizing the homogenous production technology estimates. Moving labour out of the state sector contributed 15.39 per cent of the total average labour productivity growth. Allowing for heterogeneous production functions, the contribution is less at 0.78 percentage points of total labour productivity growth of 9.16 percentage points or just 8.5 per cent of labour productivity growth, around half of the homogenous production function estimates. As these are the upper limits of the allocative effect, the predominant factor (accounting for around 85–92 per cent) in labour productivity growth in the 2000s is due to improvements in technical efficiency.

3.7 Corporate Restructuring

Turning now to what has affected the efficiency of capital, incorporation or corporatization involves the transformation of enterprises from public/state-owned or privately held firms into companies defined by shares. This is different from privatization, which is the change in ownership from the state into private hands. Both have been used across countries to try and improve firm performance across countries. This section investigates whether such reforms have been successful in China during the 2000s—at a time that coincides with one of the periods of strongest economic growth.

For incorporated firms, legal protections such as limited liability can be applied via the corporate laws. This process of establishing companies defined by shares has been seen over the past two centuries—ranging from the advanced economies of Europe and the United States to the transition economies of the former Soviet Union to developing countries in Africa. It has promoted the development of a modern corporate sector through laws that govern such entities and define their obligations to shareholders whilst permitting companies to enjoy legal protections such as limited liability. In the United States at the end of the nineteenth century, corporate laws were passed that supported the legal rights and provided for the obligations of its emerging industrial firms. Notably, restructuring public firms as corporations with private shareholders has been used as a method of privatization in both developed economies (Britain in the 1980s), transition economies (Eastern Europe in the 1990s), and developing countries (Kim 1981; Adam, Cavendish, and Mistry 1992; Bishop and Thompson 1993; Gedajlovic and Shapiro 1998).

For China, this was the strategy that was eventually the preferred avenue for reforming its state-owned enterprises and collectively owned enterprises (COEs) in the 1990s. The initial experiments with incentivizing output through managerial incentives met with some success (see Hay et al. 1994), but they failed to stem the inefficiencies of state ownership (Yueh 2010a). Short of mass privatization, the government sought to introduce ownership reform through incorporating state firms with the aim of separating management from ownership so as to make the managers more accountable for the firm's performance financially as well as legally. However, such corporate governance reforms were plagued with problems, including a lack of legal enforcement and continued state dominance in the control of the enterprise (see Lin 2001).

The intent of these reforms is that, as has been found in other economies, corporatization should improve firm performance through creating various legal forms that include the benefits of limited liability protection and recognized property rights that can reduce the cost of transactions, improve corporate governance, and enable the firm to raise capital from stock markets, among others (see for example, Himmelberg, Hubbard, and Palia 1999). For state-owned enterprises, corporatization can instil market discipline if shareholders other than the state can exert influence (see, for example, Tian and Estrin 2008).

As corporate laws and regulations were passed, the corporatization framework eventually encompassed private firms—a hitherto neglected category. In other words, during the 1990s China both developed a modern corporate sector whilst utilizing the laws to initially restructure its state-owned firms during the 1990s. By the 2000s, China's enterprise sector consisted of a range of incorporated firms, limited liability companies (LLCs), partnerships (LLPs), foreign-invested firms (FIEs), and others. The non-state sector had become more important than SOEs in industrial output. The non-state sector comprises reformed SOEs and collectively owned enterprises, and some entirely new firms. A change in the law in 1999 to recognize the legality of private sole proprietorships granted private firms the right to utilize corporate laws. They were then able to benefit from the various protections afforded by laws and regulations. For instance, the reforms of the Contract Law in the same year extended the legal protections of contracting parties to individuals for the first time, enabling the self-employed legal backing for their contractual dealings. Particularly for private firms, legal recognition as a corporate entity can also help these companies to raise finance from capital markets since they have articles of incorporation and accounts specifying assets and liabilities that can be scrutinized for investment and lending purposes, among other traits. In summary, by the 2000s, sole proprietorships were recognized as legal entities and contracting law applied that should strengthen their property rights and contracting security, whilst SOEs were largely restructured into shareholding companies including listed firms that should increase their market discipline.

However, given the weakness of the Chinese legal system (Allen, Qian, and Qian 2005), there is an open question as to how much legal recognition under such an imperfect system would matter. A number of deficiencies—such as a banking system characterized by financial repression (in which the laws and policies favour SOEs) and lingering doubts over the status of private property since it was only recognized in the Constitution in 2004—suggest that the *de jure* system may not translate into *de facto* improved firm performance. For instance, the extent of financial repression and the underdevelopment of the financial sector due to the continuing dominance of state-owned commercial banks raise further questions over the benefits of incorporation as they pertain to accessing such distorted capital markets (Yang 2001). The 'thin' capital market with bourses dominated by non-tradable shares implies that the stock market is unlikely to exert the expected disciplining influence on firms if the state retains control of listed SOEs, whilst incorporated private firms would still operate in a system of financial repression whereby the still dominant, state-owned banks favour state-owned enterprises.

There are a large number of studies of the impact of reforming SOEs, including the effects of public listing (see, for example, Li and Rozelle 2003; Song and Yao 2004; Dong, Putterman, and Unel 2006). Successful structural transformation depends on a number of factors related to privatization and ownership reform. By contrast, given the recent nature of the reforms permitting private firms to incorporate and list on stock markets, there is little study of that impact. One of the contributions of this chapter, therefore, will be to assess the effects of incorporating private firms and whether the recent push to create a modern corporate sector in China has succeeded in bolstering the performance of all corporations. Firms will be differentiated into those which have become shareholding companies and those which have not in order to assess the broader impact of corporatization. The relative performance of privatized but unincorporated firms will be compared as well as the impact of listing.

Section 3.8 will cover incorporation and ownership reform in China. Section 3.9 will state the hypotheses for testing, followed by sections on the data and the empirical approach. Section 3.10 will present the findings, while Section 3.11 will present a simple simulation exercise to calibrate the impact of having incorporated firms. The concluding Section 3.12 will assess the corporatization policy in China and answer the main questions posed in the chapter: what has driven productivity improvements for firms and labour?

3.8 Incorporation and Ownership Reform

Corporations defined by shares can have controlling shareholders or widely dispersed owners, and can be publicly listed and traded. What differentiates a corporation from a privately held firm is its corporate governance. Corporate governance both defines a set of relationships between a company's management, its board, its shareholders and other stakeholders, and provides the organizational structure through which the objectives of the company are set, promoted, and monitored (OECD 2004). Owners exercise property rights to maximize shareholder value, conduct financial audits, and establish executive compensation based on performance and threat of removal. For listed firms, the capital markets serve a further role whereby strongly performing firms are rewarded and badly run ones suffer via share price movements that determine market capitalization and through 'the market for corporate control' whereby potential mergers and acquisitions act as a further disciplining device (Hua, Miesing, and Li 2006).

Corporatization and privatization, therefore, can be different (Shirley 1999). Privatization is defined as the sale of state-owned assets; thus, a company is no longer state owned when control of management (measured as the right to appoint the managers and board of directors) passes to private shareholders. The aim is to make state-owned enterprises operate as if they were private firms operating by market forces, or, if monopolies, efficient regulation (Shirley 1999). In the Chinese context, corporatization thus differs from privatization: in the former case, the government can remain as a large shareholder, and in the latter, the government has little or no ownership.

In China, the SOE contribution to industrial output has declined steadily since 1978; in the initial stages, this was the result of neither privatization nor corporatization in the initial stages. Instead, the rapid expansion of the non-state sector, especially the township and village enterprises and foreign-invested enterprises (including investors from HMT), served to diminish the relative importance of SOEs throughout the 1980s and 1990s. Following the government decision to accelerate corporatization, a corporate system began to take shape that reformed SOEs and also eventually supported that burgeoning non-state sector. In 1993, 100 SOEs were selected to experiment with corporatization or transformation into shareholding companies under a new Company Law. Some were selected to become listed firms on the new stock exchanges formed in 1990 (Shanghai) and 1991 (Shenzhen), the so-called share issue privatization (SIP) process. By the mid-1990s, the experiments gave way to significant restructuring or *gaizhi* of SOEs as well. During the period 1996–2000, the 9th Five Year Plan implemented the large-scale restructuring of SOEs and privatization of the small- and medium-sized ones (the 'save the large, let go of the small' policy). By the 2000s, China had a diverse corporate sector consisting of state-owned enterprises, collectively owned firms, and private firms, all of which could take the form of being a shareholding company, limited liability company, partnerships or be privately held. The landscape had fundamentally changed.

This creation of a framework for corporate entities was initially limited to SOEs and collectives though foreign firms had enjoyed similar legal recognition during the late 1970s and 1980s laws governing Chinese–foreign joint ventures (JVs) and wholly foreign-owned enterprises. Private Chinese firms were granted minimal formal legal protection by contrast, and the self-employed or *getihu* were not officially counted until the early 1990s. However, in 1999, the Law on Individual Wholly-owned Enterprises was passed that granted private firms the coverage of the corporate laws, including incorporating as limited liability companies, partnerships, and other incorporated vehicles. Sole proprietorships were also recognized with the 1999 revisions to the Contract Law offering individuals and not just legal entities the right to contract. Some of these so-called private firms were indeed privatized state-owned and collectively owned firms, but many were *de novo* firms started by entrepreneurs. Indeed, self-employment—a clear measure of new private firms—grew rapidly, starting in the 1990s. By 2000, these private firms began to take the various legal forms and *getihu* ceased to exist—to be replaced by the legal category of sole proprietorships. They could also register as limited liability companies or partnerships and even list on the bourses (subject to permission of the China Securities Regulatory Commission) by the third decade of reform.

Corporatization emphasizes the new corporations' independence, profit-orientation, clearer property rights, and good corporate governance. The question is whether and to what extent this new enterprise form can improve firm performance, as a measure of whether incorporation results in productivity improvements.

The chapter will investigate the hypothesis that incorporation results in better firm performance in the context of China's corporatization policy during the 2000s, a period when significant improvements have been made in the corporate legal structure as well as extending the benefits of company and contract laws to private firms in addition to state-owned and collectively owned enterprises. With governance improving over time, a study of the 2000s may well find a stronger effect than do studies of the 1990s.

The benefits of legal recognition through incorporation which include reducing transaction costs of contracting and denoting property rights should improve firm performance. Although the legal system remains underdeveloped and there exists financial repression, incorporation even in such an imperfect system increases firm productivity. The protection and security that incorporation brings—specifically limited liability—means that firms may be more willing to take on risks in their growth strategies that could explain the stronger performance of incorporated firms. Incorporation could also make it easier to raise finance, even in the distorted financial markets. One of the strong findings for China and other transition economies is that competition is important for firm performance (see, for example, Vining and Boardman 1992; Pivovarsky 2003). By separating ownership from management in a corporatized firm, managers are more responsible for firm performance and could be incentivized to improve when faced with growing competition from privatized SOEs, COEs, and did so as well as private and foreign firms.

The evidence from other countries, and some for China, suggests that those benefits improve firm productivity. A number of studies on incorporation improving firm performance can be found in both developed and developing countries (see, for example, Shirley 1999; Djankov and Murrell 2000). However, there is a perennial concern about the endogeneity of the ownership form. For instance, Demsetz and Villalonga (2001) investigate the relationship between the ownership structure and performance of corporations in the United States and find no statistically significant relationship between ownership structure and firm performance once endogeneity is accounted for. It may not be corporatization that improves firm performance, but either unobserved factors that lead better performing firms to incorporate or other traits that characterize both productive and incorporated firms (see also McConnell and Servaes 1990). This issue can radically change the findings. To identify the effect of incorporation and evaluate China's corporatization policy will require careful treatment of the endogeneity issue.

For China, there is a large number of studies on the effects of privatization and corporatization of SOEs and collective firms. Hu and Zhou (2006), Sun and Tong (2003), Jefferson and Su (2006), Song and Yao (2004), Aivazian, Ge, and Qiu (2005) all focus on the ownership transformation of SOEs, while Dong, Putterman, and Unel (2006), Xia, Li, and Long (2009) examine collectively owned firms after reform. The predominant view is that the restructuring of SOEs has improved their performance. For instance, Jefferson and Su (2006), using a firm-level panel dataset covering 1994–2001, analyse the performance impact of conversion on state-owned enterprises and conclude that the conversion of SOEs to shareholding enterprises increased productivity. Similar results were found by Huang and Yao (2010) covering the late 1990s and early 2000s. In terms of the SIP policy, Sun and Tong (2003) evaluate the performance changes of 643 SOEs listed on China's two stock exchanges in the period 1994–8 and find that firm performance improved after listing.

Separating out the effects of privatization from corporatization, Aivazian, Ge and Qiu (2005), using data on 442 SOEs from 1990 to 1999, find that corporatization had a significantly positive impact on SOE performance even without privatization. They conclude that corporate governance reform through incorporation is potentially an effective way of improving the performance of SOEs. With improved governance in the 2000s, the effect may well be stronger for this study.

The picture for collectively-owned enterprises is broadly similar. Xia, Li, and Long (2009), using a sample of collectively owned enterprises in manufacturing industries from the National Industrial Census covering 2000 to 2005, find that the transformed firms, either through privatization or corporatization, achieved better performance than the untransformed COEs by mitigating agency problems, including those in the years after transformation. Their results echo those for SOEs in that corporatization without privatization for COEs also increases firm performance.

Finally, due to the relatively recent nature of private firms being able to incorporate (only since 2000) and to list on the bourses (only since 2001), the effect on private firms is yet to be much explored in the literature. This chapter aims to provide a more complete picture of the effects of incorporation on firm performance in China.

3.9 Data

3.9.1 *Panel Dataset*

The primary dataset is a representative firm-level panel dataset from China's National Bureau of Statistics (NBS) annual enterprise survey covering 2000 to 2005. There are 1,268 firms from 12 cities (province in parenthesis): Beijing (municipality), Changchun (Jilin), Chifeng (Inner Mongolia), Dandong (Liaoning), Hangzhou (Zhejiang), Shijiazhuang (Hebei), Shiyan (Hubei), Shunde

(Guangdong), Wujiang (Jiangsu), Xian (Shaanxi), Zibo (Shandong), and Chong-qing (municipality). The NBS takes considerable care with its annual enterprise survey such that the figures match data obtained independently by the Chinese tax authorities.

Observations with incomplete information were eliminated, so the data com-prise an unbalanced panel of 1,201 industrial firms. The information was also checked against provincial-level data, which revealed that the sub-sample is broadly in line with the provincial averages. Comparison with the averages for other studies using the large NBS firm-level dataset (Dougherty, Herd, and He 2007) yielded similar results. Also in line with most enterprise firm studies, the survey, following NBS practice, covered only firms with an annual sales volume larger than 5 million Yuan. The NBS dataset includes only firms in industry, and does not include construction and transportation companies. Thus, the major-ity of firms operate in the manufacturing sector, with a small number in mining or utilities. Given the sample size, the two-digit (37 sectors) or three-digit-level sector identifiers (188 sectors) are applied, rather than four-digit-level ones (481 sectors) in the estimations, although the results are robust for the other sectoral splits.

As was noted above, this panel dataset is unbalanced; however, the appear-ance (disappearance) of a firm in (from) the dataset cannot be equated with firm entry into (exit from) the market. In order to avoid any systematic bias in the estimations, dummy variables are included for each year 2001 to 2005 which take a value of one (1) if the firm first appeared in the dataset in this specific year, and zero (0) otherwise (the omitted category is firms which appear in 2000). In addition, there are standard year dummies to pick up average TFP evolution over time.

To avoid influential observations that result from reporting error, the produc-tion data are cleaned using standard procedures of 'windsorizing': for the pooled data on firm-level value-added, capital stock and labour, the values at the first and ninety-ninth quantile of the distribution are first determined. Then, all observed values below the former cut-off are replaced with that of the first quantile and all observed values above the latter cut-off with that of the ninety-ninth quantile. Additional information available allows for identifica-tion of firms which are multi-plant groups. Data for multi-plant enterprises may lead to bias in the estimates, and are controlled for with a separate dummy variable in the estimations, as is the age of the firm. Standard errors clustered at the firm-level are used in all the regressions.

3.9.2 Ownership Forms

Firm ownership type is constructed based on the NBS registration code, which has twenty-two ownership types ranging from SOEs to foreign-invested firms. As FIEs have always enjoyed legal recognition, they will not be the focus.

For collectives, some have become transformed into shareholding companies but usually with state partners; for example, state–collective joint ventures. For

SOEs and private firms, there are various categories. SOEs can be unreformed, privatized but not corporatized, incorporated, or LLCs—all of which can be listed companies as well. Therefore, a control variable is always entered for listed firms when they are not separately entered in the estimations, although the limited number of non-SOEs which are publicly traded effectively restricts the analysis to SOEs. For private firms, the corporatized firms are the LLCs, partnerships, and incorporated privately held firms, while the unincorporated ones are registered as sole proprietorships.

Incorporated firms are defined as follows: privatized SOEs that have become LLCs or incorporated firms, shareholding cooperative firms, private partnerships and private LLCs, and incorporated firms. Around 30 per cent of the firms have been incorporated. Table 3.15 presents the transformation of firms of each type. About 5 per cent of the sample comprise listed firms, mostly state-owned enterprises which have been transformed into LLCs or incorporated firms.

Most firms in the sample have never changed ownership type (62.7 per cent), around one-quarter have changed legal form once (24.3 per cent), and a few have changed multiple times (13 per cent). A control variable is always included for multiple changes and a set of estimations omit those which have changed multiple times; that is, those that convert from SOEs to incorporated firms and then convert again to some other ownership type.

Table 3.16 provides the summary statistics, while Table 3.17 presents the difference in performance measures before and after incorporation. Mean values

Table 3.15 Transformation into incorporated firms

Transformed from	Transformed to
SOEs Privatized SOEs Collectives Shareholding cooperative firms State and collective joint ventures	State LLCs and incorporated firms
SOEs Collectives State-owned LLCs and incorporated firms Private LLCs and incorporated firms	Shareholding cooperative firms
Private sole proprietorships Private LLCs and incorporated firms	Private partnerships
Privatized SOEs Collectives Shareholding cooperative firms State-owned LLCs and incorporated firms Private sole proprietorships Private partnerships Hong Kong-, Macao-, Taiwan-invested firms Foreign-invested firms	Private LLCs and incorporated firms

Table 3.16 Summary statistics

	N	Mean	Median	Standard Deviation	Minimum	Maximum
Value-added (in logarithm)	4354	8.921	8.783	1.572	3.414	13.521
Capital (in logarithm)	4472	9.416	9.309	1.882	4.057	14.475
Employment (in logarithm)	4484	5.513	5.389	1.296	0.000	9.472
Sales (in logarithm)	6744	7.176	9.681	5.278	0.000	17.892
Sales to asset ratio	4476	7.040	2.299	65.856	0.000	4159.500
Sales growth rate	3228	1.506	1.185	2.499	0.004	63.762
Profit (in logarithm)	3640	7.490	7.570	2.195	0.000	15.633
Profit to asset ratio	4474	0.256	0.066	1.425	−42.453	44.000
Welfare cost per worker (in logarithm)	4484	1.901	1.329	3.826	−2.960	111.504
Capital-to-labour ratio	4484	100.283	52.891	265.442	0.000	10772.729
Firm age	5385	12.695	8.000	14.373	0.000	101.000

are reported for the year before incorporation and the year of incorporation; for example, if a firm was incorporated in 2004, then the table reports the mean difference between profits in 2004 and in 2003. A one-sample t-test is conducted to determine the significance of the measured differences. This is a raw measure and firm performance may not improve immediately, but it gives a picture of the firms immediately after incorporation. Interestingly, although the first column suggests that there are no significant mean differences in performance from incorporation, the picture changes when the specific form of incorporation (such as to a state LLC or a private partnership) is accounted for. For all incorporations other than those which become state LLCs and incorporated firms, the mean difference in performance registers a significant improvement in the year of incorporation. It suggests that, unlike the case of privatization, it may not take years for the effects of incorporation to improve firm performance, and that legal standing can generate immediate benefits. By contrast, privatization involves fundamental organizational change that takes time to implement.

3.10 Drivers of Firm Performance

The question of whether corporatization improves firm performance requires addressing several sources of bias before isolating the impact of the institutional transformation, including selection bias and unobservable fixed effects. The impact of incorporation with a time lag has also to be accounted for as well as the effect of being a listed company.

This dataset covering 2000–5 will permit us to investigate the effects of incorporation for all firms in China. Particular attention is paid to the selection bias of the institutional form and takes into account the period since restructuring to capture the lag in organizational changes that may accompany incorporation which can affect firm performance. Selection of certain firms into a

Table 3.17 Mean differences in performance measures before and after incorporation (t-value in parentheses)

	Incorporation	Incorporation as state LLC and incorporated firm	Incorporation as a shareholding cooperative firm	Incorporation as a private partnership	Incorporation as a private LLC or incorporated firm
Value-added (100 RMB)	3,143	217	1,781	5,340	4,596
	(1.789)	(0.038)	(2.106)*	(2.961)*	(7.005)
Return on assets (ROA)	0.019	−0.174	0.161	0.347	0.083
	(0.158)	(−0.502)	(1.613)	(1.891)	(0.851)
Sale to asset ratio	−7.927	−2.800	1.341	5.094	−12.065
	(−0.862)	(−0.405)	(1.340)	(2.416)*	(−0.818)
Sales growth (%)	1.384	0.909	1.128	1.459	1.639
	(10.845)*	(6.223)*	(6.237)*	(3.658)*	(8.463)*
Output (100 RMB)	30,301	−0.352	19,866	33,667	56,749
	(1.565)	(−0.590)	(3.044)*	(4.003)*	(5.735)*
Profit (100 RMB)	−302.338	−6,623	1,025	3,639	2,489
	(−0.101)	(−0.672)	(1.494)	(2.084)*	(5.333)*

Note: The significant mean differences are denoted by *.

particular ownership form (incorporated or not) is corrected by using a two-stage probabilistic model that corrects for sample selectivity bias before the firm production function is estimated, mainly through the combination propensity score regression method (Imbens 2004). Further, isolating the impact of ownership change utilizing techniques such as differencing can control for the unobserved fixed effects of a firm that can also induce a higher propensity to incorporate. Without these corrections, the measured effects may be exaggerated. It helps to control for omitted variable bias, observed in the literature, that can increase the effects attributed to incorporation. Comparing firm performance before and after transformation as well as accounting for the time since transformation would further capture the expected lagged effects.

In order to isolate the effect of incorporation on firm performance, there are several sources of bias to contend with in a panel estimator. First, there could be selection bias because the firms which incorporate may not be typical of the population of firms. For instance, if the SOEs chosen to become corporations were the better performing ones before the change, then the stronger performance measures of incorporated SOEs could simply reflect the tendency to select higher quality firms for restructuring. Applying probit/logit analysis, selection bias can be estimated by determining the probability of incorporation based on different performance-related characteristics.

Another possible source of endogeneity is unobservable fixed effects, like managerial quality, that are correlated simultaneously with both the dependent performance variable and with the explanatory variables; for example, the firm's assets (see, for example, Bloom and Van Reenen 2007). Even though firm fixed effects are included, such omitted variables as managerial quality will lead to biased coefficients. For instance, private firms which changed status to become incorporated could have more motivated work staff, implying that their stronger productivity is not a result of incorporation. An attempt to control for unobservable, time-invariant characteristics can be done by using differenced estimators; that is, first differences, one year time lag, or longer lags. Therefore, using differenced estimators that control for these unobserved firm-specific traits can reduce the bias in measuring the effect of incorporation.

It could also be the case that some time is needed after incorporation to adjust to the new governance arrangements. This lagged effect can be assessed through introducing a time trend for the number of years after incorporation.

Therefore, the panel estimator takes the following form:

$$y_{i,t} = \beta_1 INCORP_i + \beta_2 YEARS_{i,t} + \beta_{i,t} V_{i,t} + a_1(\alpha_i) + a_2(\varphi_t) + \varepsilon_{i,t}, \qquad (5)$$

where $y_{i,t}$ represents firm performance of firm i in year t, $INCORP_{i,t}$ represents incorporation (which is a dummy variable equal to 1 in the years after incorporation and 0 otherwise), $YEARS_{i,t}$ is the number of years after incorporation, and $V_{i,t}$ is a vector of firm characteristics (capital, employment, industrial sector, locale, firm age). The time-invariant, firm fixed effects is denoted by α_i, year effects are ϕ_t and $\varepsilon_{i,t}$ is the random error term.

This dynamic panel is estimated in both OLS and the semi-parametric Levinsohn-Petrin (LP) forms. The latter controls for the simultaneity of productivity shocks and input choices through using intermediate inputs as the proxy for unobserved productivity shocks which have been shown to cause bias in OLS (Levinsohn and Petrin 2003). To control for selection bias in the LP results, a two-stage estimation where the residual from the first stage of the LP production function that did not include the incorporation and incorporation year variables was included in the second stage regression was run. The coefficients on β represent the effect of incorporation in the year of its occurrence (β_1), and the effects of incorporation in subsequent years (β_2).

The introduction of the term for the years since incorporation would address the lagged effect of incorporation. But, the endogeneity biases of sample selection and omitted variables would still plague the above estimation. There are various ways to cope with these issues, including addressing the endogeneity of the institutional form in a two-step process following the combination propensity score regression method (Imbens 2004).

The first step is to estimate the propensity of a firm to become incorporated as a logistic function of the firm's characteristics, including capital (in logarithm), employment (in logarithm), profit (in logarithm), welfare cost per worker (in logarithm), capital to labour ratio, firm age (in logarithm), provincial and industry characteristics. The values from the year, $T-1$, before incorporation (T is the year of incorporation) are used; that is, if the firm is incorporated in 2004, the firm characteristics estimator values for this particular firm is from 2003. For the firms which are not incorporated during the sample period, values from 2001 are used. The propensity score, which is the predicted probability from the logistic estimation, is computed as:

$$\Pr(INCORP_i) = f(\mathbf{V}_{i,T-1}), \tag{6}$$

where $\mathbf{V}_{i,T-1}$ is the vector of firm i's characteristics from the year, $T-1$, before incorporation. Using the propensity score $p(\mathbf{V}_i)$ predicted from equation (6), regression weights for the second stage are generated as follows:

$$\lambda_i = \sqrt{\frac{INCORP_i}{p(\mathbf{V}_i)} + \frac{(1-INCORP_i)}{\left(1-p(\mathbf{V}_i)\right)}}. \tag{7}$$

By using a Kernel matching process, firms with different propensity scores are given different weights in equation (5), which allows the incorporated firms to be more closely matched to those likely to become incorporated but did not do so and for the unincorporated firms to be matched with those less likely to become corporations and yet did so.

The result is that the two-stage combination propensity score regression largely, but not completely, addresses the endogeneity bias where better-performing firms or those with unobserved characteristics are more likely to become incorporated. Based on available information and by matching the firms to those which share their characteristics, it is an attempt to reduce the

endogeneity bias that can over-attribute the observed improved firm performance to incorporation.

To address omitted variable bias (for example, unobserved managerial quality
that motivates the labour force better), the second-stage combination propensity score regression is also run using first differences; that is, one year lags of the
estimators to control for the time-invariant unobservable traits likely to cause an
upward bias in the estimated effect of incorporation. The α_i terms are eliminated
in the differenced version of equation (5). The $YEARS_{i,t}$ terms capture the effects
of time since incorporation.

Using the estimated coefficients from the first stage, the differenced equation
for $T-1$, the year before incorporation, to 2005 is as follows:

$$
\begin{aligned}
(y_{i,2005} - y_{i,T-1}) = {} & \beta_1(INCORP_{i,2005} - INCORP_{i,T-1}) + \beta_2(YEARS_{i,2005} \\
& - YEARS_{i,T-1}) + \beta_i(V_{i,2005} - V_{i,T-1}) + a_2(\varphi_{2005} - \varphi_{T-1}) \\
& + (\varepsilon_{2005} - \varepsilon_{T-1}).
\end{aligned}
\tag{8}
$$

Dividing the log differences by $(2005-(T-1))$, it is the annual rates of change, so
equation (8) becomes:

$$
\begin{aligned}
gr(y_{i,T-1to2005}) = {} & \delta_1 D(INCORP_{i,T-1to2005}) \\
& + \delta_2 D(YEARS_{i,T-1to2005}) + \delta_i gr(V_{i,T-1to2005}) \\
& + \delta_4 D(\varphi_{T-1to2005}) + D(\varepsilon_{T-1to2005}),
\end{aligned}
\tag{9}
$$

where $gr(y_{i,T-1to2005})$ is the annual rate of growth from $T-1$ to 2005 of the
performance variable, y, for firm i, and $gr(V_{i,T-1to2005})$ represents the annual
rate of change of the vector of inputs, while $D(\phi_{T-1to2005})$ indicates the change
in time-varying factors common to all firms, and $D(\varepsilon_{T-1to2005})$ is the change in the
error term. For the key variables, $D(INCORP_{i,T-1to2005})$ represents the incorporation of the firm as between $T-1$ and 2005, $D(YEARS_{i,T-1to2005})$ is the additional effect of incorporation on the number of years since the corporate
transformation.

These variables in the differenced equation measure the performance differential from before incorporation to 2005. A standard fixed effects regression is also
run where each observation is differenced from the firm's mean value to control
for firm fixed effects. The results are similar. The annual rates of change of the
firm performance allow us to assess the effect of incorporation whilst controlling
for the different lengths of time of incorporation of different firms. Equation (5)
therefore provides the key coefficients: δ_1 (for the effect of incorporation), and δ_2
(the lagged effect of incorporation).

Table 3.18 shows the first-stage propensity score matching results. Firms
which become incorporated have less capital and labour than firms which do
not. They are also less profitable, but there are no significant differences in
welfare cost per worker, capital-to-labour ratio, or firm age. Relative to the
omitted category of the coal industry, most of the industrial sectors showed an
increased propensity to incorporate (not shown in table). Notable exceptions
were the paper and furniture industries as well as leather, fur, and feather
goods. Firms in Hangzhou and Changchun showed a stronger propensity to

Table 3.18 First-stage propensity score matching

Dependent variable: D(INCORP)	Full sample (1)	Excluding listed firms (2)	Controlling for privatization (3)	Controlling for SOEs and private firms (4)
ln(capital)	−0.091**	−0.071	−0.091**	−0.091**
	(0.042)	(0.043)	(0.042)	(0.042)
ln(labour)	−0.205***	−0.201***	−0.205***	−0.205***
	(0.053)	(0.054)	(0.053)	(0.053)
ln(profit)	−0.112***	−0.102***	−0.112***	−0.112***
	(0.021)	(0.022)	(0.021)	(0.021)
ln(welfare per worker)	0.022	0.009	0.022	0.022
	(0.042)	(0.043)	(0.042)	(0.042)
Capital-to-labour ratio	−0.001	−0.001	−0.001	−0.001
	(0.000)	(0.000)	(0.000)	(0.000)
ln(firm age)	0.010	0.022	0.010	0.010
	(0.029)	(0.032)	(0.029)	(0.029)
Observations	2104	1884	2104	2104
Industry dummies (36)	Yes	Yes	Yes	Yes
Year dummies (5)	No	No	No	No
Province dummies (11)	Yes	Yes	Yes	Yes

Note: Omitted variables Shiyan in Hubei, the industrial sector of coal mining and cleaning, and the standard errors are adjusted for clustering at the firm level. Significance is denoted as: *** $p < 0.01$, ** $p < 0.05$, * $p < 0.1$.

incorporate while those in Beijing and Dandong were less likely, reflecting the market-orientation of Zhejiang and Jilin and the larger presence of the state/ state-owned enterprises in Beijing and Liaoning. The firms which have a greater propensity to become incorporated appear to be smaller and less profitable, suggesting that it is not the better performing firms which are corporatized and that any positive effect of incorporation may be more attributable to the change in legal status than to selection bias. Estimates in the second stage included controls for ownership type (SOEs, private firms) based on column (4), but as those dummy variables were insignificant, they are not reported in the following tables.

Table 3.19 shows the second-stage results of the propensity score matching process: incorporation has a positive and significant effect on value-added and output. Referring to the usual productivity measures of value-added and output, column (1) reports the average annual increase in firm productivity for an incorporated firm is 0.180 percentage points. The number of years after incorporation has an insignificant effect. Output registers a smaller (0.029 percentage points) but significantly positive impact of corporatization. Value-added can produce larger estimates than the output measure as it can underestimate improvements in intermediate inputs, but it effectively measures firm productivity across industrial sectors as it does not have to account for differences in intermediate inputs across industries. Both are reported and show a similar significance of incorporation. Thus, legal registration can involve corporate governance improvements, which appear to be achieved without a radical overhaul of existing production structures, for instance, by instead adding

Table 3.19 The impact of incorporation on firm performance

Dependent variable: $gr(y_{i,T-1to2005})$	ln(value-added) (1)	ln(output) (2)
$D(INCORP_{i,T-1to2005})$	0.180**	0.029**
	(0.089)	(0.013)
$D(YEARS_{i,T-1to2005})$	−0.027	−0.002
	(0.017)	(0.002)
Y1	−0.037	−0.008
	(0.043)	(0.006)
Y2	−0.074*	−0.001
	(0.043)	(0.006)
Y3	−0.169**	−0.032**
	(0.079)	(0.013)
Y4	−0.119	−0.011
	(0.097)	(0.015)
Y5	0.008	0.017
	(0.200)	(0.025)
Firms	692	692
Observations	2082	2082

Note: Other variables not reported for brevity include capital, labour. In column (2), material inputs are also included. Y1–Y5 refers to the years since incorporation. Significance is denoted as: *** $p < 0.01$, ** $p < 0.05$, * $p < 0.1$.

independent directors to the Board. The benefits of a recognized legal form can be quickly realized. To explore this issue further, a sub-sample that excludes those firms which have changed legal ownership form more than once during the sample period was estimated. The results were similar but the size of the productivity gain is slightly smaller. This suggests that firms which change ownership more often are those which capitalize on the boost from corporate reorganization and thus supports the above interpretation.

Table 3.20 offers further evidence that the effects of incorporation on increasing firm productivity are apparent. Incorporation adds an average annual improvement of around 0.6 percentage points (0.613–0.661 percentage points) to value-added (depending on the control variables) with a small negative effect from the years since incorporation (about 0.1 percentage point). Nevertheless, the net effect of incorporation is positive and within the range of estimates in Table 3.5. This is true even without propensity score matching and only controlling for the selectivity bias of those with firms which chose to incorporate versus those which did not.

Table 3.21 excludes listed firms and the results are largely unchanged. Incorporation is associated with an increase in average annual value-added of 0.180 percentage points while the years after incorporation generates no significant effect. For output in column (2), the coefficient on incorporation is slightly smaller at 0.024 percentage points. This suggests that isolating the effect of listing does not fundamentally change the impact of incorporation on output except to reduce it by a very small 0.004 percentage points, or on firm productivity by less than 1 per cent. Thus, incorporation's positive impact is not due to

Table 3.20 Estimations using Levinsohn-Petrin production function

Dependent variable: $gr(y_{i,T-1to2005})$	Full sample	Excluding listed firms	Controlling for privatized firms
$D(INCORP_{i,T-1to2005})$	0.637***	0.613***	0.661***
	(0.141)	(0.148)	(0.144)
$D(YEARS_{i,T-1to2005})$	−0.124***	−0.122***	−0.130***
	(0.028)	(0.029)	(0.029)
Privatized firms			−0.124*
			(0.073)
Y1	−0.143***	−0.130***	−0.148***
	(0.046)	(0.048)	(0.047)
Y2	−0.220***	−0.209***	−0.229***
	(0.050)	(0.051)	(0.053)
Y3	−0.313***	−0.292***	−0.331***
	(0.095)	(0.100)	(0.101)
Y4	−0.332**	−0.306**	−0.354**
	(0.143)	(0.146)	(0.145)
Y5	−0.275	−0.260	−0.268
	(0.278)	(0.280)	(0.273)
Firms	1025	956	1025
Observations	2961	2719	2961

Note: Other variables not reported for brevity include capital, labour. Y1–Y5 refers to the years since incorporation. Significance is denoted as: *** $p < 0.01$, ** $p < 0.05$, * $p < 0.1$.

Table 3.21 The impact of incorporation on firm performance excluding listed firms

Dependent variable: $gr(y_{i,T-1to2005})$	ln(value-added) (1)	ln(output) (2)
$D(INCORP_{i,T-1to2005})$	0.180**	0.024*
	(0.089)	(0.013)
$D(YEARS_{i,T-1to2005})$	−0.026	−0.001
	(0.017)	(0.002)
Y1	−0.036	−0.006
	(0.043)	(0.005)
Y2	−0.075*	0.001
	(0.045)	(0.006)
Y3	−0.120*	−0.025*
	(0.062)	(0.013)
Y4	−0.108	−0.007
	(0.097)	(0.014)
Y5	0.032	0.021
	(0.206)	(0.025)
Firms	632	632
Observations	1866	1866

Note: Other variables not reported for brevity include capital, labour. In column (2), material inputs are also included. Y1–Y5 refers to the years since incorporation. Significance is denoted as: *** $p < 0.01$, ** $p < 0.05$, * $p < 0.1$.

Table 3.22 The impact of incorporation on firm performance controlling for privatization

Dependent variable: $gr(y_{i,T-1to2005})$	ln(value-added) (1)	ln(output) (2)
$D(INCORP_{i,T-1to2005})$	0.175*	0.029**
	(0.091)	(0.014)
$D(YEARS_{i,T-1to2005})$	−0.025	−0.002
	(0.018)	(0.002)
Privatized firms	−0.015	−0.000
	(0.030)	(0.004)
Y1	−0.035	−0.008
	(0.044)	(0.006)
Y2	−0.065	−0.001
	(0.046)	(0.007)
Y3	−0.156*	−0.032**
	(0.084)	(0.014)
Y4	−0.108	−0.011
	(0.101)	(0.016)
Y5	0.024	0.018
	(0.203)	(0.025)
Firms	692	692
Observations	2082	2082

Note: Other variables not reported for brevity includes capital, labour. In column (5), material inputs are also included. Y1–Y5 refers to the years since incorporation. Significance is denoted as: *** $p < 0.01$, ** $p < 0.05$, * $p < 0.1$.

the influence of listing. This adds robustness to the findings using the full sample.

Table 3.22 attempts to isolate the effects of privatization. Again, the picture does not significantly change. Incorporation exerts a positive impact on firm productivity of 0.175 percentage points on value-added and 0.029 percentage points on output. This suggests that it is not the effect of privatization that explains the improved firm performance, but of incorporation.

In summary, incorporation has a positive and significant impact on firm productivity. Even though controls are introduced for multiple changes of ownership type, the further estimations that exclude the multiple changes yield similar results. Isolating the impact of listing and privatization, incorporation has a robust impact in increasing firm value-added that is also not the result of the sample selection bias which would occur when better performing firms become incorporated. Indeed, the propensity score-matching estimations suggest that it is the less capitalized and less profitable firms which are more likely to become incorporated.

3.11 Implications for Industrial Output

The results suggest that the establishment of a diversified corporate sector and the granting to private firms of equal legal rights and obligations contributed to industrial efficiency over the strong economic growth period of 2000–5.

Industrial output grew in real terms by an average of 23.2 per cent from 2000–8, nearly twice as high as the 1990s, both higher than the 1980s (9.64 per cent from 1981–9). Correspondingly, China's economic growth averaged 10 per cent in the late 1990s to 2000s, a percentage point higher than the first two decades of the reform period. Numerous factors could explain the higher growth rates, but corporatization may have played a part by strengthening property rights and offering legal protection to incorporated firms.

The overall contribution of incorporated firms to gross deflated industrial output increased gradually from 27.9 per cent in 2000 to 33.95 per cent in 2006. A simulation exercise is run to determine how much lower industrial output would have been if there were no corporatized firms, so firms would still exist but as unincorporated firms; that is, no corporatized SOEs, no reformed COEs, and no incorporated private companies. Since private sole proprietorships comprise a legally recognized category, this estimate is upwardly biased as the real comparator should be *getihu* or unregistered privately owned businesses.

Figure 3.10 simulates the level of industrial output by assuming that all incorporated firms are unincorporated; for example, ensuring that industrial output would have been lower without the positive productivity differential from incorporated firms. If incorporated firms grew at the average rate of unincorporated firms, which was 17.1 per cent, the estimates imply overall industrial output would be 30 per cent lower in 2006. Using instead the *Chinese Statistical Yearbook* data, if incorporated firms grew at the rate of unincorporated firms, then industrial output would have grown at 15 per cent on average and industrial output in 2006 would have been 38.4 per cent lower. Reassuringly, the estimates are close to the raw data in the *Chinese Statistical Yearbook*.

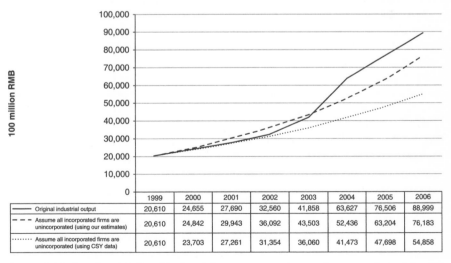

	1999	2000	2001	2002	2003	2004	2005	2006
Original industrial output	20,610	24,655	27,690	32,560	41,858	63,627	76,506	88,999
Assume all incorporated firms are unincorporated (using our estimates)	20,610	24,842	29,943	36,092	43,503	52,436	63,204	76,183
Assume all incorporated firms are unincorporated (using CSY data)	20,610	23,703	27,261	31,354	36,060	41,473	47,698	54,858

Figure 3.10 Simulated deflated industrial output assuming no incorporation of firms

Instead of 23 per cent per annum growth, industrial output growth would have averaged between 15–17 per cent in the 2000s. Incorporation, therefore, appears to have contributed to the high industrial output that formed part of the stronger GDP growth rate of the 2000s, itself a percentage point higher than the previous two decades.

3.12 Conclusion

The finding that the reallocation of labour accounts for a small proportion of labour productivity growth provides support that the higher levels of labour productivity in the 2000s is due more to gains in technical efficiency than the allocative effects of shifting labour from SOEs to the non-state sector. Trend growth rates of labour productivity are high, around 3–5 per cent per annum, but the firms with higher labour productivity are not growing more quickly. Therefore, although technical efficiency related productivity gains are more sustainable than factor reallocation as the latter will eventually run out, the mechanism driving those technological improvements needs to be understood and developed as well.

Indeed, this chapter also identifies the avenue for the improvements in technical efficiency, which appears to include the drivers of technology transfers from foreign investors and R&D spending. Chinese–foreign joint ventures with technology transfers have the highest labour productivity, followed by privatized SOEs which have the highest TFP growth rates, the latter suggesting both an allocative and a technical efficiency gain. R&D spending also improves labour productivity if there is technology in place as does a more marketized locale. The presence of foreign firms in an industry and interactive effects were insignificant, suggesting limited scope for spillovers in the area of labour productivity.

By focusing on Chinese–foreign joint ventures established with a transfer of technology, this chapter shows that such transfers can improve labour productivity and positively interact to enhance the positive impact of R&D spending. To sustain such productivity gains in the future would therefore entail gaining more transfers of advanced technology and promoting spending on R&D such that these improvements can be sustained once the factor reallocation process in China comes to a halt.

The findings suggest that foreign capital infusion embodying technological know-how, R&D, as well as market-oriented reforms in factor and product markets have made significant contributions to improving labour productivity in the 2000s. In particular, China's policy of obtaining technology in its FDI and industrial strategies appears to be successful in improving labour productivity.

Labour productivity is a key factor in China's continuing growth prospects. Promoting technology, as well as encouraging competition and further market reforms would be fruitful. Sustaining China's development will therefore require attention to maintaining the momentum of its market-oriented reforms as its firms seek to increase their value-added per worker which will induce longer term growth effects if the improvements take the form of sustained productivity enhancements.

Plus, in China in the 2000s, the latitude to incorporate, and the corporatization policy, has created a modern, corporate sector protected by laws and regulations. Not only with SOEs but private firms benefited in that they were able to become legally recognized entities and take on the various ownership forms of partnerships, LLCs, etc.

By controlling as much as possible for sample selection and unobservable heterogeneity bias, incorporation increases firm productivity. It is the smaller and less profitable firms which become incorporated, so that selection is not the explanation for the effects observed. The estimates under a number of specifications (controlling for the effect of listing, privatization without incorporation, and the type of corporation if it was an SOE or private firm) show that there is a significantly positive impact from incorporation. The hypothesis explored is therefore answered in the affirmative: incorporation does increase firm performance. The additional legal protection associated with being a recognized corporate entity improves firm productivity. The effects are quite immediate and may fade a little with time, but the boost to firm performance is significant and suggests that incorporated firms remain more productive than unincorporated ones. The division between ownership and management in corporatized firms could make managers more responsible for firm performance and so more incentivized to improve performance.

If the still imperfect legal system and capital markets improve, the impact could be even larger. Corporatization appears to have been successful in improving firm performance in China, in line with the conclusions for other countries that incorporation offers numerous benefits. For China, it supports the policy of *gufenhua* to reform its SOEs and has generated positive benefits for private firms as well in the process. Incorporation can help to explain the high industrial growth rate during the best decade of economic growth thus far.

4

Endogenous Growth: Human Capital and Labour Market Reforms

4.1 Introduction

Following from the previous chapter, one of the key drivers of economic growth in China will be to continue with labour market reforms to improve the level of human capital that can generate sustained productivity improvements. The development of the labour market has been one of the most wide-ranging reforms for China. In less than thirty years, its employment system was transformed from the 'iron rice bowl' to a more competitive one. These reforms have been instrumental in raising labour productivity and therefore drive endogenous economic growth, where efficiency improvements are wrought from improving and better rewarding human capital; that is, skills, education, etc. More reforms are needed, especially as China's labour market is still characterized by numerous inefficiencies such as migrant employment. It is critical, as China's growth must increasingly rely on productivity rather than factor accumulation, making human capital investment a crucial driver of endogenous growth.

4.2 Labour Reforms

Before the 1980s, state labour agencies exercised a virtual monopoly over the allocation of urban labour (see, for example, Bian 1994a). Governmental planning, rather than the market, dictated the supply of and demand for labour. Allocations to enterprises were aimed at avoiding unemployment. Job assignments were made without much reference to the needs of enterprises or the characteristics of workers. The initial job assignment was crucial as the first job was typically the only job, the so-called 'iron rice bowl'.

When reforms started in the 1980s, the state monopoly of labour allocation was replaced by a somewhat more decentralized system. Central and local labour authorities continued to plan the labour requirements of state- and large collectively owned enterprises and remained responsible for the placement of college graduates. However, labour exchanges began to be established for the registration of job vacancies, job placements, and training. By the 1990s, recruitment quotas for state enterprises were abolished and firms were largely allowed to choose their employees.

In the latter part of the 1990s, the attempts to resolve the problem of inefficiency of the state sector include downsizing and layoffs of workers by a quarter or more within four years (1997–2000). This was a drastic change from the official policy of full employment. In 1996, an estimated 5.25 million urban state workers were officially registered as unemployed. By the end of 1998, the official figure of laid-off workers was 15.7 million, which included 8.8 million *xiagang* workers (see, for example, Yang and Xin, 1999; Lee, 1998). Giles, Park, and Zhang (2005) report that 'aggressive economic restructuring led to the layoff of 45 million workers between 1995 and 2002, including 36 million workers from the state sector'.

Xiagang workers are laid-off workers who are officially registered as part of their enterprise or work unit, but do not go to work or receive a wage. They are registered as *xiagang* by their work unit and are officially entitled to minimum income support, although they often do not receive any such support in practice. This classification was newly created as part of the five-year restructuring programme of reforming inefficient SOEs. These laid-off workers epitomize the changes in the labour market from the mid to the late 1990s related to labour market and wage reforms. There are other forms of unemployment not captured by official statistics, including those that are classified as youth waiting for work, and even early retirement at unreasonable ages, such as in a person's mid-30s. Some are simply considered 'not in post' or *ligang*, defined as taking a long vacation without pay. These forms of lack of employment have caused the Chinese government to launch re-employment policies primarily geared toward developing labour-intensive sectors, such as food services, transport, retail, and tourism. By the mid-2000s, unemployment in China had fallen substantially and the *xiagang* workers were largely re-absorbed into the fast-growing private sector. Nevertheless, the Chinese urban labour market is, in short, characterized by many imperfections. It is underdeveloped in that workers still face some restrictions on moving from one city to another on account of the household registration system (*hukou*).

Increased competition with the move to a more market-oriented economy should be associated with more variation of wages with productivity if accompanied by appropriate reform of the wage structure. Wages in urban China have indeed been reformed.

4.3 Wage Reforms

There were two waves of wage reforms prior to 1978. The first of China's wage system reforms occurred in 1950, one year after the Communist Revolution. It was aimed at transforming the food supply system of wartime communism into a wage system. Under the reformed system, government and military officials and employees in the newly established state-owned enterprises began to receive cash salaries and compensation according to job titles and ranks. The second wage reform in 1956 was part of an overall plan to nationalize the economy. The aim was to regulate wages for an expanded work force in both the state and collective sectors. Salary standards were patterned after the Soviet model and centrally regulated according to regions, occupations, industries, sectors (state or collective), level of management of enterprises (central or local), and characteristics of workplace (for example, technology and size). The core of this wage system was a complex structure of salary standards for more than 300 occupational classifications. These wage reforms apply to state-owned enterprises (SOEs) and collectively owned enterprises, but not to private or foreign-owned enterprises. The latter categories are free to set their wages within the confines of the Labour Law. The focus is on the third wave, which consisted of three sets of reforms promulgated in 1985, 1992, and 1994, and the most recent overhaul of the wage structure implemented between 1996 and 2000.

In 1985, the Ministry of Labour (MOL) determined that the budget to be allocated for wages will be linked to the economic performance of SOEs and collectively owned enterprises. It was to be measured by enterprise profitability or a combined indicator of economic returns. The indicators vary by region and reflect local economic conditions, such as unemployment, the consumer price index, and regional growth. The goal is to provide profit-oriented incentives. Under the previous system, these enterprises turned over all profits, and paid workers with wages redistributed by the state. Except for a small amount of bonus funds linked to limited above-quota output, there was little incentive to be profitable. With these reforms, however, wage budgets were linked to an enterprise's profitability and performance. Basic wages and profit quotas were projected from an enterprise's performance from the previous three years and they were allowed to retain, after taxes, above-quota profits for investment in plant capacity, employee welfare programmes, 'floating' salaries (that is, bonus-type, temporary salary increases), raises, and bonuses. These incentives have appeared to stimulate profit-oriented behavior in state-owned enterprises and have been investigated (see Groves et al. 1995).

In 1992, the State Council issued a circular stating that enterprises were permitted to set their internal wage structure within the confines of the overall wage budget established by the government. There were two methods available to enterprises. The first was that wages would be linked to enterprise perform-ance. If the wage bill exceeded the governmental standard wage bill that would be implied by the aggregate positions established by the Ministry of Labour, the enterprise must pay a Wage Adjustment Tax of 33 per cent to the Department of Taxation. The second method is for the enterprise to propose a wage budget and then submit it for approval to the Ministry of Labour and the Ministry of Finance, which then consider the proposal in the context of the consumer price index and local wages. The primary difference is that if an enterprise chooses the latter method, it is not liable for the Wage Adjustment Tax. These policies are designed to ensure that profits accrue to the state, but also that profit-oriented incentives are maintained.

Beginning in 1994–5, enterprises that are publicly listed companies, that is, companies which have issued shares that are listed on one of the two stock exchanges in China (Shenzhen or Shanghai), were permitted to set their own wages subject to two standards. The first is that the growth rate of total wages must be lower than that of after-tax profitability, and the second is that per capita wage growth is lower than the rate of growth of labour productivity. In addition, the Ministry of Labour suggested to enterprises that wages are set not only according to occupation and rank, but also based on skills and productivity. Of the estimated 100,000 SOEs, approximately 40,000 have issued shares and set wages under this regime. Non-stock enterprises are still subject to the previous system.

There was then an overhaul which was part of the 9th Five Year Plan (1996–2000). Previously, there were six components to wages in enterprises, including the basic wage, bonuses, benefits and subsidies, overtime wages, supplementary wages, and an 'other' component, primarily based on hardship. These categories have been replaced by two components of wages, fixed (*guding*) and variable (*huo*). The fixed portion includes the basic wage, seniority wage, insurance (medical, unemployment, and pensions), and a housing fund. The variable portion includes bonuses, based on both individual productivity and enterprise profitability. Enterprises continue to pay for training and other in-kind compensation, such as firm outings and gifts of daily goods. The standard working week is forty hours with 50 per cent overtime pay on weekends and 300 per cent overtime pay on national holidays, such as Lunar New Year, for hourly workers.

In summary, these reforms are intended to create a more market-oriented wage structure. The rate of compliance by enterprises to the reforms and new regulations is thought to be high, paving the way for returns to human capital essential for endogeneous growth.

4.4 Human Capital Investment

Becker (1993) in his book, *A Treatise on the Family*, identified the parental role in developing the human capital of children. The investment in children's human capital, under credit constraints, necessarily entails forgone current consumption for the household. There is a strand of literature—intra-household resource allocation models—that can test the extent to which parents will forgo consumption to spend on children's education (see Deaton 1989; Haddad, Hoddinott, and Alderman 1997, for overviews). The degree to which expectations of returns from children will vary among societies, but parents invest in their children with an eye toward their own future utility as well as the utility of their offspring. These intertemporal considerations can generate differential investments in the human capital of sons versus daughters that are unrelated to preference or bias particular to a society.

Extending Becker's three-period model, the below set-up introduces a final-period retiree who does not earn income and whose utility comprises consumption only, which is a function of transfers from his children and returns from assets, such as pension schemes. The utility function of parents of two children in the tth period is

$$U_t = u_t + \delta(W^m_{t+1} + W^f_{t+1} + U_{t+1}), \tag{1}$$

where u_t is their utility this period from consumption, W^m_{t+1} is the future income of their son, W^f_{t+1} is the future income of their daughter, U_{t+1} is the next period's utility, and δ is the discount rate or subjective rate of time preference. The utility derived from their children is assumed to be separable from the utility produced by their own consumption. Utility next period, U_{t+1}, comprises consumption in the form of returns from savings invested in assets, A_{t+1}, and transfers from their son's future household, B^m_{t+1}, and from their daughter's future household, B^f_{t+1}.

The marginal yield on assets, A_{t+1}, is R_a, while the marginal yields on investments in the human capital of the son and daughter with respect to the returns to their future income (R^m_h, R^f_h) and the portion of that which will generate transfers to parents in the next period (R^m_h, R^f_h) are given by:

$$R^m_h = \partial W^m_{t+1}/\partial \gamma^m_t, R^f_h = \partial W^f_{t+1}/\partial \gamma^f_t, R^m_b = \partial B^m_{t+1}/\partial \gamma^m_t, R^f_b = \partial B^f_{t+1}/\partial \gamma^f_t, \tag{2}$$

where γ^m_t and γ^f_t denote the proportion of household income, Q_t, expended on the human capital of their son and daughter, respectively.

The intertemporal budget constraint is

$$Z_t + \gamma^m_t + \gamma^f_t + A_{t+1}/R_a + B^m_{t+1}/R^m_b + B^f_{t+1}/R^f_b = PV(Q_t) \tag{3}$$

where $PV(Q_t)$ is the present value of parental household income, comprising Q_t and expected Q_{t+1}. In other words, parental household income this period consists of expenditures (Z_t) that include consumption, transfers to their parents, savings invested in assets for retirement, and forgone consumption invested in children's education $(\gamma^m_t$ and $\gamma^f_t)$. Household resources next period (Q_{t+1}) is equal to the discounted value of all expected sources of consumption $(A_{t+1}/R_a + B^m_{t+1}/R^m_b + B^f_{t+1}/R^f_b)$, that is, assets and transfers, which are the result of savings and investment in children's human capital.

The allocation between investing in assets or children when contemplating consumption next period is determined by a first-order condition equating the marginal yields on the three sources of income in the third period:

$$\delta A'_{t+1} + \delta B^{m'}_{t+1} + \delta B^{f'}_{t+1} = \lambda_u/R_k = \delta U'_{t+1}, \tag{4a}$$

where λ_u is the marginal utility of income. The yields on human capital are expected to decline as more resources are invested, $\partial R^m_h/\partial \gamma^m_t \leq 0, \partial R^f_h/\partial \gamma^f_t \leq 0, \partial R^m_b/\partial \gamma^m_t \leq 0,$ and $\partial R^f_b/\partial \gamma^f_t \leq 0$, and will eventually equal returns to assets in this model, R_a assumed to be constant. Since $\partial R^m{}_h/\partial R_a < 0$, $\partial R^f{}_h/\partial R_a < 0$, $R^m{}_h > R_a$ and $R^f{}_h > R_a$, the marginal rate of return is denoted R_k.

The next first-order condition maximizes parental utility and determines their optimal consumption in periods two and three:

$$U'_t = \delta R_k U'_{t+1} = \lambda_u. \tag{4b}$$

The last first-order condition determines investment in children's human capital in terms of the utility derived from the future income of the children:

$$\delta R^m{}_h W^{m'}_{t+1} = \lambda_u, \delta R^f{}_h W^{f'}_{t+1} = \lambda_u. \tag{4c}$$

Combining the first-order conditions gives

$$\lambda_u/R_a = \lambda_u/R^m{}_b = \lambda_u/R^f{}_b = \lambda_u/R^m{}_h = \lambda_u/R^f{}_h, \tag{5}$$

which shows that the marginal rates of return on human capital for both the children's future income and expected transfers equal the return on assets in both periods.

The empirical analysis is in three parts. First, the intra-household resource allocation approach is used to model the decision of parents to forgo consumption to spend on education as a measure of direct investment in children. The equation for the proportion of household expenditure on the eth item is given by

$$\gamma^e_t = \beta_0 + \beta_1 \ln (Z_t/n) + \beta_2 \ln (n) + \sum_{g=1}^{G-1} \beta_3 (n_g/n) + \beta_4 X_t + \varepsilon_t, \tag{6}$$

where γ^e_t denotes the share of household expenditures spent on the education of children, Z_t is total household monetary expenditure, n denotes household size, n_g is the number of individuals of age–gender demographic group g, $\sum n_g/n$ represents the proportion of individuals of demographic group g in the household, X_t is a vector of control variables, and ε_t is the error term. If β_3 is significant and different for boys and girls, then two further approaches will attempt to explain the findings.

To investigate the rate of return to education, a Mincerian-type formulation of the logarithm of earnings is formulated as the dependent variable and a set of personal and other characteristics as the independent variables (Mincer 1974). The second set of returns derives from the implications of favourable assortative mating; that is, individuals of comparable educational attainment are more likely to marry each other (Becker 1981). If this holds, then there is support for the expectation that investing in daughters will generate more transfers than from sons, given the same gender earnings differentials that are causing unequal returns to education.

In Table 4.1, not surprisingly, there is a 4.98 percentage point increase in the proportion of household resources allocated to children's education associated with two-generation households. Turning to the age–gender household composition variables, the proportions of boys and girls aged 13–15 and 16–18 affect the proportion of household resources expended on children's education, but

Table 4.1 Intra-household resource allocation model of expenditure on children's education

Dependent variable: proportion of household resources expended on children's education	Coefficient (t-statistic)	Mean value or percentage (standard deviation)
Intercept	−0.0776	0.0469
	(−0.374)	(0.0898)
Household characteristics		
Log of household expenditure per capita (predicted)	−0.0088	8.1370
	(−1.119)	(0.3157)
Log of number of household members (predicted)	0.1366	1.1062
	(1.119)	(0.2016)
Communist Party membership of any member of the household	0.0051	0.4564
	(1.135)	(0.4981)
One-generation household	0.1186	0.1552
	(1.291)	(0.0871)
Two-generation household	0.0498	0.7816
	(1.706)*	(0.3622)
Three-generation household	0.0052	0.0555
	(0.377)	(0.2291)
Characteristics of household head		
Male	−0.0072	0.6593
	(−1.548)	(0.4740)
Educational level	−0.0033	3.8015
	(−3.373)***	(1.5173)
Occupation	−0.0012	5.5657
	(−1.631)	(1.9401)
Age–gender composition of household		
Male aged 0–6	−0.0096	0.0256
	(−0.233)	(0.0862)
Male aged 7–12	0.0583	0.0382
	(1.349)	(0.1046)
Male aged 13–15	0.1465	0.0270
	(3.719)***	(0.0894)
Male aged 16–18	0.1434	0.0209
	(6.180)***	(0.0785)
Male aged 19–55	−0.0027	0.2893
	(−0.147)	(0.1711)
Male aged 56–65	−0.0440	0.0653
	(−2.061)**	(0.1503)
Male aged 66 and over	−0.0404	0.0299
	(−1.398)	(0.1101)
Female aged 0–6	−0.0191	0.0235
	(−0.466)	(0.0831)
Female aged 7–12	0.0636	0.0402
	(1.418)	(0.1071)
Female aged 13–15	0.1317	0.0237
	(3.852)***	(0.0844)
Female aged 16–18	0.1998	0.0212
	(9.348)***	(0.0780)
Female aged 19–55	0.0136	0.3094
	(0.589)	(0.1634)
Female aged 56–65	0.0052	0.0593
	(0.168)	(0.1492)

Provinces

Beijing	−0.00004	0.0721
	(−0.007)	(0.2587)
Shanxi	−0.0106	0.0937
	(−1.324)	(0.2915)
Liaoning	−0.0207	0.1010
	(−4.242)***	(0.3013)
Anhui	−0.0095	0.0721
	(−1.695)*	(0.2587)
Henan	−0.0265	0.0865
	(−3.465)***	(0.2812)
Hubei	0.0018	0.1070
	(0.391)	(0.3091)
Guangdong	−0.0070	0.0787
	(−0.875)	(0.2694)
Sichuan	−0.0049	0.1223
	(−1.261)	(0.3277)
Yunnan	−0.0100	0.0935
	(−2.021)**	(0.2911)
Gansu	−0.0040	0.0577
	(−0.616)	(0.2331)
R^2	0.0905	
Adjusted R^2	0.0861	
$F_{(32, 6555)}$	26.17***	
Number of observations	6588	

Source: *China Urban Household Survey*, 1995.

Notes: (1) Omitted dummy variables are: female household head, households without any Communist Party members, females aged 66 and over, Jiangsu province and other types of households. (2) The mean of the natural logarithm of household expenditure per capita (actual) is 8.1366 with a standard deviation of 0.7323. The mean of log of number of household members (actual) is 1.1063 with a standard deviation of 0.2682. (3) *** denotes statistical significance at 1% level, ** at 5% level, and * at 10% level. (4) Instruments are ownership of telephone and type of house.

not children aged 7–12. As education is heavily subsidized, this is not surprising for the younger age groups (see Knight and Li 1996). The proportion of boys aged 13–15 increases household expenditure on children's education by 14.65 percentage points, while girls aged 13–15 increase expenditure by a smaller amount (13.17 percentage points). The situation is reversed for boys and girls aged 16–18, in which the effects on household educational expenditure are respectively 14.34 percentage points and 19.98 percentage points.

Other significant variables include the education of the household head and the proportion of men aged 56–65 in the household, along with a number of province dummy variables. The education of the household head and the proportion of men aged 56–65 both have negative effects on children's educational expenditures. There are numerous possible explanations. Regarding the education of the household head, it is possible that only direct expenditure on children's education and not indirect spending has been captured. In other words, parents will invest a set amount of time and resources in their children. More educated household heads may spend more time investing in their children by helping them with homework, or perhaps spend time and resources on cultivating *guanxi* to further the children's future opportunities. Less educated

117

household heads may not be able to invest in these other respects and thus their spending is direct, while indirect expenditures and time spent are not captured in this estimation. The proportion of men aged 56–65 in the household probably include retirees who are not now earning income but may require additional expenditure on their consumption that will take away from spending on children's education. This corresponds to other studies in which the number of adult men in the household is associated with an increase in spending on alcohol and cigarettes and a decrease in spending on education and health (for example, see Haddad, Hoddinott, and Alderman 1997). Finally, as compared with the omitted province of Jiangsu, poorer provinces such as Liaoning, Anhui, Henan, and Yunnan have significantly negative coefficients.

The results of this model suggest that there are differential patterns of household expenditure on the education of boys and girls that are significant for middle-school children (ages 13–15 best correspond to lower secondary school, while ages 16–18 best correspond to upper secondary school). Household expenditure patterns appear to favour boys aged 13–15, but girls aged 16–18.

Table 4.3 shows that 82.3 per cent of women of each level of educational attainment marry at or above their own educational level, while it is less (55.5 per cent) for men. In the absence of perfect assortative mating, parents have only a probabilistic expectation that a child will marry a spouse with comparable education based on the distribution of the educational attainment of spouses in the current cohort of married couples. The implications for children's expected future household income are explored.

Using the earnings functions estimated in Table 4.2, the mean annual income for men and women with each level of educational attainment standardizing for the characteristics of their respective samples are first predicted. The predicted annual mean income of the children's likely future spouse is the predicted annual mean income of men and women weighted by the probabilities of marrying a spouse who has attained each educational level based on Table 4.3. In other words, a woman with educational attainment at or above the college level has a 60.47 per cent chance of marrying a man who has attained the same level of education, a 15.28 per cent chance of marrying a man with a professional school education, a 7.31 per cent chance of marrying a man of middle-level professional school educational attainment, a 7.64 per cent chance of marrying a man who has completed upper-middle school, a 3.65 per cent chance of marrying a man who has completed lower-middle school, a 0.66 per cent chance of marrying a man with a primary school education, and probability of nought of marrying a man with less than primary school education. These weights are multiplied by the respective predicted annual mean income of men who have completed each level of education. The combined income of the child and that of his or her likely future spouse generates an expectation of the child's future household income from which parents may obtain transfers, shown in Table 4.4.

The smallest difference between the expected future household income of sons and daughters is for those who have completed lower-middle school, while the largest difference is for those who have completed middle-level professional

Table 4.2 Determinants of income for working-age individuals

Dependent variable: log of annual income	Coefficient (t-statistic)			Mean value or percentage (standard deviation)
	Probit	Corrected MLE	Uncorrected OLS	
Intercept	1.0259	5.9030	6.3440	8.3313
	(1.185)	(42.611)***	(45.457)***	(0.5074)
Personal characteristics				
Years of education	0.0302	0.0437	0.0424	11.1290
	(1.343)	(15.579)***	(15.184)***	(2.6608)
Male	0.0998	0.1331	0.1304	0.4858
	(1.024)	(13.350)***	(13.088)***	(0.4998)
Age	0.0488	0.1050	0.0818	37.7866
	(1.156)	(16.052)***	(12.911)***	(9.6625)
Age squared	−0.0008	−0.0014	−0.0011	1521.184
	(−1.536)	(−17.549)***	(−14.556)***	(720.6569)
Experience	0.0287	0.0200	0.0219	19.0589
	(2.825)***	(10.910)***	(11.825)***	(9.3082)
Occupation	0.0463	−0.0280	−0.0293	5.8788
	(2.044)**	(−6.308)***	(−6.615)***	(2.0064)
Communist Party membership	4.6682	0.1004	0.1037	0.2123
	(—)	(8.223)***	(8.472)***	(0.4090)
Have children	−0.6602	—	—	0.1953
	(−4.231)***			(0.3964)
Provinces				
Beijing	0.2520	0.2614	0.2553	0.0233
	(0.633)	(7.645)***	(7.503)***	(0.1509)
Shanxi	4.5034	0.2621	0.2626	0.0279
	(—)	(9.782)***	(9.778)***	(0.1648)
Liaoning	0.0706	0.1962	0.1970	0.0311
	(0.245)	(5.393)***	(5.411)***	(0.1736)
Anhui	−0.2429	−0.1414	−0.1420	0.0244
	(−1.029)	(−3.747)***	(−3.782)***	(0.1544)
Henan	−0.1305	−0.3649	−0.3665	0.0271
	(−0.460)	(−9.939)***	(−9.949)***	(0.1624)
Hubei	−0.2445	−0.0544	−0.0522	0.0392
	(−1.186)	(−2.289)**	(−2.193)**	(0.1942)
Guangdong	4.4828	0.0531	0.0586	0.0226
	(—)	(1.697)*	(1.877)*	(0.1485)
Sichuan	−0.2337	−0.2060	−0.2071	0.0384
	(−1.208)	(−6.004)***	(−6.033)***	(0.1922)
Yunnan	4.4686	0.1381	0.1389	0.0285
	(—)	(4.910)***	(4.919)***	(0.1665)
Gansu	4.4744	0.1925	0.1946	0.0161
	(—)	(5.880)***	(5.974)***	(0.1261)
Inverse Mills Ratio	—	−0.0269	—	0.0151
		(−2.676)***		(0.0253)

(continued)

Table 4.2 Continued

Dependent variable: log of annual income	Coefficient (t-statistic)			Mean value or percentage (standard deviation)
	Probit	Corrected MLE	Uncorrected OLS	
R^2	—	—	0.2355	
Pseudo R^2	0.1840	—	—	
X^2 (18)	163.89***	—	—	
Wald X^2 (17)	—	2933.07***	—	
F(17, 5976)	—	—	171.43***	
Log likelihood	−363.3931	−10791.37	—	
Number of observations	12,016	11,943	11,943	

Source: *China Urban Household Survey*, 1995.

Notes: (1) Omitted dummy variables are: female, non-Communist Party members, and Jiangsu province.
(2) *** denotes statistical significance at 1% level, ** at 5% level, and * at 10% level.
(3) Heteroscedasticity-consistent robust standard errors adjusted for clustering at the household level are computed.
(4) Wald chi-squared values are computed because of the lack of the assumption of homoscedasticity in the error terms (see Greene 2003 [1993]).

school. This coincides with the finding that parents invest more in sons than daughters aged 13–15 (corresponding to lower-middle school) but more in daughters than sons aged 16–18 (corresponding to upper-secondary school).

The proposed model of human capital posits that insofar as expenditures on children's education entail forgone consumption, parents are likely to be efficient rather than altruistic in their decisions. This is reinforced by the expectation that parents will live in retirement and will depend on transfers from children, as well as on assets, for consumption.

This model of parental investment in children's human capital considers two returns that motivate parental choices regarding expenditure on children's education. Future labour market discrimination will cause investment to differ for sons and daughters. Given perceived gender earnings differentials, parents will invest more in the human capital of sons, in accordance with standard returns to education analyses. A second consideration in the model is expected transfers. Even if all offspring have an equal probability of providing transfers, favourable assortative mating will generate higher returns from investments in daughters than in sons. This is owing to the same gender earnings differentials that will cause daughters to marry spouses with higher returns to human capital and augment their future household income more than for sons. Parents will thus be expected to invest more in the human capital of daughters. These two effects are simultaneous and there will be a range over which one effect dominates the other.

This approach to parental investment in children's human capital is not dependent on altruism or guilt but on two sets of returns. The circular nature of perceived future labour market discrimination will affect the investment decision in counteracting ways. For growth, increased investment is essential.

Table 4.3 Educational attainment of spouses in urban China (number of observations of married couples)

Women/Men	College and above	Professional school	Middle-level professional school	Upper-middle school	Lower-middle school	Primary school	Less than primary school
College and above	**60.47/24.76** (182)	15.28/4.22 (46)	7.31/2.30 (22)	7.64/1.79 (23)	3.65/0.55 (11)	0.66/0.39 (2)	0.00/0.00 (0)
Professional school	18.51/16.87 (124)	**41.04/25.25** (275)	15.07/10.55 (101)	12.23/6.37 (82)	8.51/2.83 (57)	1.19/1.54 (8)	0.30/3.33 (2)
Middle-level professional school	18.51/16.87 (148)	23.69/21.21 (231)	**22.97/23.41** (224)	15.08/11.41 (147)	16.92/8.18 (165)	1.74/3.28 (17)	0.21/3.33 (2)
Upper-middle school	8.04/15.51 (114)	16.57/21.58 (235)	13.61/20.17 (193)	34.70/**38.20** (492)	21.72/15.27 (308)	1.48/4.07 (21)	0.00/0.00 (0)
Lower-middle school	4.92/15.10 (111)	10.34/21.40 (233)	12.69/**29.89** (286)	16.90/29.58 (381)	**45.70/51.07** (1030)	5.90/25.63 (133)	0.49/18.33 (11)
Primary school	4.20/5.03 (37)	5.44/4.41 (48)	11.45/10.55 (101)	12.47/8.54 (110)	35.60/15.57 (314)	25.17/**42.77** (222)	1.13/16.67 (10)
Less than primary school	2.67/1.09 (8)	3.67/1.01 (11)	6.00/1.88 (18)	9.67/2.25 (29)	27.33/4.07 (82)	**32.67**/18.88 (98)	10.00/**50.00** (30)

Source: *China Urban Household Survey*, 1995.

Note: The largest percentage within each educational level is in bold type, where the percentage of women of each level of educational attainment in rows that marry men of the educational level corresponding to each column is denoted first. The percentage of men by educational attainment in columns that marry women of each educational level corresponding to each row is denoted second. The notation is the percentage of women of each educational level that marry men of each educational level/percentage of men of each educational level that marry women of each educational level.

Table 4.4 Predicted mean annual household income of children (in Yuan)

Children's level of educational attainment	Sons' future household (1)	Daughters' future household (2)	Difference between daughters' and sons' household income (2)–(1)
College and above	13,260.69	13,692.83	432.14
Professional school	12,324.15	12,545.25	221.10
Middle-level professional school	11,487.05	12,033.03	545.98
Upper-middle school	10,897.64	11,152.58	254.95
Lower-middle school	10,782.10	11,001.24	219.14
Primary school	10,299.27	10,555.30	256.03

Source: China Urban Household Survey, 1995.

4.5 Job Mobility

Another key issue for growth stemming from when China had an administered labour system was the lack of job mobility. Urban labour was allocated bureaucratically and wages were determined institutionally, according to a centralized and egalitarian system of wage grades and scales. Labour mobility was not permitted, neither across cities nor across employers within a city so that one's first job was often one's last. The relationship between a worker and his *danwei* (work unit), was close and pervasive; the enterprise provided lifetime employment within a mini welfare state, which was denoted as the iron rice bowl. Hence, labour mobility or labour turnover in urban China was not studied.

With the reform of the state-owned enterprises (SOEs) in the late 1980s and 1990s, managers acquired some freedom to manage their employees; they had greater power to set wages and to decide recruitment and employment. At the same time, workers acquired more rights to move from one employer to another. However, voluntary mobility continued to be impeded by the employer-specific provision of social welfare, services, such as pensions, medical care, and housing, which were gradually being privatized.

A labour market in transition from a planned to a market-oriented system experiences increased mobility from a low level. Initially, involuntary mobility results from enterprises discarding surplus labour and producers adjusting to market demand and prices. As the transition progresses, the proportion of voluntary quits increases as individuals move to jobs that match their productive characteristics better and reflect expanding activities. Urban China is arguably in the first stage of this transition because labour mobility has risen recently from very low levels. In developed economies, mobility in labour markets is characterized by long-term employment relationships, most new jobs ending early, and the probability of a job ending declining with tenure (Farber 1999). The labour market in urban China may exhibit only the first of these characteristics.

Table 4.5 Average and median tenure for select countries

Country	Average tenure (years)	Median tenure (years)	Distribution of tenure (percentage)	
			Under 2 years	Over 20 years
China (urban residents)	19.9	19.0	5.6	45.5
Poland	17.5	17.0	5.7	43.9
Japan	11.3	8.3	23.6	21.4
Germany	9.7	10.7	25.5	17.0
United Kingdom	7.8	5.0	30.3	9.4
United States	7.4	4.2	34.5	9.0
China (migrants)	4.5	3.0	39.2	1.3

Sources: OECD, China Urban Household Survey, 1999.

Notes: (1) The data relate to 1995, except for the US (1996) and China (1999).
(2) The tenure of migrants in China is measured from the time of entry into the urban labour market.
(3) For both urban residents and migrants, the data for China on the distribution of tenure include those with two years of tenure, which biases upwards both figures slightly.

The rate of job mobility is likely to be inversely related to the length of job tenure. Table 4.5 reports the length of tenure, that is, job duration, in China and in various other countries, ranked by average length of tenure. Chinese urban residents are at the top of the list, having the longest average tenure at 19.9 years while Chinese rural–urban migrants are at the bottom, having the shortest at 4.5 years. The figures for median tenure and for the distribution of tenure show almost identical patterns. Poland, the other transition economy for which data are available, is closest to Chinese urbanites, followed by Japan. The European countries occupy intermediate positions and the United States, with its flexible labour market, is closest to Chinese migrants. The reasons for the relatively long job tenure of urban residents and the relatively short tenure of migrants will be examined.

A household-based urban data set is used to examine labour mobility for urban and rural workers. The data cover both urban residents having an urban *hukou* (registration certificate), and rural–urban migrants living in the city but having a rural *hukou*. The dataset permits the tracing of the employment history of each worker including job tenure, job mobility, voluntary versus involuntary mobility, and the determinants of mobility over time.

Labour turnover is the number of quits per period as a percentage of the workers in a firm. Since the data are household-based, labour mobility has that focus and can be measured as the number of quits per period by a worker. At various times, tenure of workers is also examined, that is, job duration, whether complete or incomplete, as an inverse measure of mobility between employers. A second distinction can be made between voluntary and involuntary mobility. In a competitive labour market with free choice, voluntary mobility occurs in response to changes in information, skills, tastes, or wages. Under the system of labour allocation and lifetime jobs in China, a high degree of job mismatch was

123

inevitable and tempered only partially by intra-firm mobility. With greater labour market freedom, there should be increased voluntary mobility as a market response to the inefficient arbitrary job assignment of the past. The causes of involuntary mobility are related to the job or to the individual. The distinction between employee- and employer-induced quits is difficult to draw in practice. On the one hand, if workers recognize that their jobs are at risk, they have an incentive to search for another job and may quit before they are fired. On the other hand, workers intending to quit may volunteer for a retrenchment programme if it will provide benefits. For that reason, involuntary mobility may be understated or overstated.

The analysis of labour mobility is based on theories of firm-specific capital and theories of job-matching so that mobility may be socially desirable or not. On the one hand, mobility results in the loss of firm-specific human capital. On the other hand, it can improve job matches and raise labour productivity by matching better individual skills and abilities or by movement to higher-productivity jobs as the economy changes. Do private economic agents left to pursue their own interests generate the optimal mobility rate for the economy, given its institutions and conventions? A worker's decision to quit depends on the associated private costs and benefits to him; similarly, a firm's decision to fire depends on its private costs and benefits. In either case, termination can impose costs and benefits on the other party or on third parties so that social and private net benefits may not coincide. In this situation, the degree of labour mobility will not be optimal, as Greenwald and Stiglitz (1988) and Hosios (1990) discuss. For example, a firm will not take into account the short-term or long-term income loss that it imposes on a fired worker nor will a departing worker take into account the hiring and training costs that he imposes on his firm.

Labour mobility among employers depends partly on the degree of flux in the economy. In an entirely static economy in equilibrium, zero mobility is optimal. However, in an economy subject to rapid structural transformation and growth, substantial job change is likely as some firms and sectors decline while others expand. As goods and factors are reallocated in response to developing product and factor markets, the inherent productivity of some jobs falls and that of others rises. Even standardizing for structural change, the individual productivity of workers in their jobs may be below the potential productivity of the jobs; such a shortfall offers workers and firms opportunities for improved matching. The mobility rate depends on the relative importance both of firm-specific skills and of the scope to improve idiosyncratic matching through job mobility. However, these factors depend on the nature of the labour market and its institutions. The boundary between firm-specific and general human capital is defined by marketability, which is determined not only by the intrinsic content of the skill but also by the conventions that sustain or inhibit a market. Similarly, the scope for matching by inter-firm mobility depends on the scope for matching within firms. Japan and the United States provide an interesting contrast as Collier and Knight (1985), Hashimoto and Raisian (1985), and

Mincer and Higuchi (1988) show. Hence, the rate of job mobility varies across countries or over time.

In the context of urban China, potentially highly beneficial job matching was prevented under the planning system. Even in the late 1990s, the provision of social services was often attached to the work unit; the process of reform and marketization was incomplete and ongoing because these arrangements continued to deter advantageous voluntary mobility. On the other hand, the draconian redundancy programme imposed on state-owned enterprises in the late 1990s created too much mobility. Many specific skills were lost to the economy and retrenched workers bore a heavy loss of income, both while unemployed and on re-employment (Appleton et al. 2002; Knight and Li 2006). However, the loss of production was minimal because the government had kept unemployment disguised in the enterprises rather than allowing it to be visible. Nevertheless, the losses borne by redundant workers were not internalized fully in the decision processes that led to these retrenchments.

Under central planning, the migration of rural people to urban areas was strictly curbed and, even during the reform period, only the temporary migration of rural people is normally permitted. Rural *hukou*-holders are allowed into the residual jobs that urban *hukou*-holders do not want and the number of migrants that urban enterprises can employ is restricted (Knight, Song, and Jia, 1999). Generally, migrants are employed on short-term contracts. Regarding access to housing and to social services like education and health care, rural *hukou*-holders are discriminated against, so deterring them from settling in the cities. A pattern emerged in which migrants spend brief periods in urban employment, engaged on one or two short-term contracts, and then return to their rural homesteads. This pattern is changing only gradually as more migrants attempt to bring their families to the still inhospitable cities. In these circumstances, employers have little incentive to train their migrant workers. Therefore, labour mobility among rural–urban migrants may be too substantial to promote efficient human capital formation.

4.5.1 Modelling Differential Mobility

Before the policies concerning employment in the Chinese urban labour market were loosened, urban *hukou* workers were favoured by placement in good jobs, that is, permanent, secure iron rice bowls, while migrants were discriminated against and restricted to bad jobs, that is, jobs that were temporary and had little job security and few non-wage benefits. To analyse differential mobility that reflects only these discriminatory arrangements, a segmentation model is considered. If all urban and migrant workers are employed, and all vacancies are filled, good jobs are taken by urban workers and bad jobs are taken by migrants. Institutional arrangements ensure that jobs held by urbanites last longer than jobs held by migrants. The rate at which jobs turnover is the reciprocal of job duration. Hence, the rate at which vacancies occur for good jobs, and thus for urban workers, is less than the rate of vacancies for bad jobs, and thus for migrants. Therefore, in any period, the mobility rate of urban workers is less than that of migrants.

To include imperfect job matching in a labour market characterized by informational asymmetries and costly search for both individuals and firms, the determinants of differential mobility are examined by considering not only the role of institutions but also the importance of search motivation and of firm-specific skill acquisition. The Chinese labour market resembles the search models in which there are good and bad jobs and different types of job-seekers. For example, Pissarides (1994) develops a model of equilibrium unemployment in which those in good jobs search for and accept only good jobs, and those in bad jobs search for and accept both types of job. Occupants of good jobs stop searching when the returns to tenure offset the expected gains from search; similarly, occupants of bad jobs stop searching beyond a certain length of tenure. This model is adapted to the Chinese case by assuming that migrants are allocated initially to bad jobs and urban workers are in good jobs.

The total number of matches between firms and workers is given by the matching technology, $f = f(v, m + u)$, where v is the number of vacancies, m is the number of migrant job-seekers, and u is the number of urban *hukou* job-seekers within a constant labour force. Initially, the following are the simplifying assumptions. First, there are two types of job-seekers, urban and migrant, and two types of jobs, good and bad, distinguished by their attractiveness to the worker. Second, the matching technology is the same for both types of jobs. Third, all urban job-seekers seek good but not bad jobs, whereas all migrants seek both types of jobs. Fourth, all matches sought by employers result in job offers. Fifth, urban job-seekers reject bad jobs. The number of matches between good job vacancies and job-seekers is given by $f_g = f(v_g, m + u)$. For bad jobs, the number of matches is given by $f_b = f(v_b, m)$, which indicates that urban job-seekers do not cause congestion for migrants by taking bad jobs.

Assuming initially that the matching rate into good jobs (r_g) is the same for urban workers (r_{u_g}) and migrants (r_{m_g}):

$$r_g = r_{u_g} = r_{m_g} = f_g/(u + m).$$ (5)

Moreover, the matching rate of migrants into bad jobs is:

$$r_{m_b} = f_b/m,$$ (6)

whereas r_{u_b} is zero. Hence, the overall matching rate of migrants ($r_m = r_{m_g} + r_{m_b}$) exceeds that of urban workers ($r_u = r_{u_g} = r_{m_g}$) and, in equilibrium, $r_u < r_m$. This result occurs because urban workers are allocated initially to good jobs and migrants are allocated initially to bad jobs. From equations (5) and (6), the difference between r_u and r_m depends on the extent to which r_{mb} exceeds r_g. The institutions that provide secure employment for urban workers and impose insecure short-term contracts on migrants, lower v_g and raise v_b. In turn, good job matches are reduced relative to bad matches so that r_u falls relative to r_m.

The basic model can be modified to make it more applicable to China by changing all but the first assumption. Matching technologies for good and bad jobs differ and it is easier to find a match for a bad job because idiosyncratic skills are less important. If f_g generates fewer matches than f_b, the initial inequality $r_u <$ r_m is accentuated. Moreover, the decision to search is assumed to be a function of the prospective wage relative to the current wage of an individual. Because urban workers are initially in good jobs, their incentive to search is reduced. By contrast, migrants have a strong incentive to search for good jobs because they are initially in bad jobs. The current wage depends on both the length of job tenure and the returns to tenure. If there are returns to tenure that result from firm-specific skill acquisition, some workers are deterred from job search by the prospect of losing this premium. Since $r_u < r_m$ implies longer tenure for urban workers leading employers to invest more firm-specific skills in urban workers, a higher proportion of urban workers choose not to search, which reduces further r_u relative to r_m. In addition, urban workers receive preferential treatment in hiring for good jobs so that not all potential matches for migrants result in job offers. This discrimination against migrants reduces their offer rate for good jobs, which lowers their mobility rate relative to that of urbanites. *Ceteris paribus,* this effect suggests that $r_{u_g} > r_{m_g}$, which weakens the prediction that $r_u < r_m$. Finally, if some urban workers have been laid-off and remain unemployed, they may not reject all bad jobs. However, the basic result is maintained so long as $r_{u_b} < r_{m_b}$.

The matching rate for an individual worker is the number of matches in a particular period; for the economy, it is the number of matches in that period expressed as a proportion of the number of workers. These theoretical concepts correspond closely to the empirical measure of an annual mobility rate given by the number of job changes per year of employment experience averaged across workers. Having provided the basic hypothesis that the annual mobility rate of migrants exceeds that of urban residents, this is tested empirically by contrasting the desire and ability of urban residents and migrants to move. In addition, search behaviour, including latent mobility and actual mobility, is related to tenure and returns to tenure, as well as to actual and expected wage levels.

4.5.2 *Measuring Mobility*

The dataset is a national urban household survey designed by the Institute of Economics, Chinese Academy of Social Sciences (CASS) in collaboration with foreign scholars and conducted by the National Bureau of Statistics (NBS) in early 2000; it pertains mainly to 1999 but contains much information on work histories. The total sample size is 4,000 urban households, 2,500 of which are urban *hukou* households drawn from the NBS urban household survey and the remainder are from a representative sampling frame begun in 1999 that includes urban-residing households without urban *hukou*. In addition, independent samples were drawn of 500 households from the NBS urban survey in which a member had experienced a lay-off, and of 800 migrant households. The survey covers six provinces and thirteen cities. The provinces are Beijing, which is chosen to represent the four cities that are independently administered munici-pal districts; Liaoning, which represents the north-east; Henan, which is in the interior; Gansu, which is in the north-west, Jiangsu, which is a coastal province; and Sichuan, which is in the south-west. In addition to Beijing, the capital of each province is taken as a city within the sampling frame; a total of three cities are chosen in Sichuan and Henan, and two cities are considered in each of the other provinces.

Normally, empirical analysis of labour turnover is conducted at an aggregate level. Therefore, aggregate variables that influence mobility, such as the growth of total employment, the growth of the labour force, and structural change, are used. Since this analysis is conducted at the individual level, non-individual variables are excluded, except as proxies from available information in the survey, such as city dummies and ownership categories of employer.

In the representative urban sample, which excludes the additional 500 households that were selected because a member had experienced unemployment in the previous five years, the most notable feature of this sample is a general lack of mobility. As many as 78 per cent of respondents had only one job and a further 16 per cent had two jobs. Thus, only 6 per cent had three or more jobs. No less than 74 per cent of current employees with thirty or more years of employment experience were still in their first jobs. For the select minority of workers who changed jobs, the average length of their completed tenure was 5.5 years. For the urban sample as a whole, the average length of first job tenure, including incomplete tenure, was 21.3 years. Considering only current job tenure, that is, omitting completed jobs, the average length was 16.6 years. Allowing for future tenure in continuing jobs, the predicted duration of completed tenure for the sample as a whole would be extremely long.

The analysis of migrants is based on workers in a sample of rural–urban migrant households, that is, households that establish residence in the survey cities but retain their rural *hukou*. Because they live in resident households, these migrants are unlikely to be representative of all rural–urban migrants. Migrants who leave their rural homesteads and come to the cities on their own to work temporarily, often living with other migrants at their workplaces or in dormitories, are likely to be under-represented in this sample. The mobility rate of this group is likely to be higher than that of migrants who establish urban roots. Regarding mobility, the migrants appear to be similar to the urban workers. As many as 77 per cent had only one job, another 10 per cent had two jobs, 7 per cent had three jobs, while only 6 per cent had more than three jobs. However, these similarities are misleading. For urban workers, the data consider the period since entry to the labour force, but for migrants, the data refer to the period from entry into the city labour market only. Thus, the average length of employment experience of urban workers is 22.8 years, whereas the average length of city employment experience of migrants is 5.9 years. This difference is due partly to migrants being younger (28.6 years of age compared with 38.4 years), and partly to migrants not coming to the city immediately when they entered the labour force because most were engaged in rural household economic activities.

The average completed employment duration of migrants is 2.2 years; it is lowest for migrants in their twenties at 1.3 years and highest for those in their fifties at 4.1 years. The first job tenure, including incomplete spells, averages 5 years; the average length of the current job tenure is 4.5 years. Each of these tenure figures requires careful interpretation. First, briefly employed migrants are more likely to be unsuccessful and may have returned to the village. Second, predicting the length of incomplete spells is difficult because it may be misleading to double the length of the average current tenure from 4.5 to 9 years, as would be appropriate for a steady-state process. If migrants are more welcomed as urban residents, they will remain at their workplace longer than in the past. Nevertheless, even the figure of 4.5 years is high by comparison with the conventional wisdom about migrant employment tenure in China. Examining migrants and urban residents with comparable labour market experience at less than six years, migrants have a mobility rate of 0.1230, which is almost twice as high as that of urban residents at 0.0689. Even when the iron rice bowl no longer existed, entering urban residents had distinctly lower mobility rates than migrants with comparable amounts of urban employment experience.

Table 4.6 presents estimates of the determinants of mobility rates among urban residents aged 16 and over from tobit regressions. The overall mobility rate is defined as the number of job changes over years of employment experience, the mean value of which is 0.019. The involuntary rate is computed from a question that asked respondents whether they had been laid-off in the previous five years and, if so, how many times. Hence, there is a record of the number of involuntary moves reported during the period 1995 to 1999. All other moves are assumed to be voluntary. Using that information, a rate of voluntary mobility equal to 0.015 and a rate of involuntary mobility equal to 0.008 are derived. As Table 4.6 indicates, age up to 38 years, years of education, being self-employed, and locating one's current job through market avenues or referrals through one's social network all increase significantly the overall mobility rate. In addition, being a non-manual worker with more human capital, a homeowner who is less tied to the employer, and working currently in the preferred state and private sectors increase significantly the voluntary mobility rate.

The use of social networks in job searching increases the mobility rate for urban residents, especially if it is voluntary. Having larger social networks and more connections improves employment prospects by learning about jobs, receiving referrals to jobs, and having the relationships facilitating job moves in an administered labour system. Those with more human and social capital have more opportunities, which may be reflected in greater mobility. Factors that reduce significantly the involuntary mobility rate are being a non-manual worker, working in the state sector, and being a Communist Party member. Each of these characteristics provides relative protection against job loss. In addition, age increases the involuntary mobility rate so that older workers are more likely to be laid-off. Unfortunately, with one exception, no determinants of the migrant mobility rate or of the number of jobs held by migrants are both interesting and statistically significant. For migrants who have located their current job by a referral through a social network, mobility is reduced significantly. In summary, the determinants of the mobility of urban workers can be

Table 4.6 Urban residents: determinants of mobility rates (Tobit estimates)

Dependent variable: mobility rates	Coefficient (t-statistic)		
	Overall	Voluntary	Involuntary
Intercept	−0.2385	−0.4526	−0.3239
	(−3.120)***	(−4.622)***	(−2.226)**
Personal characteristics			
Gender	−0.0075	−0.0011	−0.0143
	(−1.168)	(−0.136)	(−1.255)
Age	0.0070	0.0107	0.0163
	(3.524)***	(4.403)***	(3.415)***
Age squared	−0.0001	−0.0001	−0.0002
	(−3.659)***	(−4.178)***	(−4.053)***
Years of education	0.0037	0.0045	−0.0021
	(3.353)***	(3.446)***	(−0.966)
Married	−0.0232	−0.0416	0.0053
	(−0.981)	(−1.544)	(0.095)
Occupation			
Non-manual worker	0.0125	0.0355	-0.0513
	(1.204)	(2.670)***	(−3.217)***
Production worker	−0.0036	−0.0013	−0.0199
	(−0.335)	(−0.092)	(−1.300)
Self-employed	0.0716	0.1147	−0.0224
	(2.780)***	(3.472)***	(−0.508)
Ownership of employer			
State	0.0025	0.0241	−0.0589
	(0.269)	(1.866)*	(−4.383)***
Private	0.0195	0.0423	−0.0246
	(1.302)	(2.185)**	(−1.058)
Household characteristics			
Head of household	−0.0053	0.0193	−0.0337
	(−0.102)	(0.282)	(−0.429)
Number of people in household	−0.0031	−0.0027	−0.0004
	(−0.775)	(−0.574)	(−0.053)
Homeowner	0.0070	0.0139	−0.0118
	(1.114)	(1.814)*	(−1.095)
Guanxi			
Communist Party member	0.0069	0.0092	−0.0264
	(1.049)	(1.187)	(−2.006)**
Social network	0.0013	0.0020	−0.0010
	(3.089)***	(3.926)***	(−1.095)
Avenue of job search			
Market forces	0.0326	0.0326	0.0255
	(3.514)***	(2.877)***	(1.597)
Referral through social network	0.0814	0.1037	0.0575
	(5.576)***	(5.865)***	(2.367)**
Self-employment	0.0409	0.0530	0.0038
	(1.537)	(1.573)	(0.094)
Cities	Yes	Yes	Yes
Pseudo R^2	0.2299	0.2228	0.2653
$X^2(31)$	247.58***	265.34***	239.66***
Mean of dependent variable	0.0192	0.0149	0.0079
Number of observations	3437	3216	3454

Source: China Urban Household Survey, 1999, China Rural Hukou Migrant Household Survey, 1999.

Notes: (1) The omitted dummy variables are male gender, unmarried, unskilled worker, urban collective sector, not head of household, non-homeowner, not Communist Party member, obtained current job through state allocation, and Pingliang.
(2) The symbols *** denote significance at the 1% level, ** at the 5% level and * at the 10% level, respectively.
(3) Heteroscedasticity-consistent robust standard errors adjusted for clustering at the household level are computed.
(4) As an avenue of job search, market forces refers to searching in newspapers, using job centres and employing methods that are not dependent on state allocation or on referral through one's own social network. The latter category includes hearing about job information and receiving a recommendation for a position.

explained by predicted factors, but the mobility of migrants appears to depend on unobserved variables; for example, rural household characteristics, short-term contracts coming to an end, or luck.

4.5.3 Impact of Reforms

The objective is to determine the extent to which mobility rose as labour market reforms progressed. The Western literature suggests that job separations are highest in the first years of employment and decrease thereafter (see, for example, Farber 1999), so a control must be set up for this effect. The data can date the most recent job change of urban *hukou* residents and be used to analyse mobility in a disaggregated manner. Unfortunately, the rural *hukou* sample is not sufficiently large, nor sufficiently dispersed in the relevant variables, to permit an equivalent analysis of migrants.

For each entry cohort, Table 4.7 shows the percentage that has never changed jobs, the percentage that has done so more than once, and the percentage that has only one job change. For the last group, the period within which the single job change was made is reported. Hence, there is a period-specific, first-job mobility rate by entry cohort.

The matrix in Table 4.7 can be read down the columns, which standardizes for the period in which separation occurred, across the rows, which standardizes for entry cohort, or along the diagonals, which standardizes for duration of tenure. Examining the columns, the familiar tendency for mobility to decline with employment experience is observed. In contrast to the Western pattern, the rows indicate that separation rates uniformly rise with time for post-1970 entrants. This result can be attributed to the increasing flexibility of the labour market over time, which is verified by the diagonals exhibiting an almost monotonic increase in mobility standardizing for the duration of employment. For example, whereas the 1965–9 entry cohort had a 1.4 per cent separation rate over the subsequent five-year period from 1970 to 1974, the 1990–4 entry cohort had a 12.1 per cent separation rate in the corresponding five-year period from 1995 to 1999. To distinguish between voluntary and involuntary mobility, the worker's reported reason for leaving a job is considered. 'Why did you leave your previous job?' The following responses were taken to indicate voluntary separations: low income, lack of job security, unsatisfactory work conditions, insufficient benefits, and to start own business. The following responses were assumed to represent involuntary separations: contract expired, laid-off by work unit, and became *xiagang*. A residual category of 'other' was available as a response. The job separation of those who are currently unemployed is assumed to be involuntary because in current market conditions, employees are unlikely to quit voluntarily unless they have obtained another job.

The voluntary mobility rate tends to be higher the more recent the cohort but also the more recent the period, whether or not duration of employment is standardized. Involuntary separations were far higher from 1995 to 1999 than in

Table 4.7 Job separations for urban residents (row percentages)

Period of entry	Period of job separation								Never changed	Multiple changes
	One job change									
	1960–64	1965–69	1970–74	1975–79	1980–84	1985–89	1990–94	1995–99		
1960–64	1.5	2.8	1.1	1.5	2.3	1.5	1.1	1.0	71.4	15.5
(724)	(11)	(20)	(8)	(11)	(17)	(11)	(8)	(7)	(517)	(112)
1965–69	—	1.8	1.4	2.9	3.2	3.3	1.9	2.2	72.1	10.4
(1472)		(26)	(21)	(42)	(47)	(49)	(28)	(32)	(1061)	(153)
1970–74	—	—	2.2	2.9	2.9	3.0	3.6	6.0	67.5	9.7
(1256)			(28)	(37)	(36)	(38)	(45)	(75)	(848)	(122)
1975–79	—	—	—	3.6	3.2	3.9	4.2	8.6	68.6	4.9
(1517)				(54)	(48)	(59)	(64)	(130)	(1040)	(74)
1980–84	—	—	—	—	3.4	4.9	5.7	8.8	70.0	3.5
(1198)					(41)	(59)	(68)	(105)	(839)	(42)
1985–89	—	—	—	—	—	4.2	5.1	10.5	71.3	3.1
(897)						(38)	(46)	(94)	(640)	(28)
1990–94	—	—	—	—	—	—	5.4	12.1	72.8	4.2
(626)							(34)	(76)	(456)	(26)
1995–99	—	—	—	—	—	—	—	7.7	82.1	6.8
(532)								(41)	(437)	(36)

Source: China Urban Household Survey, 1999

Notes: (1) The rows do not sum to 100 because there is no information on the year of the separation for some people who changed job once. (2) The number of observations is in parentheses beneath the cohorts designated by year of labour market entry. (3) The matrix contains workers with only one job change.

any previous five-year period. The iron rice bowl became increasingly fragile over time and was effectively broken in the period from 1995 to 1999.

Those who had never changed jobs were asked whether they had ever wanted to do so. Their responses enable an examination of the latent demand for mobility using a logit analysis in Table 4.8. Importantly, 77 per cent of the urban sample never wanted to move, possibly because they did not view it as a feasible option. The urban workers who are more likely to want to move even though they have not yet done so are the self-employed, possibly because self-employment is not a preferred activity, unskilled workers, because they are possibly in unattractive jobs, and those who report larger social networks of contacts and acquaintances, possibly because the possession of a large social network raises expectations of mobility among those not yet mobile. State employees and Party members, who may be already better positioned, and homeowners, the dissatisfied among whom may already have moved, are more likely to be content with their jobs. By predicting wages using the observable characteristics of urban workers, those non-movers whose actual wage exceeds their predicted wage are significantly less likely to be frustrated in their jobs, which suggests that the wage residual represents economic rent.

A high proportion, namely 72 per cent, of migrants who changed their job once, did so voluntarily. 'What was the main reason for your leaving your previous job?' The following reasons were taken to indicate voluntary separations: low income, the job was not stable, working conditions were poor, benefits and social securities were not good, wanted to start own business, and increased family burden. The following were assumed to indicate involuntary departure: contract expired, dismissed, and other. In addition, mobility is more likely to be voluntary for migrants than for urban workers. Table 4.9 reports a logit analysis of latent mobility among migrants. Of those who had never changed their job in the city and answered the question, 33 per cent wanted to change job and 67 per cent did not. Only two explanatory variables have significant coefficients. More education increases the desire to change jobs, probably because the job is ill-suited to the education, whereas working in the private sector reduces the desire to change jobs.

Table 4.9 explores latent mobility by comparing those who have moved and those who have never moved but want to do so. The dependent variable in the logit analysis consists of 59 per cent of the urban sample and 23 per cent of the migrant sample, representing individuals who have changed jobs. For the urban sample, the chance of changing jobs declines, at an increasing rate, with length of tenure. This suggests that more recent recruits have fewer disincentives, or greater opportunities, to move. *Ceteris paribus*, non-manual workers and those classified as others are more likely to move than manual workers, both skilled and unskilled, indicating that the availability of opportunities is important. The other human and social capital variables, namely education, Party membership, and social network, have positive coefficients as expected, but they are not significant. Home ownership, which is likely to reduce the cost of changing employers, increases the chances of moving. An excess of the current actual

Table 4.8 Determinants of latent mobility for immobile individuals

	Coefficient (z-statistic)	
	Urban sample	Migrant sample
Intercept	0.8094	0.1251
	(0.704)	(0.097)
Personal characteristics		
Gender	–0.1105	–0.1191
	(–0.809)	(–0.432)
Years of education	0.0292	0.1144
	(1.175)	(2.170)**
Years of tenure	–0.0068	–0.0249
	(–0.232)	(–0.203)
Years of tenure squared	–0.0009	0.0016
	(–1.247)	(0.210)
Married	–0.4870	–0.4124
	(–0.837)	(–0.388)
Occupation		
Non-manual worker	–0.4028	–0.6736
	(–2.081)**	(–1.327)
Production worker	–0.3541	–0.1470
	(–1.726)*	(–0.236)
Self-employed	2.6319	—
	(3.318)***	
Other occupations	–0.3884	–0.4383
	(–1.021)	(–1.291)
Ownership of employer		
State	–0.5800	–0.2310
	(–3.277)***	(–0.493)
Private	–0.2300	–0.7214
	(–0.762)	(–1.954)*
Household characteristics		
Head of household	–0.6959	0.2361
	(–0.783)	(0.825)
Number of people in household	0.1402	–0.0116
	(1.461)	(–0.409)
Homeowner	–0.2628	–0.5455
	(–2.105)**	(–1.030)
Guanxi		
Communist Party member	–0.2512	–0.5633
	(–1.835)*	(–0.627)
Social network	0.0191	–0.0029
	(2.028)**	(–0.571)
Wage residual (actual minus predicted wage)	–0.2753	–0.0213
	(–3.106)***	(–0.113)
Cities	Yes	Yes
Wald X^2 (26)	—	44.54***
Wald X^2 (29)	165.38***	—
Mean of dependent variable	0.1983	0.3573
Number of observations	1906	362

Source: *China Urban Household Survey*, 1999

Notes: (1) The dependent variable equals one if the individual has never changed jobs but wants to and zero if the individual has never changed jobs and does not want to.

(2) The omitted dummy variables are male gender, unmarried, unskilled worker, urban collective sector, not head of household, non-homeowner, not Communist Party member, and Pingliang. Social networks are defined as the number of people with whom a person regularly associates.

(3) *** denote significance at the 1% level, ** at the 5% level and * at the 10% level, respectively.

(4) Heteroscedasticity-consistent robust standard errors adjusted for clustering at the household level are computed.

(5) The coefficients for domestic worker and for Jinzhou cannot be estimated for the migrant sample.

(6) The predicted wage in this and the next table is estimated excluding the mobility rate.

Table 4.9 Determinants of mobility for mobile and potentially mobile individuals

	Coefficient (z-statistic)	
	Urban sample	Migrant sample
Intercept	−3.8672	−4.8539
	(−2.424)**	(−4.511)***
Personal characteristics		
Gender	−0.1659	0.3634
	(−1.010)	(1.277)
Years of education	0.0413	0.0352
	(1.265)	(0.685)
Years of tenure	−0.1321	0.4530
	(−3.730)***	(5.213)***
Years of tenure squared	−0.0024	−0.0132
	(−2.491)**	(−3.349)***
Married	0.5098	−0.4223
	(0.564)	(−0.780)
Occupation		
Non-manual worker	0.6090	0.2268
	(2.423)**	(0.535)
Production worker	0.0691	−0.0213
	(0.247)	(−0.043)
Self-employed	0.9372	0.7152
	(1.212)	(0.491)
Other occupations	1.0064	0.2366
	(2.387)**	(0.718)
Ownership of employer		
State	0.4440	−0.2321
	(1.867)*	(−0.479)
Private	0.4007	0.9204
	(1.156)	(2.712)***
Household characteristics		
Head of household	0.2495	0.2590
	(0.199)	(0.886)
Number of people in household	−0.1189	−0.0306
	(−0.922)	(−0.679)
Homeowner	0.3131	−0.2371
	(1.967)**	(−0.534)
Guanxi		
Communist Party member	0.1911	−0.9270
	(1.154)	(−0.674)
Social network	0.0157	−0.0021
	(1.335)	(−1.063)
Wage residual (actual minus predicted wage)	0.7518	0.0258
	(5.271)***	(0.163)
Cities	Yes	Yes
Wald X^2 (26)	—	70.13***
Wald X^2 (29)	185.76***	—
Mean of dependent variable	0.5949	0.2278
Number of observations	1049	742

Source: China Urban Household Survey, 1999

Notes: (1) The dependent variable equals one if the individual has changed jobs and zero if the individual has never changed jobs but wants to do so.
(2) The omitted dummy variables are male gender, unmarried, unskilled worker, urban collective sector, not head of household, non-homeowner, not Communist Party member, and Pingliang. Social networks are defined as the number of people with whom a person regularly associates.
(3) *** denote significance at the 1% level, ** at the 5% level and * at the 10% level, respectively.
(4) Heteroscedasticity-consistent robust standard errors adjusted for clustering at the household level are computed.
(5) The independent variables necessarily relate to the current position of those who changed jobs and must be interpreted accordingly. For example, occupation and ownership sector show the destinations of movers and the origins of non-movers. Moreover, years of employment experience and social network reflect the current position and not that at the time of the move.

wage over the predicted wage also promotes mobility, implying either that the movers gain rent from their moves or that unobserved productivity assists movement. Therefore, whereas non-movers whose current wage exceeds their predicted wage are less keen to move, movement itself is associated with having a current wage above the predicted wage.

Only two variables are significant in a corresponding equation for migrants, also shown in Table 4.9. Unlike for urban residents, years of tenure increase the likelihood of changing jobs for migrants. Although the squared term is negative and significant, implying that migrants eventually become less mobile, the combined effect of tenure is positive over the relevant range. Most migrants would like to move and those with more labour market experience in urban areas have a greater likelihood of doing so. Current employment in the private sector is associated with success among the would-be mobile migrants, whereas immobile migrants are less likely to want to move if they work in the private sector. Hence, employment in the private sector appears to be the preferred choice for migrants.

Table 4.10 reports coefficient estimates of the determinants of earned income for employed individuals in the urban and migrant samples in equations that include the mobility rates. For urban workers, seniority in the firm is rewarded. From column (5), ten years of tenure adds 22 per cent to earnings, whereas ten years of schooling adds 31 per cent. The opposite sign of tenure squared indicates a non-linear relationship between tenure and wages, which is reflected in the estimates of returns to tenure. This result is consistent with urban workers acquiring substantial firm-specific skills but it does not provide conclusive evidence. State enterprises had no profit incentive to train their workers so that, if the coefficient reflects administratively based seniority scales rather than the reward for higher productivity, workers lacked an incentive to acquire skills. Nevertheless, the many urban workers having long tenure do receive a substantial earnings premium, for example, 32 per cent for those with the average current tenure of 16.6 years, which discourages them from engaging in job search.

The coefficient on the overall mobility rate for urban workers is slightly positive but insignificantly so. The voluntary mobility rate has a positive coefficient, as expected, but it is not significant. In contrast, the coefficient on the involuntary rate is negative, but it too is not significantly different from zero. The results for the selectivity corrected estimates in columns (5) and (6) imply that the mobility rate resulting from a voluntary change of jobs every four years raises earnings by 7 per cent and lowers earnings by 7 per cent if the change is involuntary. These estimates are qualitatively similar to those of Keith (1993) who finds that the overall mobility rate in the US is not significant, whereas the voluntary rate has a positive impact on earnings, while the involuntary rate has a negative effect, and both are significant. In essence, workers quit voluntarily in expectation of better-paid jobs whereas those who are fired have difficulty finding equivalent jobs. However, the possibility that some unobserved characteristics, like motivation, that influence both earnings and mobility cannot be

	Urban sample Uncorrected OLS (1)	Migrant sample Uncorrected OLS (2)	Urban sample Selection-corrected MLE (3)	Migrant sample Selection-corrected MLE (4)	Urban sample Uncorrected OLS (5)	Urban sample Selection-corrected MLE (6)
			Coefficient (t-statistic)			
Intercept	1.8717 (25.418)***	2.7803 (15.617)***	1.8920 (25.820)***	2.6653 (11.336)***	1.7839 (25.588)***	1.8090 (26.060)***
Personal characteristics						
Gender	-0.1752 (-10.627)***	-0.1394 (-3.000)***	-0.1717 (-10.451)***	-0.1869 (-1.930)*	-0.1803 (-11.343)***	-0.1750 (-10.893)***
Years of education	0.0311 (8.445)***	0.0111 (0.672)	0.0304 (8.321)***	0.0145 (1.200)	0.0311 (8.440)***	0.0302 (8.225)***
Years of tenure	0.0256 (6.671)***	0.0271 (2.173)**	0.0252 (6.585)***	0.0222 (2.027)**	0.0285 (7.202)***	0.0279 (7.016)***
Years of tenure squared	-0.0006 (-5.818)***	—	-0.0006 (-5.706)***	—	-0.0007 (-6.443)***	-0.0007 (-6.163)***
Occupation						
Non-manual worker	0.2548 (8.295)***	0.4342 (2.576)**	0.2518 (8.248)***	0.4571 (3.885)***	0.2617 (8.555)***	0.2591 (8.534)***
Production worker	0.0959 (2.855)***	0.3050 (2.143)**	0.0951 (2.844)***	0.2929 (1.894)*	0.0993 (2.923)***	0.0987 (2.917)***
Self-employed	0.2842 (1.985)**	0.1107 (0.304)	0.2969 (2.081)**	0.1267 (0.221)	0.4465 (3.214)***	0.4761 (3.442)***
Other occupations	0.0461 (1.066)	0.2134 (2.150)**	0.0448 (1.041)	0.2184 (2.514)***	0.0682 (1.582)	0.0685 (1.592)
Ownership of employer						
State	0.2559 (8.913)***	-0.2928 (-2.418)**	0.2511 (8.798)***	-0.2616 (-2.557)**	0.2741 (9.455)***	0.2678 (9.270)***
Private	0.3170 (7.225)***	0.0589 (0.527)	0.3120 (7.145)***	0.0479 (0.569)	0.3183 (7.035)***	0.3124 (6.924)***
Guanxi						
Communist Party member	0.1318 (6.535)***	-0.1970 (-0.444)	0.1302 (6.491)***	-0.1635 (-0.637)	0.1218 (6.275)***	0.1207 (6.241)***
Social network	0.0068	-0.0008	0.0068	-0.0007	0.0063	0.0063

(continued)

Table 4.10 Continued

	Urban sample	Migrant sample	Urban sample	Migrant sample	Urban sample	Urban sample
				Coefficient (t-statistic)		
	Uncorrected OLS (1)	Uncorrected OLS (2)	Selection-corrected MLE (3)	Selection-corrected MLE (4)	Uncorrected OLS (5)	Selection-corrected MLE (6)
Mobility rate	(4.873)***	(−1.350)	(4.915)***	(−1.243)	(4.692)***	(4.759)***
Overall	0.0219 (0.358)	0.3739 (4.017)***	0.0217 (0.353)	0.3025 (1.838)*	—	—
Voluntary	—	—	—	—	0.2655 (1.023)	0.2722 (1.046)
Involuntary	—	—	—	—	−0.3739 (−0.353)	−0.2637 (−0.251)
Cities	Yes	Yes	Yes	Yes	Yes	Yes
Inverse Mills ratio	—	—	−0.0280 (−1.812)*	0.6757 (0.562)	—	−0.0467 (−1.818)*
R^2	0.2618	0.2336	—	—	0.2782	—
$F_{(23, 334)}$	59.83***	—	—	—	—	—
$F_{(25, 2877)}$	—	20.34***	—	—	—	—
$F_{(26, 2775)}$	—	—	—	—	57.29***	—
Wald $X^2(25)$	—	—	1461.73***	—	—	—
Wald $X^2(28)$	—	—	—	539.01***	—	—
Wald $X^2(47)$	—	—	—	—	—	1418.76***
Mean of dependent variable	2.9499	0.8216	2.9499	0.8216	2.9499	2.9499
Number of observations	5015	1006	5015	1006	4740	4740

Source: China Urban Household Survey, 1999

Notes: (1) The dependent variable for the urban sample is the log of daily earned income and it is the log of hourly wages for the migrant sample.
(2) The omitted dummy variables are male gender, unskilled worker, urban collective sector, not Communist Party member, and Pingliang.
(3) Sample selection bias may result because wages for those who do not participate in the labour market are not observed. The two-stage least squares estimation with a valid exclusion restriction addresses this issue. The exclusion restriction for equations (2), (4), and (6) is a dummy variable that equals 1 if not in good health. Health is a valid exclusion restriction because it is a significant predictor of labour market participation but it is not correlated with wages. In China, with a high level of participation by both men and women, being healthy will determine the probability of employment.
(4) *** denote significance at the 1% level, ** at the 5% level, and* at the 10% level, respectively.
(5) Heteroscedasticity-consistent robust standard errors adjusted for clustering at the household level.

discounted so that they could explain both the positive and the negative coefficients.

The earnings functions for migrants, also shown in Table 4.10, are estimated using both ordinary least squares (OLS) and two-stage least squares (2SLS) with correction for selectivity into employment. Since the two sets of results are similar, the latter is discussed. The coefficients confirm that private-sector employment is the preferred state for migrants; they receive significantly higher pay in the private than in the state sector. Migrants may look to the private sector because of an institutional distinction; namely, good jobs have been more tightly restricted to urban residents by the state than by the non-state sector. Interestingly, women are at a considerable disadvantage as they receive an hourly wage lower by 17 per cent. Neither education nor the proxies for possession of social capital are significant. However, one form of human capital is rewarded, namely, occupation, as non-manual jobs are the highest paid relative to unskilled workers. This result may indicate skills acquisition by moving either within or between firms. The coefficient on the mobility rate is positive and significant at 0.31. By comparison with migrants who remain in the same job, a move every four years results in an 8 per cent increase in earnings. Thus, mobility may improve job matches for migrants. Interestingly, the inverse Mills ratio is not significant for migrants as it is for urban residents who are perhaps more able to choose to participate in the labour market.

The coefficient on tenure at 0.027 is positive and significant at the 5 per cent level in column (2). Hence, the earnings premium for migrants with the mean current length of tenure at 4.5 years is 13 per cent, which is much smaller than the premium for urban residents so that migrants have less incentive to remain with their employer. However, this coefficient may not represent the productivity gain from longer tenure. On the one hand, it may indicate improved matching within the firm or a process of good workers selecting or being selected to stay on rather than skills formation. On the other hand, the actual return to tenure is likely to understate potential return because firms are discouraged from investing in migrants by the institutions favouring urban residents for the more skilled jobs. A vicious circle may arise in which short tenure discourages investment in skills and the lack of skills encourages short tenure because of lower earnings. Such a low-level equilibrium would be stable if an exogenous rise in tenure fails to induce sufficient investment in skills to raise tenure further.

A matrix of transition among ownership sectors can be estimated for the urban sample but not for the migrant sample. Table 4.11 presents a transition matrix for those urban workers who changed jobs once with four ownership sectors; namely, state, urban collective, self-employed, and private, distinguished for both origin and destination. Voluntary and involuntary mobility are combined. Of those who moved from one employment to another, 84 per cent moved from one state sector job to another. Only 13 per cent of those leaving the state sector and 26 per cent of those leaving the urban collective sector, entered the self-employed or private sectors. Whereas 73 per cent of the voluntary movers went to the state sector, only 33 per cent of the involuntary

Table 4.11 Transition matrix for urban residents (row percentages)

Previous sector	Current sector				
	SOE	Urban collective	Self-employed	Private	TOTAL
SOE	84	3	4	9	100
	(555)	(22)	(27)	(61)	(665)
Urban collective	41	33	14	12	100
	(38)	(31)	(13)	(11)	(93)
Self-employed	33	8	42	17	100
	(4)	(1)	(5)	(2)	(12)
Private	65	5	0	30	100
	(28)	(2)	(0)	(13)	(43)
TOTAL	77	7	6	11	100
	(625)	(56)	(45)	(87)	(813)

Source: China Urban Household Survey, 1999

Notes: (1) The matrix reports the percentage of job changes from one sector to another. The number of observations is in parentheses.
(2) The information is available only for those urban residents who have changed jobs once.
(3) SOE represents central, provincial, and local state-owned enterprises.
(4) Private includes partnerships, Chinese–foreign joint ventures, foreign companies, state share-holding companies, other share-holding companies, rural individual enterprises, and other enterprises.

movers did so, indicating that the state sector is the preferred destination. When urban workers who remain unemployed are added to the re-employed, 65 per cent came from the state sector, 31 per cent from urban collectives, and 4 per cent from the self-employed or private sectors. By contrast, among those currently employed, 77 per cent were employed in the state sector, 15 per cent in urban collectives, and 8 per cent in the self-employed or private sectors. Hence, the propensity to move is highest from the urban collective sector in which wages are the lowest, as Table 4.6 indicates, and employment has declined. Official statistics record a fall by 52 per cent from 1990 to 1999. This implication that the urban collective sector is disliked is consistent with the positive and significant coefficients for both state and private employment, with the collective sector being the omitted category, in the earnings functions for urban workers in Table 4.10.

In conclusion, a simple model of the determinants of mobility in the Chinese case supports the basic hypothesis that the mobility rate of migrants exceeds that of urban workers. Before the urban reforms began in earnest, mobility among urban workers was negligible. Effectively, these workers had lifetime employment with their work unit so that any improvements in the matching of workers and jobs occurred only within the work unit. By contrast, mobility among rural–urban migrants was extremely high, with migrants tending to leave their rural households temporarily for work on short-term contracts before returning home. The evidence confirms that these patterns have not changed greatly. The vast majority of urban workers have had only one employer. A labour market is emerging gradually for urban workers, but many workers are not affected directly. Employment duration among migrants is now higher than conventional wisdom suggests. This result is due partly to the sample, which is drawn from rural migrants with urban households. As in other developing countries, migrants who establish urban roots are likely to be more rooted to their jobs.

The mean mobility rate of migrants is almost six times that of urban workers, which confirms the basic hypothesis. Even considering only those who entered the labour market after the iron rice bowl had been smashed, the mean mobility rate of migrants is nearly double that of urban workers. These contrasting rates reflect the norms, rules, opportunities, and restrictions on choice faced by the two groups. Their mobility rates are unlikely to be equalized if they continue to be treated differently. As the restrictions on the mobility of urbanites and the rules that impose mobility on migrants are lifted, the equilibrium degree of mobility in a unified market is likely to lie between the two current rates. Taking first urban *hukou* residents and standardizing for time period, mobility is higher among young people, as in other countries. Standardizing for entry cohort, mobility tended to rise over time as labour market reforms advanced. However, the state sector, rather than the growing non-state sector, remains the preferred destination. Among the immobile, the wish to move is related to proxies indicating that the current job is unattractive. Among would-be movers, success is related to proxies indicating the availability of opportunities to move. In particular, voluntary mobility is raised by the human and social capital variables; involuntary mobility is lowered by characteristics that have provided relative protection against job loss. Voluntary mobility increases and involuntary mobility decreases earnings, while a high earnings premium associated with tenure reduces the incentive to search.

Whenever possible, the same questions were posed for migrants. The great majority of their job changes have been voluntary. In contrast to urban workers, who show preference for the state sector, migrants appear to choose private sector employment. Employment in the private sector both deters further search and is the object of past successful search. In contrast to urban workers, longer tenure raises the chances that migrant search will be successful. The fact that education and tenure increase mobility suggests that human capital improves migrants' opportunities for advantageous job change. Mobility raises migrant earnings, reflecting improved inter-firm matching. Length of tenure also has a positive effect on migrant earnings, reflecting skill acquisition or improved intra-firm matching. However, in contrast to urban workers, the low average tenure of migrants blunts their incentive to stay with the firm.

Several policy issues underlie any evaluation of labour mobility. First, mobility involves a social cost because it destroys firm-specific human capital. Second, mobility, especially if involuntary, can create the hardship and social costs associated with unemployment. Third, mobility provides a social benefit in that it permits better matching of workers and their characteristics to jobs. Fourth, mobility should be high enough to create competitive market wages with their allocative social benefit. To judge whether the mobility rate is socially optimal, the private costs and benefits must be adjusted to include the social costs and benefits. In urban China, the private costs and benefits of both residents and migrants do not correspond to the social costs and benefits of mobility. For example, tying various non-marketed facilities, such as housing and pensions, to employment has imposed private costs on quitting that are not equal to social costs. The artificial restrictions under which rural–urban migrants work in the cities, which are the prohibition on or impediments to urban settlement, restricted access to skilled jobs, and the system of short-term contracts, may have generated an excessively high migrant mobility rate. The voluntary mobility rate of urban workers and the mobility rate of migrants are converging, but they are still far apart. What is important for economic growth is that the former are too low and the latter are too high.

4.6 Migrants and Discrimination

In China, urban residents have traditionally been protected against labour market competition from rural–urban migrants. Over the period of urban economic reform—beginning in the mid-1980s and accelerating in the 1990s—rural–urban migration was allowed by government to increase in order to fill the employment gap when growth of labour demand outstripped that of the resident labour force in the urban economy. However, as the reform process gained pace and controls were lifted, it is plausible that migrants and urban residents increasingly competed. It is therefore important to discover whether the relationship between the two groups of workers is one of complementarity in a still-segmented labour market or of substitutability in an emerging competitive labour market.

During the period of the communes and central planning, the movement of labour in China was tightly controlled and restricted. During the period of economic reform and transition to a market economy, rural–urban migration became important, reflecting a growing urban need for migrant labour but also a weakening in the power of the authorities to control labour. Despite their greater freedom, it remains difficult for rural workers to acquire urban registration (*hukou*) and thus permanent urban residence. Government attempts to maintain continuing control over the 'floating' population of temporary rural–urban migrant workers. Generally, migrants have been permitted only in the 'residual' urban wage jobs not wanted by residents. These tend to be the lowest-wage, lowest-skilled, least-pleasant jobs. Nevertheless, migrant urban wages are found greatly to exceed standardized rural alternative incomes (Knight and Song 2003). Although rural households thus have a strong economic incentive to send out workers to the cities and towns, migrants are still at a considerable disadvantage in the urban labour market by comparison with urban workers, with respect both to job opportunities and to terms and conditions of employment.

Permanent migration is controlled through the *hukou* registration sysem. A *hukou* confers legal rights to be resident in the locality and to share the resources of that community. In the case of cities it involves rights to a package of benefits, and in the case of villages it involves rights to land for farming and housing. The *hukou* system has been preserved over the years but its effectiveness has declined. It has become possible for a rural person to buy a *hukou* in a town or small city although restrictions on settlement in a large city remain tight.

In some developing countries of Asia and Africa, the system of 'circular' or 'oscillating' migration can be a voluntarily one, especially when permanent migration would involve the loss of land rights (see, for example, Hugo 1982; Cordell, Gregory, and Piche 1998; Gaetano and Jacka 2004). In China, village land is generally allocated on a rent-free, contract basis, thus implying that withdrawal from the village can involve an opportunity cost. However, temporary migration in China is hardly voluntary. The combination of the security provided by access to land, the cost of withdrawal from the village, the relatively low income from farming, the lack of security in the city, and the difficulties of urban settlement, means that for many rural households, the best available option is to send out a migrant on a temporary basis. The evidence for China suggests that the removal of restrictions on urban settlement would result in faster urbanization. A survey of rural–urban migrants in a particular city found that, if a satisfactory job could be secured, 78 per cent would like to work in it as long as possible, 90 per cent of the sample would like their family to join them either immediately or when a long-term well-paid job was found, and 70 per cent wanted an urban *hukou* (Knight and Song 1999). In a 1995 national survey of migrants employed in urban enterprises, 42 per cent wanted to work as long as possible in their current job, and only 21 per cent wanted to work for less than two years (Knight and Song 1999). Since those surveys were conducted, China has indeed witnessed a process of increasing urban settlement, albeit still constrained, made difficult, and often unofficial.

There is evidence that city governments have pursued these regulatory policies in order to protect their residents. For instance, Solinger (2004) reported that regulations in various cities across China excluded workers without local *hukou* from a range of occupations and required employers to obtain permits for hiring such labour. Knight, Song, and Jia (1999) found that no less than 81 per cent of their surveyed enterprises reported to be officially restricted in recruiting migrant workers. Policies on migrant employment were common to all four survey cities but the authors reported on one of them in detail. The labour bureaux in this city classified jobs into three types: urban *hukou* jobs, rural migrant jobs, and jobs open to all, but with urban workers receiving preference. They also imposed quotas on the number of migrants that each enterprise could employ. The restrictions were sensitive to the state of the city labour market, being tightened if unemployment among city residents rose. It is to be expected, therefore, that migrant employment would be curtailed as a policy response to rising urban unemployment in China, but would be relaxed as and when labour market conditions permitted.

Table 4.12 Change in the urban labour market, 1994–2000

	1994	2000	Increase 1994–2000	2000 (1994=100)
Registered urban unemployment (million)	4.76	5.95	1.19	125.0
% of urban labour force	2.8	3.1	0.3	110.7
Xia gang employment (million)	1.58	9.11	7.53	576.6
% of urban labour force	0.9	4.7	3.8	522.2
Total urban unemployment (million)	6.34	15.06	8.72	237.5
% of urban labour force	3.7	7.8	4.1	210.8
Total urban employment (million)	184.13	212.74	28.61	115.5
Employment in urban units (million)	152.59	116.1	−36.46	76.1
% of total urban employment	82.9	54.6	−28.3	65.9
Migrant employees of urban units (million)	13.72	8.97	−4.75	65.4
% of employment in urban units	9.0	7.7	−1.3	85.6

Source: China Labour Statistical Yearbook.

The urban labour market changed rapidly from the mid-1990s onwards. Table 4.12, comparing 1994 and 2000, shows the changes. Registered urban unemployment was very low in 1994 (2.8 per cent of the urban labour force), and redundant workers (not classified as unemployed) negligible (0.9 per cent). Central and city governments preferred to keep unemployment off the streets, where it could take an open form, and to keep it instead in the factories, where it took a disguised form. Economic reform brought the state-owned enterprise sector under increasing pressure, with the growth of competition from rural industry, the urban non-state sector, and imports. The profitability of state enterprises declined, and many of them began to make losses. The initial response—permitting soft budgets and increasing public subsidies—threatened the public finances. Reform of the state sector was forced upon government.

One policy response was the imposition of labour redundancies, known as *xia-gang*, on trial from 1994 and extended in 1997. Only urban *hukou* workers who had been made redundant from jobs guaranteed for life were accorded *xiagang* status. They remained on the books of the firm and received a low income (funded in three parts—by the employer, the local government, and the unemployment insurance scheme) but did not have to attend work. *Xiagang* employees retained their status for three years, or for less if they were recruited by another registered urban employment unit.

A quarter or more of state workers were to be laid-off within the four years, 1997–2000. By the end of 2000, the official figure of the accumulated laid-off workers was 41.13 million, representing 28 per cent of the workers who had been at risk. By that date, 9.11 million workers remained *xiagang*, implying that 32.02 million had, after three years, ceased to enjoy *xiagang* status or had been re-employed—mainly in the private and self-employment sector, which grew by 18.47 million over the period. The sum of registered plus *xiagang* unemployment at the end of 2000 was 15.05 million (7.8 per cent of the urban labour force).

In 2000, urban employment totalled 212.74 million, having risen, by 28.61 million, from 184.13 million in 1994. However, at the end of 2000 only 116.13 million were recorded as being employed in urban 'registered employment units'. Urban units mainly comprised the state-owned and collective enterprises, which traditionally contained surplus labour. Their employment fell sharply, by 36.46 million, from 152.59 million in 1994. It is very likely that this sharp fall, at a time of rising urban GDP, reflects the state-imposed fall in demand for urban resident labour resulting from the redundancy policy.

There was a large transfer of workers away from urban units, partly into unemployment but also into new activities and enterprises. The sharp rise in urban unemployment at this time can safely be attributed to the redundancy policy and its consequences. There is information on the number of 'rural employees' recorded in urban units. This figure fell from 13.72 million (9 per cent of employment in urban units) in 1994 to 8.97 million (7.7 per cent) in 2000. The decline of 4.75 million may have reflected a policy of tightening controls on the recruitment and re-employment of migrants in response to the plight of unemployed urban residents. During the period of the *xiagang* policy, there were numerous protests by laid-off workers, especially the many who did not receive their income support, and this induced the government to introduce the so-called 'putting out fires' fund to placate them. The tightening of controls on migration was a further policy response.

Appleton et al. (2002) examined a fairly representative survey of urban residents conducted in 1999 to analyse the incidence and extent of redundancy and re-employment among them. Eleven per cent of urban workers had been retrenched since 1992. Certain personal characteristics were associated with a greater risk of redundancy—including having little education, being female, being middle-aged, and having a manual or unskilled occupation. The typical retrenched worker could be expected to remain unemployed for about four years, but the young, the healthy, and the educated were likely to endure shorter spells of unemployment.

Each of the as yet few studies of rural–urban migrants in the urban labour market provides evidence of segmentation between them and urban residents. In a review article, Zhong (2005) finds elements of the exclusion of migrants in the work, inter alia, of Knight, Song, and Jia (1999), Wang, Maruyam, and Kikuchi (2000), Cai, Du, and Wang (2001), Meng and Zhang (2001), and Yao (2001).

Gender and region are two dimensions of migrant employment that might affect the relationships between the two groups of workers. Research has found that women are less prone to migrate than men (Zhao 1997, 1999; Hare 1999). This partly reflects the nature of the urban demand for migrant labour—much of it manual—but in addition women's mobility, and scope for training, is relatively constrained by family obligations and cultural expectations, and this tends to depress their wages (Lee 1998). Female migrants might thus be less effective than males insofar as there is competition with urban *hukou* workers.

The demand for migrant labour first emerged and developed in the coastal region, especially in Guangdong and in the Special Economic Zones (SEZs) where foreign investors were encouraged to produce for export. This fast-growing and fast-privatizing region has a large proportion of migrants in total employment, a high proportion of whom are female operatives, and migrants are able to move higher up the job ladder. For instance, the migrant density in Shenzhen—neighbouring Hong Kong—in 1995 was as high as 35 per cent, and the proportion of migrants who were skilled manual or non-manual employees no less than 32 per cent (Knight, Song, and Jia 1999). Given reports of migrant shortages and rising wages for migrants in the private sector of this, the most dynamic region, it is likely that migrants are less a threat to, and thus more able to compete with, urban residents than in other parts of China.

Insider–outsider models of the labour market distinguish between entrenched insiders, who have influence over the wage setting process and are protected against competition, and outsiders, whose wages are governed by market forces (Cain 1976). Thus insiders are in 'good' jobs, enjoying wages above the market-clearing level, whereas outsiders are in 'bad' jobs, with wages, although market-determined, depressed below the level that would prevail were the market not segmented. The segmentation can arise because insiders use their bargaining power to protect and separate themselves from the outsiders.

Segmented labour market theory suggests that insiders and outsiders are employed in different segments of the labour market or, if employed by the same firm, on different terms and often in different jobs (Cain 1976; Dickens and Lang 1988). An increase in the demand for labour is likely to raise the demand for both insiders and outsiders. They can be complements in the sense that a rise in the employment of one group has no effect on output unless it is accompanied by an increase in employment of the other; that is, the isoquants are rectangular in shape. They can be substitute factors of production (similar to capital and labour, or skilled and unskilled labour) if they perform different functions; that is, the isoquants are downward-sloping. However, they cannot be substitute individuals if segmentation prevents an outsider from taking the job of an insider. The substitution of individuals requires that the barriers to labour market competition be eliminated or at least eroded.

Applying these ideas to the Chinese labour market, urban *hukou* workers can be treated as insiders and rural *hukou* workers as outsiders in a segmented labour market characterized by institutional barriers. The protection of urban workers stems partly from their membership of the (mainly state-owned) work unit (the *danwei*) and partly from the underlying political economy that creates 'urban bias' and protects urban residents as a group. The decentralization of power enables city officials to favour local *hukou* people in spite of central government calls to reduce such discrimination (Solinger 2004). Despite the erosion of their job security and social security during the late 1990s, their incumbent status and their potential to ferment discontent and social unrest continued to protect urban insiders against rural outsiders.

A redundancy programme has two potential effects on real wage behaviour. By improving the profitability of enterprises, it can strengthen the bargaining power of remaining employees. By raising urban unemployment, however, it can weaken their bargaining power within the enterprise. In fact, the real wage of 'staff and workers' grew on average by no less than 9 per cent per annum between 1995 and 2000. This remarkable increase in real wages over the period of the redundancy programme suggests that the former effect is more powerful than the latter.

The concern is to analyse the relationship between the employment of urban residents and the employment of rural migrants. The fact that total employment in urban units fell by more than five times the fall in migrant employment in urban units, with the proportion of migrant employment also falling, but only slightly (Table 4.12), superficially suggests a positive rather than a negative relationship.

A positive relationship between the employment levels of the two types of labour can arise in various ways. First, an increase in the general demand for inputs into production requires an increase in both of the factors of production, urban resident labour and migrant labour. Second, migrants and urban workers can be complementary if, for instance, the employment of more urban residents, doing jobs specific to urban residents, requires the employment of additional migrants, doing jobs specific to migrants, for output to be increased. Third, although a fall in demand for urban workers need have no effect on migrant employment if the reason for the fall is the retrenchment of surplus labour that exists only among urban residents, the underlying political economy of urban bias can generate a policy response to the redundancy programme and the ensuing rise in the unemployment of urban residents. As urban workers are made redundant, city governments reduce the employment and re-employment of migrant workers, so giving redundant workers more opportunities to find alternative jobs. In that case, migrants continue to be residual employees, permitted only into the jobs that urban workers do not want. Moreover, insofar as the successful retrenchment programme raises the bargaining power of the remaining urban employees, this may strengthen their protection against migrant competition for jobs.

Alternatively, the relationship between resident and migrant employment can have a negative sign. As the institutional policies imposing segmentation are dismantled, the relaxation of restrictions on migrants increases competition in the labour market. The loosening of controls over migration and migrant employment thus generates a substitution of migrants for urban employees. Such increased competition for jobs means that a rise in the employment of migrants can produce a fall in the employment of urban workers and increased unemployment among them.

There are two sources of attitudinal evidence drawn upon: one based on the views of urban employers of migrant labour at the start of the redundancy programme, and the other based on the views of urban workers after the programme was in full swing and its effects were apparent. The former came from a 1996 survey (relating to 1995), designed and conducted by the Ministry of Labour. It covered 118 enterprises located in four cities, all of which employed migrants as well as urban workers. Within each city, enterprises were chosen from a sample frame stratified by ownership and by sector. In addition to much information about the enterprise and its employees, various attitudinal questions were asked of management.

Managerial attitudes are summarized in Table 4.13. The responses suggest that migrants and urban residents were not in competition. Two-thirds of respondents denied that rural workers could be replaced with redundant urban workers, the main reasons being that urban workers did not want the jobs and that the work was too hard for them. These reasons, rather than cost cutting, were also cited as the motive for recruiting migrants. Although most managers were satisfied with the quality of their rural employees, and many stressed the need for training them and employing them on a long-term basis, the migrants were perceived as complementary to, rather than substitutes for, their urban employees.

The second source is the urban household survey conducted in 2000 (relating largely to 1999) that is referred to above. The survey was designed by the Institute of Economics, Chinese Academy of Social Sciences in collaboration with an international team of researchers including the author, and conducted by the National Bureau of Statistics (NBS) early in 2000, pertaining mainly to 1999. The sample contains 4,000 households, being a sub-sample of the NBS

Table 4.13 Managerial attitudes towards migrants

	Percentages of respondents
Why do you recruit rural workers?*	
can bear hardship	61
urban workers not available	40
they are more manageable	33
lower cost	30
Can rural workers be replaced with redundant urban workers?	
yes	35
no	65
If not, why not?*	
the work is too hard for urban workers	51
urban workers do not want the job	49
urban workers are inadequate for the job	15
Are you satisfied with the quality of migrant workers?	
yes	61
No	39
Training of migrant workers:	
must be trained strictly before starting	47
short-term training is enough	40
no training is needed	13

Source: *China Survey of Urban Units*, 1996.

Notes: * denotes that figures may add up to more than 100% because more than one answer was permitted.

Table 4.14 Urban worker attitudes towards migrants

Percentage answering yes to each question	Total	Never unemployed	Been unemployed
Possession of an urban *hukou* is less important now for job search	73.6	73.3	74.7
Migrants are no less efficient than urban workers in the same position	80.8	80.4	82.5
I would rather stay unemployed/*xiagang* than work alongside migrants	17.9	17.5	19.9
Migrants are competitors and should leave when unemployment is high	57.8	57.5	58.9
Migrants caused the high redundancy rate	32.3	31.9	34.0

Source: China Urban Household Survey, 1999.

Notes: There are somewhat different response rates to different questions. Non-responses are excluded: the percentage who answered no to a question can be derived as a residual.

annual household survey. The survey covers thirteen cities in six provinces, chosen to be as nationally representative as possible. In addition to a rich set of household and individual characteristics, various attitudinal questions were asked of urban *hukou* workers.

The basic attitudinal results are shown in Table 4.14. In addition to the sample as a whole, those who had been continuously employed and those who were made redundant or became unemployed are distinguished but there are no notable differences in the responses of these two groups. There are signs that, by 1999, migrants were being viewed as potential competitors. Over 70 per cent of urban workers regarded possession of an urban *hukou* as being less important for job search than in the past; over 80 per cent considered migrants to be no less efficient than urban workers in the same position; more than 80 per cent said that they were prepared to work alongside migrants rather than remain unemployed or *xia gang*; and over 50 per cent said yes to the statement: 'Migrants are competitors and should leave when unemployment is high.' It is true, however, that only a third of the respondents saw migrants as the cause of the high redundancy rate.

Although there was continuing recognition that migrants were willing to take the jobs that urban residents shunned, there was also a perception among some urban workers that the labour market was becoming more competitive. An illustrative case is that of a female respondent aged 26 with a professional school qualification who had left her first job in a state-owned enterprise (SOE) because she feared redundancy. Through a referral by a friend, she had secured her then current job in a wholly foreign-owned enterprise employing migrants alongside urban residents. She stressed the need to acquire more skills as protection against the greater competition that she now faced.

Table 4.15 presents the results of a logit analysis of the determinants of urban worker attitudes towards migrants. Column (1) shows the characteristics that make them more likely to regard migrants as 'competitors who should leave

Table 4.15 Logit estimation of the determinants of urban workers' beliefs

	Coefficient (t-statistic)				
	(1)	(2)	(3)	(4)	(5)
Intercept	−1.404	−2.564	−1.7863	−3.1104	−1.6342
	(−4.218)***	(−7.46)***	(−5.33)***	(−6.77)***	(−6.03)***
Female	0.5220	0.416	0.4388	0.5096	0.471
	(9.877)***	(6.37)***	(7.18)***	(5.99)***	(9.62)***
Experienced unemployment	0.3340	0.3001	0.3453	0.1195	0.3283
	(3.740)***	(2.73)***	(3.42)***	(1.41)	(3.92)***
Years of employment experience	0.0433	0.025	0.0342	0.0259	0.0317
	(9.374)***	(4.56)***	(6.59)***	(3.63)***	(7.39)***
Years of age	−0.0091	0.0019	−0.0084	−0.0012	−0.0003
	(−2.307)***	(0.40)	(−1.89)*	(−0.19)	(−0.07)
Years of education	−0.0250	−0.0349	−0.0582	−0.0272	0.0302
	(−2.717)***	(−3.07)***	(−5.39)***	(−1.84)*	(3.54)***
Communist Party member	0.0467	−0.0005	−0.0587	−0.0645	0.1079
	(0.768)	(−0.01)	(−0.82)	(−0.66)	(1.91)*
Type of ownership of employer	0.0057	−0.0466	−0.0047	−0.0457	0.0094
	(0.331)	(−1.99)**	(−0.23)	(−1.49)	(−0.59)
Cities	Yes	Yes	Yes	Yes	Yes
Pseudo-R^2	0.0396	0.0354	0.0383	0.033	0.029
LR χ^2 (21)	385.59***	249.42***	298.38***	156.03***	312.68***
Number of observations	8540	8540	8540	8540	8540

Source: China Urban Household Survey, 1999.

Notes: (1) In column (1), the dependent variable = 1 if migrants are viewed as competitors and = 0 otherwise. In column (2), the dependent variable = 1 if migrants should not receive equal treatment in the workplace because they do not have urban *hukou* and = 0 otherwise. In column (3), the dependent variable = 1 if migrants are the cause of lay-offs in urban areas and = 0 otherwise. In column (4), the dependent variable = 1 if the respondent would rather remain unemployed than work alongside migrants and = 0 otherwise. In column (5), the dependent variable = 1 if the belief is held that urban *hukou* has declined in importance and = 0 otherwise.
(2) The omitted dummy variables are: male, never experienced unemployment, not Communist Party member, and ownership sector of employer is urban collectives.
(3) *** denotes statistical significance at the 1% level, ** at the 5% level, and * at the 10% level.

when unemployment is high'. The dependent variable takes a value of one if migrants are perceived as competitors and of zero if not. Length of employment experience, being female, and having experienced unemployment significantly increase the probability of taking the competitive view. By contrast, years of age (but with a much smaller coefficient than years of employment experience) and years of education reduce the probability of holding this view. These results correspond well to those on the determinants of redundancy in the same sample (Appleton et al. 2002). In both studies, the greater the risk that urban workers will be made redundant, the more likely they are to fear the potential competition of rural migrants. Possible endogeneity issues are unlikely to alter the interpretation. For instance, if high personal ability increases educational attainment, education appears to do some of the work attributable to unobserved ability. However, both low ability and low education are likely to increase vulnerability to migrant competition.

The results of the logit analyses for the other attitudinal questions reveal similar patterns. Column (2) indicates that the same set of characteristics promotes the view that migrants should not receive the same treatment in the workplace as urban residents. There are two exceptions: age is no longer a significant determinant, and ownership of the work unit now matters. The ownership variable is ranked according to the degree of state influence on the employer—from state-owned enterprises to joint ventures and private firms, the higher values being assigned to the units in which the state has less control. The coefficient is negative and significant, suggesting that migrants are less feared by workers in those ownership sectors that are more subject to government policy directing the employment of migrants.

Column (3) estimates the traits of those who believe that lay-offs can be attributed to the presence of rural–urban migrants. The determinants of this view and those of the view that migrants are competitors are virtually the same. They reflect the insecurity of workers who are more vulnerable to being laid-off. Column (4) examines what sorts of urban residents would rather remain unemployed than work alongside migrants. The determinants are again very similar to those in column (1), with one notable exception. Previous unemployment is no longer significantly positive, suggesting that people who have experienced unemployment are realistic about their options.

Column (5) shows the attributes of respondents who believe that possession of an urban *hukou* has declined in importance. Again, being female, long employment experience, and previous unemployment significantly increase the belief that the *hukou* is now less important. These characteristics make people more vulnerable to competition from migrants. For the first time, however, education is significantly positive instead of significantly negative, and membership of the Communist Party also has a significantly positive effect. As these two variables have been shown both to reduce the probability of being made redundant (Appleton et al. 2002) and to raise wages (Knight and Yueh 2004), it is possible that workers protected by their human capital or social capital see *hukou* status as becoming less relevant to them.

It is notable that in the answers to each question analysed in Table 4.15 women are significantly more likely than men to view migrants as labour market competitors, to feel vulnerable to that competition, and to want institutional protection against it. These attitudes are predictable from the findings of Appleton et al. (2002) from the same survey that women are indeed at greater risk than men of being made redundant. The cities with the highest positive coefficients in column (1) (viewing migrants as competitors) were Shenyang in Liaoning, Zhengzhou in Henan, and Beijing. Possible explanations can be found: in 1999 Liaoning and Henan had very high unemployment—12.8 and 15.3 per cent respectively (Knight and Xue 2006, table 4.4). The capital city attracts people of high quality from across the nation: migrants to Beijing tended to be more skilled, to receive more training, and to come from more distant provinces (Knight, Song, and Jia 1999, table 3).

From this attitudinal evidence it seems that in the mid-1990s, firms perceived urban workers and migrants to be complements in a segmented market rather than substitutes in a competitive one. Towards the end of the decade, however, an element of competition for jobs had emerged, at least in the minds of urban workers; the more so, the more reason they had to fear redundancy.

Whereas employment in 'urban units' fell by 36 million between 1994 and 2000, total urban employment rose by 29 million or by 2.4 per cent per annum. Given that the urban *hukou* labour force grew by less than 1 per cent per annum, migrant employment clearly grew, although not in urban units but in small-scale wage employment and self-employment. This section aimed to explain migrant employment in urban units, which fell by 5 million or 7 per cent per annum, over the period.

Some city governments did indeed make arrangements to restrict migrant employment in order to protect their unemployed and *xiagang* citizens. At the start of the period under consideration, enterprise managers tended to perceive migrants as complementary to, and not competitive substitutes for, their urban employees—filling the jobs that urban workers did not want. The 1995 survey suggested that the urban labour market was sharply segmented.

The 1999 survey presented a rather different picture. The majority of urban workers viewed migrants as potential competitors, and this view was more common among women, the less educated, and those with long employment experience—the same variables that have been found to increase the probability of being laid-off. In fact, the same set of characteristics also make people less willing to work alongside migrants and promote the related views that lay-offs can be attributed to the presence of migrants, that migrants should not receive equal treatment, and that the possession of an urban *hukou* has become less important. The differences are revealing: the experience of unemployment makes workers more prone to view migrants as competitors, but it also makes people more willing to work alongside migrants; that is, they become more realistic about their options. Migrants appear to be less feared if the employer is more subject to government controls on migrant employment, and if workers are protected by their human capital or social capital.

At the end of the period under study, therefore, some urban workers did appear to view migrants as potential competitors, especially those among them who were at greater risk of being made redundant. It is likely that there were by then elements of both segmentation and competition in China's urban labour market.

4.7 Conclusion

There is a long march towards a labour market in China. Its formation is slower than for most product or factor markets, essentially because of the underlying political economy. This accords urban residents disproportionate political power, albeit latent rather than overt, and thus serves to protect their interests.

Nevertheless, it is possible to envisage how a less segmented and more competitive urban labour market will emerge. Projections of demand and supply in the urban labour market suggest that migrant employment will grow in relative importance. As the demand for migrants increases and they are accordingly able to move up the job ladder into jobs requiring more training, skills, and experience, so the system of temporary migration will become economically inefficient. The solution to the problem which governments and employers around the world have adopted is to permit and encourage the stabilization of the migrant labour force. The economic imperative will be to permit urbanization. City living encourages the adoption of urban attitudes and the transfer of the migrant's social reference group from the village to the city, and this process may well give rise to feelings of relative deprivation. As more migrants are transformed into proletarians, so the pressure on government to treat them on par with urban residents will grow, and *hukou* privilege will accordingly be eroded.

This isn't the only impediment in the Chinese labour market. This chapter also examined low job mobility, reasons for differential investments in human capital, and ongoing wage and labour reforms. The picture shows significant progress since the 1980s, but it also points to the still-lagging reforms in the factor markets. While product market reforms have progressed quickly, labour and capital reforms (discussed in the last chapter) lag. However, to sustain its growth rate, human capital is crucial as it is a source of endogenous growth. China has come a long way, but there is still some distance to go.

5

'Catch-up' Growth: Technology
Transfers and Innovation

5.1 Introduction

One of the enduring assumptions in economic growth is that developing countries will be able to 'catch up' with rich countries through the process of technology transfer as capital moves from developed to developing ones. Through foreign direct investment (FDI), the more advanced technology embodied in capital from developed countries induces faster growth in developing ones. Specifically, FDI spillover occurs when foreign direct investment increases the productivity of domestic firms and the value of the benefits is not completely internalized by the multinational corporation (MNC).

China is the leading destination for FDI among developing countries and has a reasonably skilled labour force that makes spillovers more likely. It is also far from the technology frontier. Its FDI policy is geared at developing joint ventures and attracting technology to improve productivity of domestic firms; evidenced by the Special Economic Zones (SEZs). And, the bulk of FDI is invested in the form of joint ventures, which are thought to have a greater likelihood of inducing technology-related spillovers to domestic firms. The prospect for such productivity gains is strong in China, although there is limited direct evidence for both it and other economies.

This chapter first analyses an original, national Chinese enterprise survey designed to provide such evidence. The survey investigates a key trait of Chinese–foreign joint ventures (JVs), which is the signing of a technology transfer agreement at the time of establishing the JV. This provides a rare instance of a direct measure of technology transfers, while most studies infer transfers from foreign presence in the sector or province, percentage of foreign equity ownership, or some other indirect evidence. In other words, indirect effects are often measured but direct ones are not. The sample is drawn from a large and comprehensive panel of enterprises held by the National Bureau of Statistics, which permits the creation of a panel that allows for rigorous estimation of productivity differences between firms which benefit from technology transfers and those which do not. The data will allow for a direct measure of technology spillover in the form of transfer, along with value paid. It thus goes to the core of the question of whether such transfers occur. In China's case, they do and they generate significant improvements in productivity.

Innovation, though, can also be generated through investment in R&D, perhaps building on the initial FDI spillover of knowledge. There has been a rapid increase in patents in China since the 1990s despite an underdeveloped legal system of protection for intellectual property rights (IPRs). This chapter will also examine whether China's patent laws are effective in producing innovation and explores the contextual factors that generate innovation within such a system, like R&D and, FDI. It will examine patent success rates across provinces at different levels of development; ask whether FDI matters, following the focus of developing and transition economies in seeking foreign capital and technology transfers to help them to achieve technological progress; determine whether China's R&D spending has generated innovation captured in patents, akin to the organisation Economic Cooperation and Development OECD) focus on increasing expenditure on research and development to foster productivity; and whether increasing research personnel will result in technological advancement, along the lines of the studies of the US where innovation was found not to be clearly linked to the number of researchers.

5.2 Foreign Direct Investment Spillovers

Certainly, there are both direct and indirect channels for FDI spillover. Direct channels are explicit technology transfers, such as technology transfer agreements between the foreign and Chinese partners in a joint venture. Indirect channels are copying products produced by an MNC in a local market, hiring workers trained by the MNC, or pro-competitive effects such as through horizontal and vertical linkages. Horizontal spillovers may take place when local firms improve their efficiency by imitating the technology of foreign firms in the local market through observation or hiring workers trained by the foreign company. Another type is the introduction of competitive forces if the presence of a multinational corporation increases the competition in a market or sector in the host country and induces local firms to become more productive or seek out new technology. Multinationals will wish to protect their position and have an incentive to prevent technology leakages and spillovers from taking place. Further, there are two types of vertical linkages: upstream and downstream. There are fewer incentives for MNCs to protect against backward links with upstream suppliers of their intermediate inputs. Local suppliers can receive direct technology transfers, indirect transfers through observation, and benefit from larger markets and scale improvements in productivity. Downstream or forward linkages from an MNC can benefit a local firm by providing more advanced and better intermediate goods, and create a market for complementary services. Clustering of FDI into SEZs in China provide another sort of effect that is worth investigating; namely, network externalities which generate the prospect of knowledge diffusion and the creation of external economies by firms.

Theories of FDI spillover and the role of MNCs include Rodríguez-Clare's (1996), and specifically as a catalyst or hindrance for industrial development (see, for example, Markusen and Venables 1999; Lall 1978). In the empirical literature, there is some evidence of limited FDI spillover in OECD countries (Blomström 1998), although given the proximity of these countries to the technology frontier and their similar levels of development, it is perhaps not surprising to not find large effects. There is also some evidence from developing countries. These studies have found minimal or negative effects (Haddad and Harrison 1993 for Morocco; Aitken and Harrison 1999 for Venezuela; Djankov and Hoekman 2000 for the Czech Republic; Konings 2001 for Bulgaria, Romania, and Poland). By contrast, other studies find positive effects (Blomström 1986 for Mexico; Javorick 2004 for Lithuania). These findings suggest that contextual factors will affect whether a country benefits from FDI, but also raise measurement issues. For China, there are studies which find that FDI both improves firm productivity and contributes to economic growth. For instance, Hu, Jefferson, and Qian (2005) and Chuang and Hsu (2004) find that FDI improves firm productivity. Felmingham and Zhang (2002) find that FDI contributes positively to economic growth. The mechanisms, however, are inferred as foreign ownership share or presence of MNCs are used as a proxy for technology transfers. The studies are largely only able to proxy FDI spillover due to the lack of a direct measure. In some instances, measures of technology licensing are used, though they are subject to issues of endogeneity as they are signed by firms which are willing to pay for the licence due to their being more productive.

This specifically designed dataset allows for measurement of technology transfer at the inception of a firm. The legal agreements that include technology transfers set up at establishment of the JV are measured which provide a unique opportunity to assess a direct effect of gaining technology at the start of a firm. It will also shed light as to whether the vehicle of FDI matters (if the foreign investment is in the form of a joint venture with more opportunities for knowledge sharing as compared with a wholly foreign-owned entity) and most importantly, whether explicit technology transfers result in more significant FDI spillover, increased firm productivity, and thus constitute a mechanism to induce 'catch-up' growth in developing countries.

This section will examine whether FDI spillover effects can be found in China, and if joint ventures are found to be more productive than domestic firms, and thus contribute to its 'catch-up' economic growth. The research questions will comprise the following set of queries. Is there evidence of positive FDI spillover in China? Are Chinese–foreign joint ventures which signed technology transfer agreements more productive than domestic firms? This will permit a direct channel of FDI spillover to be investigated. Are domestic firms in sectors with a foreign presence more productive? This will allow for an exploration of indirect channels, specifically horizontal spillovers. Are domestic firms in sectors with upstream and downstream linkages more productive? This examines another indirect channel; namely, vertical spillovers. Does it matter if the foreign presence is a joint venture or wholly foreign-owned enterprise? This will permit an investigation of the importance of implicit transfers such as learning by doing or sharing of know-how.

5.3 Chinese–Foreign Joint Ventures

The primary dataset is composed of a national firm-level survey from 2000–5. The survey pertained to 2005 which was then matched by China's National Bureau of Statistics (NBS) to their annual enterprise survey to create a panel. The survey questionnaire was designed by an international research team including the author, and carried out by NBS with support from the World Bank. The survey was conducted in the summer of 2006 on 1,268 firms in 12 cities (province in parenthesis): Beijing (municipality), Changchun (Jilin), Chifeng (Inner Mongolia), Dandong (Liaoning), Hangzhou (Zhejiang), Shijiazhuang (Hebei), Shiyan (Hubei), Shunde (Guangdong), Wujiang (Jiangsu), Xian (Shaanxi), Zibo (Shandong), Chongqing (municipality). The data is fairly evenly spread across the twelve cities. The smallest sample is for Wujiang (Jiangsu province) with 7.7 per cent, the largest is for Zibo (Shandong province) with 11.14 per cent of total observations. The survey data was then matched to the enterprise panel and is a representative sub-sample of that large-scale dataset. The NBS takes considerable care with their annual enterprise survey such that the figures match data obtained independently by the Chinese tax authorities.

After matching the data to the NBS panel, observations with incomplete information were eliminated, so the data used comprises unbalanced panel data from 1,201 industrial firms for the years 2000–5, for which 2005 provides survey information as well as the NBS data. The information was also checked against provincial-level data, which revealed that the sub-sample is broadly in line with the provincial averages. Comparison with the averages for other studies using the large NBS firm-level dataset (Dougherty, Herd, and He 2007) yielded similar results. Also in line with most enterprise firm studies, the survey only covered firms with an annual sales volume larger than 5 million Yuan following the NBS practice (see, for example, Jefferson and Su 2006). The mean descriptive information is provided in Tables 5.1 and 5.2.

The NBS dataset only includes firms in industry, and does not include construction and transportation companies. Thus, the majority of firms operate in the manufacturing sector, with a small number of firms in mining or utilities (Table 5.2). Given the sample size, the two-digit (37 sectors) or three-digit-level sector identifiers (188 sectors) are used, rather than four-digit-level ones (481 sectors) in the estimations. In all cases where sector dummies are included in the regressions, the garment sector is the omitted category.

As was noted above, this panel dataset is unbalanced; however, the appearance (disappearance) of a firm in (from) the dataset cannot be equated with firm entry into (exit from) the market. In order to avoid any systematic bias in the estimations, dummy variables for each year 2001 to 2005 are included which

Table 5.1 Ownership types

Ownership type	SOE (state-owned enterprise)	Privatized SOE	Private Chinese	JV (joint venture) Greater China	JV Other	IV TT (with technology transfer)	WFOE (wholly foreign owned enterprise) Greater China	WFOE (other)	Total
Share	37.0%	13.8%	29.2%	5.0%	6.3%	2.3%	3.2%	3.2%	100%
Firms	470	175	370	63	80	29	41	41	1269

Note: Ownership type of each firm relates to initial ownership. Greater china includes Taiwan, Hong Kong, and Macau.

Table 5.2 Firm, provincial descriptive statistics

	Value-added	Number of workers	Capital stock	Value-added per worker	Capital stock per worker	% managers with higher education	Firm age	Provincial FDI/total investment
	Y	L	K	Y/L	K/L	% college	Age	FDI
Mean	30,241.433	687.813	72,951.809	49.469	96.258	1.500	12.695	99.023
Median	6113.566	218.000	10,974.416	28.187	52.852	1.000	8.000	78.456
s.d.	92,487.605	1644.721	232,877.325	67.568	208.248	0.773	14.373	88.156
Observations	4490	4491	4490	4346	4346	5405	5385	5231

Note: Monetary values are in 100 RMB.

take a value of 1 if the firm first appeared in the dataset in this specific year and 0 otherwise (the omitted category is firms which appear in 2000). In addition, there are standard year dummies to pick up average TFP evolution over time.

To avoid influential observations due to reporting error, the production data is cleaned using standard procedures of 'windsorizing': for the pooled data on firm-level value-added, capital stock, and labour, the values at the first and ninety-ninth quantile of the distribution is first determined. Then, all observed values below the former cut-off are replaced with that of the first quantile and all observed values above the latter cut-off with that of the ninety-ninth quantile. Additional information available allows for identification of firms which are multi-plant groups. Data for multi-plant enterprises may lead to bias in the estimates, and are controlled for with a separate dummy variable in the estimations, as is the age of the firm.

From the ownership data, it is also evident when firms changed owner during the sample period. Around 10 per cent of observations are for firms which changed ownership at any point during 2000–5. All possible ownership changes are accounted for with separate dummy variables to control for their productivity effects. There is also a small number of firms changing ownership twice or even three times—given the lack or slow emergence of legal regulations relating to bankruptcy during the period of observation, these firms (typically Chinese-owned, shifting between private and public ownership) revert to state-ownership as they cannot exit the market. In order to control for their impact, they are identified with two separate dummy variables for two and three ownership changes respectively (data for these firms comprise around 6 per cent of observations).

There is also matched survey data for the above 1,201 firms, collected in June 2006. The survey data comprises a large number of variables related to social trust and responsibility, government supervision, firm-internal management, labour, production and environmental management, as well as market environment and additional information on infrastructure, investment, and innovation. With the exception of the latter, the survey questions refer to the year 2005. For infrastructure, investment, and innovation, there is recall data for 2001 to 2005 detailing investment categories such as ICT spending and R&D investment, and innovation data on new product lines and patents.

There is also additional information on joint venture (JV) firms where the Chinese partner entered into a technology transfer agreement with a foreign partner. This variable is unique to the dataset and to my knowledge has not been analysed formally before. This aside, the survey data can distinguish private Chinese firms established during the reform era of the 1990s from privatized, formerly state-owned enterprises (SOE).

As a result of this information, firms are divided into eight ownership categories: 1: SOE, 2: privatized SOE, 3: private Chinese, 4: JV with partners from Greater China (foreign partners from Taiwan, Hong Kong, or Macao), 5: JV with partners from other countries, 6: JV which signed a technology transfer agreement, 7: wholly foreign-owned enterprise (WFOE) from Greater China, 8: WFOE from other countries. These categories are mutually exclusive. The three

JV categories are also combined in some of the analysis. For instance, the JV variable is then made up of categories 4–7 (that is, 14.8 per cent, N=153). In addition, there is information on whether firms are listed on a Chinese stock exchange, which is not mutually exclusive with the ownership types cited involving Chinese partners and will be added to the regressions as an additional control.

There is incomplete data coverage on the firm's year of establishment: this information is available for most foreign-invested enterprises (JVs, WFOEs) and the private Chinese firms, with data for SOEs and privatized SOEs mostly missing. Given the considerable institutional changes during the reform period from the late 1970s to the present, whereby China transformed itself from a planned to a primarily market-driven economy, firm age for enterprises established prior to 1978 cannot be interpreted in the same way as in a Western market economy. Therefore, SOEs with missing data are coded as established in 1978. A firm age variable is constructed from the information on year of establishment—if firm age results in a negative value due to reporting error it is replaced with the value 1.

The survey data further contains information on worker characteristics for 2005. These data include information on the share of shop-floor workers with secondary and tertiary education respectively and also the share of managers with tertiary education. For each of these variables the raw data is in categories (for example, 1 = 0–20 per cent, 2 = 20–40 per cent, etc.). The median value for the reported category (in logs) is used. Additional information reveals the number of training exercises per annum, the average monthly wage (in RMB), days of paid leave, and the average tenure of shop-floor workers (all in logs). Since these data are time-invariant, standard errors clustered at the firm level are estimated in all regressions.

In order to convincingly argue for a causal effect of ownership on firm productivity, there needs to be valid and informative instruments for ownership in the 2SLS estimations. Thus, the instrumentation strategy is for JVs versus non-JVs, where the OLS results suggest a sizeable total factor productivity advantage for the former. A number of potential instrumental variables aims to predict JV ownership by province-level variables for the year the firm was established. These province-level variables are the available time-series for:

(a) Province-level foreign direct investment actually utilized (in US$10,000)

(b) Province-level foreign exchange income from tourism (in US$million)

(c) Province-level value of domestic technology contracts (in 100 million RMB)

(d) Province-level public funding for science and technology (in 100 million RMB)

(e) Provincial exports (in US$)

(f) Provincial imports (in US$)

In all cases, these instruments are normalized by either:

  (a) Province-level total investment in fixed assets (in current 100 million RMB)

or

  (b) Province-level total employment (in 10,000 workers).

These two variables (in logs) are also included in all first- and second-stage regressions. The sources for the provincial data are: *China Yearly Provincial Macro-Economy Statistics*; *China NBS Provincial Statistics Yearbooks*; China Ministry of Science & Technology (MOST), *Science & Technology Statistical Yearbooks*.

5.4 Estimating Technology Transfers

The empirical model is based on the simple production function approach

$$q_{ijt} = \beta D_{ij} + \alpha_l l_{ijt} + \alpha_k k_{ijt} + \alpha_m m_{ijt} + \gamma x_{ijt} + u_{ijt} \qquad (1)$$

where q_{ijt} is ln(output), l_{ijt} is ln(labour), k_{ijt} is ln(capital) and m_{ijt} is ln(materials) of plant i in province j at time t. The key variable is D_{ij} which indicates whether the firm is involved in a foreign joint venture including a technology transfer agreement (or in some specifications, any foreign joint venture). The x_{ijt} is a vector of control variable such as age, skills, whether the firm is multi-plant, whether the firm is listed, and a set of three-digit industry, province, and time dummies.

D_{ij} does not vary over time, so an empirical challenge is how to identify the causal effects of ownership type on productivity. In order to argue convincingly for a causal effect of ownership on firm productivity, valid and informative instrumental variables are needed. Once in place, a joint venture rarely changes over time, thus policy conditions at the start of the firm's birth are likely to be the critical factor in determining whether or not an international joint venture was formed. Since the Chinese government allowed provinces to conduct different policies towards foreign FDI (for example, a much more liberal approach in the Special Economic Zones), proxies for the policy conditions at time of firm set up are used as the instrumental variable. Since the year and province in which every firm was set up, such variables are defined for all firms.

To be precise provincial-level FDI at time of start-up is used, which is likely to reflect the openness of the province to foreign investment. Provinces with more liberal policies are likely to have more FDI and therefore more JVs than those with less foreign investment. It is unclear why historical FDI would have a direct effect on current productivity, but it may have an indirect effect through affecting other productivity relevant variables. These are controlled for in the regressions. For example, a full set of province dummies are included so this non-parametrically controls for the current stock and flow of FDI in the province as these are likely to both affect productivity and be correlated with FDI at time

161

of birth. Alternative policy proxies such as exports and imports in the province at the time of the firm's start-up were also investigated.

The first stage of the instrumental variables (IV) equation is:

$$D_{ij} = \pi z_{ij} + \delta' w_{ijt} + e_{ijt} \tag{2}$$

where z_{ij} is a measure of the provincial policy towards foreign JVs and w_{ijt} are all the exogenous variables in equation (1). The amount of FDI in the province at year of the firm's start-up as a measure of this, as provinces with more liberal approaches to FDI (for example, special economic zones) would be much more likely to generate a start-up forming as an JV.

Since provinces vary in size, FDI is normalized with respect to total provincial investment and include this variable as an additional control in equations (1) and (2). The instrument's variation is essentially an interaction between firm age and provincial characteristics. The equation carefully conditions on other confounding influences like the linear effect of age and province effects, but there is no time-varying instrument for JV (since these do not vary over time).

Before turning to the results, the extent of FDI in China over the past thirty years is worth examining. China has been remarkably successful in attracting inward FDI since its open-door policy took off in 1992. As Table 5.3 shows, it has received on average US$62 billion per annum in FDI since then, vastly outpacing all emerging economies and around the levels of major economies. Nevertheless, FDI accounted for only 15 per cent of total investment on average, underscoring China's high savings rate which averaged between 40–50 per cent during this period. Aside from the initial period of 1992–6 when FDI made up as much as one-third of total investment in China, FDI has contributed less than 10 per cent since 1997. For China, the aim is now less to attract overseas investment funds to supplant inadequate savings. Instead, the nature of FDI in China is to attract technology and know-how to help its own firms learn and become more productive and competitive.

The preferred FDI vehicle, therefore, had been Chinese–foreign joint ventures, since these enable a Chinese firm to partner with a foreign one and thus enhance the prospect of positive spillovers of knowledge to China. Prior to WTO accession in 2001, JVs (both equity and cooperative) accounted for the bulk of FDI, around two-thirds from the early 1990s to 2000. At their peak during the 1990s, JVs accounted for as much as 35 per cent of total investment and for 10 per cent on average over the past thirty years, or two-thirds of the total share of FDI in Chinese investment.

Since WTO membership, JVs declined from half to just over one-fifth of FDI in 2007, reflecting the increase in the number of wholly owned foreign enterprises which do not have Chinese partners and are also geared more to the greater liberalization of China's domestic market. Although the share of JVs has fallen as China opens up, the absolute amount of FDI in the form of joint ventures remains robust at nearly US$20 billion per year, as compared with US$20–30 billion in the pre-WTO years.

Table 5.3 Total domestic and foreign direct investment in China, 1984–2007

	(1) Total investment (US$bn)	(2) Domestic investment (US$bn)	(3) FDI (US$bn)	(4) JVs (US$bn)	(5) JV share of FDI	(6) Number of JVs	(7) Number of foreign firms	(8) FDI share of total investment	(9) JV share of total investment
1984	36.82	32.03	2.87	2.55	88.72%	n/a	n/a	7.81%	6.93%
1985	50.62	35.30	10.09	5.53	54.76%	n/a	n/a	19.94%	10.92%
1986	57.71	45.97	2.83	2.73	96.43%	n/a	n/a	4.91%	4.74%
1987	65.33	53.19	3.71	3.23	87.17%	n/a	n/a	5.68%	4.95%
1988	83.45	67.45	5.30	4.76	89.82%	n/a	n/a	6.35%	5.70%
1989	92.71	81.23	5.60	3.74	66.83%	n/a	n/a	6.04%	4.04%
1990	98.78	78.28	12.61	3.96	31.38%	n/a	n/a	12.77%	4.01%
1991	115.19	93.97	13.17	8.22	62.38%	n/a	n/a	11.44%	7.13%
1992	147.67	78.23	58.12	42.38	72.92%	n/a	n/a	39.36%	28.70%
1993	230.11	106.84	111.44	80.67	72.40%	n/a	20,058	48.43%	35.06%
1994	297.80	204.04	82.68	60.49	73.17%	n/a	29,101	27.76%	20.31%
1995	372.89	269.69	91.28	57.57	63.06%	39,350	49,559	24.48%	15.44%
1996	421.42	339.81	73.28	46.17	63.01%	32,816	43,412	17.39%	10.96%
1997	438.74	377.68	51.00	32.79	64.29%	31,580	42,881	11.62%	7.47%
1998	458.45	399.89	45.46	28.07	61.74%	n/a	26,442	9.92%	6.12%
1999	482.42	429.76	40.32	24.06	59.68%	n/a	26,837	8.36%	4.99%
2000	510.11	450.75	40.71	20.94	51.43%	n/a	28,445	7.98%	4.10%
2001	582.24	532.56	46.88	21.95	46.83%	n/a	31,423	8.05%	3.77%
2002	667.09	612.07	52.74	20.05	38.01%	n/a	34,466	7.91%	3.01%
2003	819.32	763.18	53.51	19.23	35.94%	n/a	38,581	6.53%	2.35%
2004	1,012.65	948.57	60.63	19.50	32.16%	n/a	57,165	5.99%	1.93%
2005	1,180.69	1,116.88	60.33	16.45	27.26%	n/a	56,387	5.11%	1.39%
2006	1,377.70	1,310.62	63.02	16.32	25.89%	26,604	60,872	4.57%	1.18%
2007	1,623.89	1,545.55	74.77	17.01	22.75%	28,622	67,456	4.60%	1.05%

Source: China Statistical Yearbook.

Note: Domestic investment figures in RMB were converted using 1.00 CNY = 0.146403 USD. Column (5) = (4)/(3). Column (1) is not equal to (2) and (3) as there were other types of foreign investments; namely, loans.

Table 5.4 Production functions (OLS)

Dependent variable: ln(value-added), ln(Y)	(1)	(2)	(3)	(4)	(5)	(6)
JV (joint venture)		0.203*** (0.074)	0.228*** (0.066)			
JVTT (JV with technology transfer agreement)				0.737*** (0.194)	0.759*** (0.195)	0.572*** (0.164)
JV other (all other JVs)					0.125* (0.065)	0.072 (0.060)
Privatized SOE		0.037 (0.061)				
Private Chinese firm		−0.043 (0.061)				
Foreign firm (Greater China)		−0.147 (0.115)				
Foreign firm (other)		−0.114 (0.100)				
Omitted base category: SOE						
ln(labour)	0.607*** (0.028)	0.608*** (0.028)	0.606*** (0.028)	0.606*** (0.028)	0.606*** (0.028)	
ln(capital)	0.278*** (0.018)	0.274*** (0.018)	0.272*** (0.018)	0.276*** (0.019)	0.273*** (0.019)	0.199*** (0.020)
% college educated	0.281*** (0.034)	0.274*** (0.034)	0.270*** (0.033)	0.272*** (0.032)	0.267*** (0.032)	0.230*** (0.029)
ln(wage bill)						0.342*** (0.017)
Firms	1,155	1,155	1,155	1,155	1,155	1,155
Observations	4,204	4,204	4,204	4,204	4,204	4,204
R-squared	0.740	0.743	0.743	0.745	0.746	0.782

Notes: * significant at 10%; ** significant at 5%; *** significant at 1%. Estimation by OLS in all columns with standard errors clustered by firm in parentheses below coefficients. All columns include firm age, a full set of three-digit industry dummies (187), a multi-plant dummy, year dummies, year of entering sample dummies, and province dummies. SOE is state-owned enterprise. Great China includes Taiwan, Hong Kong, and Macao. % college educated is the proportion of managers with a college degree.

Table 5.4 presents the basic OLS estimates of the value-added production function. In column (1) the conventional factor inputs of labour and capital are significantly positive and similar to the factor shares of revenue. There are slightly decreasing returns to scale as the sum of the coefficients on labour and capital is 0.9. Note, however, the estimations are also conditioned on the proportion of managers with higher education ('per cent college educated') which is positive and highly significant, suggesting that human capital is important for productivity. Column (2) includes all the ownership types (privatized state-owned enterprises, private Chinese firms, and two forms of wholly owned foreign enterprises—Greater China and elsewhere) the omitted base being state-owned enterprises. The key ownership variable of interest is JV (Joint Ventures). The coefficient on JV is positive and highly significant whereas the coefficients on all the other ownership types are individually and jointly insignificant. The F-test of the joint significance of all the non-JV ownership dummies is 0.92 (p-value = 0.45). In column (3) all the other (insignificant) ownership types are dropped. In this column an JV is associated with 20.3 log points (22.5 per cent) higher productivity. Column (4) repeats the specification of column (1) but includes only those JVs that had technology transfer agreements ('JVTT') and column (5) includes all other JVs (joint ventures that do not include technology transfers). It is clear that the coefficient on the technology transfer JVs is much larger than other JVs, although both are significant at conventional levels. In the final column, the wage bill is used as a measure of labour services instead of employment to reflect differential skill levels of the workforce. This is a very conservative specification in the sense that including the wage bill may condition out some of the effects; for example, if very profitable firms share some of their 'rents' from technology with workers, then the wage bill can rise even if human capital remains constant. As expected, this variable has a coefficient that is positive and highly significant. The coefficient on JVs is now much smaller suggesting that the ownership dummies partially reflect higher human capital in the workforce. Additional human capital characteristics of the workers such as average education, days off for training, and tenure were also included. These were insignificant when added to column (6) and did not materially change the coefficients on the JVs. In fact, although technology transfer JVs remains positive and significant, other forms of JVs are insignificant.

A major problem with estimates of Table 5.4 is that the ownership dummies are endogenous. Consequently the IV results in Table 5.5 start with a specification that pools all JVs together. The OLS coefficient in column (1) is 0.27. The first instrument is FDI in the province at the time of the firm's birth as this will reflect the policies of that province towards foreign firms. Since FDI will be larger in larger provinces, it is normalized by total investment in the province and present the first stage in column (2). The instrument is highly informative with an F-statistic of over 31. Note total provincial investment is included in all columns to make sure the equation is only identifying from the interaction between firm birth and policy variables. The second stage is presented in column (3) and shows that the coefficient on JV is positive and significant with a magnitude that is larger than the OLS coefficient.

Since it is clear from Table 5.4 that technology transfer agreements are more strongly associated with productivity than other JVs, the specifications in the first three columns in columns (4)–(6) are repeated but use JVTT instead of JV. The OLS coefficient for JVTT is 0.737 and this rises in the IV specification of column (3) to 2.62. The pattern persists across the table—the IV results are above the OLS results.

These estimates were subjected to a range of robustness tests. First, normalizing on provincial employment instead of investment made little difference: in the specification of column (3) the IV estimate on JV was 0.870 with a standard error of 0.287. Second, conditioning on the wage bill again brings down all coefficients, but only to a minor degree. The qualitative results on the large causal effects of technology transfer agreements on productivity remains robust.

165

Table 5.5 Production functions (instrumental variables)

Dependent variable:	(1) Ln(Y)	(2) JV	(3) Ln(Y)	(4) Ln(Y)	(5) JVTT	(6) Ln(Y)
		1st Stage	2nd Stage	1st Stage	2nd Stage	1st Stage
Method	OLS	OLS	IV	OLS	IV	OLS
JV (joint venture)	0.228*** (0.066)		0.812*** (0.290)			
JVTT (JV with technology transfer agreement)				0.737*** (0.194)		2.620** (1.053)
ln(FDI) in province in year of birth		0.026** (0.011)			0.011** (0.004)	
Dummy: FDI = 0 in province in year of birth		-0.275*** (0.058)			-0.065*** (0.024)	
ln(labour)	0.606*** (0.028)	0.020 (0.015)	0.603*** (0.030)	0.606*** (0.028)	0.005 (0.008)	0.605*** (0.032)
ln(capital)	0.272*** (0.018)	0.024** (0.011)	0.257*** (0.021)	0.276*** (0.019)	0.003 (0.005)	0.270*** (0.022)
% college educated	0.270*** (0.033)	0.039** (0.017)	0.242*** (0.033)	0.272*** (0.032)	0.009 (0.010)	0.251*** (0.035)
F-statistic of excluded IV		31.2			8.08	
Firms	1,155	1,155	1,155	1,155	1,155	1,155
Observations	4,204	4,204	4,204	4,204	4,204	4,204
R-squared	0.743	0.168	0.726	0.745	0.065	0.711

Notes: * significant at 10%; ** significant at 5%; *** significant at 1%. Estimation by OLS in all columns with standard errors clustered by firm in parentheses below coefficients. FDI is ln(investment in province at firm's year or birth/total investment in province). All columns include ln(investment in province in province at firm's year or birth), firm age, a full set of three-digit industry dummies (187), a multi-plant dummy, year dummies, year of entering sample dummies, and province dummies. % college educated is the proportion of managers with a college degree.

Third, provinces' export (and import) intensity at time of firm start-up were used as another proxy for policy at birth. These lead to qualitatively similar results to those reported in Table 5.5. For example, using the specification of column (3) and exports over investment at the time of set-up as the instrument the coefficient on JV was 1.156 with a standard error of 0.413. The F-statistic in the first stage of the excluded instruments was 17.6, so these have less power than the FDI instruments.

Next, the mechanism through which technology transfer agreements raised TFP in Chinese firms was examined. From the survey there is a wide range of indicators of innovation, so the question was whether conditioning on these indicators reduces the coefficient on JV technology transfer agreements. These indicators included the number of patents, R&D expenditure, the use of information and communication technologies, the use of a number of brands, the use of trademarks, and the introduction of new products. The broad answer was 'no'. Although many of the innovation indicators were positively and significantly associated with productivity, the coefficient on JVTT was broadly unchanged. For example, replicating the specification of Table 5.4 column (5) on the 2,330 observations where there are data on ICT leads to a coefficient (standard error) of 0.803(0.184) on JVTT. The coefficient on the ln (ICT expenditure) variable is 0.039 with a standard error of 0.013. But the coefficient (standard error) on JVTT falls to 0.798(0.185)—basically unchanged. The technology transfer mechanism is not well proxied by conventional observable measures of technology or innovation. One possibility is that it reflects the transfer of managerial know-how, that is valuable but hard to measure (see Bloom and Van Reenen 2007). Another possibility is that all of these conventional measures of technology are rather poor indicators of innovation in a Chinese context where the market is still underdeveloped. The implication is that JVs that included a transfer of technology imitated the existing technology, which is consistent with the 'catch-up' mechanism where the recipient firm/country does not expend further resources but is more productive by producing with the foreign partner's know-how.

5.5 Economic Growth Implications

Capital accumulation accounted for 3.2 percentage points of the 7.3 per cent growth in output per worker from 1979–2004 with TFP accounting for 3.6 percentage points (Bosworth and Collins 2008). From 1993–2004 since the take-off of the 'open-door' policy, capital accumulation has accounted for 4.2 percentage points of the higher 8.5 per cent growth in China, and interestingly outweighs the contribution of TFP (3.9 percentage points). Both estimates suggest that capital accumulation has contributed around half of China's economic growth, which is in line with other estimates that find that most of China's growth is accounted for mostly by capital accumulation rather than TFP growth. For example, see Zheng, Bigsten, and Hu (2009) who find that TFP growth falls to 3 per cent after the mid-1990s, while Young (2003) argues that on official figures it is 3 per cent but would adjust it downwards to 1.4 per cent from 1978–98.

Working on the premise that capital accumulation has accounted for about half of China's real GDP growth of 9.6 per cent per annum since 1979, the contributions of JVs of 9 per cent and FDI as a whole accounting for 15 per cent of investment translate into between 0.42 to 0.71 percentage point additions to growth. In other words, had China not attracted FDI, China would have grown slower by up to three-quarters of a per cent, bringing the average growth rate down to 8.9–9.2 per cent. Adding in the productivity boost of JVs, JVs are 23 per cent more productive as compared with other firms and JVs with technology transfer agreements hold a 73 per cent productivity advantage (from the OLS estimates). JVs are 15 per cent of all firms in the 2000s, so China's GDP has been increased by between 3.45 per cent and 10.95 per cent, respectively. Translating this into growth terms (and assuming a cumulative process starting in 1979 for the increase in GDP by 2009) means that average growth would have been lower by 0.43 per cent per annum by 2009 if there had not been JVs.

Putting all this together, had China not attracted FDI and JVs in particular with their potential to allow for 'catching up' via technology transfers and other indirect avenues of learning, then China's annual GDP growth could have been between one-half to over a percentage point lower (that is, as low as 8.5 per cent) over the past thirty years. As JVs were more important as a share of investment during the 1990s, accounting for around one-quarter of total investment, this is a conservative estimate. The contribution of joint ventures is therefore sizeable, as one percentage point in compound growth terms translates into large differences in income levels, as countries like India which has grown at 7–8 per cent instead of China's 9–10 per cent over the past few decades can attest.

Chinese–foreign joint ventures have increased productivity in China. The Chinese government, like many other countries, has had an explicit policy to boost the amount of such international joint ventures (and technology transfer agreements in particular) to boost growth. Despite this, there are few assessments of the impact of joint ventures on productivity.

This chapter has tackled this lacuna by using a new survey of ownership and joint ventures in China and matched this to administrative data. It sought to identify the causal impact of JVs by using policy variables at the time of firm start-up in the province where the firms were born. OLS and IV estimates of the impact of joint ventures suggest a large effect on firm productivity, especially for those that have explicit technology transfer agreements.

China's 'catching up' is facilitated by JVs and points the way for other developing countries. The evidence presented suggests that JVs and technology transfer agreements in particular can contribute to the faster growth of developing countries and thus provide some direct evidence that there is the potential for 'catching up' as envisioned in economic growth models.

5.6 Innovation and Patents

Technology transfers could also induce more domestic innovation, a key part of 'catch-up' growth. Innovation leading to technological progress is thought to be crucial to the long-run growth potential of an economy. Difficult to measure, economists look at patents, or formally captured innovation, as one gauge. With China's underdeveloped legal system, the effectiveness of patents in generating technological progress and therefore growth is also an open question.

Indeed, patent laws establish a system of intellectual property rights (IPRs) that secure returns on an innovation and provide protection against expropriation which in turn should increase the propensity to innovate. The lack of strong productivity gains in China throughout its otherwise remarkable period of growth during the post-1979 reform period underscores the importance of assessing the determinants of innovation in its economy (Borensztein and Ostry 1996).

China's first patent law was passed in the same year as urban reforms began; 1984. With accession to the World Trade Organisation (WTO) in 2001, China adopted the associated trade-related aspects of intellectual property rights (TRIPs) agreement and has harmonized its IPR system with international standards. However, ineffective enforcement of IPRs has been an issue. Despite the imperfect legal system, patents have nevertheless increased rapidly in China in the 2000s (see, for example, Hu and Jefferson 2009).

This section examines the effectiveness of the patent law system in China. An assessment of the effectiveness of patent laws in producing innovation should also consider the determinants of patents. In other words, technology-oriented policies particularly in developing countries such as China, are likely to affect the success of patents under any system. Further, given the size and diversity of China's provinces in terms of economic development and the importance of provincial authorities in forming industrial policies, regional differences are also explored. This section develops a patent production function for China which is similar to the ideas function in the endogenous growth literature (Romer 1986). An innovation function in China would include the inputs into innovation (researchers) and other factors which could increase the propensity to innovate, such as through FDI, under its IPR system.

With its incomplete legal system characterized by weak enforcement, the effectiveness of patent laws in China is an interesting question, particularly as the number of patents has grown steadily over the past decade. As China emerges as a significant economy among the largest in the world, the scope for comparing the drivers of its innovation with OECD countries will also be of interest. With its successful record of attracting FDI, the contribution of foreign capital to innovation would be important to determine, particularly for other transition and developing economies.

The questions raised include whether China's patent laws are effective in producing innovation, and explore the contextual factors that generate innovation within such a system, like R&D researchers and FDI. The section examines patent success rates across provinces at different levels of development; asks whether FDI matters, following the focus of developing and transition economies in seeking foreign capital and technology transfers to help them to achieve technological progress; determines whether China's R&D spending has generated innovation captured in patents, akin to the OECD focus on increasing expenditure on research and development to foster productivity; and looks at whether increasing research personnel will result in technological advancement, along the lines of the studies of the US where innovation was found not to be clearly linked to the number of researchers.

China's patent law was enacted in 1984 and promulgated in 1985. In 1992, it was revised to extend the length of patent protection from fifteen to twenty years for invention patents, and from five to ten years for process patents; for example, model and design patents. In 2000, it was further revised in anticipation of accession to the World Trade Organisation which occurred in 2001. In 2001, China adopted TRIPs as part of its WTO obligations whereby its IPR standards were harmonized with international rules. Since the passage of the patent laws, there have been dozens of regulations and guidelines adopted to promote innovation. The patent law amendments also included conditions on the granting of compulsory licences and prohibiting the unauthorized importation of products which infringe on the patents.

China's copyright law was promulgated in 1991 and has been amended several times since and limits protection to works that do not harm China's 'public interest'. Enforcement of copyright laws was further strengthened to step up criminal prosecutions in 2004. Finally, China's trademark law was promulgated in 1983 with significant revisions in 1993, which permit registration and provide protection for service marks and also criminal sanctions for trademark infringement.

Patent laws are promulgated through an IPR system that centres on a set of regulators which examine patent applications. Thus, as elsewhere, innovation is determined by the formal laws that establish IPRs as well as the regulatory system that affects those laws. Imperfection in the legal and regulatory system can refer to both the formal written laws or the regulations and regulators entrusted with their enforcement. The IPR system in China is centralized around the State Intellectual Property Office (SIPO) founded in 1980 as the Patent Office and renamed in 1998, the Trademark Office started in 1982 and the 1985 agency, National Copyright Administration. The Ministry of Commerce has a department that deals with trade-related intellectual property issues and the Chinese People's Court system addresses enforcement in this national IPR system.

China's set of patent laws appears largely to meet the standards of international law, as do the processes of its IPR system. However, the adoption of laws does not necessarily imply effective enforcement, which will come under increasing scrutiny with the implementation of TRIPs. TRIPs should strengthen the IPR regime in China, particularly in terms of its enforcement provisions within the WTO. Approximately 10 per cent of cases brought before the Dispute Settlement

Mechanism of the WTO relate to the TRIPs provisions, and China in 2009 lost an action to the United States over the imperfect implementation of its IPR system.

Thus, for China, TRIPs raises concerns about the development of its IPR system. It challenges China to adhere to strict standards that will place less emphasis on imitation and more on innovation by its own firms. Understanding what drives innovation under these laws will thus be important; for example, analysing whether spending on researchers is more notable than FDI policy.

When considering the effectiveness of patent laws, it is not only the *de jure* law and the *de facto* enforcement that is of interest, but also the contextual factors which influence the propensity to innovate. These would include industrial policies, such as China's creation of Special Economic Zones (SEZs) geared to attracting FDI, as well as domestic factors, such as R&D spending and focus on research personnel.

Enforcement certainly matters, and the poor enforcement of laws in China is well known. However, China has managed growth with weak institutional bases, namely, the lack of well-defined property rights and an incomplete legal system with which to enforce rights, such as those granted by patents. Nevertheless, China has focused a great deal of effort in developing industrial policies to utilize the technology embodied in FDI and increasingly spend on R&D and accumulating researchers to foster innovation. Thus, the conclusions surrounding the economic impact of the patent laws are likely to be heavily linked to the determinants of patent production in China. An investigation of patent laws and innovation would need to encompass both the impact of the laws and the factors which influence their effectiveness.

Furthermore, the vast disparities in the levels of development among China's provinces and the autonomy that they have in terms of law and policy suggest that any study must also differentiate between provinces. The early opening of some coastal provinces is associated with faster growth, more FDI, and more innovation. However, the policy aimed at developing the interior in the past decade coincides with the focus on technological progress such that SEZs that are focused on high technology (the High Technology Development Zones or HTDZs which are located throughout China). Assessing patent laws in China must therefore further consider the contexts of the provinces and regions.

5.7 Patents, Foreign Investment, and Growth

Technological innovation, such as those captured in formal intellectual property rights, holds significant implications for economic growth. As innovation generates technological advancement, it is the crucial driver of long-run economic growth.

Another major area surrounds the potential for FDI to bring with it advanced technologies to developing countries. The relationship between foreign direct investment and economic growth is an enduring question in development, and relates to the nature of technology transmission and possible positive spillover effects from multinational equity investments (Rodríguez-Clare 1996). FDI is thought to allow developing countries to 'catch up' in the growth process by closing the technology gap through imitation and adoption of established technologies. The evidence, though, is limited (Rodrik 1999). The lack of convergence of the growth of rich and poor countries suggests that the process of capital and technology flows still needs to be understood better (Yueh 2007).

There are a number of studies which have examined possible spillover effects of inward FDI on host countries (see Bloomström and Kokko 1998 for a survey). Of the potential spillover effects from establishing foreign direct investment, there is only limited empirical evidence as to whether FDI improves the technological capability and productivity of local firms particularly in countries in the early stages of development (Javorcik 2004). Establishing and understanding this link would perhaps shed light on the key for developing countries to achieve longer-term growth. In particular, the means through which technology is transferred between multinational corporations and the host countries is not well understood. The possible avenues include explicit transfers, such as contracts, and implicit transfers, including 'learning by doing', and transmission of skills from foreign skilled labour to domestic employees working in the same factory.

There is also a large volume of literature on innovation production functions and increasing returns which characterize endogenous growth models (see Romer 1986). Empirically, these studies attempt, among other things, to discover if increasing the number of researchers increases innovation at a progressive rate (since an invention can generate a multitude of other innovations, so there is a 'standing on shoulders' effect), or if more researchers merely duplicate research. For the United States, Jones (1995) finds the evidence of the latter. As China attempts to increase innovation through spending more on R&D, this relationship is unknown but also crucial to discover.

Despite the relatively well-defined IPR system, the attractiveness of China to FDI and the evidence of its impressive technological upgrading in manufactured goods over the past two decades, there are few empirical studies related to innovation in China. A main reason is due to data limitations, although there are studies emerging at the firm level (see Hu, Jefferson, and Qian 2005). Also, a positive and significant effect of FDI on the number of patent applications has been found. Using data from 1995 to 2000, provinces with more FDI are found to have more patent applications (Cheung and Lin 2004). The difficulty with using patent applications filed rather than granted rests with filing as not being necessarily consistent with innovation. This section examines patents that have been granted, so the criteria for patents that usually include original and non-obvious innovation are more likely to have been met. A province which received substantial FDI could generate incentives to file patents, but does not necessarily capture innovation seen more readily through the amount of patents that are granted than by the number of applications. This section will focus on patents that have been granted and a rich set of determinants in a model of patent production generated from China's patent laws. The estimation strategy will also utilize count models typically used for patents rather than OLS with its biases.

5.8 Effectiveness of Patent Laws

China has an imperfect patent law system due to problems with enforcement, which is not uncommon among developing countries. However, it was established fairly early in the reform process and provides for a formal system of IPRs when many other rights in China tend to be informal, including private use of communal property such as the Household Responsibility System. It also provides a measure of formal innovation so that a patent production function can be formulated for the economy. Moreover, China has had a successful history of attracting FDI on its own terms and is at a low level of economic development, which makes FDI more likely to embody advanced technology that could be transferred to the country's benefit. In addition, the government's explicit policy of targeting technology and creating science and industrial parks gives further evidence on which to judge the determinants of innovation similar to those which are found in more developed economies, notably the impact of R&D spending and researchers. The combination of law and policy within a national framework that also exhibits regional variation allows for an exploration of both the formal and contextual factors that determine innovation.

In terms of regional variation, China's development path has been skewed toward the coastal provinces. This can be seen in the regions that have been permitted to experiment with market-oriented reforms, which were primarily urban areas in the eastern region that have contributed to rapid GDP growth. China's 'urban bias' and regional disparities are well documented. The resultant variation in regional and provincial growth is thus a product of government policy which has focused on the urban areas and coastal regions.

Its FDI policy follows a similar pattern where the 'open-door' policy only applied to Guangdong and Fujian initially in 1978, and the latter areas, still primarily coastal and for the most part eastern, did not receive foreign investment until the mid-1980s, with the rest of the country opening up in the early 1990s after Deng's southern tour. Further, China's marketization path is such that particularly with respect to FDI, the location of foreign investment and the clustering of economic activity would be highly conducive to agglomeration or network externalities, well-known in the new trade theory literature (Fujita, Krugman, and Venables 1999). In particular, since the mid-1990s, the HTDZs created 'science parks' or 'industrial parks' which aggregate economic activity in specified areas, such as the Haidian area of Beijing and the Pudong area of Shanghai. The HTDZs are geared towards attracting more sophisticated technologies to China, and given the rise in FDI and the increase in the technological components of Chinese manufactured exports in recent years, the initial evidence looks supportive (Lall and Albaladejo 2004).

The data used in this chapter are drawn from the *China Statistical Yearbooks* and the *China Statistical Yearbooks of Science and Technology* for several years. The data cover the years from 1991–2003 and twenty-nine provinces (not including Tibet due to lack of data), and all figures are in 1990 prices.

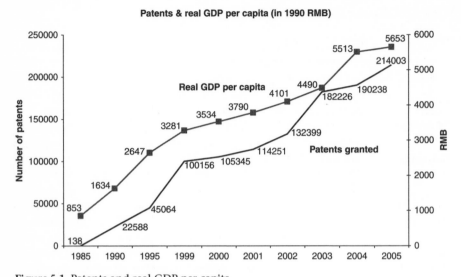

Figure 5.1 Patents and real GDP per capita

Source: China Statistical Yearbook, China Statistical Yearbook of Science and Technology.

There is rapid growth in patents during the reform period, from just 138 patents granted in 1985 with the passage of the patent law, to around 20,000 two decades later. Figure 5.1 plots GDP per capita and patents awarded in China, and it is evident that patents have grown exponentially in the past few years alongside national incomes.

Table 5.6 gives the number of patents filed and granted along with the GDP per capita data for each province. There is evidence of wide variation among provinces both in terms of GDP and patents. Looking at patents granted per capita, the variation remains, so it is not a result of population differences. For instance, Shanghai is nearly 50 per cent richer than Beijing per capita, but Beijing has twice as many patents granted per capita. Comparing two of the poorest provinces, Anhui and Ningxia, with per capita incomes that are virtually identical, Ningxia has twice as many patents per capita. Although patents have grown alongside national income, provincial variations cannot be explained simply by reference to per capita GDP. Again, in terms of total patents granted in 2002, Guangdong holds 111,874. It is also the richest province with a GDP per capita of 5,876 RMB. By contrast, Qinghai, one of the poorest interior provinces of China, has a per capita GDP of 3,208 RMB and the fewest number of patents, just 1,067. However, the rates of patent application to granted patents did not differ a great deal across provinces, suggesting that the reasons for the smaller number of patents are not necessarily the result of fewer successful applications.

Table 5.7 gives the patent grant rate for selected years and the average success rate. The average rate of patents granted to patents filed is similar across provinces despite vastly different amounts of patents granted and levels of economic development. The lowest success rate is 52 per cent in Hubei while the highest is

Table 5.6 Patents and GDP per capita by province, 2002

Province	Patents filed	Patents granted	Success rate (granted/filed)	GDP per capita (RMB)	Patents granted per capita
Beijing	111,065	60,826	54.77%	14,205	0.004398
Tianjin	30,758	16,951	55.11%	11,174	0.001688
Hebei	44,434	26,750	60.20%	4,551	0.000399
Shanxi	16,012	9,308	58.13%	3,069	0.000284
Inner Mongolia	11,031	6152	55.77%	3,661	0.000259
Liaoning	80,134	45,965	57.36%	6,484	0.001096
Jilin	27,594	14,672	53.17%	4,161	0.000545
Heilongjiang	39,194	20,986	53.54%	5,085	0.000551
Shanghai	76,986	36,474	47.38%	20,295	0.002260
Jiangsu	84,880	51,960	61.22%	7,185	0.000706
Zhejiang	91,119	56,119	61.59%	8,407	0.001217
Anhui	18,599	11,229	60.37%	2,891	0.000177
Fujian	36,523	22,150	60.65%	6,739	0.000644
Jiangxi	17,645	9,382	53.17%	2,910	0.000224
Shandong	93,836	54,088	57.64%	5,814	0.000598
Henan	39,953	22,367	55.98%	3,214	0.000234
Hubei	37,148	19,221	51.74%	4,154	0.000322
Hunan	49,366	26,336	53.35%	3,278	0.000399
Guangdong	168,363	111,874	66.45%	7,482	0.001437
Guangxi	19,183	10,581	55.16%	2,546	0.000221
Hainan	3,860	2,037	52.77%	4,030	0.000256
Sichuan	62,911	36,918	58.68%	3,586	0.000315
Guizhou	10,038	5,239	52.19%	1,574	0.000138
Yunnan	16,035	10,275	64.08%	2,586	0.000281
Shaanxi	27,775	16,397	59.04%	2,847	0.000637
Gansu	8,612	4,724	54.85%	2,243	0.000903
Qinghai	1,988	1,067	53.67%	3,208	0.000204
Ningxia	3,344	1,879	56.19%	2,898	0.000334
Xinjiang	10,459	5,917	56.57%	4,185	0.000315

Source: China Statistical Yearbook, China Statistical Yearbook for Science and Technology.

Note: GDP per capita is deflated where 1990 is the base year.

Guangdong with 67 per cent. Hubei is not the poorest province, while Guangdong is not the most innovative. Zhejiang is typically viewed as the most driven by private sector activity and its rate of patent success lags behind that of Guangdong. When considering regions, the interior has the highest success rate of patent applications on average (61.04 per cent) followed by the coast (60.51 per cent) and the central region (57.28 per cent) despite incomes in the coastal region being more than double that of the central and interior regions over this period (5,447 RMB as compared with 2,426 RMB and 2,024 RMB, respectively). However, these figures are very close and given the small number of patents in the interior, they most likely reflect insignificant differences in success rates.

Success rate is one measure of the economic effect of IPR rules. Applications are considered nationally and it seems that the patent grant rate is fairly uniform across provinces despite their very different levels of development. Although not conclusive, the substantial differences in patent outcomes must be viewed within the context of underlying economic differences across provinces and not

Table 5.7 Patent grant rate by province, selected years

Province	1995	1998	2001	Average grant rate, 1995–2003
Beijing	63.27%	60.12%	51.31%	57.02%
Tianjin	62.74%	70.17%	59.36%	58.82%
Hebei	58.37%	63.43%	59.45%	63.08%
Shanxi	62.05%	60.19%	71.08%	63.07%
Inner Mongolia	64.14%	66.62%	68.35%	59.29%
Liaoning	61.70%	56.03%	59.20%	58.06%
Jilin	59.32%	53.62%	54.93%	53.62%
Heilongjiang	54.61%	56.29%	50.95%	57.31%
Shanghai	58.47%	68.27%	42.04%	57.50%
Jiangsu	59.17%	64.97%	59.49%	63.39%
Zhejiang	52.72%	63.19%	64.80%	62.87%
Anhui	55.95%	62.87%	62.49%	61.49%
Fujian	47.15%	68.32%	66.30%	63.50%
Jiangxi	50.50%	60.76%	56.19%	55.69%
Shandong	61.87%	54.32%	60.21%	58.28%
Henan	47.99%	57.00%	63.08%	57.78%
Hubei	50.75%	48.12%	50.99%	52.70%
Hunan	57.65%	50.33%	55.94%	54.63%
Guangdong	59.66%	79.47%	66.17%	67.59%
Guangxi	54.02%	64.77%	59.79%	59.49%
Hainan	59.02%	51.07%	77.69%	59.67%
Sichuan	63.37%	58.15%	86.86%	63.81%
Guizhou	48.75%	52.25%	67.58%	56.22%
Yunnan	59.33%	73.24%	75.13%	67.65%
Shaanxi	63.04%	65.53%	58.21%	62.16%
Gansu	47.07%	58.36%	69.75%	59.00%
Qinghai	65.00%	45.26%	62.35%	56.45%
Ningxia	65.68%	53.63%	56.07%	59.45%
Xinjiang	51.23%	47.24%	69.52%	59.00%

Source: China Statistical Yearbook, China Statistical Yearbook for Science and Technology.

only as a result of institutional differences within the patent system. Therefore, the patent production process should be considered within the context of relevant policies and factors that affect innovation, such as R&D spending, as well as the provincial environment including its level of education and extent of openness and market development. FDI is another notable factor and China has enjoyed a rapid rate of growth of inward FDI since the 'open-door' policy geared up in the mid-1980s. China had become not only the leading destination for inward FDI among developing countries, but was one of the top three destinations for global FDI, often ranking just behind the US.

Also, in the early 1990s when FDI began to pour into China primarily through the SEZs, during the early efforts to establish China's export capacity, the divergence between contracted and utilized FDI was significant. As China's technological capabilities in those areas of investment—namely, light industry and low technology products—increased, it was thought to have improved its use of the agreed FDI, and thus the gap between contracted and utilized FDI began to close. A similar pattern may be emerging corresponding to China's initiatives in the mid-1990s geared to attracting more sophisticated technologies through

Economic and Technological Development Zones (ETDZs) and HTDZs. There is again a trend of divergence between the amount of contracted for FDI and the amount that can be used. This interpretation is consistent with the evidence of the increasingly complex technological make-up of China's exports while China's domestic capacity lags somewhat behind.

5.9 Determinants of Innovation

Next, the determinants of patent production will be explored. This section will present a simple model, followed by a discussion of the estimation approach, and then present the empirical results for the nation as a whole, and by region.

The determinants of patents can be thought of as a production function that follows a Poisson process. As seen in Table 5.7, the success rate of patent applications is similar across provinces despite vast differences in the level of development and the stock of innovation. The provincial variation allows for comparisons to be made within a national patent law system.

This patent production function would equate to the ideas/innovation production function in an endogenous growth framework (Jones 1995). This is not an attempt, however, to estimate the contribution of innovation to economic growth, but to determine the parameters of the ideas/innovation production function for China.

To address the over-dispersion problem whereby the standard errors for the Poisson estimator are too small, the Poisson quasi maximum likelihood (PQML) estimator will be used. A negative binomial model will also be reported, which tests for the existence of the over-dispersion issue. Thus, the negative binomial models are provided in the national estimates, although the more robust PQML estimates are interpreted in the chapter.

To estimate the patent production function, the main production input of R&D personnel is first entered in logs. Other factors that could affect the propensity to innovate, such as FDI, GDP per capita, degree of openness of the province, human capital, average firm size of above-size firms (*guimo yishang*) measured in terms of sales, the extent of private-sector development measured as the proportion of non-state-sector firms' contribution to output in a province as well as the share of manufacturing output in a province, are also included. Year and province dummy variables are also included.

From the *Science and Technology Yearbooks*, measures of the number of researchers can be obtained. R&D personnel, resulting from spending on R&D, can be a measure of a region's R&D stock. R&D expenditure has been shown to increase innovation in OECD economies (Bloom, Griffith, and Van Reenen 2002). The number of R&D personnel would be a relevant determinant of innovation since individuals innovate and greater numbers of researchers could lead to more patents. However, the relationship would depend on whether having more innovators increases or duplicates existing research (Jones 1995). Labour is, therefore, an ambiguous input in such functions and must be empirically determined.

Once the innovation input of R&D is controlled for, provincial characteristics may influence the productivity of the innovation process, either via knowledge spillover or an incentive effect. These variables are obtained from the *China Statistical Yearbooks*. FDI is measured as the annual flow reported by the provinces. FDI is often associated with the transfer of more advanced foreign technologies to a developing country such as China, although the evidence of its effects can also be ambiguous as to whether it contributes to innovation. FDI can either increase know-how or introduce competition that decimates domestic competition. The mixed evidence surrounding the effects of FDI as well as the criticism that Chinese technological upgrading in exports is not a result of innovation but of the significant contribution of FIEs to producing exports.

Other provincial characteristics can also increase the propensity to innovate if not the amount of resources that end up in the patent production process. Per capita GDP reflects the level of economic development of the province. The variable for per capita GDP is deflated by the consumer prices index (CPI) so that the reported figures are in 1990 prices. The degree of openness is also included because a province that exports may be more affected by pro-competitive forces derived from international trade which can influence the propensity to innovate due to greater competition. Human capital in the usual form of educational enrolment of school-aged children is also entered as a measure of the level of education in the province, which can also increase the inclination to innovate by providing a skills base. Key firm characteristics such as the average firm size, the share of private sector, and share of manufacturing output in provincial output are all included as they can influence the propensity to innovate. Again, the relationship is determined empirically since there is a long-standing debate as to whether larger or smaller firms innovate. Average firm size is measured by sales of industrial firms in a province. After 1998, the category used is the newly created category of above-size firms (*guimo yishang*), which refers to firms that report annual sales of 5 million RMB or more. Private-sector development can suggest more competition that affects the propensity to innovate, while the state-owned sector could have more resources and be a direct instrument of the state in promoting innovation. Finally, manufacturing firms are the ones that often undertake innovation, so how industrialized a province is would also influence the tendency to innovate. Year dummies are entered to account for any overall trends in productivity during the period, 1991–2003, as well as a provincial dummy to control for other unobserved fixed effects. This chosen period coincides with the 'open-door' policy taking off in China and accession to the WTO. This is also the period of significant economic growth in China deriving from reform of the state sector and increased opening to the global economy, which makes it an appropriate period of study. Finally, as FDI can be realized with delay, a lagged FDI variable is included. For instance, time is required between signing a contract to take over a factory in China and making it operational.

First, there is evidence of over-dispersion in the data, seen in the significance of the alpha parameter reported in Table 5.8. Therefore, the PQML estimator will be relied upon. The results show that more R&D personnel significantly increase

Table 5.8 Determinants of patents in China (z-statistics in parentheses)

	Poisson (PQML) model (1)	Poisson (PQML) model with lagged FDI (2)	Negative binomial model (3)	Negative binomial model with lagged FDI (4)
R&D personnel	0.0814	0.0690	0.4511	0.4588
	(2.12)***	(2.01)***	(12.03)***	(11.56)***
Foreign direct investment	−0.0886	—	0.1970	—
	(−1.30)		(7.08)***	
Foreign direct investment (one year lag)	—	−0.1742	—	0.2141
		(−2.43)***		(5.81)***
Per capita GDP	1.6979	1.7325	0.0873	0.1126
	(5.91)***	(5.70)***	(0.84)	(1.04)
Openness	0.0152	0.0158	0.0087	0.0079
	(1.29)	(1.39)	(2.89)***	(2.47)***
Educational enrolment	0.0183	0.0261	0.0578	0.0614
	(0.85)	(1.28)	(2.09)***	(2.16)***
Average firm size	−0.0139	−0.0140	0.0097	0.0140
	(−1.25)	(−1.15)	(0.60)	(0.83)
Share of non-state sector in provincial output	−0.4576	−0.03219	0.4401	0.3650
	(−0.74)	(−0.55)	(1.47)	(1.15)
Share of industry in provincial output	0.0107	−0.0290	−0.1334	−0.1293
	(0.07)	(−0.21)	(−1.05)	(−0.95)
Over-dispersion parameter	—	—	0.2190	0.2294
			(10.57)***	(10.37)***
Wald $X^2(8)$	361.69***	249.76***		
LR X^2 (10)			423.39***	386.40***
Pseudo R^2			0.1133	0.1075
N	212	203	212	203

Source: China Statistical Yearbook on Science and Technology, China Statistical Yearbook.

Notes: (1) Dependent variable: patents granted. Mean is 2121.

(2) Independent variables are: log of number of R&D personnel, log of foreign direct investment and with a one year lag, log of per capita GDP, export-to-GDP ratio is the measure of openness, educational enrolment rate of school-aged children, average firm size including above-size firms (guimo yishang) measured by sales from 1998 onward, share of non-state (for example, not state-owned or controlled) firms in the output of the province as well as the share of industry in provincial output. Dummy variables for province and year are also included to control for time-invariant and time-varying effects.

(3) The over-dispersion parameter is a t-test of the alpha variable specified in the negative binomial model.

(4) Coefficients are followed by z-statistics, where*** denotes statistical significance at the 1% level, ** at the 5% level, and * at the 10% level.

the number of patents. This is evident in column (1) and also in (2) where FDI is entered with a lag. The fixed effect negative binomial model produces the same significant result for R&D personnel. As such, the innovation input of more provincial R&D expenditure on research personnel is associated with more patents granted in a province. The marginal effect of R&D is a positive 8 per cent improvement in the innovation process, holding other factors constant.

Among the other provincial characteristics that might increase the propensity to innovate, only per capita GDP is significantly positive. Richer provinces are associated with a greater propensity to innovate, which is consistent with higher income creating incentives for technological improvements to produce more sophisticated output to suit the more developed market.

Unlike the effect of R&D spending, which is a fairly straightforward input into producing patents, the estimate for FDI likely reflects the more complex relationship of foreign investment to patents. FDI can increase the propensity to innovate through knowledge spillovers, but the impact of FDI may also be of shielding proprietary knowledge or making it available through licensing so that domestic firms either do not learn or simply imitate the more advanced technology, and thus do not patent. Foreign firms can also dominate the sector or market so that the competition they introduce relegates domestic firms to less innovative functions in the production/supply chain. It is not possible to disaggregate these effects, which attests to the conflicting evidence surrounding FDI spillovers. FDI is not a significant determinant when entered contemporaneously, but is a negative factor when entered with a lag. It appears that when foreign investment is established rather than just contracted, there is an effect. Therefore, FDI may produce exports with increasing amounts of technological improvement but does not increase the propensity to innovate in the province and instead reduces the tendency for Chinese firms to undertake innovation.

Turning to other control variables, the average size of above-size firms (*guimo yishang*), the ownership composition of the province in terms of share of private sector, and the share of manufacturing output in a province are not significant. At the firm level, these are likely to be significant factors but at a more aggregated level, these provincial traits are not significantly associated with a greater propensity to innovate.

Given the earlier opening of China's coastal provinces and their accounting for the bulk of GDP, there could be regional differences that are obscured by the aggregate estimations. This table divides the provinces into the coastal region which includes earliest opened provinces such as Guangdong, the central region with provinces such as Hunan, and the interior region that includes some of the least development provinces like Qinghai which does not have a High Technology Development Zone.

Not surprisingly, there are significant differences in the mean number of patents awarded in the regions. For the coast, the average number of patents during this period was 3,492, while it was 1,117 for the central region, and 841 for the interior. However, the average success rate of patent applications is similar across regions. Indeed, the interior has a marginally higher rate of patents granted than the coast, which is slightly higher than the central region. Thus, there is no correlation between the number of patents held and the grant rate. The regions exhibit rather different determinants of innovation.

Table 5.9 presents the estimates which confirm that for every region, R&D is a significant determinant of innovation but differently so in each. The findings for the coastal region are that the number of R&D personnel determines innovation with a similar magnitude (5–7 per cent marginal effect) as the national estimates. Similar to the national estimates, FDI has a significantly negative effect on the propensity to innovate, as does FDI entered with a lag. This suggests that FDI in the coastal region, which receives the bulk of the investment, does not increase the innovation tendency of the province. It has the opposite effect such that innovation in China's coast increases when there is

R&D personnel undertaking innovation, rather than expectations around spill-overs from foreign investment.

Per capita GDP continues to promote innovation, and this effect is robustly evident across all regions. Unlike the national estimates, average firm size reduces the propensity to innovate, suggesting that smaller firms are more likely to innovate rather than the larger ones in the more developed coastal region. This is after controlling for private sector and manufacturing sector develop-ment, as well as openness and education, which are not significant factors.

The evidence for the central region is notably different from the coast. For these provinces, the number of researchers reduces innovation, while larger firms and the state-owned sector increase the propensity to innovate. Per capital GDP continues to show that innovation tendencies follow from greater economic development. FDI, openness and educational environment do not matter. The centre of China is poorer than the coast and it is firm characteristics that matter instead of spending on researchers. There is thus some evidence that there is 'crowding out' in that increasing the number of researchers does not increase patents produced, but rather results in duplicative effort. Larger average size of above-size firms also increases innovation, suggesting that larger firms have the resources and capacity to innovate. The importance of the state-owned sector which is dominated by larger firms renders further evidence. These findings together suggest that it is the state-owned or state-controlled enterprises (SOEs) that are likely to be the larger firms that innovate. The central region has retained a number of large SOEs that have the resources to innovate in a range of industries in which they still dominate, including telecommunications, while smaller, pri-vate firms that produce for export could be marketing goods that are lower in the technology spectrum and competing on price rather than innovative quality.

Finally, the evidence for the interior provinces is again dissimilar to the coastal and central provinces. There are some similarities in that as with the national picture and the coast, R&D personnel and GDP increase the number of patents for these provinces. Larger firms are associated with a greater propensity to innovate, probably due to their having more resources. As many of the western provinces are among the poorest and underdeveloped in China, those with a greater share of industry in their economy are also more likely to innovate. This increased propensity can be traced to most innovation being conducted by manufacturing firms.

The regional differences are notable, but R&D personnel is consistently a significant factor. Also robust is per capita GDP which shows across all provinces that more developed markets have a greater tendency to innovate. This is consistent with evidence that rich countries around the world are the most innovative; for example, the United States. FDI also has the same negative effect in the coast as with the national estimates, although with no effect in the poorer central and interior parts of China which receive less FDI and may also be less able to absorb the more advanced technology associated with it. Regional differ-ences therefore abound and show that the determinants of patents are associ-ated with varying factors across China.

Table 5.9 Determinants of patents in China by region: Poisson (PQML) model (z-statistics in parentheses)

	Coast (1)	Coast (2)	Central (3)	Central (4)	Interior (5)	Interior (6)
R&D personnel	0.0745 (2.69)***	0.0535 (1.99)**	-0.2307 (-2.95)***	-0.1997 (-1.89)*	0.1859 (2.19)**	0.1593 (2.21)**
Foreign direct investment	0.01739 (-1.88)*	—	0.0725 (1.33)	—	0.0314 (0.56)	—
Foreign direct investment (one year lag)	—	-0.2460 (-2.52)**	—	-0.0066 (-0.14)	—	-0.0778 (-1.49)
Per capita GDP	2.2864 (6.66)***	2.3733 (6.38)***	1.0123 (4.62)***	1.0367 (4.24)***	0.5142 (2.23)**	0.4248 (1.92)*
Openness	0.0048 (0.36)	0.0053 (0.43)	-0.0523 (-1.51)	-0.0569 (-1.41)	0.0133 (0.77)	0.0109 (0.56)
Educational enrolment	0.0250 (0.97)	0.0336 (1.65)*	0.0328 (1.48)	0.0380 (1.68)*	0.0314 (1.19)	0.0319 (1.12)
Average firm size	-0.0273 (-2.48)**	-0.0314 (-3.06)***	0.1354 (2.90)***	0.01219 (2.47)***	0.2590 (3.92)***	0.2329 (5.06)***
Share of non-state sector in provincial output	-0.6063 (-0.97)	-0.05093 (-0.94)	-0.6944 (-2.61)***	-0.6076 (-1.92)*	-1.3957 (-1.16)	-0.8622 (-0.82)
Share of industry in provincial output	0.1650 (0.88)	0.01403 (0.90)	-0.2410 (-1.75)*	-0.2355 (-1.53)	1.1552 (1.86)*	0.8021 (1.93)*
Wald X^2(8)	537.65***	917.37***	7679.66***	6048.80***	5241.29***	4649.07***
N	86	84	55	52	71	67

Source: China Statistical Yearbook on Science and Technology; China Statistical Yearbook.
Notes: (1) Dependent variable: patents granted. For the coastal region, the mean is 3,492. For the central region, the mean is 1,173. For the interior region, the mean is 841.
(2) Independent variables are: log of number of R&D personnel, log of foreign direct investment and with a one year lag, log of per capita GDP, export-to-GDP ratio is the measure of openness, educational enrolment rate of school-aged children, average firm size including above-size firms (guimo yishang) measured by sales from 1998 onward, share of non-state (for example, not state-owned or controlled) firms in the output of the province as well as the share of industry in provincial output. Dummy variables for province and year are also included to control for time-invariant and time-varying effects.
(3) Coastal region includes Beijing, Tianjin, Hebei, Liaoning, Heilongjiang, Shanghai, Jiangsu, Zhejiang, Fujian, Shandong, Guangdong, Guangxi, and Hainan. Central region includes Shanxi, Inner Mongolia, Jilin, Anhui, Jiangxi, Henan, Hubei, and Hunan. Interior region includes Sichuan, Guizhou, Yunnan, Shaanxi, Gansu, Qinghai, Ningxia, and Xinjiang.
(4) The over-dispersion parameter is a t-test of the alpha variable in the negative binomial model.
(5) *** denotes statistical significance at the 1% level, ** at the 5% level, and * at the 10% level.

5.10 Conclusion

Innovation as captured by patents has been increasing in China. The expectation of the implementation of TRIPs most likely increases this incentive to patent, although the rate of successfully innovating is roughly the same as before WTO accession. Nevertheless, the amount of formally captured innovation in the form of patents is indeed growing in China despite a much-criticized, imperfect legal system. Moreover, in spite of vastly different levels of regional economic development, the patent laws in China have produced a steady rate of growth of patents across the country.

Despite similar grant rates, there remain vast differences among provinces in terms of their levels of innovation. Contextual factors and industrial and R&D policies likely play a role in explaining innovation. Innovation in China is posited to be determined not only by the legal system but also by factors that affect the production of patents, such R&D personnel, and provincial traits that could influence the propensity to innovate.

R&D personnel is indeed found to be a significant determinant of innovation, although the effects vary notably across China's regions. The number of researchers matters in the coast and interior, while increasing R&D stock depresses innovation in the central region, which relies instead on SOEs and larger firms. Per capita income in a province is positively associated with a greater tendency to innovate across all regions, while smaller firms on the coast are more likely to innovate in contrast to larger firms that increase this propensity in the poorer central and interior regions. Interestingly, openness and educational enrolment do not matter, nor does FDI except on the coast where it reduces the propensity of a province to innovate, leaving no evidence of positive spillovers measured in terms of patents.

Therefore, the key drivers of innovation are found to be closely related to China's R&D expenditures on researchers. Regional differences exist, reflecting the complexity of promoting technological advancement across a nation as large as China.

The determinants of innovation are difficult to assess for any country, and the measurement of patents underestimates the level of innovation. China's patent laws have created these formal measures of innovation despite a much criticized IPR system. Moreover, it has a growing stock of patents which has accompanied its economic growth. The very different determinants for the coastal, central, and interior regions of China confirm that an economic analysis of the impact of patent laws on innovation must also consider that the relevant factors will be likely to depend on the context of the region. China's patent laws have produced innovation despite their imperfections and innovation is found to be largely affected by R&D personnel and not by FDI or other policies such as openness to trade. As China contends with TRIPs and its policies are scrutinized by developed and developing countries—the latter coping with adjusting to an increasingly harmonized international IPR regime—there is evidence of the importance of domestic spending on R&D in generating innovation that will ultimately influence long-run economic growth.

6

Informal Growth Determinants: Self-employment and Social Capital

6.1 Introduction

Starting self-employment, including the role played by social capital, is one of the most significant factors in understanding what has propelled China's economic growth. These factors do not fit neatly into economic growth models, but are crucial. For China, it is particularly the case as its transition from central planning was characterized by a 'dual track' path where a non-state track developed to allow for the gradual reform of the less efficient, existing state-owned sector. This, as well as the long-standing importance of social capital or *guanxi* relationships played an important economic role that will be explored in this chapter.

6.2 Social Capital and *Guanxi*

The role of social capital in the economy has attracted widespread attention (for example, Dasgupta and Serageldin 2000). The work spans many areas, including economic growth and development (for instance, Putnam, Leonardi, and Nanetti 1993; Knack and Keefer 1997), inter-firm links (for instance, Fafchamps and Minten 2002), and the labour market (for instance, Granovetter 1995 [1974]; Montgomery 1991; Rebick 2000).

A distinction can be drawn between the operation of social capital through social networks and through social norms. The term 'social capital'—with its connotation of current sacrifice for future gain—is not necessarily appropriate in either case. According to Arrow (2000, pp. 3–5) '...the essence of social networks is that they are built up for reasons other than their economic value to the participants...that much of the reward for social interactions is intrinsic...'. He went on to say, '...this is not to deny that social networks and other social links may also form for economic reasons. One line of reasoning is that the social networks guard against market failure...'.

Similarly, the behaviour that generates such social norms as trust, reciprocity, and cooperation need not be interpreted as the outcome of investment decisions. Nevertheless, the term 'social capital' is often used, implying that social networks or social norms are economically valuable assets.

An important aspect of Chinese society—whether in traditional China (–1949), in the period of central planning (1949–78), or in the period of economic reform (1978–)—is the Chinese variant of social capital known as *guanxi*. The social relationships that constitute *guanxi* are pervasive in both economic and non-economic life. Is social capital important for success in the labour market; that is, does it raise labour incomes? The Chinese urban labour market is in a process of transition from an administered system, in which labour was allocated and wages were set institutionally, to one in which market forces play a role. In principle, *guanxi* can be used in either system. Therefore, is social capital more or less important in the more competitive parts of the labour market?

The economic literature is divided between those who model social capital at the community level (for instance, Knack and Keefer 1997; Narayan and Pritchett 1998; Dasgupta 2000), and those who do so at the individual or household level. The latter approach is adopted here: the effects of social capital acquisition by individuals, whether motivated by social or economic considerations, are examined. The main contributions are twofold: the measures of social capital and its value in the Chinese labour market, and the comparative analysis of its value in different parts of this transitional labour market.

The notion that social institutions can address labour market failure has been investigated in the contexts of imperfect information and transaction costs. Various beneficial effects in the labour market have been attributed to social capital. Among them is better information (Granovetter 1995 [1974]; Waldinger 1996), decreased transaction costs (Abraham and Medoff 1982), increased efficiency (Burt 1992), or improved trust and other normative values (Akerlof 1982). Montgomery (1991) develops an adverse selection model in which a referral system using the contacts of current employees results in higher profits for the firm as well as in higher wages for the employees who have the requisite social contacts to make referrals. Social networks may thus assist job search and promotions and give rise to earnings premiums. Moreover, there is empirical evidence to support the arguments that social capital is valuable. Studies in the United States show the importance of referrals in recruitment (Granovetter 1995 [1974]; Waldinger 1996), and of associational affiliation (Bartlett and Miller 1985), or contacts (Mortensen and Vishwanath 1994), in raising wages.

Social capital and in particular *guanxi*—the relationships that an individual maintains in social networks—have been emphasized in the analysis of Chinese economic transactions (for instance, Bian 1994b; Wank 1995) as well as social life (for instance, Kipnis 1997; Yang 1994; Yan 1996). Oi (1999, p. 132) regards *guanxi* as the 'operational code' for how best to get things done in China. The traditional strength of *guanxi* may stem from the lack of a comprehensive legal structure (McMillan 1997), and its more recent economic importance may be due to the inconsistent enforcement of laws (Yang 1994; Lee 1998), risk reduction in an uncertain socio-politico-economic environment (Walder 1986; Oi 1989, 1999), risk spreading in an economy characterized by shortages (Yan 1996; Kipnis 1997; Chang 1999), information sharing when information is imperfect (Knight and Song 1999), and rent-seeking in imperfectly competitive labour markets (Knight and Song 1995). Meals and gifts are common and effective methods of cultivating *guanxi* (Yan 1996; Kipnis 1997; Oi 1999). The associated gift economy is prevalent in both urban and rural China (Yang 1994).

Turning specifically to the Chinese labour market, Bian (1994a) argues that *guanxi* was a determinant of employment success in the system of allocated jobs. In his case study, over half of the state sector workers who were allocated their first job had used *guanxi* to help obtain the assignment; according to Bian (1994b), half of another sample of state-sector workers who had changed jobs had used a contact to do so; Oi (1989) finds that contacts are important in hiring; Lee (1998) concludes that managers use referrals from current employees to generate goodwill and to reduce the chance of hiring undesirable workers; Knight and Song (1999) argue that the use of contacts improves the information of both recruiting firms and searching workers in an imperfect labour market. *Guanxi* can also raise earnings. Promotions and pay rises can depend on inside information and connections (Bian 1994a; Lee 1998). The only empirical approach to *guanxi* is made by Bian (1994a, 1994b), but it is simply to ask whether an individual used *guanxi* when seeking the above economic advantages. The contribution is to provide a quantitative measure of the size of an individual's social network. It is similar in concept to the use by Glaeser, Laibson, and Sacerdote (2002) of associational memberships as a measure of individual social capital which stands proxy for a person's intrinsic abilities and the size of his or her Rolodex in the United States.

The Chinese Communist Party has complete control of the organs of state in China, and the Party also reaches down to the lower levels of social organization. There is a Party secretary in each village and a Party organization in each work unit. Membership of the Party is not simply a matter of personal choice: recruits are vetted and selected (Bian, Shu, and Logan 2001). Membership involves acceptance of Party discipline but it may also provide information, contacts, and influence. Given the crucial importance of the Communist Party in China's society and its power structure, the access to influence which it provides makes membership the most promising indicator of associational social capital. Party membership might also be regarded as a form of 'political capital' insofar as it accords members power over the levers of economic redistribution (Nee 1989, 1996). However, this is likely to be more important in spheres other than own labour income, such as access to business opportunities. Whatever the terminology, the concern is to measure the effect of an individual's Party membership in the labour market. Whether one or both of the respondent's parents are Communist Party members can also be relevant. Parental membership can be viewed as a form of *guanxi* from which children can benefit at a formative stage of their careers, so increasing their own associational social capital.

Both social network and Communist Party membership will be explored as they capture two main facets of social capital in urban China. Three measures are used—the size of a worker's social network, the worker's membership of the Party, and the Party membership of the worker's parents—as the measures of social capital. Then, returns to *guanxi* in different parts of the labour market are measured. In principle, *guanxi* can be important in either an administered system involving labour allocation and institutional wage determination, or in a market-oriented system. In the former, *guanxi* may provide access to economic rents, and in the latter, *guanxi* may provide information and reduce transaction costs.

Two stratifications of the labour market will be analysed. First, age cohorts are contrasted: the younger age cohorts are more likely to have encountered a labour market, whereas the older cohorts generally continue to work in allocated jobs. Second, returns to social capital are thought to differ by ownership sector, as state enterprises and urban collectives are associated with the administered labour system whereas private firms and the self-employed are more subject to labour market forces.

There are two basic problems in the analysis of the causal effects of social capital on wages: the variable used to measure social capital may be inappropriate or it may be endogenous. Durlauf (2002) takes three well-known studies of the effects of social capital to task on these accounts. He argues that some of the variables that are used to proxy social capital have alternative interpretations and represent other economic mechanisms; and that some of the variables used to instrument social capital in cross-section analysis have direct effects on the outcome. The interpretation must be done carefully.

The dataset is an urban household survey designed by the Institute of Economics, Chinese Academy of Social Sciences in collaboration with foreign scholars and conducted by the National Bureau of Statistics (NBS) in early 2000; it pertains mainly to 1999. The total sample size is 4,000 urban households. The survey covers six provinces and thirteen cities. The provinces are Beijing (chosen to represent the four cities that are independently administered municipal districts), Liaoning (to represent the north-east), Henan (the interior), Gansu (the north-west), Jiangsu (the coast), and Sichuan (the south-west). The capital of each province is chosen as a city within the sampling frame—a total of three cities are chosen in Sichuan and Henan and two in each of the others, in addition to Beijing.

A module of the survey was designed to measure social capital at the individual level. The measures of social capital include the size of social network, Communist Party membership. and parents' Communist Party membership. The concept of an individual's social network typically encompasses both the size and density of the network (Burt 1992; Wasserman and Faust 1994). Size is the number of contacts in a social network and density is its interrelatedness. For instance, an individual could have a large number of social contacts, but if the contacts all know each other, the network is denser and smaller than another individual's network in which few of the contacts know each other and in which

Table 6.1 Size of social networks and Communist Party membership for urban sample (standard deviation)

Segment (number of observations)	Social networks (number)	Communist Party member (%)	Parents' Communist Party membership (%)		Father and mother Communist Party membership (%)	
			One	Both	Father	Mother
Whole sample (7,501)	6.40	23.28	29.62	8.93	34.63	11.06
	(6.6469)	(0.4227)	(0.4566)	(0.2852)	(0.4758)	(0.3137)
By age cohort						
Aged 19–30 (1,530)	5.73	7.81	38.43	14.77	45.00	19.13
	(5.6137)	(0.2685)	(0.4866)	(0.3549)	(0.4977)	(0.3935)
Aged 31–41 (2,452)	6.77	20.81	35.28	9.62	42.10	12.05
	(6.8195)	(0.4060)	(0.4779)	(0.2950)	(0.4938)	(0.3256)
Aged 42–55 (3,337)	6.35	32.63	21.25	5.27	25.31	7.22
	(6.8123)	(0.4689)	(0.4091)	(0.2236)	(0.4349)	(0.2589)
By sector of employer						
State sector (5,127)	6.62	29.36	30.80	9.38	37.15	11.65
	(6.6138)	(0.4555)	(0.4617)	(0.2916)	(0.4833)	(0.3208)
Urban collectives (925)	5.24	11.90	22.16	4.54	22.68	5.83
	(5.0885)	(0.3240)	(0.4156)	(0.2083)	(0.4190)	(0.2344)
Self-employed (219)	6.51	3.20	26.03	5.48	24.29	8.10
	(11.7954)	(0.1763)	(0.4398)	(0.2281)	(0.4298)	(0.2734)
Private firms (499)	6.53	15.63	32.36	10.62	36.42	14.99
	(6.7862)	(0.3635)	(0.4680)	(0.3084)	(0.4817)	(0.3573)

Source: *China Urban Household Survey*, 1999.

there are more potential indirect contacts. However, the data require us to concentrate on network size rather than density.

The measure of social network is the reported number of close contacts of the respondent in any context, social or economic. The survey question asked: 'In the past year, how many relatives, friends, colleagues or acquaintances did you exchange gifts with or often maintain contact?' For the working-age population in the urban sample, the mean size of social network is 6.4 persons and its standard deviation is 6.7 (Table 6.1). Working-age individuals are defined as those aged 19–55 in consideration of the different retirement ages for men and women, and the age at which urban children leave education.

Figure 6.1 shows that this variable has a reasonable dispersion. The social network is not dominated by household members. The average household size in the sample is 3.2 persons: the one-child family policy has resulted in small households. The inverse correlation between family size and network size implies that people with smaller families build larger networks. Among the age cohorts, those aged 31–41 have the largest networks (mean 6.8). Workers who are in the state sector have the largest number of contacts in their social networks (6.6) and those who work in urban collectives the smallest (5.2). However, the means across groups are not statistically different from each other. Instead,

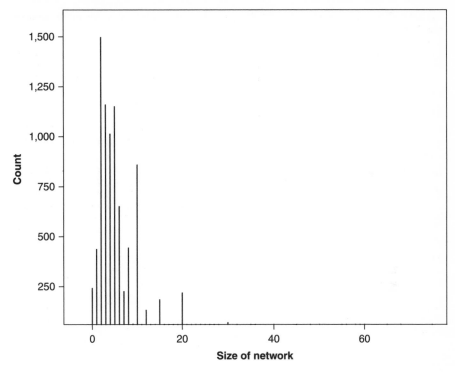

Figure 6.1 Frequency distribution of the size of network

networks are posited to differ by gender and suggest that human capital, as reflected in years of education and years of employment experience, assists network formation.

There is information on whether each working-age individual is currently a member of the Communist Party, but not on the date joined, and whether either parent was ever a member. Some 23 per cent of the sample are Communist Party members (Table 6.1). Among the age cohorts, membership increases with age: the youngest age cohort has 8 per cent and the oldest 33 per cent. No less than 29 per cent of the state-sector workers are members, whereas the figure is 16 per cent for private firms, 12 per cent for urban collectives, and only 3 per cent for the self-employed. About 30 per cent of the urban sample have one parent who is or was a Communist Party member, and another 9 per cent have both parents who are or were members. Many more have fathers who are or were Party members than have mothers. It is most common for individuals who work in the state sector to have a parent in the Party. Thus, *ceteris paribus*, male gender, human capital, and age increase the chances of Party membership. Moreover, the nature of the job is relevant; for example, employment in the state sector and in non-manual occupations can raise the value of membership to the person or the Party. It is plausible that membership of the Party can be passed on from one generation to another via attitudes or influence. Finally, are the two measures of social capital related; does Party membership expand a person's social network, and does possession of a larger social network make it more likely that a person will have joined the Party?

Using the full sample of adults, the predictors of both social network and Party membership for persons of working age (19–55) are estimated, so as to gain a better understanding of the key variables (Table 6.2). Column (1) is an OLS regression of the factors predicting the size of social network, and column (2) is a logit estimation of the probability of becoming a Communist Party member. There are few determinants of the size of social network. Aside from differences by city, the significant variables include gender, years of education, and years of work experience. Being female reduces the number of contacts in a social network (significant at the 5 per cent level), and years of education and of work experience both increase the size of social network (significant at the 1 per cent and 10 per cent level, respectively). This suggests that human capital is important in forming social networks. By contrast, age in itself has no effect. An attitudinal question asking whether the importance of political status for household income has changed is the last significant variable. The interpretation is that if the respondent thinks that political status has increased in importance, he will have an incentive to expand his social network. Notably, being a Communist Party member does not increase the number of reported contacts, nor do the variables representing Party membership of parents.

In column (2), the variables that significantly raise the likelihood of becoming a Communist Party member are shown to be years of education, years of work experience as well as age, employment in the state-owned sector, employment in a non-manual occupation, and being a household head. Party membership of one or both parents also significantly increases the probability of own Party membership, whereas female gender significantly reduces it. Again, it is notable that social networks are not a factor in the likelihood of membership. Finally, a question that asks whether the respondent hopes that her children will become members is also a significant determinant, reflecting support for the Party.

It appears that a person's social network is a phenomenon whose determinants are not well measured by an economic survey, whereas Communist Party membership is more closely determined by his or her economic characteristics. This suggests that social networks are more likely than Party membership to be entered for reasons other than economic returns, such as friendship or social relations. It is also notable that parents' membership of the Party does not influence the development of a social network. When added to the fact that neither social network nor Party membership is a determinant of the other, the estimations indicate that they are distinct phenomena. Human capital contributes to the formation of social capital and suggests that human capital may have its effects on income partly through this indirect route.

Table 6.2 First-stage instrumenting regressions: predicting social network and Communist Party membership

Dependent variable: (1) Social network: size (2) Communist Party membership: 0–1	Coefficient (t-statistic)		Mean value or percentage (standard deviation)
	(1)	(2)	
Intercept	−2.6214	−11.7840	
	(−0.62)	(−11.06)***	
Personal characteristics			
Female	−0.5689	−0.5985	0.5017
	(−2.14)**	(−8.73)***	(0.5000)
Age	−0.0563	0.0945	37.1451
	(−0.28)	(2.09)***	(9.5394)
Age squared	0.0003	−0.0007	1470.7520
	(0.12)	(−1.38)	(709.2652)
Years of education	0.1559	0.1675	10.2976
	(2.71)***	(10.56)***	(2.9891)
Years of employment experience	0.0565	0.0590	19.4816
	(1.70)*	(5.40)***	(9.1166)
Head of household	−0.4945	0.3571	0.3930
	(−1.16)	(5.22)***	(0.4885)
Ownership sector of employer			
State-owned sector	0.2531	0.3845	0.5359
	(0.47)	(2.97)***	(0.4987)
Private sector	−0.2466	−0.1941	0.2476
	(−0.41)	(−1.05)	(0.4316)
Occupation			
Non-manual worker	−0.0578	1.2095	0.3591
	(−0.09)	(8.92)***	(0.4798)
Production worker	−0.5468	−0.0361	0.1832
	(−0.84)	(−0.24)	(0.3869)
Self-employed	−0.0034	0.1544	0.0100
	(−0.04)	(0.45)	(0.0996)
Other occupations	−0.7679	0.1942	0.0485
	(−1.05)	(0.88)	(0.2148)
Guanxi			
Communist Party member	0.3724	—	0.1736
	(1.23)		(0.3788)
Social network	—	0.0056	6.4134
		(1.38)	(9.5384)
Parents' characteristics			
One parent is a member of the Communist Party	0.1414	0.3825	0.2228
	(0.52)	(4.96)***	(0.4162)
Both parents are members of the Communist Party	0.0281	0.5223	0.0664
	(0.05)	(4.23)***	(0.2491)
Father is/was a skilled worker	—	**0.3415**	0.9374
		(2.74)***	(0.2423)
Attitudinal response			
'Has the importance of political status for household income changed compared with before?' Answers: (1) decreased; (2) unchanged; (3) increased	**0.8065** (1.95)*	—	2.1401 (0.4431)
Cities	Yes	Yes	

(*continued*)

Table 6.2 Continued

Dependent variable: (1) Social network: size (2) Communist Party membership: 0–1	Coefficient (t-statistic)		Mean value or percentage (standard deviation)
	(1)	(2)	
R^2	0.0651	—	
Pseudo R^2	—	0.2460	
F(29, 2971)	14.08***	—	
Wald X^2 (29)	—	1192.39***	
Number of observations	2972	6568	

Notes: (1) Omitted dummy variables are: male, non-Communist Party member, not head of household, works in urban collective, unskilled worker, whose parents are not Communist Party members, whose father is a skilled worker, and Pingliang.

(2) *** denotes statistical significance at the 1% level, ** at 5% level, and * at 10% level.

(3) Heteroscedasticity-consistent robust standard errors adjusted for clustering at the household level are computed.

(4) Coefficients reported in bold are the instruments in the first-stage regression. For social network, the attitudinal response reflects the importance an individual places on developing connections to improve economic circumstances. Thus, the attitude is correlated with developing a social network, but possessing such views alone is not sufficient to increase economic gain. For Communist Party membership, father's level of skill is correlated with an individual's probability of joining the Party. Moreover, it is a binary variable corresponding well to the 0–1 dummy variable of Party membership. As expected, the parental characteristic is exogenous to the earned income function of the worker, and is unlikely to be affected by the worker's income.

6.3 Social Capital and Incomes

There are three possible methods of establishing the causal effects of social capital on incomes: panel data analysis, twin studies, and the use of instrumental variables. Each has its limitations. Even if panel data were available, they would not necessarily be more conclusive: as both size of social network and Party membership are likely to change infrequently (membership of the Party is normally for life) and their effects can be subject to long and unpredictable lags if opportunities are infrequent, panel analysis might fail to identify the full effects of social capital. Studies of identical twins can be subject to measurement error and consequent attenuation bias where the estimated coefficient is downwardly biased toward zero unless the relevant variable can be instrumented (Ashenfelter and Krueger 1994; Ashenfelter and Rouse 1998). Li et al. (2007), using a small sample of identical twins to control for ability and family background and so reduce omitted variable bias in OLS, found that the between-twin-pair effect of Communist Party membership on wages in China was small and not significant. The use of instrumental variable analysis involves the difficult task of finding instruments that are both relevant and valid. Three China studies have instrumented Party membership or corrected for selectivity into the Party. Liu (2003) used father's education as an instrument for own Party membership and found that the wage premium actually rose after instrumenting, whereas Lam (2003) and Appleton, Song, and Xia (2005), both using parental Party membership as the exclusion restriction, found no evidence of selectivity bias in OLS estimates, with the selection correction term being insignificant. Using the instrumental variable approach in the estimations which are similar to the approaches discussed above. Within the limitations of the data, the more appropriate and available instruments are used but given the difficulties of instrumental variable analysis, there is no inference of causality.

The analysis begins with estimating income functions for the entire urban sample to estimate if *guanxi* can affect wages in China's transitional labour market. Later the sample is partitioned into different segments concerning the differential role of social capital in different parts of the labour market. Each of the tables presents an earned income function which does not include the social capital variables, in order to indicate the returns to personal characteristics, human capital, etc. The social capital variables are then introduced to see what difference, if any, they make and whether their effects are significant in the income functions. In each formulation, the income functions are estimated by ordinary least squares (OLS), selection-corrected maximum likelihood (MLE), and two-stage least squares (2SLS) with an instrument for any endogenous variable. The exclusion restrictions for the MLE are discussed below as are the instruments for the 2SLS, as well as in the notes accompanying each table.

For the purposes of interpretation, the MLE figures are used except where the social capital variables are found to be endogenous. The MLE estimates are preferred because the OLS estimates are biased on account of selection into employment seen in the significant inverse Mills ratio coefficients. If the social capital variables are found to be endogenous, an instrument is used and 2SLS estimates are presented. The test for endogeneity is the standard Durbin-Wu-Hausman test evaluated at the 5 per cent level of significance. In Table 6.3, relating to the whole sample, all estimates are presented. For brevity, only the pertinent estimates are reported for the remaining tables.

A recurring issue in these estimations is the possibility that social capital is endogenous. In each case, the identifying instruments are well correlated with the potentially endogenous variable (relevance) and (an informal test) they are not correlated with the residual in the estimated income function (validity). However, that is not enough: there should be no theoretical reason why the chosen instruments could themselves influence income. The best instrument for Communist Party membership is whether the father has or had a manual job. Since this variable might influence income directly via inherited ability or acquired attitudes, the instrument should reduce but might not eliminate the likely upward bias in the coefficient resulting from any positive association between Party membership and productive personal traits. The variable used to instrument the size of social network was a positive answer to the question: 'has the importance of political status for household income risen?', on the grounds that respondents replying affirmatively would have a greater incentive to acquire social capital. Again, although the statistical tests were passed, there is the possibility that the exclusion restriction cannot identify exogenous variation in network size. For instance, a particular personality trait might both attract a large social network and a wage premium.

In Table 6.2, the predictors of social capital variables are presented including the instruments used for the sample as a whole. There is some variation in the instruments used for different market segments; these details are reported in the notes to the tables.

A final issue to address before turning to the results concerns the possibility of bias arising from selection of labour force participants into employment and the choice of exclusion restriction variables to eliminate that bias. Labour force participation rates for both men and women are high in urban China. As a result of the socialist legacy, the expectation is for both men and women to work on a full-time basis. Accordingly, there are few variables that are significant in determining selection into wage employment. Having a young child in the home, which has been found to be significant in the labour market participation of women in developed economies, cannot perform this role in urban China. However, the availability of childcare in the home turns out to be a valid exclusion restriction for both men and women. The first-stage regression results from the MLE estimates (not reported) confirm the a priori specification.

Table 6.3 presents the income functions for the entire urban sample of employed individuals. The dependent variable is the logarithm of annual earned income, excluding those who did not earn income for the year, thus permitting the usual corrections for selection into paid employment. Further details of the estimations are provided in the notes to the tables.

The uninstrumented estimators in Table 6.3 are first reported to give a picture of the raw relationship among these variables using OLS. The sign and significance of the social capital variables are not altered by the instrumenting or other corrections for biases such as heteroscedasticity. Compare the most appropriate equations without (column (2)) and with (column (4)) the social network variable. In column (2), regarding productive characteristics, there is a 4.9 per cent return to each year of education and a 2.1 per cent return to each year of employment experience at the mean value of employment experience. There is a large gender earnings gap: women are paid 18 per cent less than men. Ownership sector of the employer and occupation are controlled for, but focus the discussion on the human capital and social capital variables.

In the MLE estimation of column (4), social network is associated with a positive income premium of 0.34 per cent per additional contact and is significant at the 10 per cent level. When social network is instrumented (column (5)), the coefficient is actually raised—rather than lowered as might be expected if social network were simply a proxy for unobserved personal productive traits. When the social network variable is introduced, the returns to education fall, from 4.9 per cent to 2.5 per cent per annum. Returns to employment experience a similarly fall, to 1.6 per cent per annum at the mean. Interestingly, the gender gap is reduced, to 12 per cent. The findings suggest that there is a correlation between the social network and the gender and human capital variables. When the former is omitted, the returns to gender may be overstated: part of the gap can be attributed to gender differences in social network. Social network may be a vehicle by which human capital is rewarded.

Table 6.3 Income equations for working-aged employed individuals

Dependent variable: log of annual income	Coefficient (t-statistic)									
	(1)	(2)	(3)	(4)	(5)	(6)	(7)	(8)	(9)	(10)
	OLS	MLE	OLS	MLE	2SLS	OLS	MLE	OLS	MLE	2SLS
			with SN	with SN	with SN	with CP	with CP	with SN and CP	with SN and CP	with SN and CP
Intercept	7.1839 (114.10)***	7.3349 (112.98)***	7.1763 (103.76)***	7.3041 (102.76)***	6.9102 (30.09)***	7.2295 (114.86)***	7.3796 (113.55)***	7.3039 (106.27)***	7.3508 (103.06)***	6.9458 (30.13)***
Guanxi										
Social network	—	—	0.0037 (1.88)*	0.0034 (1.83)*	0.1021 (1.92)*	—	—	0.0036 (2.00)**	0.0033 (1.83)*	0.0981 (1.88)*
Communist Party member	—	—	—	—	—	0.1390 (8.01)***	0.1331 (7.59)***	0.1348 (7.23)***	0.1338 (7.11)***	0.0980 (2.06)**
Personal characteristics										
Female	-0.2057 (-15.07)***	-0.1950 (-13.98)***	-0.2073 (-14.10)***	-0.1974 (-13.19)***	-0.1326 (-2.57)***	-0.1907 (-13.66)***	-0.1809 (-12.71)***	-0.1983 (-13.17)***	-0.1833 (-11.98)***	-0.1267 (-2.61)***
Years of education	0.0513 (16.19)***	0.0490 (15.10)***	0.0515 (15.11)***	0.0503 (14.52)***	0.0245 (2.00)**	0.0478 (15.05)***	0.0455 (14.04)***	0.0463 (13.56)***	0.0467 (13.48)***	0.0231 (2.01)**
Years of employment	0.0379 (10.65)***	0.0345 (9.47)***	0.0361 (9.52)***	0.0332 (8.58)***	0.0262 (2.34)**	0.0363 (10.23)***	0.0330 (9.05)***	0.0321 (8.54)***	0.0317 (8.19)***	0.0265 (2.41)**
Employment years squared	-0.0006 (-6.93)***	-0.0005 (-5.77)***	-0.0005 (-5.71)***	-0.0005 (-5.27)***	-0.0004 (-1.46)	-0.0006 (-6.43)***	-0.0005 (-5.82)***	-0.0005 (-5.35)***	-0.0005 (-5.34)***	-0.0004 (-1.61)
Occupation										
Non-manual worker	0.3067 (12.08)***	0.2885 (11.15)***	0.2926 (10.77)***	0.2745 (9.96)***	0.2799 (3.21)***	0.2778 (10.88)***	0.2608 (10.02)***	0.2745 (10.08)***	0.2473 (8.92)***	0.2610 (3.23)***
Production worker	0.0918 (3.39)***	0.0797 (2.89)***	0.0868 (2.99)***	0.0758 (2.57)**	0.1279 (1.82)*	0.0911 (3.38)***	0.0792 (2.88)***	0.0857 (2.96)***	0.0758 (2.58)**	0.1260 (1.84)*
Self-employed	0.3938 (4.04)***	0.3658 (3.72)***	0.3779 (3.60)***	0.3558 (3.36)***	0.5338 (3.80)***	0.3820 (3.91)***	0.3548 (3.59)***	0.5188 (4.77)***	0.3451 (3.25)***	0.5315 (3.85)***
Other occupation										

(continued)

Table 6.3 Continued

Dependent variable: log of annual income	(1)	(2)	(3)	(4)	(5)	(6)	(7)	(8)	(9)	(10)
					Coefficient (t-statistic)					
	OLS	MLE	OLS with SN	MLE with SN	2SLS with SN	OLS with CP	MLE with CP	OLS with SN and CP	MLE with SN and CP	2SLS with SN and CP
	0.1123 (3.15)***	0.1085 (2.96)***	0.0983 (2.52)**	0.1023 (2.55)**	0.1664 (1.95)*	0.1037 (2.92)***	0.1000 (2.73)***	0.1182 (3.03)***	0.0946 (2.36)**	0.1628 (1.95)*
Sector of employer										
State sector	0.2867 (12.78)***	0.2492 (10.70)***	0.3073 (12.82)***	0.2728 (11.06)***	0.2819 (4.38)***	0.2787 (12.46)***	0.2416 (10.40)***	0.2625 (11.54)***	0.2638 (10.74)***	0.2740 (4.45)***
Private sector	0.3121 (9.43)***	0.2751 (8.05)***	0.3255 (8.99)***	0.2934 (7.88)***	0.3465 (4.57)***	0.3157 (9.57)***	0.2788 (8.17)***	0.3108 (7.32)***	0.2952 (7.95)***	0.3426 (4.65)***
Cities										
Beijing	0.6626 (17.60)***	0.6521 (16.86)***	0.6856 (16.62)***	0.6770 (16.01)***	0.7484 (8.45)***	0.6743 (17.92)***	0.6624 (17.10)***	0.6907 (16.47)***	0.6910 (16.21)***	0.7553 (8.83)***
Shenyang	0.1887 (4.72)***	0.1724 (4.19)***	0.1861 (4.33)***	0.1675 (3.80)***	0.2856 (3.10)***	0.1939 (4.86)***	0.1763 (4.29)***	0.1847 (4.26)***	0.1730 (3.92)***	0.2875 (3.21)***
Jinzhou	0.1381 (2.94)***	0.1204 (2.49)***	0.1558 (3.12)***	0.1363 (2.64)***	0.1525 (1.41)	0.1414 (3.01)***	0.1226 (2.53)***	0.1544 (3.05)***	0.1399 (2.70)***	0.1526 (1.44)
Nanjing	0.5375 (14.18)***	0.5140 (13.22)***	0.5598 (13.48)***	0.5381 (12.63)***	0.8715 (4.28)***	0.5562 (14.65)***	0.5309 (13.61)***	0.5711 (13.56)***	0.5565 (12.99)***	0.8717 (4.44)***
Xuzhou	0.3489 (7.61)***	0.3225 (6.90)***	0.3647 (7.61)***	0.3354 (6.86)***	0.1580 (1.22)	0.3560 (7.77)***	0.3284 (7.02)***	0.3655 (7.56)***	0.3430 (7.00)***	0.1706 (1.33)
Zhengzhou	0.1969 (4.41)***	0.2068 (4.53)***	0.2097 (4.38)***	0.2218 (4.51)***	0.4370 (3.71)***	0.1947 (4.37)***	0.2032 (4.45)***	0.1981 (4.10)***	0.2204 (4.48)***	0.4294 (3.72)***
Kaifeng	-0.2341 (-4.31)***	-0.2289 (-4.10)***	-0.2301 (-3.93)***	-0.2237 (-3.73)***	0.0665 (0.40)	-0.2137 (-3.94)***	-0.2099 (-3.77)***	-0.2157 (-3.65)***	-0.2037 (-3.40)***	0.0746 (0.46)
Pingdingshan										

	(2)	(3)	(4)	(5)	(6)	(7)	(8)	(9)	(10)
	0.2559 (5.14)***	0.2411 (4.60)***	0.2340 (4.38)***	0.0474 (0.30)	0.2533 (5.12)***	0.2498 (4.95)***	0.2372 (4.52)***	0.2329 (4.38)***	0.0583 (0.38)
Chengdu	0.2677 (6.64)***	0.2900 (6.65)***	0.2733 (6.14)***	0.1586 (1.33)	0.2779 (6.90)***	0.2590 (6.29)***	0.2947 (6.68)***	0.2839 (6.36)***	0.1704 (1.47)
Zigong	-0.0155 (-0.32)	0.0282 (0.54)	-0.0099 (-0.19)	0.0431 (0.45)	-0.0184 (-0.39)	-0.0537 (-1.11)	0.0157 (0.30)	-0.0113 (-0.22)	0.0384 (0.41)
Nanchong	0.1084 (2.31)**	0.1337 (2.67)***	0.1159 (2.27)**	0.2264 (2.08)**	0.1143 (2.45)**	0.0992 (2.06)**	0.1451 (2.88)***	0.1196 (2.34)**	0.2278 (2.15)**
Lanzhou	0.1475 (3.50)***	0.1367 (2.87)***	0.1275 (2.61)***	-0.0263 (-0.20)	0.1568 (3.72)***	0.1416 (3.27)***	0.1414 (2.94)***	0.1383 (2.83)***	-0.0073 (-0.06)
Inverse Mills ratio	-0.5024 (-18.792)***	—	-0.4862 (-13.963)***	(-17.442)***	—	-0.5002 (-13.443)***	—	-0.4843	—
R^2	0.3057	0.3110	—	—	0.3110	—	0.1647	—	—
$F_{(22, 3909)}$	131.38***	—	—	—	—	—	—	—	—
$F_{(23, 3504)}$	—	109.56***	—	—	—	—	—	—	—
$F_{(23, 2972)}$	—	—	—	29.17***	—	—	—	—	—
$F_{(23, 3907)}$	—	—	—	—	129.95***	—	—	—	—
$F_{(24, 3503)}$	—	—	—	—	—	—	108.21***	—	—
$F_{(24, 2971)}$	—	—	—	—	—	—	—	—	28.89***
Wald X^2 (22)	2482.73***	—	—	—	—	—	—	—	—
Wald X^2 (23)	—	—	2214.81***	—	—	2575.40***	—	—	—
Wald X^2 (24)	—	—	—	—	—	—	—	2293.88***	—
Number of observations	7546	6572	6572	2973	7540	7540	6568	6568	2972

Source: *China Urban Household Survey*, 1999.

Notes: (1) Omitted dummy variables are: non-Communist Party member, urban collective sector, unskilled worker, and Pingliang.

(2) *** denotes statistical significance at the 1% level, ** at 5% level, and * at 10% level.

(3) Heteroscedasticity-consistent robust standard errors adjusted for clustering at the household level are computed.

(4) The exclusion restriction for columns (2), (4), (7), and (9) is whether childcare is available in the home. It is a dummy variable that equals one if there are grandparents and a child under the age of 17 who are living in the household and zero otherwise. The exclusion restrictions are significant at the 5% level and used for all equations unless otherwise denoted.

(5) Since there is some variation in the instruments used for different labour market segments, each table reports the specific instruments used. The instrument for social network in columns (5) and (10) is an attitudinal question that asked: 'Has the importance of political status for household income changed compared with before?' Answers were (1) decreased; (2) unchanged; (3) increased. The instrument for Communist Party membership in columns (8) and (10) is a dummy variable that equals one if an individual's father is or was a skilled worker and equals zero otherwise. Social network is endogenous while Communist Party membership is not endogenous in these estimations.

In column (7), there is a 13 per cent income premium associated with Communist Party membership, which is significant at the 1 per cent level. The human capital and the gender coefficients remain largely unaffected by its inclusion. When both social network and Communist Party membership are introduced, in column (9), approximately the same effects associated respectively with each variable are found. Whereas instrumenting both social network and Party membership actually raises the coefficient on the former, it lowers the coefficient on the latter, from 14 per cent to 10 per cent (column (10)): at least part of the influence of unobserved productive characteristics is eliminated. The evidence of Table 6.3 is of consistent social capital being rewarded in the labour market.

Table 6.4 divides the full sample into three age cohorts. The oldest cohort, aged 42–55, is the group most likely to have been allocated jobs during the period of central planning, and many were in the same jobs in 1999 (Knight and Yueh 2004). The youngest cohort, aged 19–30, probably entered the labour force during the 1990s, when the allocation system had broken down or weakened and entrants generally had to search for their own jobs in the emerging labour market. Social network does not benefit the oldest age cohort, whereas Party membership, and even parental Party membership, does. Indeed, the parental variable is only significant for the oldest cohort (column (10)). The effect of parents' Communist Party membership was estimated for all age cohorts, but this variable is included only in the specification presented for the oldest cohort. Deceased parents' Party membership is included, as the benefits could have accrued to the individual on the basis of the status rather than direct action and could have accrued early on. It appears that parental Party membership was important in securing a favourable job allocation under central planning, and that own Party membership assisted the subsequent careers of the oldest cohort. Social network is significant for the youngest and middle cohorts, but the coefficient is lower for the former. For labour market entrants, parental social network (not measured in the survey) may be more important than own social network. Finally, the coefficient on own Party membership is positive, significant, and more or less the same for all three cohorts.

Four ownership sectors are distinguished in Table 6.5: state-owned enterprises (SOEs), accounting for 76 per cent of employees in the sample, urban collectives (14 per cent), private firms (7 per cent), and self-employment (3 per cent). Reforms have given greater managerial autonomy to SOEs, including a degree of freedom to manage workers. Nevertheless, this ownership sector is the one least affected by labour market forces. The difference between SOEs and urban collectives is not large, except that collectives are more likely to face 'hard' budgets. Labour market forces are most likely to be experienced in the private sector. The self-employment sector is also subject to market forces, but the nature and role of social capital is probably different for the self-employed. Indeed, Table 6.5 shows social capital does not assist the self-employed. To explain its role in this case, different measures of social capital are needed, such as networks of business associates. The social network variable is positive

Table 6.4 Income equations for employed individuals, by age cohort

Dependent variable: log of annual income	Coefficient (t-statistic)									
	Ages 19–30			Ages 31–41			Ages 42–55			
	(1)	(2)	(3)	(4)	(5)	(6)	(7)	(8)	(9)	(10)
	MLE	MLE with SN	MLE with CP	MLE	MLE with SN	MLE with CP	MLE	2SLS with SN	MLE with CP	2SLS with SN, CP, PCP
Intercept	7.6072 (48.71)***	7.273 (41.79)***	7.6206 (47.91)***	7.6174 (52.97)***	7.4717 (49.15)***	7.6474 (53.41)***	7.3706 (53.29)***	7.1544 (32.19)***	7.4159 (53.90)***	7.1844 (32.39)***
Guanxi										
Social network	—	0.0036 (2.08)**	—	—	0.0093 (4.21)***	—	—	0.0266 (0.98)	—	0.0259 (0.98)
Communist Party member	—	—	0.1605 (2.68)***	—	—	0.1346 (4.58)***	—	—	0.1376 (5.91)***	0.1229 (3.14)***
Both parents in Communist Party	—	—	—	—	—	—	—	—	—	0.1199 (1.84)*
Personal characteristics										
Female	-0.1888 (-4.85)***	-0.2288 (-5.45)***	-0.01793 (-4.50)***	-0.1963 (-8.47)***	-0.2003 (-8.16)***	-0.1813 (-7.69)***	-0.2049 (-10.75)***	-0.1373 (-3.78)***	-0.1897 (-9.70)***	-0.1296 (-3.57)***
Years of education	0.0309 (3.46)***	0.0467 (4.86)***	0.0299 (3.32)***	0.0582 (9.94)***	0.0563 (9.01)***	0.0540 (9.23)***	0.0467 (10.70)***	0.0334 (4.66)***	0.0425 (9.74)***	0.0289 (4.20)***
Years of employment	0.0681 (3.20)***	0.0607 (2.52)**	0.0667 (3.10)***	-0.0013 (-0.09)	0.0087 (0.56)	-0.0017 (-0.12)	0.0213 (2.14)**	0.0379 (2.33)**	0.0205 (2.07)**	0.0373 (2.32)**
Employment years squared	-0.0024 (-1.65)*	-0.0023 (-1.35)	-0.0025 (-1.63)	0.0005 (1.06)	0.0001 (0.30)	0.0004 (0.99)	-0.0002 (-0.94)	-0.0005 (-1.57)	-0.0002 (-0.99)	-0.0005 (-1.59)
Sector of employer	Yes	Yes	Yes	Yes	Yes	Yes	Yes	Yes	Yes	Yes
Occupation	Yes	Yes	Yes	Yes	Yes	Yes	Yes	Yes	Yes	Yes
Cities	Yes	Yes	Yes	Yes	Yes	Yes	Yes	Yes	Yes	Yes
Inverse Mills ratio	0.2415	0.0307	0.2284	0.2007	0.1712	0.1771	0.1266	—	0.1335	—

(continued)

Table 6.4 Continued

Dependent variable: log of annual income

	Ages 19–30			Ages 31–41				Ages 42–55		
					Coefficient (t-statistic)					
	(1)	(2)	(3)	(4)	(5)	(6)	(7)	(8)	(9)	(10)
	MLE	MLE with SN	MLE with CP	MLE	MLE with SN	MLE with CP	MLE	2SLS with SN	MLE with CP	2SLS with SN, CP, PCP
Partial R^2 of excluded instruments	(1.68)*	(0.16)	(1.61)*	(1.83)*	(1.36)	(1.64)	(0.47)	0.0061	(0.49)	0.0062
R^2	—	—	—	—	—	—	—	0.2204	—	0.2329
$F_{(23, 1548)}$	—	—	—	—	—	—	—	26.81***	—	—
$F_{(26, 1548)}$	—	—	—	—	—	—	—	—	—	24.27***
Wald X^2 (22)	415.18***	—	—	907.32***	—	—	1433.08***	—	—	—
Wald X^2 (23)	—	408.00***	446.26***	—	856.97***	946.81***	—	—	1463.46***	—
Number of observations	1388	1126	1383	2750	2451	2749	3603	1549	3603	1549

Source: China Urban Household Survey, 1999.

Notes: (1) Omitted dummy variables are: non-Communist Party member, urban collective sector, unskilled worker, parents who are not Communist Party members, and Pingliang.

(2) *** denotes statistical significance at the 1% level, ** at 5% level, and * at 10% level.

(3) Heteroscedasticity-consistent robust standard errors adjusted for clustering at the household level are computed.

(4) For the first and third age cohorts, the instrument for social network is an attitudinal question, which asked: 'Has the importance of social network changed as compared with before?' Answers were (1) decreased; (2) unchanged; (3) increased. For the second age cohort, the instrument for social network is a similar question: 'Has the importance of social connections for household income changed as compared with before?' Answers were (1) decreased; (2) unchanged; (3) increased. For the second and third age cohorts, the instrument for Communist Party membership is a dummy variable that equals one if an individual's father is or was a skilled worker and equals zero otherwise. For the first age cohort, the instrument for Communist Party membership is the question: 'Do you hope your children will join the Communist Party?' Answers were (1) no; (2) little; (3) some; (4) very much. Social network is endogenous, while Communist Party membership is not endogenous even at the 10% level for the third age cohort and not endogenous at the 5% level for the other age cohorts.

Table 6.5 Income equations for employed individuals, by ownership sector of employer

Dependent Variable: log of annual income										
	Coefficient (t-statistic)									
	SOEs				Urban collectives		Self-employed		Private firms	
	(1)	(2)	(3)	(4)	(5)	(6)	(7)	(8)	(9)	(10)
	MLE	MLE with SN	MLE with CP	MLE with SN and CP	MLE	MLE with SN and CP	MLE	MLE with SN and CP	MLE	MLE with SN and CP
Intercept	8.0445 (103.19)***	8.0377 (95.99)***	8.0561 (103.88)***	8.0475 (96.48)***	7.9174 (28.96)***	7.8174 (27.13)***	8.4466 (25.55)***	8.3031 (21.96)***	7.6661 (16.25)***	7.9973 (9.63)***
Guanxi										
Social network	—	0.0071 (3.16)***	—	0.0066 (3.04)***	—	0.0132 (3.16)***	—	-0.0004 (-0.77)	—	0.0146 (3.20)***
Communist Party member	—	—	0.1460 (7.78)***	0.1361 (6.74)***	—	0.1435 (2.10)**	—	-0.2520 (-1.22)	—	0.1636 (2.19)**
Personal characteristics										
Female	-0.1537 (-10.06)***	-0.1519 (-9.34)***	-0.1377 (-8.78)***	-0.1368 (-8.19)***	-0.2493 (-5.52)***	-0.2634 (-5.53)***	-0.2047 (-2.64)***	-0.2922 (-3.31)***	-0.2516 (-4.51)***	-0.2274 (-3.65)***
Years of education	0.0500 (14.42)***	0.0492 (13.45)***	0.0452 (13.04)***	0.0448 (12.24)***	0.0484 (4.58)***	0.0354 (3.31)***	0.0147 (0.81)	0.0323 (2.10)**	0.0280 (1.94)*	0.0126 (0.71)
Years of employment	0.0312 (7.15)***	0.0293 (6.44)***	0.0291 (6.69)***	0.0274 (6.03)***	0.0316 (2.85)***	0.0312 (2.68)***	0.0696 (3.58)***	0.0580 (2.95)***	0.0534 (4.15)***	0.0612 (4.13)***
Employment years squared	-0.0004 (-4.00)***	-0.0004 (-3.67)***	-0.0004 (-4.02)***	-0.0004 (-3.69)***	-0.0006 (-2.25)**	-0.0006 (-1.96)**	-0.0016 (-2.36)**	-0.0012 (-1.72)*	-0.0011 (-3.02)***	-0.0014 (-3.32)***
Occupation	Yes	Yes	Yes	Yes	Yes	Yes	Yes	Yes	Yes	Yes
Cities	Yes	Yes	Yes	Yes	Yes	Yes	Yes	Yes	Yes	Yes
Inverse Mills ratio	0.3161	0.2545	0.3196	0.2660	0.1681	0.1755	-0.4165	-0.4273	0.8455	0.7986

(continued)

Table 6.5 Continued

Dependent Variable: log of annual income	Coefficient (t-statistic)									
	SOEs				Urban collectives		Self-employed		Private firms	
	(1)	(2)	(3)	(4)	(5)	(6)	(7)	(8)	(9)	(10)
	MLE	MLE with SN	MLE with CP	MLE with SN and CP	MLE	MLE with SN and CP	MLE	MLE with SN and CP	MLE	MLE with SN and CP
	(3.40)***	(2.46)**	(3.49)***	(2.59)***	(1.20)	(1.00)	(−0.41)	(−1.31)	(1.00)	(1.10)
Wald X^2(7)	—	—	—	—	—	—	33.50***	—	—	—
Wald X^2(9)	—	—	—	—	—	—	—	31.49***	—	—
Wald X^2(11)	—	—	—	—	—	—	—	—	97.50***	—
Wald X^2(15)	—	—	—	—	250.17***	—	—	—	—	—
Wald X^2(17)	1635.86***	—	—	—	—	—	—	—	—	—
Wald X^2(18)	—	1428.37***	1707.91***	—	—	—	—	—	—	—
Wald X^2(19)	—	—	—	1484.96***	—	305.65***	—	—	—	127.82***
Number of observations	5681	4963	5676	4959	1108	971	249	208	534	446

Source: China Urban Household Survey, 1999.

Notes: (1) Omitted dummy variables are: non-Communist Party member, unskilled worker, and Pingliang.

(2) *** denotes statistical significance at the 1% level, ** at 5% level, and * at 10% level.

(3) Heteroskedasticity-consistent robust standard errors adjusted for clustering at the household level are computed.

(4) The instrument for social network is an attitudinal question that asked: 'Has the importance of political status for household income changed compared with before?' Answers were (1) decreased; (2) unchanged; (3) increased. The instrument for Communist Party membership is a dummy variable that equals one if an individual's father is or was a skilled worker and equals zero otherwise. Social network and Communist Party membership are both exogenous. Maximum likelihood estimates are reported for all estimations.

and significant in all three of the sectors offering paid employment, as is the Party membership variable. Both variables have coefficients that are no smaller in the private sector than in the SOE and urban collective sectors. As only a fifth of the employment in the private sector is in Chinese–foreign joint ventures (which are typically formed with former state-owned enterprises and probably use the same managers), the new and growing private sector seems to place similar emphasis on social capital. It appears that social capital is important in both the administered and the market-oriented parts of the labour market.

It is worth pointing out an unexpected result. Whereas the returns to employment experience are highest in the private sector, the returns to education are lowest there, and the inclusion of the social capital variables reduces them to insignificance (columns (9) and (10)). This does not fit the argument that, given the egalitarianism of the state sector, the rewards for human capital, including education, should be higher in the more market-oriented, private sector. However, it does suggest that those better able to enter the private sector have experience that is sought by new private firms which in turn reward these workers for the contacts and connections that are valuable in an uncertain market.

Both measures of social network and of associational social capital, Communist Party membership, are positively correlated with the incomes of employed persons. Social capital appears to be important, controlling for the standard set of variables like human capital and personal characteristics like gender. It is possible that the measures are correlated with unobserved personal characteristics, such as sociability. However, it is also possible that such personal characteristics enhance income through their effects in expanding social networks and encouraging associational memberships. Thus, the evidence suggests that networks and memberships play an economic role. This finding accords with the conclusions of others, such as Granovetter (1995 [1974]) and Rebick (2000), who have investigated social networks in other countries. It is also consistent with research reporting the rising importance of both human capital and Party membership in urban China (Yueh 2010a). The role of human capital in forming social capital suggests not only that social capital is itself important but also that it can be a vehicle by which human capital is rewarded.

There was a potential role for social capital both in an administered labour system, where jobs are allocated and wages are institutionally determined, and in a market-oriented system—especially an underdeveloped one—where labour market information is poor and transaction costs are high. The results were rather mixed. The measure of social network has a greater effect for the middle than for the youngest or the oldest age cohort, possibly because the forms of social capital relevant to the other two groups are different: parental Communist Party membership was important under central planning and parental social networks may be important for labour market entrants. Social networks appear to be as beneficial in the private sector as in the state or urban collective sectors. Since this is the rapidly expanding sector, the expectation must be that *guanxi* will continue to play an important role in the Chinese labour market. The evidence is consistent with *guanxi* both providing access to economic rents (especially for older workers and workers in the state sector) and also reducing informational and transaction costs (given its importance in the private sector). For China, this is an attempt to measure the pervasive phenomenon of *guanxi* and its effects in the labour market. More generally, it is unusual in providing an individual-level measure of social network, in contrast to community-level measures or binary measures of whether an individual does or does not have social capital. The relatively simple measure was successful and showed an economic impact on wage employment. It has a strong effect as well in self-employment, as the next section will detail.

6.4 Self-employment and Social Networks

Private economic activity, including starting self-employment, is an important driver of growth, particularly for an economy such as China where partial marketization relies on the rapid growth of the non-state sector in driving the transition from central planning (Fan 1994). China's gradualist reforms are associated with a high degree of market imperfection where many sectors are still controlled by the state, and private economic activity tends to be character-ized by a great deal of uncertainty. Moreover, China is a developing country where there are numerous information-related obstacles which can impede obtaining credit and starting a business.

Self-employment is a challenging proposition in a developing economy charac-terized by imperfect credit markets, supply chains, and product markets (Banerjee and Newman 1993). Existing studies focus on institutional factors, such as credit constraints, and individual traits as determinants of those who choose to enter into self-employment or start small- and medium-sized enterprises (Blanch-flower and Oswald 1998; Rees and Shah 1986). Both sets of approaches would support the importance of social networks in fostering self-employment, as well as point to motivation and attitude toward risk as determinating factors. Social networks can arise from a need to work within imperfect formal institutions, such as a regime of uncertain property rights (Frye and Zhuravskaya 2000), or evolve in the context of community and cultural factors (Portes 1998), as well as result from individual preferences (Glaeser, Laibson, and Sacerdote 2002). It is likely that social networks have both an economic and non-economic function. For instance, social networks can help ease financial constraints and provide needed contacts for operating a business in a partially marketized environment such as China (Oi 1999; Zhang et al. 2006), but can also serve a primarily social function with some economic uses (Komter 2005).

In China, the private sector has rapidly overtaken the state sector as a propor-tion of GDP even though the system is characterized by a poor legal system that provides incomplete protection of private assets, credit constraints for private enterprises, and regulatory opacity. Despite these challenges, there is a growing segment of non-state-driven economic activity that has propelled China along its gradualist transition path and helped it to achieve remarkable growth rates in the reform period. In such an imperfect legal and financial system, the characteristics of those who are able to enter self-employment are of interest. Moreover, the dominance of informal and relation-based contracting in China suggests that the elements fostering private-sector development are likely to evolve around social networks, as well as other traits associated with managing uncertainty such as motivation or drive, and traditional characteristics such as the willingness to embracing risk.

The determinants of becoming self-employed in China, particularly in urban areas, are yet to be well understood despite the growing importance of the *de novo* private sector. Studies of self-employment include analyses by Wu (2002), Zhang et al. (2006), and Mohapatra et al. (2007), as well as a survey by Djankov et al. (2006). The study of rural China by Mohapatra, Rozelle, and Goodhue (2007) emphasizes education as the key determinant of rural farmers leaving the agricultural sector and moving into self-employment and wage employment, while Wu (2002) finds that education and Communist Party membership are a deterrent to self-employment in urban areas. As with most issues in China, there are significant urban–rural differences, suggesting in this instance that the rural residents able to move into higher value-added work are the educated ones, while more educated workers in urban areas tend to remain in the institutionally favoured wage employment.

Zhang et al. (2006) and Djankov et al. (2006) concur that starting one's own business is more likely if the individual has friends or family who have done so. In the Djankov et al. (2006) study, the most robust determinant was knowing others who had tried it. This is consistent with the work on the importance of social networks. The original data, with measures of social networks, motivation, and attitudes, allow us to build upon these findings.

Therefore, *guanxi* plays a role in the rise of self-employment in China's transitioning economy which lacks significant formal institutions in the areas of property rights and other features crucial for private economic activity, such as well-functioning credit markets, certainty in contracting, and investment protection. Moreover, China has traditionally had a cultural and historical emphasis on interpersonal relationships or *guanxi*, which informs business dealings both within and outside of China. This suggests that networking is possibly an important factor in determining non-state sector development in transitioning China.

Self-employment should require many of the same personal traits as employed persons working for a wage, such as education, in a transition labour market. However, the self-employed must also contend with the need to obtain credit to start a business and buy inventory, gain access to suppliers and distributors, as well as the knowledge to navigate the uncertain regulatory and legal environment in China where licences are often required for starting a business. Social networks would be useful in all these respects.

6.4.1 *Credit and Supply Networks*

In China, self-employed persons often encounter severe credit constraints due to the credit allocation system which is skewed toward SOEs (Fan 1994; Lin 2007). Small and medium enterprises find it difficult to obtain credit and often rely on family and friends, including remittances from migrated family members, to start a business (Oi 1999). Alternatively, self-employed persons use their social networks to arrange for inventory to be issued without advance payment. Anything which is sold is then split between the vendor and the supplier of the inventory, such as pedlars receiving their goods in advance. The author encountered this type of trust-based relationship in conducting the household survey in China, notably in Liaoning which has a substantial proportion of heavy industry that was hard hit by the large-scale downsizing of the SOEs in the mid-1990s. Access to suppliers and distributors is a significant challenge in a partially marketized economy, and having a social network would facilitate self-employment by helping to overcome such obstacles (see for example, Wu 2002). With the stagnation of the state-owned sector during this period and the beginning of market liberalization facilitating the growth of the non-state sector, it is also likely that urban workers began to seek other sources of income and thus became self-employed.

When asked the main reason why the respondent started his or her own business, 37 per cent of the survey respondents said that it was because he or she had the requisite skills and experience, 7 per cent had funds, 11 per cent had real estate, and 17 per cent started a business by joining in with relatives. The remaining chose 'other'. As this was during the period of the *xiagang* policy where there were large-scale lay-offs in the SOE sector, it is likely that some became self-employed or, more likely, small goods pedlars out of necessity. Given the small proportion of the self-employed who started with their own funds, credit is likely to be a constraint that social networks can help with by improving information flows to attain credit or indeed access credit from personal networks. This figure may be understated since having funds may be a subsidiary reason because respondents were limited to one response. Having real estate in China suggests a social network because all urban land is state-owned and land/buildings were only beginning to become privatized. Those who had the resource of real estate would most likely have had the connections to attain such an asset. This finding supports the argument that one of the motivations for entering self-employment is having overcome credit constraints.

6.4.2 *Navigating an Uncertain Institutional Environment*

China has an imperfect legal system with a great deal of regulatory complexity (Chen 2003; Clarke 2003c). In such an environment, having the contacts and know-how to obtain a licence would be important (see for example, Oi 1999). Indeed, licences and permissions are needed not only for starting the business but also for the transport of goods at the city and provincial levels. A social network would help in this instance. Interpersonal relationships would also reduce the costs of enforcement in such a system where trusted individuals are preferred in the absence of an effective legal system (see for example, Yang 1994; Yan 1996; Kipnis 1997). Networking would increase information flows and reduce the transaction costs of starting a business.

The second most important reason for starting one's own business reported in the survey was the opportunity to join in with relatives as well as knowing others who will also become self-employed. This is consistent with the self-employment literature which emphasizes the importance of knowing friends or relatives who have already done so (Blanchflower and Oswald 1998; Djankov et al. 2006), and joint ownership with relatives which resolves a number of obstacles. Starting a business with relatives and others who have experience of self-employment supports the contention that networking can assist with navigating an uncertain institutional environment if the self-employed knows others who have knowledge of how to conduct business in an uncertain context, such as help in obtaining licenses to operate. Joining with relatives also reduces the transaction costs of enforcement should problems arise. Thus, networking should help with self-employment in urban China.

The above factors suggest the importance of social networks and where they might perform an economic function. Having a social network is likely to be important in the choice to become self-employed in urban China. It may well be that some people are more entrepreneurial; they have greater drive or embrace risk more willingly than others. This can be measured separately in some segments of the dataset to see if networks still have an effect if these often observed traits are accounted for.

6.5 Choosing Self-employment

The household dataset is original and collected in urban China in 2000 pertaining to 1999. It is a representative survey administered across China, enumerated by the National Bureau for Statistics (NBS) in China, and designed by a team of international researchers from the Chinese Academy of Social Sciences, Japan, Australia, and the UK, including the author. The detailed information on type of employment and personal characteristics as well as original measures of social networks allow for estimations of the traits of the self-employed in urban China. The total sample size of the 1999 survey is 4,500 urban households and around 9,000 working-aged people. There is also a group of around 1,500 persons who have experience of unemployment in the previous five years. The massive layoff policy from SOEs began in the mid-1990s and caused urban unemployment to rise, so the previous five years from the 1999 survey year would correspond to the introduction of the *xiagang* policy. This group is interesting as those who have experienced unemployment as a result of the downsizing of the state sector could have different motivations for entering self-employment, and therefore employ their social networks, which are worth investigating.

NBS sample households excludes migrants residing in urban areas without urban *hukou*, so a limitation of this study is that it excludes rural persons who are working in the informal sector or are temporary migrants. The survey covered six provinces and thirteen cities. The provinces are Beijing (chosen to represent the four cities that are independently administered municipal districts), Liaoning (to represent the north-east), Henan (the interior), Gansu (the north-west), Jiangsu (the coast), and Sichuan (the south-west). The capital of each province is chosen as a city within the sampling frame—a total of three cities are chosen in Sichuan and Henan and two in each of the others, in addition to Beijing. Given the breadth of the survey, there is no need to attempt to normalize the sample as with smaller scale data typically used in this type of study.

Table 6.6 provides the descriptions of the dependent and explanatory variables for the main sample and for the sub-sample of individuals who had experience of lay-off during the previous five years and had answered a further set of attitudinal questions which measure their motivation and drive to some extent.

There are 359 individuals who are self-employed, where 56 per cent are men and 44 per cent are women. This constitutes approximately 4 per cent of all urban workers. There are another eighty individuals who are both employed and also report themselves to be self-employed, suggesting that they are working for themselves as secondary employment. During the late 1990s when employment was becoming increasingly insecure, this is perhaps not surprising. It is also possible that they are temporary workers and turn to self-employment during periods when they are out of work. They constitute just under 1 per cent of all urban workers, so taken together the self-employed (solely and as second jobs) constitute around 5 per cent of all urban workers.

There are more men in self-employment than in wage employment, with no differences between the self-employed as the sole or secondary job. Both the wage-employed and the self-employed have just over nine years of education (compulsory education in China is nine years), whereas the secondarily self-employed have had significantly more education of over ten years. There are no gender differences. Where they differ is in age and years of employment experience. Self-employed men are on average three years older than women, and have over five years more employment experience. They are also less likely to be married, and the self-employed have less formal-sector work experience.

Those who are self-employed as a second job are similar in profile to the self-employed, although they are slightly younger on average, have fewer years of employment experience, and fewer are married. Notably, nearly one-third had experienced unemployment in the previous five years, perhaps explaining why this group seeks out additional income to stave off insecurity in employment. Those who are solely self-employed also have greater experience of lay-off; around 27 per cent of the sample. There are no differences between men and women in terms of the proportion who have experienced being laid-off (a quarter of men as compared with slightly more for women). Membership of the Chinese Communist Party provides a stark contrast with urban workers: whereas nearly 18 per cent of employed persons are Party member, only 6 per cent of self-

Table 6.6A Descriptive values: main sample

Variable	Sample size	Mean	Std. dev.	Minimum	Maximum
Self-employed	8,536	0.0398888	0.1539149	0	1
Self-employed as second job	8,536	0.0058954	0.0765574	0	1
Social network	6,889	6.165203	7.139347	0	152
Variance of income	8,536	9481437	9.74e + 07	0	0.99e + 09
Gender	8,535	0.4989946	0.5000199	0	1
Age	8,536	35.84305	10.46876	19	55
Years of education	8,510	10.30362	2.923238	0	23
Years of wage employment experience	7,757	19.43551	9.15153	0	47
Communist Party member	8,525	0.1630818	0.3694558	0	1
Experienced lay-off	8,536	0.1446131	0.3302919	0	1
Married	8,536	0.6927045	0.4613899	0	1
Spouse in wage employment	8,536	0.1604274	0.3670155	0	1
Spouse in self-employment	8,536	0.0031688	0.0562045	0	1
Father's educational attainment					
College and above	8,536	0.03972	0.1953077	0	1
Professional school	8,536	0.0714812	0.2576364	0	1
Secondary school	8,536	0.2134856	0.4097827	0	1
Primary school	8,536	0.2096536	0.4070764	0	1
No schooling	8,536	0.1801032	0.3842875	0	1
Mother's educational attainment					
College and above	8,536	0.0123803	0.1105797	0	1
Professional school	8,536	0.0439941	0.2050895	0	1
Secondary school	8,536	0.1445099	0.3516190	0	1
Primary school	8,536	0.1639646	0.3702571	0	1
No schooling	8,536	0.3509211	0.4772759	0	1
Father is/was Communist Party member	7,766	0.2866817	0.4522348	0	1
Mother is/was Communist Party member	7,773	0.0905362	0.2869632	0	1
Father's occupation	7,773	6.706096	3.334315	1	12
Mother's occupation	7,773	8.57897	3.311557	1	12
Father's work unit	7,773	6.875513	5.156912	1	16
Mother's work unit	7,107	8.151652	6.024444	1	16

employed are members, and 7 per cent of the secondarily self-employed are. The percentage is lower for self-employed women, of whom only 4 per cent are Party members. If Party members are more likely to be allocated desirable jobs and less likely to be laid-off, then that could contribute to the lesser likelihood of them leaving the more secure lifetime employment for self-employment, which is riskier.

Around 27 per cent of fathers of the self-employed were Communist Party members, while only 9 per cent of mothers were. More fathers were skilled (22 per cent) as compared with mothers (8 per cent). Both parents have on average educational attainment at the lower-secondary-school level. The interesting statistic is regarding self-employment. Although the previous generation was squarely within the administered economy era, nearly 4 per cent of fathers

Table 6.6B Descriptive values: sample with experience of unemployment

Variable	Sample size	Mean	Std. dev.	Minimum	Maximum
Self-employed	1691	0.0372561	0.1894446	0	1
Self-employed as second job	1691	0.0147842	0.1207236	0	1
Social network	1426	5.513324	8.335098	0	152
Variance of income	1691	7122460	5.41e + 07	0	1.62e + 09
Gender	1691	0.5659373	0.4957798	0	1
Age	1691	38.8105	7.663141	19	55
Years of education	1685	10.02603	2.293683	1	17
Years of wage employment experience	1629	18.06066	8.058186	1	40
Communist Party member	1690	0.1044686	0.3059599	0	1
Married	1691	0.6927045	0.4613899	0	1
Spouse in wage employment	1691	0.1604274	0.3670155	0	1
Spouse in self-employment	1691	0.0031688	0.0562045	0	1
Father's educational attainment					
College and above	1691	0.0390302	0.193724	0	1
Professional school	1691	0.0869308	0.281817	0	1
Secondary school	1691	0.2879953	0.4529628	0	1
Primary school	1691	0.3270254	0.4692654	0	1
No schooling	1691	0.2312241	0.4217401	0	1
Mother's educational attainment					
College and above	1691	0.011236	0.1054338	0	1
Professional school	1691	0.048492	0.2148670	0	1
Secondary school	1691	0.1939681	0.3955211	0	1
Primary school	1691	0.2613838	0.4395185	0	1
No schooling	1691	0.4577173	0.4983563	0	1
Father is/was Communist Party member	1644	0.2785888	0.4484411	0	1
Mother is/was Communist Party member	1652	0.0756659	0.2645428	0	1
Father's occupation	1637	6.420281	2.943316	1	12
Mother's occupation	1556	8.448586	3.143399	1	12
Father's work unit	1624	6.624384	4.822855	1	16
Mother's work unit	1496	7.937166	5.801977	1	16
Do you agree with the following statements in order to secure a stable household standard of living in the long run? 0. Disagree, 1. Agree					
Try to improve my abilities to be more competitive	1040	0.8586538	0.3485459	0	1
Earn as much as possible while working in order to save for the future	1039	0.8806545	0.3243508	0	1

(same as the total proportion of self-employed in the current sample) are or were self-employed. A much smaller percentage (less than 2 per cent) of mothers are or were self-employed. The profile is similar for the secondarily self-employed, although few of these traits of the self-employed as a group are significantly different from the wage-employed. The significant differences are that a greater number of the wage-employed have mothers who are or were professionals

(14 per cent) as compared with 8 per cent for the self-employed and a large 21 per cent for the secondarily self-employed. There is also a difference in the father being a professional as between the two types of self-employed: 22 per cent versus 18 per cent. In terms of gender differences, there are no differences in the socio-economic backgrounds of men and women who are self-employed. All of the parental characteristics are similar for both genders.

The self-employed earned around 9,526 RMB on average in the survey year, and 7,673 RMB on average over the previous four years. The self-employed made 40 per cent more than the wage-employed on average. The gender differences here are notable. Self-employed men earned 12,508 RMB, which is more than twice as much as women who made 5,903 RMB on average. Over the previous four years, men earned 9,967 RMB on average as compared with women who earned almost half that amount at 4,789 RMB. The gender difference in incomes is a significant difference in their conditional mean income after controlling for age, education, employment experience, occupation, employment sector, and locale (cities). The total income for those who reported themselves as self-employed in a second job was 5,361 RMB on average which is nearly 50 per cent less than the incomes of the wholly self-employed. The disparity in income is confirmed by the average income that the secondary self-employed earned in the previous four years, which was 3,606 RMB, which is again nearly half of the average previous income of the self-employed. For this group in the sample year, the mean salary from their primary job was around 35 per cent of their total income (1,860 RMB), with the remainder from secondary earned income through self-employment which was as important as earned income. However, compared with the self-employed income of the wholly self-employed, these are small amounts. With increasing numbers of state-owned sector workers who are underemployed and a greater likelihood of becoming redundant without adequate unemployment benefits, these respondents appear to be doing what they can to increase their income.

The size of social networks is determined by asking the reported number of close contacts of an individual in any context, social or economic. The survey question asked: 'In the past year, how many relatives, friends, colleagues or acquaintances did you exchange gifts with or often maintain contact?' The mean size of social network is 8.2 persons, as compared with the non-self-employed who have social networks of 6.4 persons on average. This suggests that social networks may be linked to self-employment. Interestingly, for those who report self-employment as a second job, they have smaller social networks (5.4 persons), which suggest that this group seeks supplementary income perhaps not out of entrepreneurial spirit but out of necessity. Self-employed men have significantly larger social networks (9.5 persons) than women (6.8). Men and women who are self-employed as a second job have similarly sized social networks (5.1 persons versus 5.7, respectively).

Figure 6.1 shows that there is a small number of large social networks of over 100 persons in the sample. A number of studies of social networks from a variety of disciplines find a rule of 150 as the mean size of networks; for example, 150 is known as Dunbar's number. Anthropologists have doubled the mean size of social networks typically observed in field work; for example, Bernard, Shelley, and Killworth (1987) find a mean of 290 for the USA. Much depends on what questions are posed to find out the network size. For instance, Glaeser, Laibson, and Sacerdote (2002) use a person's Rolodex as the measure of a social network, which could figure in the hundreds. The measure used here focuses on interpersonal interactions so it should be smaller, but it is possible for self-employed individuals to have business-related networks of that magnitude and three of those surveyed have networks of around 150–2. It is a small percentage but one that reflects the fact that self-employed individuals are likely to need to maintain networks for their business; for example, supply and distribution chains which require regular interactions when operating in an uncertain institutional environment such as China where disputes are not adequately settled in courts or by an ombudsman. Thus, removing them would lose valuable observations concerning the sample of the self-employed. Nevertheless, outliers in the range of 200 and over were removed. Also, eliminating all of these observations in the tail does not affect the results.

The multinomial logit equation to be estimated is:

$$SELFEMPLOYED_i = \alpha + \beta X_i + \delta H_i + \chi SB_i + \gamma SN_i + \tau Risk_i + \varepsilon_i, \qquad (1)$$

where self-employment equals 0 if person i is wage employed, 1 if he is self-employed as a second job, and 2 if he is solely self-employed. The choice of multinomial logit is conditional on the assumption of the Independence of Irrelevant Alternatives (IIA) as not violated. The Hausman test examines the null hypothesis that the difference in coefficients is not systematic. If the Chi-squared test statistic is significant, then it would indicate a violation of the IIA assumption. The IIA assumption is found to hold (the Chi-squared test statistic is 0.872), so the multinomial logit model is the appropriate estimation approach. The Wald and LR chi-squared test results confirm the validity of the estimations and the pseudo-R^2 gives an indication of goodness of fit.

Self-employment is determined by a vector of observable characteristics associated with occupational choice, including a vector of personal traits (X_i) such as education, age, gender, Communist Party membership, years of employment experience, and having experienced unemployment which can induce self-employment, and two vectors of variables capturing spousal characteristics (H_i), such as marital and employment status of one's spouse, and socio-economic background (SB_i), such as parental education, occupation, and sector of employer. Controls for the city of the respondent are also included. Marital status is measured as whether single or married, and employment status of the spouse is whether he/she is in wage employment or self-employment. Parental education is measured in educational level attained and entered as dummy variables each corresponding to a particular educational level, such as college and above, secondary school, and primary school. Parental occupation is a continuous variable that is ranked from skilled to unskilled occupations, and sector of employer or work unit is also a continuous variable that is ranked from the extent of state involvement; for example, from the state-owned to the private sector. Given the possibility of the clustering effect of using a household dataset to estimate individual outcomes, robust standard errors that are also adjusted for clustering at the household level are computed.

Spousal characteristics, such as marital status and employment status of one's spouse, could also influence the decision to become self-employed. This is particularly the case since joining with relatives was one of the reasons for choosing to become self-employed. For instance, married individuals could rely on their spouse's network or income to help them obtain the necessary permissions or funds to enter self-employment. Having a spouse who is employed with regular income may also matter to reduce the risk of self-employment. Measuring whether one's spouse is also self-employed is also significant since familial labour and other forms of support could be important, as there is no information regarding whether these are family businesses. Spousal social network could also be important, but the variable was not significant in the estimations. It could be that the income or expertise a spouse supplies is more important than the use of their network since spouses are likely to share contacts, so the inclusion of this measure turns out not to be significant and is omitted. Socio-economic background could be important for similar reasons. Parental connections and influence could manifestly affect whether a respondent starts his or her own business. Both sets of traits could also provide avenues for social networks whereby familial networks help an individual accomplish self-employment.

Indeed, self-employment is also thought to be associated with having a social network, and possessing certain attitudes such as having drive or motivation and contending with risk. The logit equation will be modified to first include a measure of social network (SN_i). Next, given the importance placed on attitude toward risk as a defining characteristic of those who have entrepreneurial spirit, a measure of risk will be included to determine if social network remains a significant and robust determinant of self-employment once attitudes such as whether one embraces risk is accounted for. More risk-averse people would prefer wage employment even if the rewards were smaller if the variance of the income was less. On the other hand, if the self-employed are risk-loving, then variability of income would not deter them. Attitude toward risk could thus be proxied by the variance of income over the past five years (see for example, King 1974). There is recall income data from the previous five years in this survey. Although there is concern about the reliability of recall data, the sample is of NBS survey households who are required to keep detailed records of their income and expenditure to be inspected every ten days (Appleton, Song, and Xia 2005). Thus, this data will be used for the limited purpose of measuring the variance of income.

One of the motivations for entering self-employment may be the experience of job loss and therefore the involuntary motivation of starting a business if wage employment is difficult to find due to scarring from the experience of

213

unemployment or perhaps provide an impetus to strike out on one's own. The sample of those who have experienced unemployment is therefore an interesting group to investigate. Also, it is often believed the measures of social capital merely pick up certain unobservable motivations such as simply being more driven. Although measures of motivation and drive are not available in the main sample, they are found in this sub-sample. The question asked was: 'Do you agree with the following statements in order to secure a stable household standard of living in the long run? (0) Disagree or (1) Agree.' The indicated statements were: '(a) Try to improve my abilities to be more competitive'; and '(b) Earn as much as possible while working in order to save for the future'. Agreement would indicate motivation to improve one's own skills to earn more money and a drive to work hard for the same purpose. Proxies are not perfect, but this estimation will test whether these responses reflect any motivation or drive on the part of the self-employed.

The baseline model will be modified for this sub-sample as follows:

$$SELFEMPLOYED_i = \alpha + \beta X_i + \delta H_i + \chi SB_i + \gamma SN_i + \tau Risk_i + \upsilon Drive_i + \varepsilon_i. \quad (2)$$

Social networks are thought to be relatively stable over time in that there are not significant changes in the size of networks from year to year, but it is not possible to rule out the fact that there are omitted variables which simultaneously predict self-employment and networks, or that reverse causality could exist. Thus, endogeneity will be tested for by using an instrumental variable (IV) approach (Smith and Blundell 1986).

The reduced form first-stage regression is:

$$SN_i = \varphi + \gamma GIFTS_i + \eta X_i + \sigma_i, \quad (3)$$

where the instruments are the value of gifts given in the survey year. Gifts are often exchanged to build relationships in China, particularly gifts given to family and friends. It can be as much personal- as business-driven. In fact, the mean value of gifts given was higher for non-self-employed (654 RMB) than for the self-employed (336 RMB), as was the maximum value (55,000 RMB versus 4,200 RMB). The large number of outcomes possible under the social networks and gifts variables is also preferable.

To establish whether an instrumental variable approach is unbiased, the instrument must be informative and valid. The gifts variable should be correlated with the potentially endogenous variable: $cov(GIFTS,SN) = 0$, so the instrument is informative. Second, the instrumental variable should not be correlated with the residual in the structural equation: $cov(GIFTS,\varepsilon) \neq 0$, so the instrument is valid. Table 6.2 gives the first-stage regression results.

Table 6.7 shows that the value of gifts given is positively and significantly correlated with social networks at the 1 per cent level. However, there may still be a weak instrument problem. If the correlation between gifts given and social networks is very small and close to zero, and the instrument is valid, it can still be the case that the IV approach produces biased estimates. Staiger and Stock

Table 6.7 First-stage regression results for instrumental variable approach (t-statistics)

Dependent variable: social network	
Gifts given in the survey year	0.0003
	(2.96)***
F(33, 3761)	11.60***
Anderson test	22.455***
Cragg-Donald F-statistic	22.319*
Number of observations	3762

Notes: (1) Only the coefficient of the instrument is reported.
(2) Robust standard errors adjusted for clustering at the household level are computed.
(3) *** indicates significance at the 1% level, ** at the 5% level, and * at the 10% level.

(1997) propose a rule of thumb to detect if there could be a weak instrument problem. If the F-statistic in the first-stage regression is more than 10 in the case of one potentially endogenous variable, then there is not a weak instrument. An F-statistic of 11.60 is computed which is significant at the 1 per cent level, suggesting that there is not a weak instrument problem. The Cragg-Donald F-statistic further suggests that the instrument is relevant (Cragg and Donald 1993). According to the Stock-Yogo test critical values, this means that with 90 per cent confidence, the IV estimates have less than 10 per cent of OLS bias (Stock and Yogo 2005). Finally, the Anderson test for IV relevance rejects the null hypothesis at the 1 per cent level, indicating that the instrument is good in the relevance sense (Anderson 1986).

Validity is implied through a null hypothesis that the instrument is not correlated with the residuals in the structural equation. After calculating the residuals from the first-stage regression, they are included as a regressor in the structural equation. A t-test of the coefficient indicates a t-statistic of 0.98, which is not significant at even the 10 per cent level. The null hypothesis is therefore not rejected.

Having established the relevance and validity of the instrument, the Smith-Blundell test of exogeneity for probit regressions is applied (Smith and Blundell 1986). The null hypothesis is that all explanatory variables are exogenous. The Smith-Blundell test statistic is evaluated with respect to a chi-squared distribution in the number of potentially endogenous variables, and the associated p-value either rejects or does not reject the null hypothesis. If the null hypothesis is not rejected, then equation (2) is the appropriate formulation.

The second-stage logit regression uses the predicted value of social networks from the first stage, and equation (2) is re-formulated as follows:

$$SELFEMPLOYED_i = \alpha + \beta X_i + \delta H_i + \chi SB_i + \gamma \hat{S}N_i + \tau Risk_i + \upsilon Drive_i + \upsilon_i. \quad (4)$$

The Smith-Blundell test statistic for exogeneity was 0.0125465. For a chi-squared distribution of one, a p-value of 0.9108 is computed. This p-value does not reject the null hypothesis that all explanatory variables are exogenous at any conventional level of significance. Therefore, social networks can be entered in the

215

probit regressions with some assurance, and equation (2) is the appropriate model for estimation.

Nevertheless, any significant effects would be interpreted as reflecting not a causal relationship between self-employment and social networks, but rather a correlation between being self-employed and networking in a transition labour market, and whether this association holds even after other observable traits identified above are controlled for. Finally, gender differences will be considered and the traits of the self-employed men and women will be investigated separately, particularly as gender differences are notable in social networks.

This section now turns to the determinants of self-employment and investigating the role of social networks for two types of the self-employed. As already outlined, there are likely to be different characteristics and drivers for those who are self-employed in addition to their paid employment job, so the empirical findings separately analyse those who are entirely self-employed and developing China's private sector from the ground level, from those who are self-employed as a second job to supplement their income. The latter would be interesting to examine as those who take advantage of China's marketization to develop opportunities. There may be different traits that influence self-employment for the solely self-employed who leave the security of paid employment, and start private-sector activities. Also, with the high rate of experience of unemployment in this sample, there might also be different determinants for those who entered self-employment after experiencing periods of unemployment. As such, these three groups will be assessed separately.

Tables 6.8–6.10 identify the factors influencing the likelihood of becoming self-employed based on equation (2) for three groups; for example, wholly self-employed, self-employed as a second job, and those who become self-employed after experiencing unemployment. Separate estimations will be undertaken for men and women within each table. The multinomial logit regressions allow for three outcomes: wage-employed, self-employed as a second job, and self-employed. The coefficients on the explanatory variables, notably of social networks, represent an increase or decrease in the probability of self-employment. The significance of the social network variable is of greatest interest, having reviewed a number of factors that suggest that relationships are important in establishing self-employment, even after accounting for all other relevant characteristics.

6.5.1 *Determinants of Self-employment*

The findings of the main sample of the self-employed are generally consistent with studies of self-employment that find knowing people who are entrepreneurial or having connections increases the likelihood of starting one's own business (see for example, Rees and Shah 1986; Djankov et al. 2006; Zhang et al. 2006). The social network variable is significantly positive and remains robustly so for the entire sample and for the sub-samples of men and women. As seen in Table 6.8 columns (3)–(5), a single-person increase in the size of a social network will

Table 6.8 Determinants of self-employment, urban sample, multinomial logit regression (robust standard errors in parentheses)

Self-employed	(1)	(2)	(3)	(4)	(5)	(6) Men	(7) Men	(8) Women	(9) Women
Social network			0.0191*** (0.0063)	0.0192*** (0.0072)	0.0191*** (0.0072)	0.0218** (0.0090)	0.0198* (0.0105)	0.0162* (0.0085)	0.0175* (0.0103)
Personal characteristics									
Gender	-0.6298** (0.2714)	-0.9490*** (0.1542)	-0.7394*** (0.1488)	-1.0108*** (0.1689)	-1.0031*** (0.1907)				
Age	-0.0066 (0.0228)	0.0194** (0.0094)	0.0201** (0.0095)	0.0249** (0.0100)	0.0249** (0.0120)	0.0354*** (0.0118)	0.0355** (0.0156)	0.0039 (0.0147)	0.0097 (0.0200)
Years of education	-0.1011* (0.0577)	-0.1069*** (0.0337)	-0.1014*** (0.0350)	-0.0992*** (0.0369)	-0.1014*** (0.0361)	-0.1287*** (0.0420)	-0.1631*** (0.0478)	-0.1016* (0.0578)	-0.0488 (0.0633)
Years of wage employment experience	-0.1459*** (0.0268)	-0.1524*** (0.0147)	-0.1383*** (0.0135)	-0.1511*** (0.0159)	-0.1527*** (0.0152)	-0.1197*** (0.0181)	-0.1319*** (0.0206)	-0.1931*** (0.0216)	-0.2125*** (0.0266)
Communist Party member	-0.3669 (0.4969)	-1.2939*** (0.3690)	-1.2486*** (0.3716)	-1.1777*** (0.3805)	-1.2054*** (0.3658)	-1.3351*** (0.4268)	-1.2966*** (0.4315)	-0.9060 (0.7984)	-0.6736 (0.7585)
Experienced unemployment in previous 5 years	0.5052 (0.3507)	0.2993 (0.2080)	0.3876* (0.1991)	0.4857** (0.2195)	0.4837** (0.2070)	0.5303** (0.2519)	0.6068** (0.2775)	0.2548 (0.2935)	0.2581 (0.3350)
Spouse characteristics									
Married		0.4480 (0.2807)		0.4316 (0.3225)	0.4643 (0.2953)		0.2663 (0.3673)		0.8046 (0.5374)
Spouse in wage employment		0.2681 (0.2032)		0.2995 (0.2271)	0.2754 (0.2246)		0.0918 (0.3437)		0.2059 (0.3439)
Spouse in self-employment		5.1171*** (0.5117)		5.1220*** (0.4896)	5.0946*** (0.5150)		6.6538*** (1.0703)		4.8282*** (0.6849)
Socio-economic background									
Father's educational attainment									
College and above	0.5558	0.7248	0.4856	0.6689	0.6262	0.7501	0.9186	-0.0453	0.2452

(continued)

Table 6.8 Continued

Self-employed	(1)	(2)	(3)	(4)	(5)	(6)	(7)	(8)	(9)
						Men	Men	Women	Women
	(0.7670)	(0.4423)	(0.4563)	(0.4593)	(0.4810)	(0.5359)	(0.5915)	(0.9539)	(0.9165)
Professional school	0.2305	0.1082	-0.2635	-0.1160	-0.0977	-0.3138	-0.0420	-0.3919	-0.2661
	(0.5713)	(0.3419)	(0.3401)	(0.3569)	(0.4004)	(0.4525)	(0.5175)	(0.6297)	(0.6581)
Secondary school	-0.2833	0.1099	-0.1172	-0.0558	-0.0383	-0.1759	0.0085	-0.0622	-0.1469
	(0.4418)	(0.2752)	(0.2759)	(0.2964)	(0.2972)	(0.3495)	(0.3966)	(0.4504)	(0.4728)
Primary school	-0.1797	0.0612	-0.1423	-0.0879	-0.0686	-0.3553	-0.2169	0.1451	0.0863
	(0.4396)	(0.2463)	(0.2494)	(0.2605)	(0.2683)	(0.3266)	(0.3565)	(0.3861)	(0.4375)
Mother's educational attainment									
College and above	-0.1707	-0.6176	-0.8978	-0.8618	-0.8192	-0.4624	-0.4860	—	—
	(1.1786)	(0.7255)	(0.8503)	(0.8576)	(0.8584)	(0.9163)	(0.9358)		
Professional school	-1.2328	-0.9848**	-0.7996	-0.7766	-0.7646	-0.9135	-0.9594	-0.4624	-0.3435
	(0.8394)	(0.4613)	(0.5258)	(0.5006)	(0.5015)	(0.6445)	(0.6582)	(0.8472)	(0.8300)
Secondary school	-0.0723	-0.5121*	-0.3888	-0.2532	-0.2710	-0.1268	-0.2546	-0.7264	-0.4992
	(0.4443)	(0.2874)	(0.3064)	(0.3135)	(0.2998)	(0.3615)	(0.3940)	(0.5444)	(0.4925)
Primary school	0.1980	-0.5818***	-0.3269	-0.4039	-0.4018	-0.6496*	-0.7987**	0.0039	-0.0221
	(0.4366)	(0.2525)	(0.2725)	(0.2808)	(0.2662)	(0.3828)	(0.3841)	(0.3824)	(0.3960)
Father is/was a Communist Party member	-0.3159	-0.2388	-0.0692	-0.0884	-0.1111	0.0693	-0.0086	-0.2076	-0.2746
	(0.3396)	(0.2051)	(0.2069)	(0.2091)	(0.2137)	(0.2438)	(0.2805)	(0.3413)	(0.3598)
Mother is/was a Communist Party member	0.0930	0.3249	0.2880	0.2505	0.2770	0.4170	0.5823	-0.0454	-0.3819
	(0.4639)	(0.2973)	(0.2982)	(0.3012)	(0.3165)	(0.3745)	(0.3723)	(0.5198)	(0.6420)
Father's occupation	0.0433	0.0127	0.0070	0.0007	-0.0007	-0.0145	-0.0329	0.0214	0.0228
	(0.0569)	(0.0325)	(0.0325)	(0.0339)	(0.0353)	(0.0380)	(0.0466)	(0.0610)	(0.0575)
Mother's occupation	0.0638	0.0688*	0.0672*	0.0670*	0.0690*	0.0949**	0.0980*	0.0217	0.0265
	(0.0572)	(0.0370)	(0.0380)	(0.0399)	(0.0384)	(0.0476)	(0.0503)	(0.0685)	(0.0636)
Father's employment sector	-0.0405	0.0040	-0.0054	-0.0000	0.0001	0.0114	0.0146	-0.0325	-0.0265
	(0.0340)	(0.0190)	(0.0188)	(0.0201)	(0.0206)	(0.0258)	(0.0268)	(0.0313)	(0.0332)
Mother's employment sector	0.0110	-0.0021	-0.0032	0.0054	0.0049	-0.0267	-0.0225	0.0244	0.0399
	(0.0289)	(0.0173)	(0.0171)	(0.0184)	(0.0186)	(0.0240)	(0.0250)	(0.0263)	(0.0290)

Variance of income					9.02e10***		9.01e-10***		-4.49e-09
					(2.60e-10)		(2.70e-10)		(7.41e-09)
Cities	Yes	Yes	Yes	Yes	Yes	Yes	Yes	Yes	Yes
Constant	-1.4020	-1.0476	-0.8239	-1.4069*	-1.3950*	-1.4760*	-1.2446	-0.2612	-1.8209
	(1.2475)	(0.7202)	(0.7522)	(0.7476)	(0.8210)	(0.8652)	(1.0285)	(1.2674)	(1.4600)
Wald χ^2 (64)	489.48***								
Wald χ^2 (66)		19,880.40***	24,171.06***			23,359.13***		36,961.48***	
LR χ^2 (72)				495.88***	532.16***				
LR χ^2 (74)							294.41***		336.31***
Pseudo R^2	0.1821	0.2329	0.2276	0.1811	0.2410	0.1904	0.2431	0.2675	0.3379
Number of observations	8382	8382	7405	7405	7405	3769	3769	3636	3636

Notes: (1) Dependent variable: 2 if wholly self-employed, 1 if self-employed in second job, and 0 if wage employed. The results for dependent variable = 2 are reported here.
(2) Robust standard errors adjusted for clustering at the household level are computed.
(3) *** indicates significance at the 1% level, ** at the 5% level, and * at the 10% level.
(4) Instead of a Wald test, the attitude toward risk equations uses the variance of five years of income in the specification so the likelihood used for the estimation is a true distribution of the sample and a likelihood ratio test is employed.
(5) The coefficients on variables measuring parental education have been omitted where the estimates are subject to multicollinearity due to the small number of observations within the sub-sample.

Table 6.9 Determinants of self-employment as a second job, urban sample, multinomial logit regression (robust standard errors in parentheses)

Self-employed as second job	(1)	(2)	(3)	(4)	(5)	(6)	(7)	(8)	(9)
						Men	Men	Women	Women
Social network			-0.0151 (0.0269)	-0.0134 (0.0273)	-0.0134 (0.0310)	-0.0088 (0.0272)	-0.0045 (0.0360)	-0.0197 (0.0418)	-0.0237 (0.0514)
Personal characteristics									
Gender	-0.6298** (0.2714)	-0.6617** (0.2835)	-0.5610* (0.3136)	-0.5731* (0.3252)	-1.0108*** (0.1689)				
Age	-0.0066 (0.0228)	0.0004 (0.0215)	-0.0161 (0.0250)	-0.0080 (0.0245)	0.0249** (0.0100)	-0.0043 (0.0306)	0.0070 (0.0377)	-0.0317 (0.0346)	-0.0342 (0.0347)
Years of education	-0.1011* (0.0577)	-0.1045* (0.0585)	-0.1326* (0.0687)	-0.1373* (0.0702)	-0.0992*** (0.0369)	-0.1672* (0.0862)	-0.1639* (0.0870)	-0.1284 (0.0989)	-0.1324 (0.0984)
Years of wage employment experience	-0.1459*** (0.0268)	-0.1389*** (0.0269)	-0.1396*** (0.0295)	-0.1332*** (0.0298)	-0.1511*** (0.0159)	-0.1286*** (0.0352)	-0.1157*** (0.0446)	-0.1765*** (0.0478)	-0.1837*** (0.0442)
Communist Party Member	-0.3669 (0.4969)	-0.3094 (0.4980)	-0.1052 (0.5233)	-0.0449 (0.5259)	-1.1777*** (0.3805)	0.0981 (0.6470)	0.1627 (0.5780)	-0.2988 (1.0364)	-0.2128 (1.0840)
Experienced unemployment in previous 5 years	0.5052 (0.3507)	0.7291* (0.4064)	0.5972 (0.4070)	0.8163* (0.4720)	0.4857** (0.2195)	1.7459*** (0.5106)	1.9255*** (0.4538)	-0.9813 (0.7081)	-0.8739 (0.7019)
Spouse characteristics									
Married		-0.7787* (0.4589)		-0.8117* (0.5258)	-0.8084* (0.4280)		-1.2794** (0.5769)		0.0469 (0.7159)
Spouse in wage employment		0.7835* (0.4158)		0.7158* (0.4692)	0.7141* (0.3746)		0.5081 (0.6267)		0.6082 (0.5608)
Socio-economic background									
Father's educational attainment									
College and above	0.5558 (0.7670)	0.5351 (0.7603)	0.3572 (0.7452)	0.3238 (0.7233)	0.6689 (0.4593)	1.0031 (0.8767)	0.8950 (1.0032)	-1.0285 (0.9956)	-1.0542 (1.5746)
Professional school	0.2305 (0.5713)	0.2065 (0.5828)	-0.3068 (0.6383)	-0.3502 (0.6580)	-0.1160 (0.3569)	-0.5970 (1.0204)	-0.7370 (1.0284)	-0.0451 (0.9872)	-0.0129 (0.9918)
Secondary school	-0.2833 (0.4418)	-0.3263 (0.4485)	-0.4985 (0.4609)	-0.5626 (0.4655)	-0.0558 (0.2964)	-0.3238 (0.7057)	-0.4086 (0.6884)	-0.5689 (0.5918)	-0.5857 (0.7914)
Primary school	-0.1797 (0.4396)	-0.1964 (0.4428)	-0.8190 (0.5042)	-0.8644* (0.5095)	-0.0879 (0.2605)	-0.7760 (0.6449)	-0.8035 (0.6533)	-1.1587 (0.8366)	-1.1661 (0.8318)
Mother's educational attainment									

College and above	-0.1707 (1.1786)	-0.1099 (1.1845)	0.0157 (1.2235)	0.0550 (1.2159)	-0.8618 (0.8576)	—	0.0023 (0.7160)	1.6330 (1.3322)	1.8371 (1.6551)
Professional school	-1.2328 (0.8394)	-1.2427 (0.8593)	-0.9126 (0.8911)	-0.9471 (0.9148)	-0.7766 (0.5006)	—	0.1842 (0.6349)	-0.5409 (1.2988)	-0.4802 (1.2601)
Secondary school	-0.0723 (0.4443)	-0.0867 (0.4542)	-0.0168 (0.4946)	-0.0364 (0.5062)	-0.2532 (0.3135)	0.1892 (0.5952)	0.0023 (0.7160)	-0.2987 (0.7713)	-0.1605 (0.8935)
Primary school	0.1980 (0.4366)	0.2140 (0.4414)	0.5346 (0.4728)	0.5703 (0.4760)	-0.4039 (0.2808)	0.1755 (0.6844)	0.1842 (0.6349)	1.1182* (0.6590)	1.1568 (0.7419)
Father is/was a Communist Party member	-0.3159 (0.3396)	-0.3256 (0.3404)	-0.1819 (0.3614)	-0.2054 (0.3611)	-0.0884 (0.2091)	0.1417 (0.4909)	0.0518 (0.5019)	-0.4384 (0.6181)	-0.4435 (0.5753)
Mother is/was a Communist Party member	0.0930 (0.4639)	0.0825 (0.4708)	0.3823 (0.4929)	0.3812 (0.5015)	0.2505 (0.3012)	0.6707 (0.6461)	0.6600 (0.7177)	0.1262 (0.8131)	0.1407 (0.7925)
Father's occupation	0.0433 (0.0569)	0.0510 (0.0591)	0.0703 (0.0616)	0.0768 (0.0637)	0.0007 (0.0339)	0.0529 (0.0818)	0.0559 (0.0890)	0.1088 (0.0937)	0.1204 (0.0975)
Mother's occupation	0.0638 (0.0572)	0.0674 (0.0587)	0.0588 (0.0660)	0.0626 (0.0677)	0.0670* (0.0399)	0.1634* (0.0957)	0.1700* (0.0997)	-0.0518 (0.0873)	-0.0646 (0.0982)
Father's employment sector	-0.0405 (0.0340)	-0.0405 (0.0348)	-0.0413 (0.0376)	-0.0403 (0.0383)	-0.0000 (0.0201)	-0.0127 (0.0445)	-0.0093 (0.0491)	-0.0399 (0.0645)	-0.0368 (0.0572)
Mother's employment sector	0.0110 (0.0289)	0.0129 (0.0295)	0.0194 (0.0321)	0.0201 (0.0329)	0.0054 (0.0184)	0.0344 (0.0412)	0.0315 (0.0431)	-0.0335 (0.0572)	-0.0306 (0.0497)
Variance of income					-1.96e-09 (7.15e-09)		-3.18e-10 (3.31e-09)		-1.78e-08 (2.65e-08)
Cities	Yes	Yes	Yes	Yes	Yes	Yes	Yes	Yes	Yes
Constant	-1.4020 (1.2475)	-1.4334 (1.2428)	-0.7517 (1.3965)	-0.7213 (1.4025)	-1.4069* (0.7476)	-3.2704 (2.1261)	-2.9285 (2.0013)	1.6461 (1.7072)	1.4788 (2.2082)
Wald χ^2 (64)	489.48***	19,880.40***	24,171.06***	495.88***		23,359.13***			
Wald χ^2 (66)								36,961.48***	
LR χ^2 (72)					532.16***		294.41***		
LR χ^2 (74)									336.31***
Pseudo R^2	0.1821	0.2329	0.2276	0.1811	0.2410	0.1904	0.2431	0.2675	0.3379
Number of observations	8382	8382	7405	7405	7405	3769	3769	3636	3636

Notes: (1) Dependent variable: 2 if wholly self-employed, 1 if self-employed in second job, and 0 if wage employed. The results for dependent variable = 1 are reported here.

(2) Robust standard errors adjusted for clustering at the household level are computed.

(3) *** indicates significance at the 1% level, ** at the 5% level, and * at the 10% level.

(4) Instead of a Wald test, the attitude toward risk equations uses the variance of five years of income in the specification so the likelihood used for the estimation is a true distribution of the sample and a likelihood ratio test is employed.

(5) There were no spouses in self-employment among those who are self-employed as a second job. (6) The coefficients on variables measuring parental education have been omitted where the estimates are subject to multicollinearity due to the small number of observations within the sub-sample.

Table 6.10 Determinants of self-employment as a second job, urban sample, multinomial probit regression (z-statistics in parentheses)

Self-employed as second job	(1)	(2)	(3)	(4)	(5)	(6)	(7)	(8)	(9)
						Men	Men	Women	Women
Social network	-0.6298**		-0.0151	-0.0134	-0.0134	-0.0088	-0.0045	-0.0197	-0.0237
	(0.2714)		(0.0269)	(0.0273)	(0.0310)	(0.0272)	(0.0360)	(0.0418)	(0.0514)
Personal characteristics									
Gender	-0.6298**	-0.6617**	-0.5610*	-0.5731*	-1.0108***				
	(0.2714)	(0.2835)	(0.3136)	(0.3252)	(0.1689)				
Age	-0.0066	0.0004	-0.0161	-0.0080	0.0249**	-0.0043	0.0070	-0.0317	-0.0342
	(0.0228)	(0.0215)	(0.0250)	(0.0245)	(0.0100)	(0.0306)	(0.0377)	(0.0346)	(0.0347)
Years of education	-0.1011**	-0.1045**	-0.1326**	-0.1373**	-0.0992***	-0.1672*	-0.1639*	-0.1284	-0.1324
	(0.0577)	(0.0585)	(0.0687)	(0.0702)	(0.0369)	(0.0862)	(0.0870)	(0.0989)	(0.0984)
Years of wage employment experience	-0.1459***	-0.1389***	-0.1396***	-0.1332***	-0.1511***	-0.1286***	-0.1157***	-0.1765***	-0.1837***
	(0.0268)	(0.0269)	(0.0295)	(0.0298)	(0.0159)	(0.0352)	(0.0446)	(0.0478)	(0.0442)
Communist Party Member	-0.3669	-0.3094	-0.1052	-0.0449	-1.1777***	0.0981	0.1627	-0.2988	-0.2128
	(0.4969)	(0.4980)	(0.5233)	(0.5259)	(0.3805)	(0.6470)	(0.5780)	(1.0364)	(1.0840)
Experienced unemployment in previous 5 years	0.5052	0.7291*	0.5972	0.8163*	0.4857**	1.7459***	1.9255***	-0.9813	-0.8739
	(0.3507)	(0.4064)	(0.4070)	(0.4720)	(0.2195)	(0.5106)	(0.4538)	(0.7081)	(0.7019)
Spouse characteristics									
Married		-0.7787*		-0.8117*	-0.8084*		-1.2794**		0.0469
		(0.4589)		(0.5258)	(0.4280)		(0.5769)		(0.7159)
Spouse in wage employment		0.7835*		0.7158*	0.7141*		0.5081		0.6082
		(0.4158)		(0.4692)	(0.3746)		(0.6267)		(0.5608)
Socio-economic background									
Father's educational attainment									
College and above	0.5558	0.5351	0.3572	0.3238	0.6689	1.0031	0.8950	-1.0285	-1.0542
	(0.7670)	(0.7603)	(0.7452)	(0.7233)	(0.4593)	(0.8767)	(1.0032)	(0.9956)	(1.5746)
Professional school	0.2305	0.2065	-0.3068	-0.3502	-0.1160	-0.5970	-0.7370	-0.0451	-0.0129
	(0.5713)	(0.5828)	(0.6383)	(0.6580)	(0.3569)	(1.0204)	(1.0284)	(0.9872)	(0.9918)
Secondary school	-0.2833	-0.3263	-0.4985	-0.5626	-0.0558	-0.3238	-0.4086	-0.5689	-0.5857
	(0.4418)	(0.4485)	(0.4609)	(0.4655)	(0.2964)	(0.7057)	(0.6884)	(0.5918)	(0.7914)
Primary school	-0.1797	-0.1964	-0.8190	-0.8644*	-0.0879	-0.7760	-0.8035	-1.1587	-1.1661
	(0.4296)	(0.4428)	(0.5042)	(0.5095)	(0.2605)	(0.6449)	(0.6533)	(0.8366)	(0.8181)

Mother's educational attainment	(1)	(2)	(3)	(4)	(5)	(6)	(7)	(8)	(9)
College and above	−0.1707	−0.1099	0.0157	0.0550	−0.8618	−32.3364***	−32.7229	1.6330	1.8371
	(1.1786)	(1.1845)	(1.2235)	(1.2159)	(0.8576)	(0.9708)	(1.5633e+07)	(1.3322)	(1.6551)
Professional school	−1.2328	−1.2427	−0.9126	−0.9471	−0.7766	−31.8386***	−32.5743	−0.5409	−0.4802
	(0.8593)	(0.8911)	(0.9148)	(0.9148)	(0.5006)	(0.7501)	(7386618.3876)	(1.2988)	(1.2601)
Secondary school	−0.0723	−0.0867	−0.0168	−0.0364	−0.2532	0.1892	0.0023	−0.2987	−0.1605
	(0.4443)	(0.4542)	(0.4946)	(0.5062)	(0.3135)	(0.5952)	(0.7160)	(0.7713)	(0.8935)
Primary school	0.1980	0.2140	0.5346	0.5703	−0.4039	0.1755	0.1842	1.1182*	1.1568
	(0.4366)	(0.4414)	(0.4728)	(0.4760)	(0.2808)	(0.6844)	(0.6349)	(0.6590)	(0.7419)
Father is/was a Communist Party member	−0.3159	−0.3256	−0.1819	−0.2054	−0.0884	0.1417	0.0518	−0.4384	−0.4435
	(0.3396)	(0.3404)	(0.3614)	(0.3611)	(0.2091)	(0.4909)	(0.5019)	(0.6181)	(0.5753)
Mother is/was a Communist Party member	0.0930	0.0825	0.3823	0.3812	0.2505	0.6707	0.6600	0.1262	0.1407
	(0.4639)	(0.4708)	(0.4929)	(0.5015)	(0.3012)	(0.6461)	(0.7177)	(0.8131)	(0.7925)
Father's occupation	0.0433	0.0510	0.0703	0.0768	0.0007	0.0529	0.0559	0.1088	0.1204
	(0.0569)	(0.0591)	(0.0616)	(0.0637)	(0.0339)	(0.0818)	(0.0890)	(0.0937)	(0.0975)
Mother's occupation	0.0638	0.0674	0.0588	0.0626	0.0670*	0.1634*	0.1700*	−0.0518	−0.0646
	(0.0572)	(0.0587)	(0.0660)	(0.0677)	(0.0399)	(0.0957)	(0.0997)	(0.0873)	(0.0982)
Father's employment sector	−0.0405	−0.0405	−0.0413	−0.0403	−0.0000	−0.0127	−0.0093	−0.0399	−0.0368
	(0.0340)	(0.0348)	(0.0376)	(0.0383)	(0.0201)	(0.0445)	(0.0491)	(0.0645)	(0.0572)
Mother's employment sector	0.0110	0.0129	0.0194	0.0201	0.0054	0.0344	0.0315	−0.0335	−0.0306
	(0.0289)	(0.0295)	(0.0321)	(0.0329)	(0.0184)	(0.0412)	(0.0431)	(0.0572)	(0.0497)
Variance of income					−1.96e−09		−3.18e−10		−1.78e−08
					(7.15e−09)		(3.31e−09)		(2.65e−08)
Cities	Yes	Yes	Yes	Yes	Yes	Yes	Yes	Yes	Yes
Constant	−1.4020	−1.4334	−0.7517	−0.7213	−1.4069*	−3.2704	−2.9285	1.6461	1.4788
	(1.2475)	(1.2428)	(1.3965)	(1.4025)	(0.7476)	(2.1261)	(2.0013)	(1.7072)	(2.2082)
Wald χ^2(64)	489.48***								
Wald χ^2(66)		19,880.40***	24,171.06***	495.88***		23,359.13***		36,961.48***	
LR χ^2(72)					532.16***				
LR χ^2(74)							294.41***		336.31***
Pseudo R^2	0.1821	0.2329	0.2276	0.1811	0.2410	0.1904	0.2431	0.2675	0.3379
Number of observations	8382	8382	7405	7405	7405	3769	3769	3636	3636

Notes: (1) Dependent variable: 2 if wholly self-employed, 1 if self-employed in second job, and 0 if wage employed. The results for dependent variable = 1 are reported here.
(2) Robust standard errors adjusted for clustering at the household level are computed.
(3) *** indicates significance at the 1% level, ** at the 5% level, and * at the 10% level.
(4) Instead of a Wald test, the attitude toward risk equations uses the variance of five years of income in the specification so the likelihood used for the estimation is a true distribution of the sample and a likelihood ratio test is employed.
(5) There were no spouses in self-employment among those who are self-employed as a second job.

increase the probability of self-employment by 1.9 per cent. It is not a large effect, but if a social network were to be expanded by ten persons, then the probability of self-employment rises 19 per cent, and so forth.

Amongst the personal characteristics, the significant and negative coefficient on female gender implies that being a woman reduces the probability of self-employment, as do years of education and wage employment experience as well as Party membership. Age, by contrast, increases the probability. Experience of unemployment in the previous five years also raises the probability of self-employment. This variable was insignificant in columns (1) and (2) before the social network variable was included, suggesting that there was omitted variable bias. By omitting social networks, the OLS estimates would be biased. If the wrong variables were included, the estimates are inefficient but not biased. In this instance, those who had experienced unemployment are more likely to become self-employed once their social networks are also measured, as both positively increase the prospects of starting one's business and are correlated.

Only having a spouse in self-employment is important for self-employment amongst the spousal traits, not marital status, or whether a spouse is in wage employment. This variable is significant across estimations and suggests that having a spouse who is also self-employed is a strong predictor of one's own self-employment. It leads to a supposition that these are family-run businesses and strengthens the view that joining with relatives can be a strong motivator for self-employment, consistent with the responses to the questionnaire.

Among the socio-economic background factors, only mothers in more skilled occupations increase the probability of self-employment. Mothers in higher skilled occupations could provide the aspiration for their children to seek higher incomes via self-employment and step out of the lifetime job system. Father's background has no significant impact.

The attitude-toward-risk variable is also positive and highly significant. The variance of income positively increases the likelihood of self-employment. As a proxy for risk, this suggests that the self-employed are more comfortable with taking risks than employed workers, and that the variability in income increases the prospect of self-employment. The rest of the explanatory variables are virtually unchanged, implying a robustness of the results.

For both men and women, social networks increase the probability of becoming self-employed; the effect for men is slightly larger than that for women. There are other gender differences, though. Whereas having more education and work experience as well as being a Party member will reduce the probability, being older and having been unemployed increases it for men, and only employment experience reduces the probability for women. For both, having a spouse who is self-employed is important. For men, having a father who had only achieved primary school level of education attainment reduces the likelihood of self-employment while a mother being in a skilled profession increases it. For women, socio-economic background does not matter. Men who are self-employed are also more risk-loving, while it is not the case for women.

Therefore, in urban China, the probability of becoming solely self-employed is driven by social networks as well as personal and household traits, more so than socio-economic background. There are gender differences in that attitudes toward risk do not affect women nor do most personal characteristics, but social networks are significant determinants for both.

The overall finding supports the basic hypothesis that those with networks are more likely to overcome the institutional constraints in China to start a business. Those who have social networks could be more likely to attain credit, have access to suppliers and distributors, and obtain the requisite licences to operate. The social network variable in the occupational choice regression could also pick up the economic effects of personality traits that are associated with a drive for success. Indeed, the self-employed have larger networks than the wage employed.

6.5.2 Self-employed as Second Job

Examining the sample of individuals who started their own businesses as a second job, Table 6.9 reveals that their determinants are rather different from the solely self-employed group. Social networks do not matter for the entire sample or the sub-samples of men and women. There are none who have a self-employed spouse, but marriage and whether one's spouse was in wage employment are both significant, unlike those who are solely self-employed. Being married reduces the probability of self-employment, while having a spouse in wage employment increases the likelihood of undertaking self-employment as a second job. Being married could foster more security so that working a second job is less necessary, while having an employed spouse could provide the resources needed to start a business. Socio-economic background influences were similar to those in sole self-employment. Attitudes toward risk, however, did not matter for this group, including when men and women are estimated separately. This is presumably because they are self-employed as a second job, so there is less risk as they are still earning regular income. For men who are self-employed as a second job, more years of education and employment as well as being married reduce the likelihood of self-employment, while having experienced unemployment induces taking on a second job working for oneself. For women, as with those who are solely self-employed, only more employment experience deters self-employment as a second job.

The profile of this group reveals that social networks do not play a role. It may mean that this group earns some additional income through some work on the side, but the demands are less than those who are solely self-employed.

6.5.3 Unemployment Impact

Table 6.10 shows the findings for the sub-sample of the two groups of self-employed with experience of unemployment. This sub-sample was given an additional module with questions about motivation and attitudes. It is thus possible to investigate the robustness of the importance of social networks and the other identified traits related to self-employment while also adding considerations of drive and motivation. However, the additional motivation measures are not found to be significant, while social networks continue to be for the wholly self-employed and not significant for the secondarily self-employed. In column (1), the coefficient on the variable indicating a motivation to improve one's own skills was −0.7583 and a z-statistic of −0.93, while the coefficient on the other measure of seeking to earn more income was 1.5095 with a z-statistic of 1.17. The results are unchanged from their inclusion. However, the determinants of self-employment for this group are indeed different from the main sample, as seen in Table 6.10.

Table 6.10 is divided into findings for the wholly self-employed and the self-employed as a second job. Columns (1)–(3) report the findings for the first group, divided into the whole sample and then men and women for the former, while columns (4)–(5) do the same for the whole sample and men. There are only six women who are self-employed as a second job after experiencing unemployment, so the extent of multicollinearity among the explanatory variables precludes estimating the determinants of their occupational choice.

Column (1) for the solely self-employed shows that age and Party membership do not matter for self-employment in contrast to the main sample and suggests that when forced to seek work, age is not a significant factor. Party members could also be less likely to become laid-off and therefore membership would be insignificant in this estimation. Spousal characteristics, such as a spouse who is also self-employed, continue to matter and having a spouse in wage employment is also significant, suggesting that a spouse with a steady income makes undertaking self-employment more probable for those who have been unemployed. Socio-economic background and attitudes toward risk do not matter for this group either.

For men who have experienced unemployment, social networks have a larger effect on self-employment than for any other group or sub-group examined in Tables 6.8–6.10. Only education reduces that probability, while mothers in skilled professions and a willingness to take risks increase the possibility of starting a business. Spousal characteristics do not matter. As the expected breadwinner, men who have experienced unemployment appear to be willing to embrace risk and use their social networks to become self-employed. For women in the same position, social networks interestingly have a negative effect on their occupational choice. This suggests that women who have networks may be better protected in their jobs and do not need to choose the more uncertain profession of starting a business. More years of employment experience continue to deter self-employment, while having a spouse either in wage or self-employment increases the probability. Having a father in a more marketized sector of employment reduces the prospect of self-employment, suggesting that fathers would deter their daughters from entering the less certain private sphere. A further difference from men is that attitudes toward risk do not matter for women.

For those who have been unemployed in the previous five years and choose self-employment as a second job, social networks continue to be as insignificant as they were for those who do so without having experienced unemployment (Table 6.11). Gender and employment experience continue to reduce the probability, but other personal traits do not matter. Marital status affects this group as does having a spouse in wage employment, which is unlike the main sample of the secondarily self-employed. A spouse in wage employment raises the probability of self-employment but few other variables matter, and not attitudes toward risk, which is similar to the findings in Table 6.9. Men are not influenced by having a larger social network, although self-employment is negatively affected by employment experience and being married as well as positively by Party membership. Attitudes toward risk remain insignificant for starting a business on the side.

Social networks continue to influence the choice of self-employment but not self-employment as a second job for the sample of those with experience of unemployment as it did for the main sample. Gender differences abound in this sample and are more striking in many ways than for the larger population of respondents. Social networks matter but differently for men and women.

6.6 Conclusion

This chapter examined social capital and found a widespread economic impact, including on income and self-employment. The socio-economic background and attitudes of the self-employed were similar to those of the wage employed, but personal traits and incomes differed. The gender gap that has become evident in the employment market also characterizes the self-employed. Women who are self-employed earn around half the income that men earn.

Social networks are consistently significant as a determinant of self-employment except for the self-employed as a second job and for women who had experienced unemployment and then started a business. For that group of women, social networks reduced the probability that they would become self-employed after experiencing unemployment, suggesting that the nature of their networks is rather perhaps to generate information that could help them find another job rather than striking out on their own. For men who have experienced unemployment though, their social networks increase the probability of self-employment, possibly through helping them obtain the necessary permissions, credit, distribution, or production channels. This is not dissimilar to the main sample of the wholly self-employed where social networks increase the prospects of starting a business. For women who did not experience unemployment, their social networks could have prevented them from being laid off and served as conduits for their starting their own businesses. This is similar to men and dissimilar to women who lost their jobs. Spousal characteristics further suggest that family businesses are a strong factor in the burgeoning *de novo* private sector.

Table 6.11 Determinants of self-employment, unemployed sub-sample, multinomial probit regression (z-statistics in parentheses)

	Wholly self-employed			Self-employed as second job		
	Whole sample (1)	Men (2)	Women (3)	Whole sample (4)	Men (5)	Women (6)
Social network	0.0179*	0.0233*	-0.1588*	-0.0038	0.0081	-0.7470
	(0.0099)	(0.0137)	(0.0873)	(0.0373)	(0.0269)	(4,974,252.8762)
Personal characteristics						
Gender	-0.9377***			-2.8419***		
	(0.3603)			(0.8282)		
Age	0.0392	0.0261	0.0751	0.0508	0.0717	-1.9817
	(0.0336)	(0.0563)	(0.0526)	(0.0607)	(0.0710)	(1.2393e+07)
Years of education	-0.1638**	-0.2197**	-0.1859	-0.0558	-0.0832	-3.9333
	(0.0793)	(0.1103)	(0.1504)	(0.1308)	(0.1504)	(2.1382e+07)
Years of wage employment experience	-0.0880***	-0.0542	-0.1817***	-0.1329**	-0.1486**	1.7563
	(0.0329)	(0.0570)	(0.0558)	(0.0603)	(0.0742)	(1.9531e+07)
Communist Party Member	-0.2375	-0.7539	1.5344	1.5710*	1.5154*	-8.2105
	(0.6746)	(0.8825)	(1.3475)	(0.8138)	(0.9147)	(1.6934e+08)
Spouse characteristics						
Married	-0.0609	-0.4851	-0.1716	-1.7071*	-2.0185*	31.2374
	(0.7018)	(0.9323)	(1.4253)	(0.9539)	(1.1407)	(4.6182e+08)
Spouse in wage employment	1.3556***	0.8688	1.6656**	2.3487***	1.3494	60.5158
	(0.4257)	(0.8674)	(0.6514)	(0.7581)	(1.1219)	(2.7166e+08)
Spouse in self-employment	5.6808***	40.2093	7.9511**			
	(1.3501)	(0.0000)	(3.3132)			
Socio-economic background						
Father's educational attainment						
College and above	1.0503	0.8954	1.9515	1.4346	0.7681	-28.6550
	(0.9250)	(1.2408)	(1.5636)	(1.6031)	(2.4649)	(3.2904e+08)
Professional school	-0.7793	-0.1941	-43.2747	-0.0593	-42.9335	-10.7373
	(0.9197)	(1.1380)	(1.8276e+09)	(1.5818)	(1.7709e+09)	(1.1581e+08)
Secondary school	0.3338	-0.3956	0.6261	0.7340	1.0954	-31.9115
	(0.5287)	(0.8045)	(0.9494)	(0.9467)	(1.0153)	(2.1137e+08)
Primary school	-0.2818	-0.4007	-0.4548	-0.7481	-0.4909	-30.7415
	(0.5067)	(0.6717)	(0.9701)	(0.8932)	(0.9907)	(3.2389e+08)

Mother's educational attainment

	(1)	(2)	(3)	(4)	(5)	(6)
College and above	0.6339	2.1235	-44.2673	0.1650	-43.2533	99.1949
	(1.4335)	(2.0198)	(0.0000)	(1.9278)	(0.0000)	(4.9566e+08)
Professional school	0.2311	-0.1238	0.2939	-1.9755	-44.7816	33.6184
	(0.9375)	(1.3595)	(1.8710)	(1.7094)	(2.0788e+09)	(1.8029e+08)
Secondary school	0.0512	-0.8105	0.6659	-2.0354*	-1.9240	-17.2978
	(0.5718)	(0.9498)	(0.9101)	(1.1209)	(1.2043)	(1.3771e+08)
Primary school	0.3876	0.2744	0.7728	-1.8591*	-1.7768*	-51.7104
	(0.4650)	(0.7030)	(0.7735)	(0.9793)	(1.0525)	(3.0402e+08)
Father is/was a Communist Party member	0.0768	0.3750	0.0128	0.5600	0.5131	0.7393
	(0.4017)	(0.6006)	(0.7150)	(0.7193)	(0.8938)	(1.3679e+08)
Mother is/was a Communist Party member	0.6208	0.8313	0.0345	0.4922	2.0012	-73.6644
	(0.6419)	(0.8513)	(1.4508)	(1.0763)	(1.4951)	(4.5373e+08)
Father's occupation	0.0399	-0.0262	0.0761	-0.0321	-0.0900	1.6133
	(0.0678)	(0.0976)	(0.1110)	(0.1400)	(0.1816)	(2.2347e+07)
Mother's occupation	0.0944	0.287**	-0.0641	-0.0193	0.1808	-6.1302
	(0.0743)	(0.1198)	(0.1297)	(0.1401)	(0.1893)	(3.1554e+07)
Father's employment sector	-0.0339	0.0497	-0.1363**	-0.1237	-0.0740	-6.8899
	(0.0385)	(0.0571)	(0.0682)	(0.0800)	(0.0981)	(2.9058e+07)
Mother's employment sector	0.0351	-0.0419	0.0872	0.0852	0.0447	3.8758
	(0.0339)	(0.0556)	(0.0533)	(0.0658)	(0.0784)	(2.4358e+07)
Variance of income	-1.09e-09	1.26e-08	-8.17e-09	7.78e-10	9.82e-09	-8.03e-09
	(4.40e-09)	(7.40e-09)*	(1.29e-08)	(5.03e-09)	(1.47e-08)	(1.746617)
Cities	Yes	Yes	Yes	Yes	Yes	Yes
Constant	-2.4213	-2.4551	-1.1177	-21.3405	-23.7944	46.4628
	(1.7155)	(2.3883)	(3.0665)	(0.0000)	(0.0000)	(2.3119e+09)
LR χ^2(70)	148.61***	94.03**		94.03**		
LR χ^2(72)			123.08***	148.61***	123.08***	
Pseudo R^2	0.2525	0.2860	0.4981	0.2525	0.2860	0.4981
Number of observations	1219	525	694	1219	525	694

Notes: (1) Dependent variable: 2 if wholly self-employed, 1 if self-employed in second job, and 0 if wage employed.

(2) Robust standard errors adjusted for clustering at the household level are computed.

(3) *** indicates significance at the 1% level, ** at the 5% level, and * at the 10% level.

(4) Instead of a Wald test, the attitude toward risk equations uses the variance of five years of income in the specification so the likelihood used for the estimation is a true distribution of the sample and a likelihood ratio test is employed. In these estimations as well as the ones measuring attitudes, parental background was dropped as were some cities as they predicted one of the outcomes perfectly.

The growth of the non-state sector during China's gradual transition has undoubtedly been a driver of economic growth. Going into business for oneself plays an important role in the development of the non-state sector. The decision to become self-employed could be informed by institutional and personal as well as socio-economic factors. Institutional barriers to starting a business could include credit constraints, lack of access to supply networks, and regulatory complexity. Having a social network could help ease these constraints. Networks of relatives, friends, and associates could help with credit constraints, improve access to supply and distribution networks, and gain the necessary licences to operate. Family businesses are not atypical. Becoming self-employed is also likely to be associated with personal traits, such as attitude toward risk, spousal traits, and socio-economic background, such as parents' occupation that feeds into such motivations.

Therefore, the self-employed in urban China are likely to have larger social networks and there is a relationship between starting a business and having the network to do so. Those who work for themselves on the side are not affected by their networks. The evidence generally suggests that relationships are important in starting a business in China during a time when the legal and financial contexts are imperfect and uncertain, but economic development is rapid.

The finding that social networks negatively influence women's decision to become self-employed after experiencing unemployment is a surprising one. Social networks could help them gain wage employment in that instance and deter them from entering into self-employment. Women who have not suffered unemployment may have networks that are more similar to those of men, and therefore may use these in a similar fashion to start a business.

Social networks facilitate self-employment in urban China, but not for those who only undertake self-employment as a second job. The reasons for their influence could have to do with easing credit and institutional constraints to make up for an imperfect banking/financial system as well as an opaque regulatory environment. The insecurity of property rights in a country would also cause the self-employed to rely on relational-based contracting so that disputes can be resolved via trust rather than the courts. With better protection of property as evidenced by the 2007 Property Law which granted equal protection to private and public property, the reliance on social networks as an enabler of self-employment should decline. However, China's marketizing process is as yet incomplete and it will for some time have an imperfect contracting regime and credit system which suggests the continuing use of social networks. Indeed, even as China's environment for starting a business improves with marketization, social networks are likely to retain their importance. This can be seen in the reliance on relationships of the overseas Chinese diaspora in countries with very good legal systems such as the United States, as networks can still reduce transaction costs and help businesses avoid what is often an expensive and lengthy legal process.

7

Financial and Legal Development: The Role of Private Enterprises in Growth

7.1 Introduction

The rapid rise of the entrepreneurial private sector in China is one of the key reasons for the success of its transition from a centrally planned economy toward becoming a market-oriented one since the late 1970s, which was explored in part in the last chapter. At the same time, China is a country known for its incomplete legal system, including the lack of an independent judiciary and adjudication is not free from interference from the executive branch (see for example, Allen, Qian, and Qian 2005). In addition, there is evidence of financial repression whereby legal and institutional constraints impede the development of financial intermediaries, thereby retarding the development of the financial sector. In China, this is manifested insofar as the rules favour state-owned enterprises (SOEs) despite three decades of reform. SOEs still dominate credit allocation, such that the majority of private small- and medium-sized enterprises (SMEs) obtain no bank financing, even in 2006 (Lin 2007). This chapter investigates the impact of lagging financial and legal systems on private-sector development and complements the previous one.

For entrepreneurs starting private businesses in China, legal constraints—directly through the legal and regulatory system and indirectly via credit rationing due to financial repression—are factors influencing the ability to start a business. Entrepreneurship in China, therefore, is a product of not only the usual socio-economic factors such as motivation and overcoming wealth constraints, but is also affected by the legal and institutional environment (see for example, Banerjee and Newman 1993; Blanchflower and Oswald 1998).

In terms of the legal environment, there is imperfect protection of private property and commercial contracting, which adds to uncertainty for private firms (see for example, Pei 2001). For instance, private property was not granted equal protection in a formal sense as public property until the Property Law was passed in 2007. On the regulatory front, governmental permissions, rather than a transparent regulatory structure, govern the commercial sector. For example, starting a business requires obtaining numerous licences, and operating a firm requires permission to transport and distribute goods and services. With respect to another important facet of the influence of law on entrepreneurship, the enforcement of contracts in China is fraught with difficulty due to the under-developed legal system. This will tend to lead to relational contracting, which refers to the self-enforcing nature of contracts where the parties adhere to the terms of the contract due to their own future self-interest (Bull 1987; Baker, Gibbons, and Murphy 2002). This can minimize the costs of contract enforce-ment if business is contracted with known associates and on a trust basis, which is reinforced not through courts and fits with a long-standing cultural preference in China for reliance on interpersonal relationships or social networks (Bian 1994b).

The economics of starting a firm are also influenced by the extent of 'financial repression'. The banking system in China is considered to suffer from financial repression due to the significant diversion of formal credit to state-owned enter-prises via the state-owned banking system which negatively affects non-state firms. Credit constraints restrict options for entrepreneurs and reliance on savings, remittances from migrated family members, and savings of relatives tend to provide alternative sources of capital when the formal banking system is difficult to access (Oi 1999). The commonly observed wealth constraints among entrepreneurs also bind because assets were uncommon in urban China until the advent of equity investments and privatization of housing both in the 1990s. The lack of financial intermediaries due to financial repression further compromises the augmentation of assets through avenues such as venture capital funding, and means that entrepreneurs rely upon their own assets. Those who start their own businesses, therefore, confront numerous legal and financial impediments to entrepreneurship in such an environment.

Despite the uncertain institutional context, the *de novo* private sector has flourished since the 1990s with the dismantling of much of the state-owned sector and liberalization of most markets. For instance, SOEs accounted for nearly all of industrial output in the late 1970s but has fallen to account for less than half of GDP, while non-state owned firms became the major force in the economy by the 1990s and the 2000s (Yueh 2011).

However, the reasons for entrepreneurship in the midst of China's challenging legal and institutional context are not well understood. The few studies of entrepreneurs have emphasized education and other observable personal traits such as membership of the Chinese Communist Party (Wu 2002; Zhang et al. 2006; Mohapatra et al. 2007) while a cross-country survey of entrepreneurs by Djankov et al. (2006) also delves into interpersonal relationships and concludes that the most robust determinant of entrepreneurship was knowing people who had tried entrepreneurship. This is consistent with the work on the importance of social networks in other facets of Chinese society (see for example, Oi 1999). A study of rural China by Mohapatra et al. (2007) finds education to be the key factor in rural farmers leaving the agricultural sector to start their own firms or enter into wage employment, while Wu (2002) finds that education and Com-munist Party membership are a deterrent in urban areas. Education is found to be a factor that inhibits entrepreneurship in urban areas, which suggests that the preferred sector remains the more secure state sector. As with most issues in China, there are significant urban–rural differences, as rural residents never had a privileged state-owned enterprise (SOE) sector. The findings for education stand in contrast to urban studies insofar as the rural residents who are able to move into higher value-added work are the educated ones, while more educated workers in urban areas tend to remain in the institutionally favoured wage employment.

These studies focus on either rural areas or urban residents in the cities; that is, those with a rural or urban *hukou* (household registration system) in the appropriate areas. What are omitted are rural–urban migrants who face an additional set of institutional obstructions on account of not having permission to settle in urban areas (see Solinger 1999). Migrants working in the urban economy are particularly important in the development of the private sector, as they constitute the surplus labour from rural areas which was shifted to the urban non-state sector to fuel growth (Fan 1994). These workers manned the factories in China's Special Economic Zones which produce goods for export in places such as the Pearl River Delta that supported China's growth while the inefficient state-owned sector which employed urban residents was gradually reformed and dismantled. In other words, they provided a ready workforce for the nascent private sector. In spite of the key role played by migrants in China's economy, they continue to face discrimination in the urban labour market and have been prevented from competing for jobs that were reserved for urban residents (see for example, Knight and Yueh 2004). In many ways, the legal constraints and economic characteristics of these workers are more than those faced by or constituting urban residents starting their own firms.

Thus, entrepreneurship in China is likely to be driven by not only the usual set of personal and socio-economic characteristics, such as being motivated by economic gain or facing credit constraints, but is also affected by the incomplete legal and institutional environment. This is a factor also found in other countries, such as the United States, but so far relatively unexamined in marketizing economies like China which are in the process of legal as well as economic reforms (see for example, Holtz-Eakin, Joulfaian, and Rosen 1994; Djankov et al. 2006). The study of the evolution of entrepreneurship in China could thus shed light on the path for other emerging economies which often have incomplete legal systems. The interplay of economic and legal factors influencing the decision to become an entrepreneur should also be evident from the use and reliance on social networks, which provide the basis for relational contracting as well as a source of funds and entrepreneurial know-how in China's complex commercial system (see for example, Gompers, Lerner, and Scharfstein 2005, for the importance of learning from networks in fostering entrepreneurship).

In providing a law and economics picture of Chinese entrepreneurship, two types of self-started businesses will be distinguished. Different factors may determine the entrepreneurial decision of urban residents and rural–urban migrants, the latter group in particular has not been well studied despite its notable importance in forming China's non-state sector. Indeed, there are few studies of migrant entrepreneurs in urban China, so this chapter will also focus on the traits of those migrants who have been able to set up businesses and settle to some extent in the urban economy and constitute a significant segment of entrepreneurial activity.

To investigate the influence of these factors on Chinese entrepreneurship, a national urban household dataset collected in China in 2000, pertaining to 1999, will be used that has comprehensive data on the traits of entrepreneurs in China such as education and Party membership, as well as attitudinal information that constitute widely observed entrepreneurial traits; for example, motivation or drive to succeed, and also original measures of individual social networks. The latter allows for some investigation of the suspected role of informal relational contracting that arises to supplement the incomplete legal system, whereby networks can form the basis for trust in contracting to start a business, contacts can help obtain the relevant permissions, as well as provide a source of funds in a credit-constrained society. The rich data include detailed individual- and household-level information about the income and work patterns of urban workers and rural–urban migrants in China, which will allow for investigations of the characteristics of Chinese entrepreneurship for both types of residents. The data will be supplemented by city-level measures to approximate the likely influence of the legal and institutional environment, including the extent of financial repression and utilization of the legal system, on entrepreneurship.

Moreover, China has traditionally had a strong cultural and historical emphasis on interpersonal relationships or *guanxi* (see for example, Bian 1994a), which informs business dealings both within and beyond China, and helps to explain how entrepreneurs cope in an imperfect legal system and still manage to become engines of economic growth. In these respects, determining the traits of entrepreneurs in urban China can also generate wider implications for the development of a private sector in developing countries with similarly weak formal legal/regulatory systems.

7.2 China's Private Enterprises

The national urban household dataset used is an original, representative survey administered across China in 2000, enumerated by China's National Bureau for Statistics (NBS), and designed by a team of international researchers from the Chinese Academy of Social Sciences, Japan, Australia, and the UK. The selected households were randomly drawn from the NBS sample households and the questionnaire was administered by trained enumerators working for the NBS, who would often make repeated visits to ensure accuracy. Details of the dataset can be found in Li and Sato (2006). The sample size of the 1999 survey is 4,500 urban households and another 800 migrant households settled in urban areas, with around 14,000 working-aged individuals defined as those over the age of 16. Both household- and individual-level responses are recorded. The survey covered thirteen cities in six provinces, including provincial level cities: Beijing, Liaoning, Jiangsu, Henan, Sichuan, and Gansu. Given the breadth of the survey, there is no need to attempt to normalize the sample with smaller scale data typically used in studies of entrepreneurship.

There are 1,263 individuals in the sample who report that they started their own business. Eliminating the six respondents under the age of 16 (whose ages ranged from 12 to 15), the 1,257 individuals constitute around 8.7 per cent of all urban workers. Another three are over the age of 65, but were left in the sample as they report positive earnings for the sample year. Those who own their own firms need not retire at a certain age, so the inclusion of these three entrepreneurs seems appropriate. Of this sample, seven entrepreneurs had a previous business venture, while fourteen entrepreneurs reported having started a business in their prior job but are no longer running their own firms. In terms of the proportion of migrants and urban residents, some 955 (80 per cent) of all entrepreneurs are migrants, while 308 (20 per cent) are urban residents. Therefore, the picture of entrepreneurship in the urban economy quickly shifts toward considering the significant role played by migrants in developing the private sector as they constitute four-fifths of all entrepreneurs. An estimated 120 migrant entrepreneurs left their previous job specifically to start their own business within this sample.

There is no information on the size of these firms, but there is some limited information on profitability for those owned by urban residents but not migrant-owned firms. Most respondents did not answer this question in the survey, perhaps because it is phrased as reporting on the profitability of an 'enterprise' and the common conception of an enterprise is a state-owned enterprise. Of those who did (30 per cent of the sample of entrepreneurs), only 5.6 per cent reported themselves as having made 'high profit' that year. This may, however, be due to a reluctance to report profits due to concerns about taxation. The majority (62.9 per cent) reported 'marginal profit', while the remainder or 25.2 per cent declared that they were making a loss or at the edge of bankruptcy. These are the three general categories of answers allowed in the survey, so the precise quantification of such profits/losses is not available, although this gives at least a partial picture.

The average age of these firms is 5.3 years, which is higher for urban resident-owned ones (8.1 years) than migrant-owned businesses (4.4 years). This reflects two factors. In the mid-1990s, the passage of China's Company Law in 1994 recognized the corporate form for privately owned businesses and fuelled the rapid increase in the number of small- and medium-sized, privately owned enterprises that have come to dominate over 99 per cent of all Chinese firms (Yueh 2011). Also, the liberalization of the wholesale and retail sector in the early 1990s opened the market for private firms to serve the rapidly developing consumer market, which was still largely protected from foreign competition.

In terms of the sector in which these firms operate, the largest category for urban-resident-owned firms (43 per cent) is the wholesale, retail, and food services industry. This is followed by social services (19 per cent) and transportation, storage, postal, and communications sector which comprise 13 per cent. Manufacturing accounts for only 8 per cent, while the remaining firms are spread amongst construction (2 per cent), finance and insurance (1 per cent), and others. There is a more detailed breakdown of the sectors in which the migrant firms operated, but the largest sectors are the same as privately owned urban firms: 52 per cent are in the wholesale, retail, and food services industry, while 20 per cent are in the social services sector. Similarly, the next largest sector is manufacturing, but for migrants, it is the garment sector that accounts for 8 per cent of their firms, while another 3 per cent of firms operate in the production of consumer goods. Construction accounts for 2 per cent, as with the urban firms, as does transportation, storage, postal, and communications for another 2 per cent. The latter category differs from the breakdown for urban-owned firms which seem to be based more heavily in the transportation and communications business.

7.3 Motivations of Entrepreneurs

When owners of urban-resident firms were asked why they started their own business, the responses reflected the three factors most likely to influence the entrepreneurship decision in China's particular, imperfect institutional environment. The responses broke down as follows: 37 per cent said that they started their own business because they had the requisite skills and experience, 17 per cent did so by joining in with relatives, 11 per cent had real estate, and 7 per cent had funds. Another 27 per cent chose 'other', which most likely reflects an involuntary move due to this being the period of the large-scale lay-offs in SOEs which forced a number of the previous holders of 'iron rice bowls' (lifetime employment) to seek work. The primary motivation appears to be self-belief and skills, while 11 per cent were motivated by having access to an important asset; for example, real estate. A mere 7 per cent had their own funds, and 17 per cent chose to start their own business because of their personal relationships. Although it is not possible to know for certain, the large-scale lay-offs of the late 1990s from SOEs would have caused some urban residents to start their own businesses, perhaps out of necessity (see for example, Banerjee and Duflo 2007, for entrepreneurs as being driven by either profit seeking or due to unemployment). As most declared their self-belief as being important, motivation is surely a determinant of entrepreneurship. The entrepreneurial spirit often observed in other economies is the dominant factor in China, and perhaps even more so given the challenges of coping with a weak legal system and uncertain property rights.

In China, the institutional context of entrepreneurship is fraught with challenges. These include economic factors (for example, credit constraints and an underdeveloped financial system) and legal issues (for example, navigating an uncertain legal and institutional environment for operations and resolution of disputes). The two are interrelated. Moreover, China has an imperfect legal system with a great deal of regulatory complexity. In such an environment, having the contacts and know-how in order to obtain a licence would be important. This setting gives rise to the importance of relational contracting, as trust can reduce the risk of enforcing contracts in a country with a weak legal system which also suits China's traditional emphasis on relationships in business practices (see for example, Oi 1999, for the view that *guanxi* or interpersonal relationships is the operational code for getting things done in China).

Having real estate in China suggests being fairly well placed as urban land is state-owned and land/buildings were only beginning to be privatized during this period. Those who owned real estate would have needed to have had the connections to attain such an asset which also gave them credit in an economy characterized by 'financial repression', in which the legal/institutional framework reduces the depth of the market (see for example, Garnaut et al. 2001).

Some 7 per cent started a business with their own funds and another 17 per cent did so with the help of relatives', which is consistent with the rationing of formal bank credit that causes private firms to rely on the founder's savings and pooling funds with relatives. Private small and medium enterprises often find it difficult to obtain credit and often rely on family and friends, including remittances from migrated family members, to start a business (Oi 1999). With such credit constraints, it can be difficult to secure inventory for small firms. Therefore, entrepreneurs in China have been known to use their social networks to arrange for inventory to be issued without advance payment. Anything which is sold is then split between the entrepreneur and the supplier of the inventory, such as pedlars receiving their goods in advance. This type of trust-based relationship was encountered during the enumeration of the household survey in China. Access to suppliers and distributors is a significant challenge in a partially marketized economy in any event, and having a social network and the appropriate attitude to overcome these constraints would facilitate entrepreneurship.

Finally, the second most important reason for starting one's own business was to join relatives and knowing others who are also willing to become entrepreneurs. This is also consistent with the findings of the entrepreneurship literature which emphasizes the importance of both (Blanchflower and Oswald 1998; Djankov et al. 2006). Relatives are a source of finance, know-how, network of labour, and pooled wealth.

The self-declared reasons of Chinese entrepreneurs suggest that the usual considerations such as motivation and self-belief are important. However, it is also the case that interpersonal relationships are crucial in terms of providing an informal relational-based system to counteract the imperfect formal legal system. The other important factors enabling one to start one's own business reflect possessing funds or assets, giving an advantage to those who can bypass the credit-rationed banking system. The next section of this chapter will test whether the proffered reasons relating to personal traits, and legal and economic factors, significantly predict entrepreneurship in China. It should be noted that migrant entrepreneurs were not asked the same question, so there is no *prima facie* view of their decision taking, although it is likely that they face similar but even worse constraints given their less secure institutional position in urban China.

A simple model of becoming an entrepreneur includes observable personal characteristics, such as age, gender, education, years of employment experience, etc. This is followed by adding and testing various factors that are thought to influence the probability of entrepreneurship in an imperfect legal and institutional environment.

A probit estimation of the entrepreneurship decision is as follows:

$$ENTREPRENEUR_i = \alpha + \beta X_i + \gamma V_i + \varepsilon, \tag{1}$$

where entrepreneur equals 1 if person i is an entrepreneur and 0 if not. Entrepreneurship is determined by a vector of observable personal characteristics, X_i, associated with occupational choice, including education, age, gender. and other related factors, and those arising in response to the particular legal and institutional setting, V_i, which could include characteristics such as having social networks or strong motivation. Each of the latter set of variables will be entered after a baseline model is estimated.

Then, measures of the legal and institutional context in the locale will be included to test whether two facets—financial repression (measuring credit constraints) and utilization of the legal system (measuring development of the legal system)—influence the entrepreneurship decision. Financial repression (F_j) is measured as extent of financial development in province j, which is the ratio of bank credit allocated to the private sector as a proportion of total credit as measured for the province. Utilization of the legal system (U_j) is measured as the ratio of cases filed on a per capita basis which could be viewed as an indication of the extent of the development of the courts as an avenue for resolving disputes. These two variables will enter the model as follows for person i in province j:

$$ENTREPRENEUR_{i,j} = \alpha + \beta X_i + \phi F_j + \varphi U_j + \eta. \tag{2}$$

Details of all variables are reported in Table 7.1 as well as in the notes to the relevant tables. There is the possibility of heteroscedasticity induced by the selection bias into labour force participation and a clustering effect of using a household dataset to estimate individual outcomes, so robust standard errors adjusted for clustering at the household level are computed.

It is not possible to rule out omitted variable bias or reverse causality. Thus, the relationship between legal constraints and entrepreneurship will be re-estimated using instrumental variable (IV) techniques. Since the average age of these firms unsurprisingly coincides with the corporatization drive in China whereby enterprises were converted into shareholding companies and private firms began to form, the legal system for civil and commercial matters would have developed at

Table 7.1 Conditional means of entrepreneurs

Personal characteristics	Wage-employed (urban residents) (1)	Entrepreneurs (urban residents) (2)	Entrepreneurs (migrants) (3)	Significance of mean difference (1)–(2)	Significance of mean difference (2)–(3)
Age	35.8	36.5	33.3	***	***
Gender	49.7% male	58.4% male	55.6% male	***	Insignificant
	51.3% female	41.6% female	44.4% female		
Marital status	84.2% married	78.5% married	92.5% married	***	***
Education, in years	9.4	10.1	8.0	***	***
Employment experience, in years	22.8	12.7	9.2	***	**
Experienced lay-off	19.2%	28.9%	12.9%	***	**
Communist Party member	17.7%	5.8%	2.4%	***	***
Social network (size)	6.4	7.6	7.8	Insignificant	Insignificant
Income and Wealth (RMB)					
Annual income	5,986	8,425	11,227	***	***
Total household net wealth (assets minus debts)	20,250	11,778	13,511	***	Insignificant
Saved funds for family business	2,060	8,687	5,798	***	Insignificant
Debts incurred for family business	2,159	4,027	2,218	***	Insignificant

Source: China Household and Income Project, urban survey.
Notes: *** indicates significance at the 1% level, ** at the 5% level, and * at the 10% level in a two-tailed t-test for equality of means. For migrants, years of employment experience in the urban economy is reported.

the same time. Therefore, a province with a more developed legal system could lead to greater entrepreneurship and more private firm activity utilizes more of the legal system. There is thus a strong systemic element to these relationships. To address this endogeneity issue, two simultaneous equations will be estimated. One will be for entrepreneurship, and the other addressing legal constraints.

In an attempt to disentangle the potential endogeneity and feedback among the legal variable and entrepreneurship, the 3SLS (three-stage least squares) technique will be used. The 3SLS approach estimates a system which yields more efficient results than 2SLS. The 2SLS estimation produces consistent estimators, but neglects cross-equation correlations in the error terms (Greene 2003). The 3SLS achieves consistency through instrumentation and efficiency through cross-equation error covariance terms. In 3SLS, all dependent variables are explicitly taken to be endogenous to the system and are treated as correlated with the disturbances in the system's equations. The first stage of the 3SLS estimator is identical to the first stage of 2SLS, whilst the second and third stages compute the covariance matrix of the error terms and then perform a general least squares (GLS) estimation to assess the full system. Both a 3SLS full system and a 'seemingly unrelated regression estimation' (SURE) are estimated. The SURE estimator treats all variables as exogenous within the system and is a form of 2SLS. It can provide further statistical evidence, but the full system estimates are preferred for the above-stated reasons and thus will be relied upon.

In terms of identification, the variable of the number of lawyers per capita predates the take-off of *de novo* firms so has a direct impact on legal development and only an indirect one on entrepreneurship (via legal constraints) since lawyers will influence case development but not directly foster entrepreneurs except through the legal system. Second, the measure of wealth for urban residents is likely to be related to the success of being an entrepreneur in the survey year, so any interpretation concerning a significant influence of wealth constraints should be mindful of the relationship. By contrast, the measure of wealth for migrant entrepreneurs is that of assets brought from the countryside before starting a business in urban areas. This is more likely to be an exogenous measure and thus a more proximate indicator of wealth constraints on entrepreneurship. Thus, the instrumentation will use wealth brought from the countryside by migrants as directly affecting entrepreneurship but only indirectly influencing legal development (via entrepreneurship) because the monies will fund entrepreneurship but not directly influence the existent legal development in a city to which the migrant is a new entrant.

Finally, the first stage will include a further IV that is exogenous to the simultaneous equations system, appearing in the first stage, and chosen to have an effect on legal development but not on entrepreneurship, which is borne out in the estimations as being significant for the law and not the entrepreneurship variables. The measure is of legal system development between 1985 and before the mid-1990s (where data are unavailable for the 1980s), which marked the start of urban reforms and before the private-sector urban firms were permitted. Recall from the survey that these firms started in the mid-1990s. This indicator—'number of units with legal advisors'—taken on a per capita basis in a province before the mid-1990s will be associated with later legal development in the four provinces on which there are data. The difficulty of finding appropriate instruments for a system of equations will mean a focus on the direct rather than indirect relationships (such as financial repression, which is a manifestation of legal impediments on the credit system and social networks which work within the institutional framework) between law and entrepreneurship. Financial repression and social networks are both factors that work via or in reaction to the legal system on entrepreneurship, as well as potentially in reverse. They will be estimated in the probit models, but the 3SLS estimation will focus on testing the effect of the legal system on entrepreneurship decisions.

Table 7.1 presents the traits of entrepreneurs, divided into urban residents and migrants, and the wage-employed, with conditional means to assess significant differences amongst these groups. The reported figures are conditional means with the difference tested first by Levine's test to establish equality in variances. The Levine's test does not require the same sample sizes and works even if the normality assumption does not hold. In other words, the Levine's test uses the test statistic constructed for analysis of variance. By rejecting the null hypothesis, there is evidence of a difference in the population variances. If the Levine's test for the equality of variances did not result in a significant F value, then equality of variances can be assumed. This is followed by a two-tailed Welch t-test to compare conditional means between both types of entrepreneurs and non-entrepreneurs. The difference in conditional means reflects whether there is significant difference between urban-resident and migrant entrepreneurs conditional on the other observable characteristics identified in the table.

All personal characteristics except for the gender balance between migrant and non-migrant entrepreneurs and the size of their respective social networks are significant. Whereas the wage employed have a nearly 50–50 gender mix, some 58 per cent of urban firm owners and 56 per cent of migrant entrepreneurs are male, reflecting a significant male share of business start-ups in China. The size of their social networks is also not significantly different. The size of social networks is determined by asking the reported number of close contacts of an individual in any context, social or economic. The survey question asked: 'In the past year, how many relatives, friends, colleagues, or acquaintances did you exchange gifts with or often maintain contact?' The mean size of social network is 6.4 persons and has a reasonable dispersion for non-entrepreneurs. The non-entrepreneurs have around 6.4 persons as compared with 7.6 for urban entrepreneurs and 6.5 for migrant entrepreneurs. Perhaps whilst all groups value interpersonal relationships, entrepreneurs may utilize it to start a business while the wage-employed rely on networks for social utility. Social networks of migrant entrepreneurs are much larger by an alternative measure which did not specifically ask about maintaining contact, but just the number of relatives, fellow villagers (*lao xian*), which is a very important relationship in China, and friends or acquaintances that he or she has in the city. The mean size of that network is 14.4 persons, which is inflated by the assessment of the fellow-villager category. Omitting that group, the mean size is virtually identical to the urban entrepreneurs at 7.8 persons. There is no statistically significant difference between the two measures. The latter will be used as the first measure and was only asked of migrants who had obtained urban *hukou* while the latter was asked of all migrant households.

All other characteristics of entrepreneurs and non-entrepreneurs are significantly different. Migrant entrepreneurs are around three-years younger on average than urban resident entrepreneurs and non-entrepreneurs. The mean age difference between all three groups is significant. The differences indicate an age hierarchy of urban firm owners, urban wage-employed, and then migrant entrepreneurs. Over 90 per cent of migrants are married, while this percentage falls for the wage employed to 84 per cent and for urban firm owners, it declines to 79 per cent. There are also significant differences in average years of education. The most educated are the urban entrepreneurs who have completed around ten years, followed by the urban wage-employed of nine years and migrants who have eight years.

Entrepreneurs have on average a decade less experience than non-entrepreneurs. The most likely interpretation of this question in the context of China is experience in paid employment, as the lifetime employment system or 'iron rice bowl' was only gradually dismantled starting in the mid-1990s, and working in an SOE is what urban residents would consider to be employment experience when answering the question. This would suggest that entrepreneurs have around on average ten years of experience starting their own businesses which would be consistent with China's liberalization of its consumer markets in particular in the late 1980s/early 1990s, which created the opportunity for starting a business in consumer goods. The liberalization phase would also explain the average of nine years of work experience of migrants in urban areas. As the urban economy was reformed, opportunities for migrants to work in the newly liberalized joint-venture sector and private economy would explain their migration from rural to urban areas to seek work that had previously eluded them under the allocated job system that was geared toward urban residents and excluded migrants. Finally, urban entrepreneurs are also more likely to have experienced being laid-off during the large-scale restructuring of the mid-1990s of the SOEs, thus prompting them to start their own business. A smaller proportion of migrant entrepreneurs had experienced lay-off, but that could reflect their exclusion from SOE and permanent jobs which meant more short-term contracts that would terminate rather than result in redundancy.

There are notable significant differences distinguishing the entrepreneurs from the non-entrepreneurs in terms of Communist Party membership. Whereas around 18 per cent of all employed persons are Party members, only 6 per cent of urban entrepreneurs and just 2 per cent of migrants are members. If Party members are more likely to be allocated desirable jobs and less likely to be laid-off, then that could contribute to their lesser likelihood of leaving the more secure lifetime employment for starting their own businesses, which is riskier.

The final set of comparisons is of income and wealth. There are significant differences in mean incomes across the three groups, but insignificant differences in wealth as between urban and migrant entrepreneurs. Urban entrepreneurs make around 30 per cent more than non-entrepreneurs, which is a significant difference in their conditional mean income after controlling for age, gender, education, employment experience, occupation, employment sector, and locale (cities). This is despite more entrepreneurs having experienced being laid-off, which typically reduces income upon re-employment. Impressively, migrant entrepreneurs make nearly twice the income of the wage employed, and 25 per cent more than urban business owners despite having fewer years of education and facing tougher institutional constraints such as prohibitions on settling in cities. This is all the more so when their annual income prior to coming to urban areas was just RMB 1,500 compared with RMB 11,227 in the city, reflecting a substantial increase in earnings through migration. It is possible that because they are less able to claim social security support in urban areas which are granted to urban residents, such as a pension, they are more likely to work hard and seek to earn more income. However, as the conditional mean controls for differences in net assets, which includes measures of in-kind support such as social securities for urban residents, it remains a significant difference once net wealth is taken into account.

In terms of measures of wealth, there are significant differences between the wage-employed and the entrepreneurs but no significant differences between the two types of entrepreneurs. Total household net wealth, calculated as assets minus debts, is RMB 20,250 for the wage employed, while it is RMB 11,778 for urban entrepreneurs, and slightly higher at RMB 13,511 for migrants. Unsurprisingly, the entrepreneurs have a great deal more savings geared at their businesses (RMB 8,687 for urban residents and RMB 5,798 for migrants), compared to around RMB 2,000 that the wage-employed have saved for family businesses. These savings might be geared towards a future family business or it may reflect savings to lend to relatives starting a business. Urban entrepreneurs have the largest share of debt (RMB 4,027) as compared with migrant entrepreneurs who owe half of that amount (RMB 2,218). Non-entrepreneurs also report debt incurred for family businesses of around RMB 2,000, which again may reflect family pooling of resources of a future endeavour that has gotten under way. It appears that although entrepreneurs are richer than the wage-employed in terms of income, they have less wealth, presumably because their assets are tied up in their businesses in a credit-constrained environment where businesses are funded through own or familial savings.

Table 7.2 gives the marginal effects of the likelihood of becoming an entrepreneur and the influence of socio-economic factors, including the extent of social networks which can serve to ease the constraints of an imperfect institutional context, household wealth as a factor influencing the decision to start a business, as well as motivation or drive to be entrepreneurial. First, equation (1) provides the baseline model which only considers observable personal traits before turning to the hypothesized variables.

Table 7.2 Socio-economic factors influencing urban entrepreneurship (z-statistics in parentheses)

Dependent variable: 1 if entrepreneur; 0 if non-entrepreneur	(1)	(2)	(3)	(4)	(5)	(6)	(7)
Personal characteristics							
Gender	−0.0113 (−6.33)***	−0.0104 (−5.41)***	−0.0045 (−2.11)**	−0.0046 (−2.13)**	−0.0047 (−2.18)**	−0.0048 (−2.23)**	−0.0046 (−2.16)**
Age	0.0003 (2.51)***	0.0003 (2.31)**	0.0003 (2.32)**	0.0003 (2.29)**	0.0003 (2.18)**	0.0003 (2.28)**	0.0003 (2.20)**
Marital status	0.0034 (1.23)	0.0042 (1.43)	0.0024 (0.56)	0.0026 (0.62)	0.0023 (0.54)	0.0022 (0.52)	0.0021 (0.50)
Education, in years	−0.0014 (−3.58)***	−0.0014 (−3.27)***	−0.0013 (−3.00)***	−0.0013 (−3.03)***	−0.0013 (−3.07)***	−0.0013 (−3.24)***	−0.0014 (−3.23)***
Employment experience, in years	−0.0018 (−10.43)***	−0.0018 (−9.59)***	−0.0012 (−7.40)***	−0.0012 (−7.46)***	−0.0012 (−7.31)***	−0.0012 (−7.43)***	−0.0012 (−7.29)***
Experienced lay-off	0.0084 (2.96)***	0.0094 (3.05)***	0.0031 (1.31)	0.0033 (1.37)	0.0035 (1.41)	0.0035 (1.44)	0.0034 (1.41)
Communist Party member	−0.0122 (−4.22)***	−0.0111 (−3.65)***	−0.0061 (−2.10)**	−0.0060 (−2.07)**	−0.0060 (−2.06)**	−0.0058 (−2.01)**	−0.0059 (−2.05)**
Social network (size)	—	0.0002 (2.67)***	—	—	—	—	—
Attitudinal indicators: Has the importance of the following factors that influence household income changed compared with before? 1) decreased, 2) unchanged, 3) increased							
Educational level	—	—	−0.0031 (−1.69)*	—	—	—	—
Political status	—	—	—	−0.0024 (−1.19)	—	—	—
Rank of work unit	—	—	—	—	−0.0019 (−1.22)	—	—
Social connections	—	—	—	—	—	−0.0016 (−0.82)	—
Urban *hukou*	—	—	—	—	—	—	0.0038 (1.56)
Cities	Yes	Yes	Yes	Yes	Yes	Yes	Yes
Wald χ^2 (19)	275.49***	—	—	—	—	—	—
Wald χ^2 (20)	—	254.10***	122.51***	121.01***	121.92***	117.46***	115.11***
Pseudo R^2	0.1675	0.1639	0.2009	0.1992	0.1974	0.2012	0.2033
Number of observations	9729	8390	4319	4314	4313	4308	4300

Source: China Household and Income Project, urban survey.

Notes: (1) Omitted dummy variables are: male, never experienced lay-off, not a Communist Party member, and Pingliang.

For urban residents who start their own businesses, personal characteristics differ significantly from those who are wage-employed except for being married, which is not a determinant. Gender, education, employment experience, and being a member of the Chinese Communist Party all influence the likelihood of becoming an entrepreneur. Being older and having experienced unemployment increase the probability. These people are likely to have been forced into the evolving labour market due to the large-scale downsizing and lay-offs associated with the *xiagang* policy of the late 1990s. At the same time, liberalization made starting a private firm more viable than before, which could explain why having experienced unemployment is a positive determinant of entrepreneurship. Interestingly, typically those who have experienced unemployment will suffer from 'scarring' whereby they earn less than before, but Chinese urban entrepreneurs make significantly more than the wage employed. Being a woman, being more educated and more experienced all reduce the likelihood of leaving the stability of wage employment, as well as being a member of the Party. Party members have been on the rise in the reform period despite the economy being more marketized, although the proportion of Party members amongst entrepreneurs is lower than the wage-employed. The findings show that Party membership reduces entrepreneurship and fewer Party members wish to leave their positions to seek opportunities in the market-driven sector.

With the baseline model established, column (2) introduces social networks, which do not notably affect the coefficients of the baseline explanatory variables. Even controlling for observable personal traits often tested in the entrepreneurship literature, social networks significantly increase the probability of entrepreneurship. This suggests that social networks aid entrepreneurial activity, most likely through sharing information about how to start and operate a business in the imperfect legal environment.

The next six columns explore a multitude of attitudinal measures and find that most are insignificant. The one significant measure at the 10 per cent level asked respondents about whether educational attainment has increased in importance in affecting household income. The negative coefficient suggests that those who believe that education is associated with greater earnings are not entrepreneurs, which reinforces the finding that more years of education deters entrepreneurship. Both are significant in column (3), which suggests that attitudinal effects exist beyond the measured impact of years of education attained in the entrepreneurship equation.

Therefore, social networks and attitudinal positions significantly affect the decision to become an entrepreneur even when observable personal traits are controlled for. Wealth turns out not to be a significant factor, suggesting that Chinese entrepreneurs are not as wealth constrained as those in other countries (see, for example, Evans and Leighton 1989). However, social networks play a significant role, which suggests that informal relationships are a factor in enabling the start of a business and is consistent with the observed declarations of entrepreneurs across countries that knowing others who are entrepreneurial is important (see for example, Djankov et al. 2006).

Migrant entrepreneurs in urban areas have not been much studied in China, and Table 7.3 presents the findings for this group who dominate the start-up sector. Column (1) shows the baseline model. Unlike for urban residents, observable personal traits do not predict entrepreneurship for migrants. Gender, age, years of education, employment experience in urban areas, and Party membership are all irrelevant. Experience of unemployment was not estimated for this group because only urban residents who were in lifetime employment could be laid-off. Migrants worked on contracts which terminated after a period of time and were not entitled to unemployment or *xiagang* benefits. Only marital status is a significant determinant of unemployment. Being married positively increases the probability of entrepreneurship, suggesting that those who are married and have families are more likely to start their own businesses in urban areas. Indeed, a higher proportion of migrants are married as compared with urban residents, as seen in Table 7.2. Migrant entrepreneurs earned ten times their annual income after moving to the city, and remitted 20 per cent of their income (RMB 2,195) on average to the home village where their families reside.

Social networks are more significant for migrant entrepreneurs than with urban resident entrepreneurs. The coefficient on networks for migrants is substantially larger than for urban resident entrepreneurs (0.0049 versus 0.0002), suggesting a much stronger influence on the decision to start one's own business. For instance, a one unit increase in social networks would increase the probability of entrepreneurship of migrants by 0.4 per cent, while it would be only 0.02 per cent for urban residents.

Attitudinal measures are also important for migrants and underscore the importance of social networks. A question which asked whether social connections had become more important for household income indicated that migrant entrepreneurs believed that this was indeed the case. The variable retained its significance when social networks is also included in column (8). The coefficient on social networks was virtually unchanged, but the magnitude of the attitudinal variable increased, suggesting that social networks reinforced the importance of the motivational indicator and both significantly increase the likelihood of entrepreneurship among migrants. An unexpected result is that marital status ceases to be significant when social networks are included, which could be interpreted in a number of ways, including that spouses are likely to be included in one's social network for migrants so that the two are collinear. Finally, migrants who thought that the *danwei* or work-unit status mattered were less likely to be entrepreneurs. This reflects an attitude that values the paid-employment sector and the status bequeathed by the government which is one that makes a migrant less likely to strike out on his or her own.

Therefore, migrant entrepreneurs in urban areas have vastly different profiles to urban-resident entrepreneurs, although they share social networks and attitudes as drivers of the entrepreneur decision. However, all observable personal traits do not matter, including education and Party membership, which stands at odds with the findings of rural China insofar as the decision of rural

Dependent variable: 1 if entrepreneur; 0 if non-entrepreneur	(1)	(2)	(3)	(4)	(5)	(6)	(7)	(8)
Personal characteristics								
Gender	0.0150	0.0293	0.0151	0.0170	0.0157	0.0174	0.0329	0.0175
	(0.73)	(1.12)	(0.73)	(0.82)	(0.76)	(0.84)	(1.24)	(0.84)
Age	−0.0006	0.0003	−0.0007	−0.0005	−0.0007	−0.0001	0.0002	−0.0001
	(−0.27)	(0.09)	(−0.31)	(−0.22)	(−0.33)	(−0.05)	(0.06)	(−0.03)
Marital status	0.1428	−0.0366	0.1420	0.1396	0.1479	0.1317	−0.0675	0.1422
	(1.84)*	(−0.34)	(1.84)*	(1.80)*	(1.91)*	(1.65)*	(−0.61)	(1.79)*
Education, in years	−0.0017	0.0057	−0.0018	−0.0024	−0.0020	−0.0022	0.0053	−0.0024
	(−0.26)	(0.68)	(−0.28)	(−0.36)	(−0.31)	(−0.34)	(0.62)	(−0.37)
Employment experience in urban areas, in years	−0.0014	−0.0034	−0.0010	−0.0009	−0.0007	−0.0011	−0.0033	−0.0002
	(−0.40)	(−0.86)	(−0.29)	(−0.26)	(−0.20)	(−0.30)	(−0.86)	(−0.06)
Communist Party member	0.0151	0.1139	0.0217	0.0175	0.0293	0.0048	0.1026	0.0148
	(0.15)	(0.67)	(0.22)	(0.18)	(0.30)	(0.05)	(0.59)	(0.15)
Social network (size)	—	0.0049	—	—	—	—	0.0048	—
		(1.82)*					(1.79)*	
Attitudinal indicators: Has the importance of the following factors that influence household income changed compared with before? 1) decreased, 2) unchanged, 3) increased								
Educational level	—	—	−0.0185	—	—	—	—	—
			(−0.51)					
Political status	—	—	—	0.0236	—	—	—	—
				(0.52)				
Rank of work unit	—	—	—	—	−0.0867	—	—	—
					(−1.96)**			
Social connections	—	—	—	—	—	0.0892	0.1285	—
						(2.24)**	(2.40)**	
Urban hukou	—	—	—	—	—	—	—	−0.1025
								(−2.26)**
Cities	Yes	Yes	Yes	Yes	Yes	Yes	Yes	Yes
Wald χ^2 (18)	40.81***	—	38.72***	39.41***	43.66***	44.25***	—	—
Wald χ^2 (19)	—	34.36**	—	—	—	—	40.01***	—
Wald χ^2 (20)	—	—	—	—	—	—	—	44.57***
Pseudo R^2	0.0391	0.0543	0.0370	0.0376	0.0399	0.0427	0.0622	0.0426
Number of observations	2302	1374	2288	2280	2280	2274	1358	2272

Source: *China Household and Income Project, urban survey.*

Notes: (1) Omitted dummy variables are: male, not a Communist Party member, and Pingliang. (2) Robust standard errors adjusted for clustering at the household level are computed. (3) *** indicates significance at the 1% level, ** at the 5% level, and * at the 10% level.

entrepreneurs to start a business is significantly influenced by having more education and membership in the Communist Party.

7.4 Legal Constraints and Financial Repression

Table 7.4 sets out two measures of the legal environment to determine whether the wider institutional environment plays a role in entrepreneurship in China. The first measure is of financial repression, whereby the variable attempts to stand as proxy for the extent of credit constraints in the economy. The variable as constructed is the inverse of financial repression, so it is a typical measure of financial development; for example, the share of credit allocated to the private sector as a ratio of the total amount of bank credit in a province (see for example, Rajan and Zingales 1998; Lu and Yao 2009). The more credit that is allocated to the private sector, the less financial repression exists. The second measure is utilization of the legal system, which proxies for the extent that the formal legal system is invoked in solving commercial or civil disputes. Although an imperfect measure of the effectiveness of the legal system, an untrustworthy or incompetent legal system would get very few filings (see for example, Lu and Yao 2009, who use a similar measure). The variable is constructed as the number of annual filings of civil or commercial cases per capita in a province.

In Table 7.4, the utilization of the legal system is a significantly positive factor in entrepreneurship for both urban residents and migrants. Increasing the effectiveness of the legal system appears to be significantly associated with more entrepreneurship. By contrast, there is little evidence that financial repression influences entrepreneurs. There is no effect on urban residents, while there is a positive effect on migrants, as seen in column (2). However, when the variable that measures the extent of the legal system is included, then the variable ceases to be significant which suggests that the legal impediments to financial sector development are subsumed when a measure of the effectiveness of laws is included. By contrast, the legal system retains its significance and increases in magnitude when financial repression is included. Interestingly, when the social network variable is also included, it retains its significance although the size of the coefficient is reduced somewhat for urban residents though not for migrants. This robust finding for urban entrepreneurs suggests that social networks continue to perform a function in facilitating relational contracting and business formation alongside the legal system even though its importance is reduced. For migrant entrepreneurs, an actively used legal system eliminates the significant effect of social networks. What is evident is that legal development is a significant and positive determinant for both urban residents and migrants.

As discussed earlier, there is the potential issue of endogeneity. The estimators could suffer from reverse causality if legal development, for instance, did not increase the probability of entrepreneurship but more firms are likely to start up in areas where there is greater legal development. The interpretation of the

Table 7.4 Legal factors influencing entrepreneurship (z-statistics in parentheses)

Dependent variable: 1 if entrepreneur 0 if non-entrepreneur	Urban residents (1)	Migrants (2)	Urban residents (3)	Migrants (4)	Urban residents (5)	Migrants (6)	Urban residents (5)	Migrants (6)
Legal environment								
Financial development (extent of financial repression)	0.0026 (1.62)	0.0476 (1.82)*	—	—	-0.0009 (-0.85)	-0.0076 (-0.74)	-0.0006 (-0.49)	-0.0274 (-1.46)
Utilization of the legal system	—	—	0.0158 (2.70)***	0.1818 (3.04)***	0.0189 (2.75)***	0.2070 (3.00)***	0.0171 (2.24)***	0.3244 (3.26)***
Social network	—	—	—	—	—	—	0.0001 (1.74)*	0.0022 (1.24)
LR x^2 (7)	—	—	—	29.73***	—	—	—	—
LR x^2 (8)	—	—	304.64***	—	—	30.27***	—	—
LR x^2 (9)	—	—	—	—	305.35***	—	254.04***	—
LR x^2 (10)	—	—	—	—	—	—	—	19.41**
Wald x^2 (18)	275.49***	—	—	—	—	—	—	—
Wald x^2 (19)	—	40.81***	—	—	—	—	—	—
Pseudo R^2	0.1675	0.0391	0.1432	0.0114	0.1435	0.0116	0.1409	0.0132
Number of observations	9729	2302	8355	2010	8355	2010	7264	1154

Sources: *China Household and Income Project*, urban survey, 1999. *China Statistical Yearbook, China Provincial Yearbook*.

Notes: (1) Only the variables of interest are reported for brevity.

(2) Robust standard errors adjusted for clustering at the household level are computed.

(3) *** indicates significance at the 1% level, ** at the 5% level, and * at the 10% level.

(4) Financial development is measured as the ratio of bank credit allocated to the private sector as a proportion of total credit. It is measured for the cities of Shenyang and Chengdu, while all others are reported at the provincial level for 1999.

(5) Use of legal system is measured as the ratio of cases filed on a per capita basis. For Beijing, the measure is of commercial cases, while it is civil cases excluding domestic cases for the other provinces for 1998. For Henan, the figures refer to 2000, while those for Sichuan are from 2004. Gansu is not included in the estimation due to lack of information regarding the legal system.

results in this section should be an associational one. In a probabilistic estimation of whether a person becomes an entrepreneur, the probability is higher in an area (city) where there is a more developed legal system (measured through greater use of such a system). The system estimation now will attempt to address these issues of endogeneity. The same can be said for the measure of financial repression. However, the extent of financial development is not significant in the probit models, suggesting no association between financial sector development and entrepreneurship. Any effect that may be found could be via the legal development variable. Thus, in the next section, the decision uses the 3SLS estimator on the effect of the legal system on entrepreneurship as the key test.

Table 7.5 sets out the first stage and the results of the 3SLS estimation, along with the SURE estimations as a further statistical test. In the first-stage regressions, the instruments all indicate statistically significant relationships with the potentially endogenous variables. Wealth from the countryside predicts entrepreneurship for migrants but does not affect legal development, while the pre-1995 number of lawyers affects legal development but not migrant entrepreneurship. Both lawyers per capita and also the additional instrument of legal advisors in enterprises (also pre-1995) have significantly negative relationships with later legal development. This suggests that the provinces with larger numbers of lawyers and legal advisors experienced slower subsequent development of the legal system, indicating some degree of convergence whereby the provinces which had opened earlier and which were not as developed legally progressed faster as compared with those which had more lawyers and legal advisors. This would fit with studies showing the harmonization of Chinese law across the country accompanying economic growth such that the backward regions develop faster in order to catch up with the more advanced legal regions, propelled by a national legal system to which provinces reform to meet those standards (see for example, Yueh 2009, for findings that provinces have similar rates of utilization of patent laws despite starting from differential levels of legal and economic development).

The 3SLS estimations confirm the results of the earlier probabilistic models that were unable to address endogeneity. Once instrumentation is undertaken and a system of equations is estimated using the instrumented values, the key relationships can be disentangled and the hypothesis that there is a significant effect of legal development on entrepreneurship can be tested with greater confidence. In column (3), legal development is indeed found to continue to have a significant and positive effect on migrant entrepreneurship. The SURE estimation offers further support. In turn, in column (4), migrant entrepreneurship positively influences the development of the legal system, which is again echoed in column (6) of the SURE results. The other independent variables are largely unaffected (compare Table 7.4). Although this estimation was conducted solely on the sample of migrant entrepreneurs due to the lack of a comparable exogenous instrument for 'wealth brought from the countryside' for urban residents, migrants comprise 80 per cent of all entrepreneurs in urban China, so the findings would pertain to the vast majority of those starting their own

Table 7.5 Results of the 3SLS estimates (t-statistics in parentheses)

Dependent variable: 1 if entrepreneur 0 if non-entrepreneur	First stage		3SLS		SURE	
	Migrant entrepreneurship (1)	Legal development (2)	Migrant entrepreneurship (3)	Legal development (4)	Migrant entrepreneurship (5)	Legal development (6)
Legal development	—	—	0.4816*** (0.0105)		0.3520*** (0.0578)	
Migrant entrepreneurship	—	—		2.0764*** (0.0805)		0.0521*** (0.0085)
Personal characteristics						
Gender	-0.0117 (0.0252)	-0.0013 (0.0011)	-0.0118 (0.0252)	0.0245 (0.0520)	-0.0129 (0.0219)	-0.0055 (0.0084)
Age	-0.0003 (0.0016)	0.0002 (0.0001)***	-0.0008 (0.0016)	0.0016 (0.0032)	-0.0011 (0.0014)	-0.0001 (0.0005)
Marital status	0.2033 (0.0632)***	0.0053 (0.0026)***	0.1990 (0.0631)***	-0.4133 (0.1313)***	0.1375 (0.0548)***	0.0040 (0.0211)
Education, in years	0.0010 (0.0052)	-0.0004 (0.0002)	0.0037 (0.0052)	-0.0076 (0.0107)	-0.0126 (0.0042)***	-0.0028 (0.0016)
Employment experience in urban areas, in years	-0.0054 (0.0033)	-0.0007 (0.0001)***	-0.0031 (0.0032)	0.0065 (0.0067)	-0.0023 (0.0022)	-0.0016 (0.0008)**
Communist Party member	-0.0487 (0.0917)	0.0036 (0.0038)	-0.0360 (0.0915)	0.0747 (0.1889)	0.0232 (0.0692)	0.0426 (0.0266)
Instrumental variables						
Wealth brought from countryside	5.30e-06 (1.96e-06) ***	9.10e-08 (8.17e-08)	—	—	—	—
Log of lawyers per capita (pre-1995)	-0.0178 (0.0445)	-0.1402 (0.0019)***	—	—	—	—

(continued)

Table 7.5 Continued

Dependent variable: 1 if entrepreneur 0 if non-entrepreneur	First stage		3SLS		SURE	
	Migrant entrepreneurship (1)	Legal development (2)	Migrant entrepreneurship (3)	Legal development (4)	Migrant entrepreneurship (5)	Legal development (6)
Legal advisors per capita (pre-1995)	-0.0115 (0.0407)	-0.0619 (0.0017)***	—	—	—	—
Constant	-0.1036 (0.1851)	-7.7890 (0.0077)***	3.0074 (0.1193)***	-6.2451 (0.2106)***	2.4322 (0.3471)***	-5.8282 (0.0344)***
Adjusted R-squared	0.0119	0.9838	0.004	-39.402	0.010	0.006
F-test	3.01	10127.88	303.27	95.28	8.16	6.94
p value	0.0015	0.0000	0.0000	0.0000	0.0000	0.0000
Observations	1498	1498	1498	1498	2006	2006

Sources: China Household and Income Project, urban survey, 1999. China Statistical Yearbook, China Provincial Yearbook.

Notes: (1) To support the multivariate regression, small sample t-statistics and F-tests are computed instead of z-statistics and χ^2.

(2) Robust standard errors adjusted for clustering at the household level are computed.

(3) *** indicates significance at the 1% level, ** at the 5% level, and * at the 10% level. R-squared can be negative in 3SLS because the estimation is not nested within a constant-only model of the dependent variable, so the residual sum of squares is not restricted to be smaller than the total sum of squares. As such, the F-test would provide the overall model significance.

(4) Use of legal system is measured as the ratio of cases filed on a per capita basis. For Beijing, the measure is of commercial cases, while it is civil cases excluding domestic cases for the other provinces for 1998. For Henan, the figures refer to 2000, while those for Sichuan are from 2004. Gansu is not included in the estimation due to lack of information regarding the legal system.

(5) The number of lawyers per capita is measured for Liaoning and Henan provinces in 1985, in Jiangsu (1990) and in Beijing (1995). Measures before the mid-1990s were not available for Sichuan and Gansu, so they were omitted from the estimation. The number of legal advisors working for an enterprise is measured on a per capita basis for the same years and provinces as in note 4.

businesses. In conclusion, the 3SLS findings confirm the probabilistic models and suggest that a better-developed legal system would foster entrepreneurship.

7.5 Private Firms and Provincial Legal Development

Another variation would be to estimate a panel over time of the incidence of private sector development in provinces at different stages of legal development. Through a panel estimator, time-varying effects such as differential economic growth and levels of income as well as time-invariant effects such as province-specific traits can be controlled for so that the incidence of entrepreneurship in a province can be determined. A panel dataset of Chinese provinces from 1991–2006 is used in the estimates.

Across China's provinces, from virtually no entrepreneurs (around 1–2 per cent), those who have started their own businesses reached one in eight in market-driven provinces such as Jiangsu by the 2000s. The proportion is not so high for most provinces, but the upward trend since the early 1990s is evident. For most provinces, the proportion peaked in the late 1990s at the height of the restructuring of the state-owned sector that opened up the market. By the 2000s, the rate had declined somewhat probably in response to the growth of private-sector employment that offered avenues other than starting one's own business.

Table 7.6 shows those results estimated using a fixed-effect and random-effects panel estimator. The former controls for provincial fixed effects beyond that which is measured by the control variables of GDP per capita, foreign direct investment, exports as a share of GDP, and educational enrolment rates. In other words, there are still provincial-specific influences on entrepreneurship that exist. The random effects estimator assumes that the provincial effects are orthogonal to the other covariates. If the assumptions are satisfied, then the random-effects model is preferred over the fixed-effects model as it is more efficient. Using the Breusch-Pagan Lagrangian multiplier test, the null hypothesis is rejected which implies that the assumptions of the random effects model are not satisfied. Those and other test statistics including an F-test of the joint significance of the fixed-effects regressors are reported in the table. Year dummies control for macroeconomic trends over time.

Relying therefore on the fixed effects model where individual provincial effects are controlled for (though the result is unchanged in the random effects model), the number of civil cases filed per capita is indeed significant and positive in determining entrepreneurship, supporting the earlier findings. Also, the number of lawyers per capita continued to have no direct effect on the incidence of entrepreneurship, again supporting the 3SLS whereby lawyers influence the development of the legal system which increases entrepreneurial activity but not directly. These measures also include all urban and rural residents and migrants.

Table 7.6 Determinants of provincial entrepreneurship (z-statistics in parentheses)

Dependent variable = log of starting one's own business per capita	Fixed-effects model (1)	Random-effects model (2)
Log of GDP per capita	0.212	−0.296*
	(0.277)	(0.158)
Log of FDI	0.117**	0.103***
	(0.046)	(0.037)
Provincial exports-to-GDP ratio	−0.138	−0.181
	(0.192)	(0.185)
Educational enrolment (primary and secondary schooling)	−0.965***	−0.902***
	(0.158)	(0.157)
Log of lawyers per capita	0.071	0.072
	(0.097)	(0.091)
Log of civil cases filed per capita	0.283***	0.242***
	(0.084)	(0.080)
Year	−0.062**	−0.012
	(0.024)	(0.013)
Constant	120.329**	25.881
	(46.503)	(24.349)
Adjusted R-squared	0.149	
R-squared		0.025
$F_{(7, 190)}$	9.43***	
Wald χ^2 (7)		57.67***
Breusch-Pagan Lagrangian multiplier test χ^2 (1)		290.41***
Number of provinces	22	22
Observations	219	219

Sources: *China Statistical Yearbook, Census Yearbook.*

Notes: *** indicates significance at the 1% level, ** at the 5% level, and * at the 10% level. Independent variables are: log of deflated per capita GDP, log of foreign direct investment, export-to-GDP ratio, educational enrolment rate of school-aged children, log of lawyers per capita, log of civil cases filed per capita, dummies for twenty-nine provinces (except for Tibet and Chongqing is included in Sichuan) and year.

Legal and financial constraints can affect entrepreneurship due to an under-developed legal system and financial sector. For China, an economy that epitomizes institutional underdevelopment, the legal system is found to be a positive determinant in entrepreneurship while financial repression is not significant. The findings imply that entrepreneurship would be bolstered with improvements in the formal legal system, while entrepreneurs of both types are canny enough to start their businesses without being unduly influenced by China's imperfect credit markets and lack of financial depth even if the latter is caused by legal impediments. Informal institutions like networks become less significant once the extent of legal development is taken into account, suggesting that relational contracting is largely used by migrants as a substitute for a developed legal system, though there is some evidence of their continuing use by urban residents.

Entrepreneurship is explained by not only the usual set of personal characteristics, but is also affected by the particular legal and institutional environment. Specifically, a more developed legal system is found to increase entrepreneurship consistent with the notion that greater formal protection of property rights increases the propensity to develop the private sector. Further, there is evidence of feedback from entrepreneurship to further legal development. However, becoming an entrepreneur was not affected by the extent of financial repression. It may affect the further development of the business, but does not play a role in the decision to start up, probably reflecting the small scale of the private sector in the initial stages. Both migrants and urban residents in China were affected by the external legal environment when the personal traits which determine entrepreneurship otherwise differed for the two groups.

Notably, entrepreneurship in urban China is largely driven by migrants to cities who start their own businesses and a handful of urban residents. Both groups earn substantially more than the wage employed, although they share a number of similarities in personal traits, such as educational attainment. However, they differ in what drives them to become entrepreneurs.

For those starting a business in China, having the right attitude and using one's social network are important, as well as the legal environment. However, as the effectiveness of the legal system improves, it should help increase entrepreneurship. The significant rise in entrepreneurs in recent years could plausibly be traced to the a corresponding improvements in China's laws and regulations, particularly with the increased attention paid to protecting private businesses after joining the World Trade Organisation in 2001, such as the passage of the Property Law in 2007. For entrepreneurs, an entrepreneurial attitude will be needed in the meanwhile at the very least.

8

Global Integration and Growth: Rebalancing the Economy

8.1 Introduction

China has been a particularly successful example of utilizing policy to attract foreign direct investment (FDI) in order to develop manufacturing and export capacity to support its early growth. Recently, it has also begun to promote outward FDI as part of its firms' 'going global'. In the twenty-first century, China is practising a 'going out, bringing in' policy. Its 'open-door' policy has been supplemented by the 'going out' of its firms as well as 'pulling in' FDI. This is a key part of China's future growth that is dependent on the ability to produce globally competitive corporations that will help China move up the value chain and sustain its development through this new form of global integration.

There is no doubt that China's trade and FDI policies are closely intertwined with its industrial upgrading and successful 'catching up' in economic growth. China's ability to manage its global integration is one of the key reasons why the economy has grown so well. Given its size, it has also made an impact on the rest of the world. The 'China effect' on global trade and investment patterns can be clearly seen in its accelerated global integration after World Trade Organisation (WTO) entry in 2001. What is also becoming apparent is the changing impact of China on the world as it also increases its outward foreign investment as its firms 'go global'. China's outward investment is similarly motivated by a desire to learn to speed up growth, secure commodities for development, and to create competitive multinational corporations. As such, its outward investment will accentuate its current impact and raise concerns about the difficulty of separating state-directed from commercially oriented motives for emerging Chinese multinationals, and could thus determine its ultimate success with effects ranging from Europe to Africa.

As China enters its next phase of growth, though, it will need to rebalance its economy towards domestic demand. With nearly 10 per cent of global trade share, exports are unlikely to grow much more and certainly not at the rapid pace of the past. But this is a sizeable task as consumption has fallen dramatically to less than 40 per cent of GDP while the trade surplus rose rapidly during the

2000s and was part of the ultimately unsustainable global macroeconomic imbalances. Moreover, its foreign exchange reserves grew to a record US$3.3 trillion that has led China to worry over the value of its holdings with Western economies struggling in the aftermath of the 2008 global financial crisis. Also, as China seeks to create multinational companies, outward investment will grow. All of this points to an inevitable structural shift.

Rebalancing its growth drivers will add to its stability and allow it to become more like the structure of the only economy in the world larger than China's, America. The US is one of the world's top three traders, but its economy is largely driven by domestic demand. China, too, can become a large, open economy alongside the United States. China would gain greater stability and a more sustainable basis for its future growth if it continues to become more globally integrated, but be less subject to the volatility that plagues small, open economies such as those in South-east Asia, Africa, and emerging Europe.

8.1.1 *Joining the World Economy*

In 1978, the reform period began when market-oriented measures, which included the 'open-door' policy designed to encourage foreign trade and investment, were launched (Lardy 1998). China's approach to economic reforms, though, is and has been gradual as it tends to adopt policies slowly. China's reform programme progressed gradually, adopting an approach that has been referred to as 'crossing the stream while feeling the stones' (Naughton 1995). China's approach is to wait until a particular policy has been successfully implemented in one region before the 'experiment' is extended nationally. As a result, China's 'open-door' policy did not move forward until reforms were implemented in urban areas in the mid-1980s and then did not pick up until Deng Xiaoping's famous tour of the southern coastal provinces in 1992. Since then, China has been tremendously successful in attracting FDI, developing its infrastructure, and utilizing foreign investment, particularly with respect to manufacturing and exports.

The first reforms in the area of FDI policy created what are known as Special Economic Zones (SEZs). SEZs were first introduced in 1979 in the south-eastern coastal provinces of Fujian and Guangdong and located in urban areas. The SEZs are similar to special customs areas. Foreign-invested enterprises (FIEs) receive preferential treatment, including up to 50 per cent reduction in custom duties, with respect to corporate income tax, and were granted duty-free imports. This resulted in extremely rapid growth in these areas due to their attractiveness to foreign investment. Guangdong has invariably been the leading exporting province in China on account of the successful growth of the SEZ city of Shenzhen on the Hong Kong border and that of the capital city, Guangzhou. Although the SEZs were successful even at the start, the Chinese authorities believed that they tended to attract investment in low-technology and light industry sectors. These were indeed consistent with China's comparative advantage in abundant, low-cost labour. However, China was keen to attract more advanced technologies to prompt industrial upgrading and the combination of these factors paved the way for further reforms. In 1984, Economic and Trade Development Zones (ETDZ) or 'Open Port Cities' (OPC) were created. The 'Open Port Cities' were originally created to address the perceived shortcomings of the SEZs. These OPCs became ETDZs in 1985. They are located along China's eastern coastline and were granted preferential investment and import treatment. These were considered to be more successful then SEZs in attracting higher technological investments, particularly in consumer electronics and computer-related goods. Guangzhou remains a strong example of the success of this policy initiative.

In 1992, Free Trade Zones (FTZs) were created following the success of the earlier initiatives. Free Trade Zones are specially designated urban areas selected for receiving preferential treatment and trading privileges. The investment incentives in FTZs are extremely attractive since exports and imports are free of any taxes or tariffs so long as the imports are not resold in China. Items intended for resale in China were, by contrast, subject to high tariff rates. The best known FTZs are Shanghai's Pudong district, particularly Waigaoqiao, Tianjin Harbour, and Futian, an area of Shenzhen, Dalian, and Haikou on Hainan Island.

China continued its push to attract more advanced technologies by developing High-Technology Development Zones (HTDZs) in 1995, just three years after the successful creation of FTZs. The aim in creating HTDZs was to increase China's research and development (R&D) capabilities through fostering both domestic and foreign investment. With the exception of the three inner provinces (Xinjiang, and Tibet and Ningxia Autonomous Regions), every province has at least one of the fifty-three HTDZs. Each zone includes a number of 'industrial parks' and 'science and technology parks' open to domestic and foreign high-tech investors. There are also numerous zones that have not been sanctioned by the State Council, as with the ETDZs. HTDZs comprise cities or certain areas of urban China, such as the well-known 'Haidian' district in Beijing. These zones are intended to promote industrial applications of technology and tend to be located in proximity to existing or planned research institutions, or research and development centres. A characteristic of the HTDZs is the 'three-in-one' development system, whereby every zone must include a university-based research centre, an innovation centre to utilize applied technology for product development, and a partnership with a commercial enterprise to manufacture and market the products. The HTDZs are expected to contribute significantly to China's science and technology infrastructure, although there is a question as to whether domestic firms have gained in innovative ability as a result of FDI. Although more than 50 per cent of China's exports have been produced by foreign invested enterprises since the mid-1990s, an estimated 80 per cent of China's high-tech goods are currently produced by FIEs.

The result of these policies contributed to the coastal areas growing more rapidly than the inward and western regions as over 90 per cent of FDI is located in China's 'gold coast' (Yueh 2010a). Efforts to promote inland areas as potential locations for FDI have faced more obstacles as infrastructure and less dense populations deter investment, although rising wages in the coastal regions and significant investment in roads in the central region have begun to shift economic activity westward, if not yet all the way to the western regions.

Prior to WTO accession and further opening of its economy, China exerted significant control over the form and destination of inward FDI (Yueh 2011). For instance, joint ventures were not approved unless they met two criteria. First, the foreign partner must have superior technology that is of interest to China. In fact, many of the joint venture agreements included annexes designating technology transfers. Second, the manufactured products must be suitable for export and demanded in global markets. These rules governing joint ventures meant that Chinese enterprises had more potential to benefit from both explicit and implicit (such as through learning and know-how) technology transfers from the foreign partners and thus help develop China's domestic innovative capacity, in a process known as 'catching up' in economic growth. Moreover, joint ventures were usually nearly 50–50 in percentage of ownership (with the Chinese partner holding 51 per cent of shares), reducing the threat of foreign capital taking over or dominating domestic sectors. It may also be that the change in the vehicles of FDI means that China will be less able to direct the type of investment that comes in, shifting the investment potential of FDI away from manufacturing and into the retail sector where less positive spillover is likely. But, it may reflect foreign investors moving into a growing consumer market that has opened substantially since WTO accession.

China's industrial policy has focused on developing partnerships between domestic enterprises and foreign partners, usually via well-established multinational corporations. China has been remarkably successful in attracting foreign direct investment despite a lack of formal private property rights, transparent institutions, and with a significant degree of bureaucratic 'red tape'. The creation of export-oriented zones and parks was undoubtedly important in this process.

After fifteen years of negotiation, China gained entry to the WTO which made it a part of multilateral trade arrangements with other members that account for the near totality of world trade in manufactured goods. Agreeing to open up has implications for China's FDI policy, as WTO membership entailed opening up more of its domestic market to foreign competitors and removed long-standing barriers such as geographical restrictions that had previously prevented national expansion of foreign businesses in China.

On the eve of accession, China was already a strong international competitor in a large range of industrial products, led by simple labour-intensive manufactures, but quickly diversifying into complex, capital, and technology-intensive goods (Lall and Albaladejo 2004). While accession may not give China an immediate advantage in markets where it already enjoys most favoured nation (MFN) status, it gave it unprecedented access to other markets. Accession will also assure it secure access in the future and so induce more sustained investment in the development of exports.

Foreign investors have been major drivers of China's export success, and inward FDI has increased from an average of US$ 50 billion per year in the late 1990s to about double that amount in the 2000s. WTO principles call for transparency in legal rules and China's business environment has improved as it confronted the need to develop laws that govern markets with not only greater marketization in its own economy, but also to meet the expectations of foreign firms gaining access to China's domestic market. Although imperfect, the legal system has undergone a rapid number of reforms, including passing a law governing mergers and acquisitions (M&A), unifying the various codes that had governed foreign and domestic corporations separately, and passing an anti-monopoly law for the first time. Market access remains a key point of contention for foreign firms and is often the subject of disputes in summits between China and its largest trading partners of the EU/US, but the composition of FDI inflows is changing. In the initial stages, most export-oriented FDI came from neighbouring economies, particularly from Hong Kong. Over time, advanced industrial countries have accounted for larger shares of FDI, mostly in hopes of serving the domestic market.

Indeed, some view as the most significant part of WTO accession China's agreement to open its services sector, which is wide in scope, as it includes not only financial services, but also professional services such as law, accounting, etc. (Lardy 1998). This is in spite of much evidence of considerable financial weakness. However, in many respects, the restricted opening of its services sector is designed to use foreign know-how to reform its lagging banking and capital markets. China's leadership believes that competition from foreign banks can accelerate the development of a commercial credit culture in the domestic banking system. This potential is being weighed carefully against the risks associated with premature financial liberalization in the context of an admittedly weak capital market and a relatively new central bank with insufficient supervisory and regulatory experience. Adding to these concerns is the issue of full currency convertibility. The Chinese authorities are under increasing pressure to speed up currency liberalization.

8.1.2 The Exchange Rate

Since 1994, China's currency, the renminbi or RMB, has been effectively pegged to the US dollar despite its official description as a managed float. The exchange rate at that time was set at RMB 8.7 per US dollar. From 1994 to 1997, the exchange rate appreciated by 5 per cent to RMB 8.29 against the US dollar. Before the onset of the Asian financial crisis in 1998, the peg was at 8.6 to the dollar. After then and before the new peg to a trade-weighted basket in July 2009, the RMB was effectively pegged to the US dollar in a narrow band of 8.276 to 8.280. It was thought to be quietly repegged to the dollar during the global financial crisis but then again depegged in 2010. By 2011, the RMB managed a record appreciation of 4.4 per cent against the dollar, strengthening beyond 6.3 in 2012.

It is difficult to determine the fundamental value of a currency in the short run. In any case, because of China's trade surplus, in particular its significant surpluses with the US and EU, import restrictions, and attractiveness to FDI, the RMB was viewed as undervalued. The timing of reform will certainly be driven by macroeconomic fundamentals in China. Moreover, it will not be easy for China to diversify its holdings. An estimated 70–80 per cent of its reserves are US dollar holdings. If the dollar falls due to diversification, then the RMB will require more intervention. If the dollar falls in value on account of increased holdings of euros, then again, the People's Bank of China (PBOC) will need to spend more money stabilzing the peg. Amid clamours for a new global reserve currency separate from the US dollar, China is sitting uncomfortably on large dollar holdings although its exchange rate regime leads it to accumulate more dollar-denominated assets in any case.

Taken together, the concern over the accumulation of US dollar holdings and a push for the RMB to be included in a new supra-national reserve currency all point in one direction. RMB liberalization and relaxation of the exchange rate are on the cards, sometime down the road.

8.2 The China Effect

China's re-emergence in the global economy has unsurprisingly had a significant growth impact given its size. Even though China is a developing country in the midst of making the transition to a market economy, it is already emerging as a major force in the world economy—one that accounts for 20 per cent of the world's population, more than four times the size of the United States, and nearly three times that of the European Union.

China's size and integration with the world economy have contributed to uncertainty about the global inflationary environment; its currency has been a subject of contention; its trade has raised concerns for workers and firms in both developed and developing countries; its demand for energy has led to competition and conflict; it has rivalled the United States, the UK, and developing countries as a destination for foreign direct investment; and the effects of its own overseas investments have begun to be felt across the world. As a result, China has generated incremental growth in the global economy that has made its success significant for the welfare of other countries.

The 'China effect' has been acutely felt in terms of commodity prices. The reform of the state sector in the 1990s and the rise of the non-state sector have heralded a second industrialization in China, which requires energy and raw materials. While these commodities constitute a relatively small share of total Chinese imports, they are large enough to impose a major impact on world markets.

Since the mid-1990s, China has become a net oil importer even though it is also one of the top ten world producers of oil. China is the world's second largest consumer of oil after only the United States, and, in 2004, with 4.4 per cent of total world GDP, China consumed 30 per cent of the world's iron ore, 31 per cent of its coal, 27 per cent of its steel, and 25 per cent of its aluminium. Between 2000 and 2003, China's share of the increase in global demand for aluminium, steel, nickel, and copper was, respectively, 76 per cent, 95 per cent, 99 per cent, and 100 per cent (Kaplinsky 2006).

Highly speculative estimates suggest that demand from China is responsible for about 50 per cent of the recent boom in world commodity prices. One effect of this is to redistribute income between other countries in the world. Thus, primary commodity exporters have experienced dramatic improvements in their export earnings and terms of trade, which have been paid for by importers of these commodities, some of them developed countries.

At the same time, Chinese exports of a range of manufactures have resulted in some substantial price falls. China's terms of trade for manufactured goods fell by 14 per cent between 1993 and 2000 (Zheng and Zhao 2002). Its overall terms of trade worsened by 17 per cent between 1980 and 2003 (UNCTAD 2006). Moreover, in one-third of 151 industrial sectors, the prices of Chinese imports into the European Union have fallen (Kaplinsky 2006). Lower import prices have also contributed to a more benign inflationary environment. Up until the real commodity boom peaking in 2008, China's rapid global integration and remarkable growth generated a favourable terms-of-trade shock that produced lower than expected levels of inflation in the global economy (Rogoff 2006).

But China nevertheless poses a competitive threat. In some countries in Latin America (Chile, Costa Rica, and El Salvador), 60–70 per cent of exports are directly threatened by China's rise because of a similar export product mix (Lall and Weiss 2005). There remain concerns for other developing countries. For example, the phasing out of the WTO Multi-Fibre Agreement in 2005, which had previously limited China's exports of clothing and textiles through a global quota system, raised concerns for Bangladesh and Sri Lanka, whose export sectors are dominated by these goods. and while China's rise has induced more imports from its Asian neighbours, this has not been enough to offset displacement of their exports in third-country markets.

But exports of labour-intensive products like clothing, apparel, textiles, and footwear, although still significant, are a rapidly declining share of China's trade. These have dropped from 40 per cent of exports in the early 1990s to less than 20 per cent in 2006, as much of the fastest export growth has been in more advanced manufactured products, particularly electrical equipment.

A key aspect of this technological upgrading is the growth of high levels of two-way trade in similar items, particularly electronics. This 'intra-industry trade' reflects cross-border production networks. Since around half of China's exports have been produced by foreign-owned enterprises since the mid-1990s, the rise of intra-industry trade should not be surprising. Multinational corporations seek low cost manufacturing bases and often diversify their production and supply chains.

China's comparative advantage is seemingly no longer being driven simply by low cost, abundant labour. Some interior provinces may still compete on that basis, but for areas on the coast this advantage has been substantially eroded and competitive advantage is increasingly based on skills. This upgrading will alter the set of industries that experience competitive pressure from China, but relative prices and exchange rates will change, and aggregate effects will turn on terms-of-trade effects.

8.2.1 *Becoming a Large, Open Economy*

The global financial crisis of 2007/8 and the ensuing Great Recession hit China in the autumn of 2008 when exports collapsed. China suffered some losses from the failure of Lehman Brothers, but did not become embroiled in the financial crisis, and thus only suffered the real economy effects, notably the contraction in global trade. It did, though, reshape its outlook towards rebalancing its economy.

Exports collapsed during the height of the crisis. The severity of this Great Recession has meant a contraction in global trade for the first time in thirty years. Exports account for over 30 per cent of China's GDP and the closing of export-oriented factories resulted in an estimated 20 million unemployed rural–urban migrants.

It did cause China to think about achieving a more stable economic growth model; it will need to institute reforms that can boost domestic demand whilst promoting global integration. The aim of reform in the context of a weaker global economy has to be twofold: (1) to improve the structure of the Chinese economy towards a model suitable for a large, open economy; (2) to ensure stability in economic transition/development against external shocks including designing better institutional integration with the global economy in recognition that world markets are linked (capital, technology, environmental) but not governed, which limits positive spillovers and instead transmits shocks.

The structure of the Chinese economy needs to evolve to become like the USA and Japan, which are large countries whose growth is primarily driven by domestic demand, but also are the largest traders in the world. Countries with small populations are more influenced by international trade and must rely on external markets to achieve scale, which was one of the rationales for the EU single market which has become the largest economic entity in the world. China would be less subject to the volatility of the world economy by following a path that strengthens both internal and external demand which can cause the proportion of growth to be driven by domestic demand to increase even as trade expands in absolute terms. As China affects the global terms of trade (prices of exports to imports), structuring itself as a large, open economy which recognizes the benefits of global integration whilst maintaining a strong base of domestic demand to shield it from the worst excesses of external shocks is feasible.

To orient toward domestic demand means boosting consumption in China which is the same as saying that there is a need to reduce the savings motive of households and firms. The strong savings motive was evident in the 2000s. When China's current account surplus grew to double digits as a share of GDP after 2004, investment retained its share of GDP. Normally when this happens in other countries, investment is squeezed. In China, savings increased instead, such that investment retained its share of GDP with the consequence that consumption fell from around 50 per cent of GDP in the early 1990s to nearly one-third by the late 2000s. Consumption maintained its share of around 40 per cent of GDP in the 1990s until 2004 when it fell below 40 per cent and eventually to 35 per cent in 2008. Consumption as a share of GDP in market economies is around 50–65 per cent of GDP; for example, Japan's stands at 60 per cent, while US consumption, at 72 per cent before the onset of the global financial crisis, was considered to be too high. This result is not only from households but also as a result of the rapid increase in corporate savings in the 2000s.

For households, precautionary savings motives are important to address, particularly in rural areas. Increasing incomes and wealth along with improved social security provision are required. These issues are well rehearsed and the latter additions to the government's 2008 stimulus plan demonstrate a recognition of the challenges, although the funding was inadequate, particularly in the area of pensions. Other measures such as developing the service sector will boost domestic demand by increasing the non-tradable component of the economy and also create jobs along the low and high ends of the skills spectrum that suits the Chinese (urban and migrant) labour force. Increasing income, including through greater urbanization that can improve the earning potential of rural residents, would be a crucial driver in boosting consumption.

As the increase in savings by firms in the 2000s has outpaced that of households, several reforms are needed. First, taxing state-owned enterprises to reduce their retained earnings is sensible, while increasing dividend payments would be another avenue. Second, non-state firms find it more difficult to obtain bank credit, and other sources of funding from domestic capital markets are less developed, so firms grow by retained earnings. As economic growth was higher than trend at 10 per cent per annum in the 2000s, this led to high rates of savings by the non-state sector that accounts for over two-thirds of industrial output. Third, complete liberalization of interest rates will improve credit allocation to non-state sector firms and reduce the savings tendency as well as remove the distortion to investment that can happen when the internal rate of return (the interest rate represents the cost of capital) is not driven entirely by market forces. Fourth, greater, gradual capital account liberalization, in particular the 'going out' policy, will allow firms to operate in global markets including accessing credit markets that are much better developed. This will reduce the motive for corporate savings as well as the portion of the current account surplus funded by purchasing US Treasuries since capital outflow can also comprise both long- and short-term capital investments. Also, increasing the flexibility of the exchange rate would occur with greater capital account liberalization to support the 'going out' policy. Coupled with interest rate reforms, there should be a better balance between the internal (savings/investment) and external (current account) positions.

8.2.2 China 'Going Global'

Finally, the other key aspect is the 'going global' policy. State-owned enterprises and increasing numbers of private firms were encouraged by the Chinese government to 'go out' and compete in global markets. Launched in 2000, 'going out' is intended to create Chinese multinational corporations that are internationally competitive. By doing so, China aims to become more than a generic producer of low-end manufacturing goods, branded under the name of Western firms. The ability to do so is an indicator of industrial upgrading, the very thing that China needs to ensure a sustained growth rate if its firms are innovative and productive when compared with leading global companies.

For instance, Haier is the largest white-goods manufacturer in China and is sold in Wal-mart but does not command brand recognition and loyalty in world markets. The strategy of Lenovo, therefore, was to not only purchase IBM's PC business but also to licence the use of the brand name for five years so that Lenovo can eventually assume the trusted name of IBM in world markets. These are all developments which took place starting in the mid-2000s, when the first commercial outward investment by a Chinese firm was permitted in 2004 with TCL's purchase of France's Thomson.

Most outward FDI remains state-led investments in energy and commodities, but the maturing of Chinese industry indicates that the trend is changing as China seeks to move up the value chain and develop multinational companies that can follow in the footsteps of other successful countries like Japan and South Korea. These countries, unlike most developing countries, managed to join the ranks of the rich economies through possessing innovative and technologically advanced firms that enabled them to move beyond what is sometimes termed the 'middle-income country trap'. Nations start to slow down in growth when they reach a per capita income level of US$14,000. The process of growth through adding labour or capital (factor accumulation) slows or reaches its limit, and they are unable to sustain the double-digit growth rates experienced at an earlier period of development. By increasing productivity instead through developing industrial capacity and upgrading that is stimulated by international competition, it is more likely that a country can maintain a strong growth rate. The need for energy as well as the upgrading of industrial capability are motivating forces for China to invest overseas. Nevertheless, by the end of the 2000s, the share of commercial outward investment remains small whilst state-owned firms continue to constitute the bulk of outgoing FDI. The shape of things to come, though, points to China becoming a net capital exporter, and the 'going global' of its firms heralding an era of Chinese multinational corporations.

There has been explosive growth of outward FDI since the mid-2000s, which points to not only SOE investment in commodity sectors but also the commercial M&As for private companies like Lenovo which purchased the IBM PC business for the then-record of US$1.75 billion in 2005, later exceeded by Geely's acquisition of Volvo for US$1.8 billion in 2010. In 2008, outward FDI rose rapidly to US$55.6 billion, a 194 per cent increase over a year earlier of which US$40.7 billion was in the financial sector and US$11.9 billion in non-financial sector. As China receives around US$60–80 billion per annum in inward FDI, it may become a capital exporter in the next few years, especially as investments in energy, minerals, and raw materials accelerated in 2009 and its commercial firms begin to expand overseas. By 2011, China reported it had invested a record US$116 billion overseas. In addition to easing the pressures on its external account, global ambitions could mark an era of Chinese multinationals.

Becoming a net capital exporter is also viewed as a mark of a country reaching a level of industrial development as its firms are able to operate and compete on world markets. With outward FDI accelerating and close to overtaking inward FDI by the end of the 2000s, China could be on track to demonstrate that its industrial capacity is not only a function of FIEs producing its exports, but indicative of a more widespread upgrading of its industry. 'Going out' or 'going global' points to a policy aim that looks to be realized at the end of the first thirty years of reform.

It wasn't the only reform. In 2009, China began to liberalize its capital or financial account and allow for greater convertibility of the RMB with select trading partners. Specifically, its 'going out' policy formed in the mid-1990s was pursued in the aftermath of the global financial crisis. China declared that its foreign exchange reserves will be used to help finance the global expansion of its firms and thus allow capital outflows and reduce its balance of payments surplus, which has the effect of lessening reserve accumulation. At the same time, cheap equity investments in the US and Europe, both suffering a 'credit crunch' from the near collapse of the Western banking system, facilitate the global establishment of Chinese firms, which have yet to establish global brands and multinational operations.

Gradual capital account liberalization, in particular the 'going out' policy, will also help private firms if they are permitted to operate in global markets and allowed to access funding from better-developed overseas credit markets. In other words, firms can raise money on capital markets and not just rely on China's banking system with its controls on credit.

For private firms, the ability to operate in overseas markets can help them grow and gain economies of scale. In the three decades of the reform period, these firms have grown from nothing to being the largest driver of output and GDP growth in China. Private firms were the source of growth that allowed China to gradually transition away from central planning. Yet, it was not until the 2000s when they were granted legal protection, even the *getihu* sole proprietors, and began to have access to credit. Further reform is still needed.

The domestic market in China is highly competitive in numerous respects with monopolies largely in the capital-intensive industries dominated by SOEs. But, private firms still face a difficult environment in China. For China to sustain its remarkable growth rate, promoting efficient private firms and allowing them to gain scale and financing on world markets is a necessary policy move.

China can be a fast-growing, large, open economy—developing domestic demand and upgrading industry/promoting globally competitive firms—that recognizes its wider impact, as it is unlike small, open, export-led economies which do not affect the global terms of trade. Given China's still low level of development, global integration would benefit its own development as well as that of the entire world. These macroeconomic reforms will be important to position China optimally in a global economy that is changing rapidly and faces more uncertainty than before. By pursuing these reforms, China could continue to increase its growth in the years to come. It may have done something extraordinary in growing strongly for the past thirty years, but at per capita income levels of just US$5,400, there is still considerable scope for 'catch-up' growth, hence the importance of not only attracting investment via the 'open-door' policy, but also the increasing emphasis on 'going out'. By so doing, its global investments and corporations will affect the contours of the corporate sector internationally. To avoid a backlash against state-led investment, China will need to consider carefully how these reforms help its firms become multi-national corporations and how to manage the impact that its state-funded acquisitions is likely to have around the world.

8.3 Global Imbalances

Although history has always seen nations in either surplus or deficit, the magnitude of the so-called global imbalances in the 2000s provided the macroeconomic backdrop to the worst financial crisis in nearly a century. Two key players are the United States and China, but the global macroeconomic imbalances involve many more emerging economies whose integration into the global economy in the 2000s fundamentally altered the structure of the world economy.

Two key consequences of the rapid growth and integration of emerging economies are their effects on the global terms of trade (price effect), and an acceleration of the global imbalances in the 2000s that drove an increase in demand for the US dollar, the de facto global reserve currency (liquidity effect). The price effect boosted American and Western consumption since imports were less costly, while the liquidity effect hastened that trend as borrowing was cheaper due to low interest rates in the States after the dot.com bubble burst in 2000 and elsewhere in the West after the early 2000s economic slow-down. The accumulation of US dollars in foreign exchange reserves—estimated to constitute some two-thirds of global reserve holdings—tripled between 1998 and the start of the crisis in 2008, which also contributed to excess liquidity (or monetary growth over real GDP) in the United States, with consequences for consumption and borrowing.

China, for its part, practised the same export-led policies that had served its neighbours so well. However, China is sufficiently large that its integration with the world economy altered the global terms of trade; that is, prices of exports and imports. Since its 'open-door' policy took off in 1992, China exerted a deflationary impact on manufactured goods prices, contributing to the 'Great Moderation' that characterized the mild global business cycle of the late 1990s/early 2000s, a period of strong economic growth but low inflation worldwide. It, however, exerted a positive price effect on commodities whose prices rose in the 2000s and peaked in 2008; for example, oil prices increased from around US$20 per barrel to some US$150 before the onset of the global recession. However, as commodities form only a small proportion of the CPI (consumer prices index) particularly in developed economies, the typical measure of consumer prices, the predominant effect was deflationary until the commodity cycle peaked in the summer of 2008 when inflationary pressure fed through into domestic prices in developed and developing economies. Other large, emerging economies like India also played a part.

A consequence was that Western central banks targeting price stability achieved their targets of low inflation in the 2000s and kept interest rates low, which supported economic growth. Low interest rates in turn contributed to a build-up of liquidity which ultimately undermined macroeconomic stability as an unsustainable credit boom emerged. Another implication of the commodity boom of the 2000s is that traditional surplus (oil exporting) countries in the Middle East, North Africa, and elsewhere accumulated larger amounts of reserves than previously, which also fed into excess liquidity in the USA. In other words, because commodities are priced in dollars, the growing demand for energy by newly emerging economies dramatically increased the surplus in oil-exporting countries which helped enlarge global imbalances in the 2000s. A depreciating dollar since 2002 further put upward pressure on commodity prices. Therefore, as the global reserve currency, the US dollar is the predominant peg in fixed-exchange regimes in emerging economies experiencing significant current account surpluses due to low-cost exports and commodities. The resultant demand for dollar assets in reserve holdings further funnelled global savings to the United States whilst domestic interest rates were low, thereby boosting consumption as disposable incomes rose due to cheaper imports, and the low cost of borrowing hastened consumption via borrowing.

Although the genesis of the global financial crisis of 2008 is much more complex and has mostly to do with financial innovation and deregulation in the West, particularly the United States, global macroeconomic imbalances have become a focal point for the G20 group of major economies in considering a post-crisis system of global economic governance. Assessing the consequences of the changed structure of the global economy should be considered in economic policy-making and particularly in terms of identifying the effects of capital flows associated with reserve accumulation.

The reserve currency effect of the US dollar alongside an acceleration of global imbalances in the 2000s meant that the foreign exchange reserve accumulation of China and other large surplus economies contributed to excess liquidity in the US economy. The context was already set in the US with loose monetary policy used to fend off a technical recession after the dot.com bubble burst in 2000. At the same time, the price effects of the integration of emerging economies changed the macroeconomic policy-making environment where low inflation and low interest rates went hand-in-hand for a time. The acceleration of reserve accumulation in the Middle East and Asia in the 2000s and loose monetary policy by the Fed helped to fuel liquidity in US wholesale money markets. Monetary policy was focused on inflation targeting and not on asset bubbles, which meant that interest rates were kept low in the United States during the Great Moderation despite the build-up of liquidity that ultimately led to a credit boom (see also Adrian and Shin 2009). This had international implications due to the dominance of the American financial system as a source of short-term funding for, particularly, European banks as well as transmitting risk across globally linked capital markets in terms of financial products. Indeed, the developed state of US financial markets and therefore their specialization in finance is one of the frequent arguments put forward as to why liquidity flowed to America (see for example, Caballero, Farhi, and Gourinchas 2008a). Excess liquidity fed into the housing boom whose collapse in 2007 was a trigger for the ensuing global recession and the subsequent global financial crisis.

The combination of the reserve currency role of the US dollar and the 'price shocks' of the integration of large emerging economies together led to a credit boom associated with a worsening of the imbalances in the 2000s. For instance, Caballero, Farhi, and Gourinchas (2008a) argues that financial development in the US explains why emerging (and developed) economies exported savings to America after experiencing strong growth in the 1990s and 2000s (see also Chinn and Ito 2007 who argue that the stronger legal system in the US is a further attraction). The budget deficit in the United States is another determinant (Chinn and Ito 2008), while Bergsten (2009) considers the global importance of the US dollar in combination with the fiscal position as drivers of global imbalances.

The role of the US dollar is also related to the global 'saving glut' argument put forth by the US Federal Reserve Chairman, Ben Bernanke. For instance, the low US and world interest rates in the period leading up to the crisis is interpreted by Bernanke (2005) as representing excess global saving from emerging economies invested in the United States. Caballero, Farhi, and Gourinchas (2008b) likewise argue that the United States is uniquely placed to receive such investments due to asymmetric financial development around the world as other countries specialize in manufacturing/commodities and send their earnings to the US which specializes in finance.

The importance of the United States as an attractive destination for financial investments and the large fiscal deficits are linked to the willingness of fast-growing emerging economies to lend/invest in the United States. Highlighting the US fiscal position and comparative advantage in financial services culminating in the well-recognized 'twin deficits' (in the budget and trade positions) are important parts of the issue, but there are also other elements to consider. Given that these and the reserve role of the dollar are long-standing features of the US economy, what exactly was it about the 2000s that changed the picture? First, global macroeconomic imbalances worsened. This chapter provides an explanation that also brings in the structural changes in the global economy that occurred in the 2000s, which are likely to remain. Second, the magnitude of the imbalances put greater demands on the US dollar as the global reserve currency with consequences for the domestic American economy (liquidity effect). Third, the 'price effects' on global exports and imports occurred in an era of inflation targeting by central banks in developed economies. This would provide a further explanation for the credit boom and the lack of monetary tightening to combat the inflow of liquidity linked to the reserve currency role of the US dollar.

The US 'twin deficits' are long-standing, but worsened before the 2007/8 crisis. The acceleration of global imbalances is not just a result of profligate US government spending, but is also a function of private-sector spending that increased leverage in households and firms which led to the savings rate becoming negative on the eve of the crisis. The mirror is in the high savings of households and firms in surplus countries, which concomitantly determine the savings/investment and current-account decision behind global imbalances. Due to capital controls in China preventing outward investment by the private sector, for instance, this is not solely an issue of decisions taken to invest in the US as an attractive financial centre. Rather, the liquidity comes from reserve accumulation by governments. Moreover, the US is more financially developed than other economies, but this is not a unique element and had not led to crisis previously.

All of these explanations are tied to structural changes in the wider global economy in the 2000s. All of these factors are associated with the acceleration of global imbalances during this period. For instance, the 'price shocks' exerted by a large, open economy such as China after it joined the World Trade Organisation (WTO) in December 2001 were heightened as it became one of the top three traders in the world in the 2000s. The loose monetary policy conducted by the US Federal Reserve after the dot.com bubble burst in 2000 was maintained until 2004, which was too accommodating insofar as it contributed to a liquidity build-up which fed into subsequent macroeconomic instability. This stance was, though, consistent with a mandate to maintain price stability since inflation was low, though the consumer prices index (CPI) was affected by the deflationary impact on imported goods and services from low-wage, low-cost emerging economies. At the same time, the reserve currency role of the US dollar contributed to excess liquidity by attracting global savings into the United States, and monitoring such build-ups was not a focus in an inflation-targeting regime. The two sides (price effects and liquidity demands) of the accelerated integration of emerging economies like China in the 2000s affected policy-making in the US. Thus, the larger magnitude of the global imbalances was a factor in the ensuing American housing bubble whose collapse triggered the global recession and financial crisis. The cause of the financial crisis was not global imbalances, but such imbalances affected the macroeconomic context of the 2000s. Certainly, research will continue to highlight other factors in this evolving area.

8.3.1 *Changed Global Economy*

The decade up until the onset of recession in the United States at the end of 2007 was characterized by strong global economic growth of 4.2 per cent per annum on average from 1997–2007 as compared with 3.2 per cent in the previous two decades from 1980–97 and historically low rates of inflation worldwide. This period of low volatility and high growth rates has become known as the 'Great Moderation'.

Figure 8.1 also shows the ascendancy of China over this period and the unusual feature of world GDP growth exceeding that of the advanced economies in the past decade. This strong growth is the result of not just the rise of China, but also the re-emergence and integration of other large developing economies in the early 1990s.

The global economy fundamentally changed then with the take-off of the 'open door' policy in China in 1992, the firmer switch to export-oriented from import-substitution policies in India after its 1991 balance of payments crisis, and the re-engagement of Eastern Europe after the fall of Communism in the former Soviet bloc at the start of the 1990s. These nations together doubled the global labour force to 3 billion people, which effectively halved the capital-to-labour ratio in the world. Adding more labourers led to falling wages and therefore lower prices of goods and services, pushing down the cost of imports

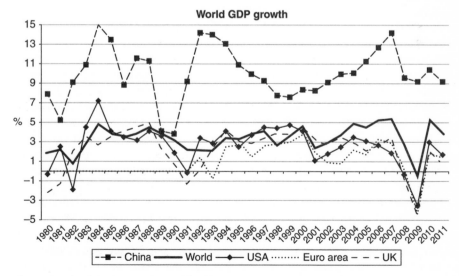

Figure 8.1 Real GDP growth, world and major economies, 1980–2011
Source: IMF.

271

into rich economies (see Kaplinsky 2006, who estimates widespread falls in import prices in developed economies). This deflationary effect on world prices, particularly of China with its 700 million labourers becoming integrated into the world trading system (referred to as the 'China price'), contributed to low inflation throughout the late 1990s/early 2000s that in turn enabled low interest rates in the West, particularly the United States, despite strong growth rates.

The other facet, though, relates to the industrialization of these emerging economies which produced upward pressure on commodities, helping to generate a boom that peaked in the summer of 2008. Coupled with a dollar that lost around one-third of its value against a floating currency such as the euro since 2002, the price of commodities (priced in dollars) increased significantly in the 2000s. The increase in energy prices further fuelled the accumulation of reserves of oil exporters, traditionally surplus countries whose current accounts also bulged with growing demand from China and India. However, as commodity prices are not a large component of CPI in advanced economies, the predominant effect of China/emerging economies was deflationary for most of the decade (Rogoff 2006). Until the onset of the 2008 global financial crisis, this period had been called the 'nice decade' or the 'Great Moderation' since it marked an era of strong growth, low inflation, and therefore low interest rates.

The 2000s, though, witnessed the acceleration of the global integration of these economies, which led to a widening of the global macroeconomic imbalances. In 2001, China joined the WTO, causing its share of global trade to increase significantly (from around an impressive 5 per cent to more than doubling to 11 per cent in less than a decade by 2007), and becoming one of the three largest traders in the world in a matter of years from accession. In 2002, net capital flows also became positive in South-east and East Asia as the region recovered from the Asian financial crisis. Rebuilding balance sheets after the financial crisis boosted savings in these countries. It is also argued that as a bulwark against future currency crises, developing Asian countries increased their reserves which can be used to defend their pegged currencies, as argued by Wolf (2009). In 2004, the European Union undertook its biggest enlargement since its 1980s 'southern expansion' adding ten countries largely from Eastern Europe (plus Romania and Bulgaria three years later) so reaching twenty-seven countries in the EU, encompassing some half a billion people and thus accelerating the integration of these economies into Europe and the world.

Figure 8.2 shows that although global imbalances have existed since the early 1980s, the 2000s marked an increase in the magnitude of the imbalances associated with the fast growth and integration of large emerging economies. The US moved from a positive current account position in 1980 and 1981 to running an average deficit of around 1.6 per cent of GDP until the 2000s, when the gap more than tripled. For their part, emerging economies in developing Asia (East and South-east) and oil exporters in the Middle East and North Africa have been surplus countries but not of the scale seen in the 2000s. The result was an enlargement of global imbalances in the 2000s: increased savings in surplus

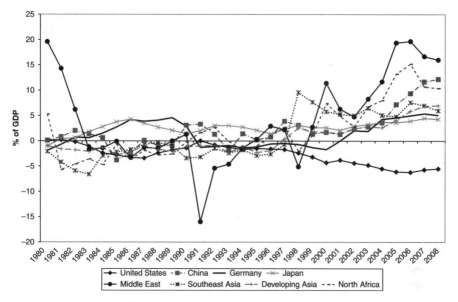

Figure 8.2 Current account balances (% of GDP)
Source: IMF.

countries versus growing consumption in the USA and expanding current account surplus in emerging economies with a mirror deficit in the USA.

Figure 8.3 shows that the US current account deficit (as a share of world GDP) rose dramatically from –0.5 per cent to –1.5 per cent at the onset of the crisis (around 3 per cent to 6 per cent of US GDP in a decade from 1997 until the 2007/8 recession), which is mirrored in the growth in the current account surpluses of emerging Asia and oil-exporting countries. The domestic counterpart was the falling US savings rate and the growing Chinese savings rate, and also that of developing Asia to a more limited extent. The Eurozone, despite including the second largest surplus country in the world after China—Germany—was roughly in internal and external balance due to its trade being predominantly within Europe itself since an estimated three-quarters of EU trade is within the single market.

The acceleration of global imbalances in the 2000s meant that export-oriented countries accumulated growing foreign exchange reserves (Figure 8.4). As the de facto global reserve currency, the US dollar was the predominant peg in the fixed exchange rate regimes of emerging economies. There was strong demand for dollar-denominated assets by these economies in developing Asia and amongst Middle-Eastern oil exporters to maintain stable exchange rates while their current account surpluses grew. The reserve currency effect of the US dollar further meant that when developing economies in South-east Asia emerged from the Asian financial crisis in the early 2000s, the demand for more reserves to protect against a repeat of the currency attack led to increased purchases of dollar-

273

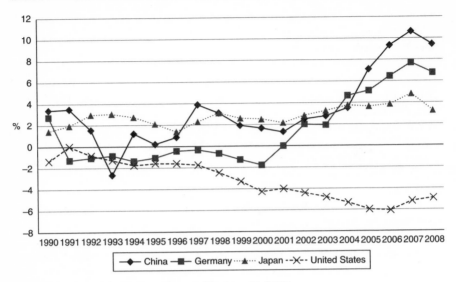

Figure 8.3 Current account balances (% of world GDP)
Source: World Bank World Development Indicators.

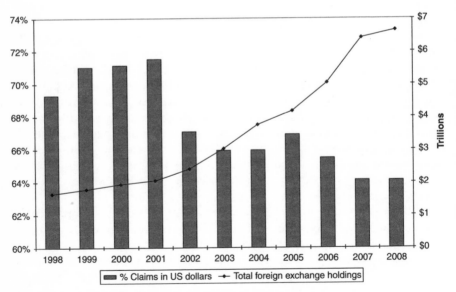

Figure 8.4 Global foreign exchange holdings, 1998–2008
Source: IMF.
Note: Claims in US$ is of allocated holdings of foreign exchange reserves.

denominated assets. For instance, Singapore increased its reserves to amount to 100 per cent of GDP after the 1997–8 crisis. This occurred despite a falling dollar since 2002, and significant budget and trade deficits in the United States. The increase in reserves was also found in Japan whose largely floating currency still led to it having the largest reserves in the world in the 2000s (overtaken by China only in 2006) because its current account surplus, added to the yen carry trade (borrowing yen at near zero interest rates and investing in higher yielding currencies), fuelled its holdings. A consequence of which was that savings from surplus countries was funnelled into purchases of dollar assets.

Therefore, although there have been surplus and deficit countries since before the 2007/8 recession and crisis, the global economic structure fundamentally changed in the 1990s. Although the reserve currency role of the US dollar contributed to its long-standing current account deficit, while export-oriented economies like Japan and Germany ran surpluses, the rise of emerging economies and the acceleration of their integration in the 2000s led to a much larger magnitude of global imbalances. For instance, the US current account deficit doubled in the 2000s while global holdings of foreign exchange reserves, including of the dollar as the main reserve currency (the US dollar accounts for between 64–72 per cent of all reserves), increased by fourfold to US$6.6 trillion by 2008 from US$1.6 trillion a decade earlier, according to the IMF Currency Composition of Official Foreign Exchange Reserves (COFER) data in Figure 8.5.

Figure 8.5 further shows how emerging economies overtook advanced economies by 2005 in reserve holdings, which is mirrored in their current account surpluses (Figure 8.3). Advanced economies held around US$2.5 trillion in reserves, while emerging economies accounted for nearly twice that amount. The foreign exchange reserves of emerging economies grew rapidly from a much smaller amount (US$634 billion) to over US$4.1 trillion in just a decade to 2008, which fuelled dollar holdings. Further, although fixed exchange rates and high savings in developing countries contributed, countries with floating exchange rates similarly added to growing global reserve holdings; for example, Japan is the second-largest holder of foreign exchange reserves after only China.

Thus, although there have been global imbalances for some time associated with the US role as the global reserve currency, the acceleration of the imbalances in the 2000s led to a significant increase in reserve holdings worldwide. The associated liquidity fed into the credit boom in the US. Although not the genesis of the crisis, the impact of the changed global economic structure formed part of the backdrop. The institutional changes in financial markets and central bank formulation of monetary policy played larger roles and were also interlinked with global macroeconomic imbalances.

8.3.2 Genesis of a Crisis

The structural changes in the global economy coincided with the early 1990s movement to create independent central banks that essentially targeted inflation. Starting in New Zealand in 1991, this model was eventually adopted by

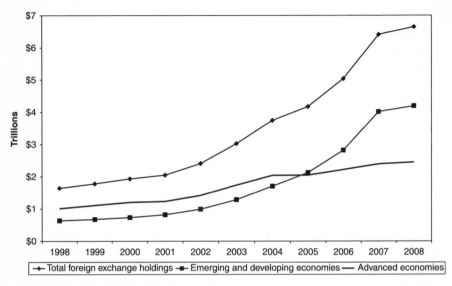

Figure 8.5 Global reserve holdings of advanced and emerging economies, 1998–2008
Source: IMF.

some two dozen major economies (Bean 2009). This regime has been credited with increasing transparency about monetary policy and effectively controlling inflation expectations that contributed to the 'Great Moderation'. However, targeting asset bubbles was not part of such mandates, and this became an evident issue when such bubbles in a deregulated financial system could lead to macroeconomic instability.

Financial deregulation since the 1970s and 1980s enabled financial innovation and was one of the reasons for central banks moving away from the previous regime that targeted monetary aggregates (for example, M2) in favour of inflation controlled through interest rates (see Bean 2009). Because of the growth of financial intermediation and the globalized nature of liberalized financial markets, the monetary transmission mechanism did not operate in a straightforward manner to transform the central bank's monetary target into the money supply of the economy. In other words, complicated high-powered money made it difficult to target money supply once banks moved away from being simple intermediaries in the credit system. Thus, central banks moved from controlling the supply of money to dictating its price in order to manage inflation and the business cycle.

Deregulating banking and capital markets also meant that financial instruments and global links became much more diverse, leading to securitization of assets which were sold and bought around the world. In 1999, the Gramm-Leach-Bliley Act repealed the Glass-Steagall Act of 1933 that had previously separated retail from investment banking. This notably transmitted the risks being undertaken by investment banks in a liberalized and globalized financial sector to retail (deposit-holding) banks and permitted more complex transactions such as the broker-dealer model of Lehman Brothers which led to the possibility of systemic banking system failure in the 2008 financial crisis that is reminiscent of the 1930s banking crisis that had led to the passage of Glass-Steagall in the first place. Around that time, European banks were also able to access US wholesale money markets to a greater extent so their lending became less reliant on deposits, and also meant that they could access the same cheap money as the Americans even though the European position is not a significant contributor to the global imbalances. The balance of payments and savings rate of the euro area have not changed dramatically in the past decade, but the losses at European banks due to troubled assets exposed in the global financial crisis have been worse than in American ones (US$1.7 trillion in Europe as compared with US$1 trillion in the US according to the IMF 2009).

In 2001, after the bursting of the US dot.com bubble, loose monetary policy in the United States fuelled a further asset bubble in sub-prime mortgages that underpinned the 2008 global financial crisis. Although this is the usual utilization of monetary policy (cutting interest rates) to forestall recession, the question (or the 'Greenspan conundrum') is why interest rates stayed low for too long and thus were allowed to fuel another bubble? With the focus on inflation and maintaining price stability, the US Federal Reserve did not act to raise interest rates because inflation was low. However, inflation was low (due in part to globalization and the deflationary effect of the reintegration of emerging economies) in spite of strong growth and excess liquidity which contributed to the underpricing of risk that was at the heart of the financial crisis.

When interest rates were increased by the Federal Reserve in May 2004, long-term interest rates remained low which helped to fuel the housing bubble until it burst in the summer of 2007 despite the efforts of the Fed to raise the base rate before then (Figures 8.6 and 8.7). The link between short-term and long-term rates is not straightforward and can consist of views about inflation expectations, future economic growth, and supply of US Treasuries. The downward movement in the benchmark ten-year Treasury bills also coincided with the rapid growth in reserves around the world and thus a lower cost of borrowing (see Cabellero, Farhi, and Gourinchas 2008b who show evidence of thirty-year mortgage rates falling in line with long-term interest rates during the Great Moderation).

The fixed exchange rates operated by emerging economies led to their accumulation of dollar assets in spite of low yields since their purchases were less related to returns and more driven by the desire to maintain their currency pegs. Moreover, demand for dollar-denominated debt was driven not just by the US balance of payments, but also by commodities priced in dollars, and international investments seeking a 'safe haven'. Thus, countries like Japan which have floating currencies, also contributed to the growth in dollar reserve holdings. For instance, the Japanese yen experienced exchange rate appreciation

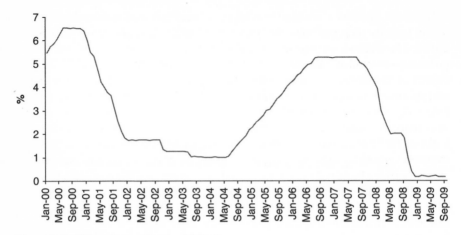

Figure 8.6 US base interest rates, 2000–9
Source: US Federal Reserve.

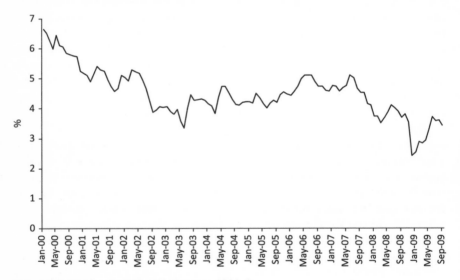

Figure 8.7 Yields on 10 Year Treasuries, 2000–9
Source: US Federal Reserve.

against the US dollar, but Japan still amassed US$2 trillion in reserves as the yen carry trade and other uses of the dollar played a large role.

Another view of global imbalances is to consider the declining US saving rate. Savings as a share of GDP have fallen steadily over the past decade while consumption grew via leverage. Low interest rates further deterred savings and led instead to a search for yields for investments other than Treasuries as housing and other assets offered higher returns.

The credit boom was likely to lead to a housing bubble. However, the bursting of the bubble need not have led to a financial crisis (McKibbin and Stoeckel 2010). The actions of central banks determine the cost of borrowing, but targeting inflation in the face of strong deflationary pressures from structural change in the global economy meant that a credit bubble was permitted to build and monetary policy was not geared at controlling such bubbles in any case. Coupled with financial deregulation and poor regulatory oversight, particularly of cross-border transactions of securitized instruments as well as unsustainable levels of leverage in systemically important players, a housing bubble led to a traumatic global financial crisis.

8.3.3 *Global Reserve Currency*

The reserve currency effect of the US dollar became the magnet for the increased liquidity associated with the structural changes of the 2000s. In the world economy this led to larger global imbalances. The imbalances were generated by changes in economic policies regarding savings and consumption, exports and reserves, in developed and developing economies alike. Despite the decline of the dollar since 2002 and falling yields on US Treasuries, the accumulation of dollar assets associated with reserve holdings led to liquidity build-up despite the Fed increasing the base interest rate between May 2004 and the onset of recession in 2007. This is evidently not only an issue of exchange rates (the Japanese yen, Germany and the euro played a role along with fixed-exchange rate countries like China and Middle East oil exporters), but of the reserve currency role played by the US dollar and, by extension, the credit conditions of the US economy associated with the reserve currency effect.

The magnification of the reserve currency effect points to the importance of global imbalances accelerating in the 2000s. Since the 1990s, there has been a transformative increase in the global labour supply, leading to lower prices of traded goods and services. This in turn enables low interest rates in Western economies as inflation is driven down by cheaper imports. There has also been a fall in the global capital to labour ratio, mirroring low interest rates, and reducing the cost of capital and increasing leverage (see Cabellero, Farhi, and Gourinchas 2008b, for calculations of low global as well as US interest rates in the 1990s and 2000s). In the US, financial liberalization and the resultant expansion of consumer credit and home ownership contributed to declining saving and increased leverage ultimately not just of households, but also firms/banks seeking yields in an environment of low interest rates. Fiscal deficits since the balanced budget of 2000 and the loose monetary policy that helped to avoid a technical recession after the 2000/1 dot.com bubble contributed further to the declining savings rate.

In surplus economies, the mirror opposite occurred where savings increased in part due to recovery from the Asian financial crisis as firms rebuilt balance sheets and commodity exporters experienced significant terms-of-trade improvements linked to the growth of large emerging economies that enlarged their reserves.

The largest, China, had capital controls and trapped high levels of savings by households and firms due to limited financial liberalization which contributed to its current account surplus that in turn led to accumulation of reserves that increased purchases of dollar-denominated assets. Ironically, the crisis has led to a credit crunch in the West, but China may well experience the 'hot money' inflows which could lead to asset bubbles in its real estate and stock markets.

Thus, monetary policy was too accommodating in the US and other advanced economies during the 2000s due in part to achieving their mandate of targeting inflation. Prices were low during this period as a result of globalization and the negative price shocks exerted by China and other large emerging economies on imported goods and services. The upward pressure on commodity prices did not become evident until the peak of the commodity boom in 2008 but was sufficient to add to the coffers of oil-exporting countries such that they also added to a much greater extent to global liquidity through larger reserve holdings. Therefore, globalization forces exerted price effects, even while global imbalances via reserve accumulation contributed to liquidity associated with the dollar. Taking account of these factors (price and liquidity effects) in the medium-term outlook for global rebalancing and maintaining stability will be important in any system set up to monitor such imbalances.

8.3.4 *Global Rebalancing*

There is already rebalancing in the global economy due to the deleveraging of the balance sheets of US firms and households. For instance, the US current account deficit is at its lowest point in a decade (under 3 per cent of GDP and roughly its expected rate given its reserve currency role and extent of deficits, according to Bergsten 2009), and the US savings rate has increased some fourfold a year since the crisis. For China, the collapse of exports has been offset by a dramatic decline in imports, so that it may well still run a current account surplus despite large-scale closures of export industries. As a result, China is experiencing significant inflows of short-term capital which, along with its own loose monetary and fiscal policies to combat the recession, is contributing to potential asset bubbles in its real estate and stock markets. M2 growth at the end of 2009 was nearly 30 per cent, for instance.

Capital account liberalization and greater exchange rate flexibility in China will ease global imbalances, similar to deleveraging and increased savings in the United States which will accomplish the same on the other side of the equation. By implementing its 'going out' policy where commercial outward investment is permitted and indeed supported by its foreign exchange reserves as of 2009 in the aftermath of the global financial crisis, China should experience more capital outflows that will reduce its foreign exchange holdings and which will have the further effect of easing liquidity in its economy. It is also a more effective way of re-allocating saving to more developed markets, including the more developed financial sector, of the US through foreign direct investment and equity investment rather than via purchases of government bonds.

As a developing country, China is likely to continue as a surplus country while the US, as a rich economy, will probably revert to running current account deficits of around 1.5 to 2 per cent of GDP (or even 3 per cent in the medium term as fiscal deficits reduce public saving), particularly as the dollar remains the predominant reserve currency. Neither economy is therefore likely to completely rebalance the global economy, particularly as other surplus countries as well as deficit ones such as the UK also play a part. Nevertheless, focusing on the liquidity associated with the reserve currency role of the US dollar in the context of a world economy characterized by many more surplus economies would go some way toward acknowledging the risks for developed and developing countries alike with insufficient monitoring capital flows across national borders. Global financial regulation and monetary policy setting should also take into account this change in the structure of the world economy.

Reformulating monetary policy to be cognizant of the destabilizing effects of excessive current account deficit of the US as the country of the global reserve currency would be a first step. Price stability may be achieved by inflation targeting, but a current account deficit can lead to capital inflows that fuel excess liquidity. This risk further points to how the Federal Reserve should incorporate the impact of not just globalization but also the reserve currency effect in its formulation of monetary policy (see for example, Adrian and Shin 2008, who argue that price and financial stability are in effect the same issue in terms of monetary policy objectives of achieving macroeconomic stability).

The IMF has been given a mandate by the G20 to monitor global imbalances and this chapter argues that it should focus on monitoring global capital flows and excess liquidity build-up as a consequence of such imbalances. In other words, focusing on the imbalances themselves will most likely be ineffective in that countries which run surpluses/deficits are driven by a range of factors, domestic and external, and are unlikely to be conducive to international coordination. However, even though global imbalances are likely to remain, excessive imbalances associated with the reserve currency effect can be moderated through a combination of monetary policy and reserve diversification strategies which in turn will prevent the magnification of such imbalances that occurred during the 2000s—a period when a confluence of factors, not obviously connected, led to crisis.

8.4 Rebalancing China

'Rebalancing' the Chinese economy away from exports by increasing the share of GDP generated by domestic demand would support a more sustainable economic growth approach. This type of rebalancing is a realistic reaction to weaker expected import demand by the West as the United States in particular recovers from the worst financial crisis since the 1930s. Figure 8.8 shows the increase in net exports alongside the decline in consumption as shares of GDP starting in the early 1990s when the 'open-door' policy took off in China. The

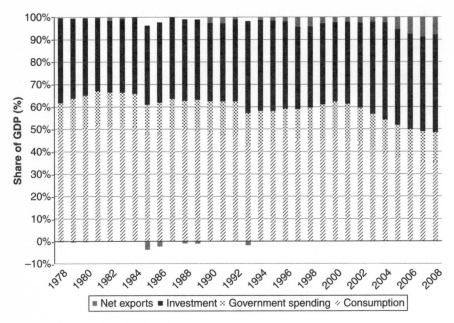

Figure 8.8 China's macroeconomy
Source: China Statistical Yearbook.

current account surplus, nevertheless, was not large until the 2000s when China acceded to the World Trade Organisation (WTO) in December 2001. This is seen in Figure 8.9, which shows that both exports and imports grew rapidly since the early 1990s, but the large trade surplus was apparent after 2002.

In 2009, China achieved a 9.6 per cent share of global trade, surpassing Germany with 9 per cent and the United States with 8.5 per cent, to become the world's largest trader. The trade shares of the three largest traders dwarfed the share of the fourth largest trader, Japan, which accounted for 4.7 per cent. Arguably for China, there is limited scope for growth from this high level because the United States, the world's largest importer, which averaged US $1.48 trillion of imports per annum since 1998 and imported US$2.17 trillion in 2008, is unlikely to maintain this level of imports as consumption has fallen from its peak at 72 per cent of GDP on the eve of the financial crisis. Those heady rates were unsustainable, as the global financial crisis reflected an unsustainable consumption boom fuelled by rapid credit expansion in the United States (Rajan 2010). As discussed earlier, the global economy has begun to rebalance since 2007. The current account deficit has fallen in the United States and the surpluses of China, Germany, and Japan have come down as well.

For China to sustain its growth rate, it will need to reorient itself more toward domestic demand. However, rebalancing China will not completely rebalance the global economy. The United States ran a current account deficit before China's integration in the world economy in the early 1990s, and is argued to

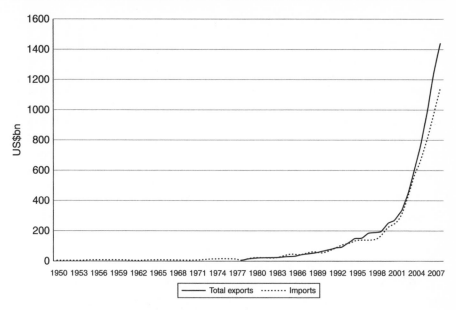

Figure 8.9 China's exports and imports
Source: China Statistical Yearbook.

continue to do so for a variety of reasons, including its fiscal and savings deficit (Bergsten 2009; Chinn and Ito 2008), financial specialization (Cabellero, Farhi, and Gourinchas 2008a,b), and reserve currency status (Yueh 2010b). The continuation of global imbalances, however, raises concerns about the management of China's current account surplus, as that surplus has hitherto generated foreign exchange reserves of US$3.3 trillion in 2012.

To do so, China should institute liberalization of the capital account and reform of the domestic capital market to reduce reserve accumulation by generating more capital outflows. Therefore, rebalancing the Chinese economy in the post-crisis environment will require both interest rate liberalization and greater exchange rate flexibility (see also Woo 2008, for a discussion about exchange rate adjustment and a wider set of reforms in the pre-crisis context; see also Bosworth and Collins 2008, estimating that US exports to China are determined by a wide range of factors and not due to the exchange rate). Rebalancing the economy toward domestic demand is also a realistic development path for China because its vast population should be able to support a large domestic consumption of goods.

China's reorientation toward domestic demand is based on the recognition of (1) the likely weakness of global trade in the aftermath of the 2008 financial crisis, and (2) the longer-term growth policy that aims to create an upper-middle-income country with a significantly larger middle class. For China to achieve a more stable economic growth model, it will need to institute reforms that can boost domestic demand while promoting global integration.

8.4.1 *Structure of the Chinese Economy*

The structure of the Chinese economy can evolve to become more akin to that of the United States and Japan, which are both large economies whose growth is primarily driven by domestic demand, but at the same time which are among the largest (third and fourth, respectively) exporters in the world. Figure 8.10 shows that in 1990, China was more similar to the structure of the economies of the United States and Japan in that exports accounted for 12.9 per cent of GDP in China and around 7 per cent in the United States and Japan. Since the 'open-door' policy took off, China's trajectory became more similar to Germany. Exports in 2007 accounted for 56 per cent of Chinese GDP and for 76 per cent of German GDP (though intra-European trade in the single market accounts for around three-quarters of German trade). In 2009, when global trade contracted for the first time since the Second World War by 12.2 per cent according to the WTO, both Germany and Japan experienced recessions that were worse than the United States (the epicentre of the financial crisis). In China's case, despite the large-scale unemployment of workers in export industries, a technical recession was avoided because of the fast implementation of fiscal and monetary stimulus that succeeded in raising domestic demand significantly.

China could reduce its exposure to the volatility of the world economy by following a path to strengthen both internal and external demand, which can cause the portion of growth to be driven by domestic demand to increase even as trade could expand in absolute terms. Such restructuring allows China to continue to benefit from global integration that includes learning from the technological advancements of developed economies and to continue its 'catch-up'

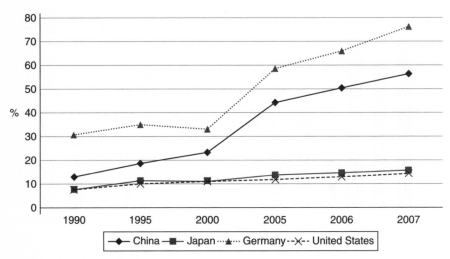

Figure 8.10 Exports as share of GDP
Source: World Penn Tables.

growth, while maintaining a larger base of domestic demand to shield it from the worst excesses of external shocks.

To orient toward domestic demand means boosting consumption in China; that is reducing the savings tendencies of households and firms. Figure 8.11 shows the increase in savings as a share of GDP, particularly notable in the 2000s. Consumption fell from around 50 per cent of GDP in the 1980s and early 1990s to nearly one-third by the late 2000s. In developed economies, consumption is typically between half to two-thirds of GDP; for example, in Germany it is 58 per cent, Japan registers 60 per cent and it was 72 per cent in the United States on the eve of the 2008 global financial crisis (the latter was generally considered to be too high; McKibbin and Stoeckel 2010).

For Chinese households, precautionary savings motives are important to address, particularly in rural areas, and so there should be a substantial improvement in social security provision if there was better social security provision. There was some provision in the government's stimulus plan of 2009, which increased health and pension spending, but more is needed. Developing the service sector will also boost domestic demand by increasing the non-tradable component of the economy and by creating jobs in the low and high end of the skills spectrum. Furthermore, greater urbanization can improve the earning potential of rural residents and boost consumption. Indeed, wage bills that have lagged behind output growth reduced the share of income to workers,

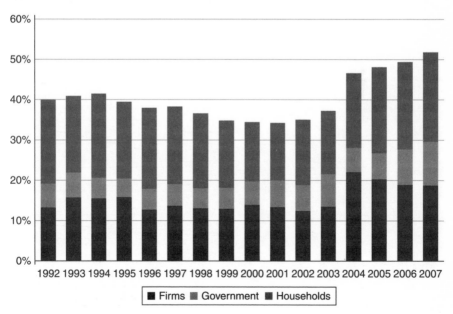

Figure 8.11 Savings in China (% of GDP)

Source: China Statistical Yearbook.

which in turn depressed consumption and caused it to shrink as a share of GDP (Bai and Qian 2009).

Figure 8.11 also shows an increase in savings by firms (state-owned and non-state-owned) during the 2000s. China's distorted financial system is biased toward state-owned enterprises (SOEs), and private firms have trouble obtaining credit—whether from banks or the underdeveloped domestic capital markets. Therefore, private firms rely heavily on retained earnings to finance their growth. Even SOEs save because of the minimal taxation of their profits. It is noteworthy that when China's current account surplus was near 10 per cent of GDP after 2004, China's investment maintained its share of GDP, even though investment is typically squeezed when countries develop a current account surplus.

Figure 8.12 shows gross capital formation as a share of GDP and its constancy for the past twenty years. Consumption dropped as the motives for saving were undiminished by the export boom, and total savings rose instead. Reforming the internal and external sectors would help to rebalance the Chinese economy.

8.4.2 The Salter-Swan Framework

In the Salter-Swan model with both a tradable and non-tradable goods sector, the relative supply and demand for tradable versus non-tradable goods determines the real exchange rate. It shows why China is experiencing appreciation pressure and how exchange rate reform can aid in rebalancing the Chinese economy away from exports toward a greater share of domestic demand in GDP.

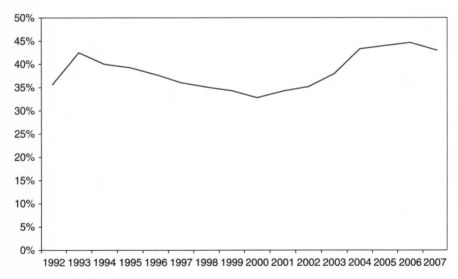

Figure 8.12 Gross capital formation (% of GDP)
Source: China Statistical Yearbook.

Following Dornbusch (1980), a small, open economy produces two goods, a traded good (T) and a non-traded good (N). The price of the traded good (P_T) is determined by the level of the nominal exchange rate E (RMB per US dollar) and of foreign tradable goods' prices (P^*). The price of the non-tradable good (P_N) is determined by the equilibrium in the market for non-tradables.

Producers in each sector maximize profits subject to declining marginal products of labour, the only variable input:

$$MaxP_iQ_i - WL_i \qquad (1)$$

subject to:

$$Q_i = Q_i(L_i)$$

$$Q'_i() > 0, Q'_i() < 0$$

$i = N,T$
$W =$ wage rate

Profit maximization in each sector leads to implicit labour demand computed as a function of real wages:

$$L_T = L_i(W/P_i) \qquad (2)$$

$$L'() < 0$$

Conditional on the prices of traded and non-traded goods, the wage rate (W) equates the sum of labour demand in the two sectors to the total labour supply:

$$L_T(W/P_T) + L_N(W/P_N) = L \qquad (3)$$

Log-differentiating, equilibrium wages (W) is a function of the changes in non-tradable prices (P_N) and tradable prices (P_T):

$$\hat{W} = \gamma\hat{P}_T + (1 - \gamma)\hat{P}_N \qquad (4)$$

Shifts in real wages in the two sectors reflect changes in relative prices:

$$\hat{W} - \hat{P}_T = (1 - \gamma)(\hat{P}_N - \hat{P}_T) \qquad (5)$$

$$\hat{W} - \hat{P}_N = \gamma(\hat{P}_T - \hat{P}_N)$$

Based on (1), (2), and (5), the supplies of traded and non-traded goods in terms of relative prices, or equivalently, the real exchange rate, θ or P_T/P_N, is given by:

$$S^T = S^T(P_T/P_N), S^{T'}() > 0 \qquad (6)$$

$$S^N = S^N(P_T/P_N), S^{N'}() < 0$$

Turning now to demand for tradable and non-tradable goods; these are determined by relative prices and domestic demand or absorption, A. Sectoral demand is decreasing in the relative price of that sector's goods and increasing in the level of total demand:

$$D^T = D^T(P_T/P_N, A) \tag{7}$$

$$\partial D^T = D^T(P_T/P_N) < 0,$$
$$\partial D^T/\partial A > 0$$

$$D^N = D^N(P_T/P_N, A)$$

$$\partial D^N/\partial(P_T/P_N) > 0,$$
$$\partial D^N/\partial A > 0.$$

Equilibrium in the markets for traded and non-tradable goods is established through (6) and (7) and depicted in Figure 8.13. The NN curve shows the combinations of the real exchange rate and absorption that generates equilibrium in the market for non-tradables. Increases in absorption (A) lead to excess demand for non-tradables and raise their relative price, that is, an appreciation of the real exchange rate.

If non-tradable prices do not move quickly to equate supply and demand for non-tradables, then the economy can be off the NN curve. The adjustment of non-tradables' prices to excess supply or demand for non-tradables will move the economy back onto the NN curve over time. If the economy is above the NN curve, there is excess demand for non-tradables and the real exchange rate is lower than its equilibrium value. At this point, demand pressures will raise the prices (P_N) of non-tradables until the real exchange rate (P_T/P_N) appreciates to move the economy back onto the NN curve. Conversely, if the real exchange rate is higher than its equilibrium value and the economy is below the NN curve, then the non-tradables' prices will fall and non-tradables deflation would move the economy back onto the NN curve and restore equilibrium.

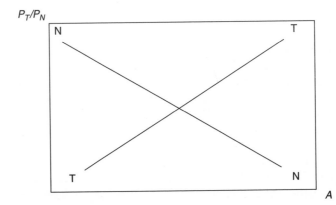

Figure 8.13 Salter-Swan framework

The TT curve completes the Salter-Swan model. It represents combinations of the real exchange rate and absorption for which the demand for tradables equal supply; that is, a balanced trade position. Greater absorption would lead to more demand for tradables and thus a trade deficit that requires depreciation of the real exchange rate to correct (if the trade balance is to be maintained). Or, low absorption would reduce the demand for tradables and lead to a trade surplus that requires appreciation of the real exchange rate to maintain the trade position.

Where there is substantial net capital flows, the Salter-Swan framework suggests much stronger forces moving the real exchange rate toward equilibrium along the NN curve than along the TT curve. This is because the equilibrium real exchange rate produces a balanced current account at a level of output corresponding to equilibriums in both the non-tradables and tradables markets (where the NN and TT curves cross). This is the real exchange rate that is sustainable in the long run, but adjustments can be very slow in the short and medium term, depending on the extent to which trade imbalances are financed by capital flows and the exchange rate regime. Excess demand or supply of tradable goods (when the economy is off the TT curve) lead initially to only trade deficits or surpluses, respectively. Imbalances in the tradable market do not affect the price of non-tradable goods or directly affect the price of tradables since those prices are fixed by the exchange rate and the price of foreign tradables. Also, trade imbalances may be associated with excess demand or supply of foreign exchange that could lead to adjustments of the nominal exchange rate, which then move the real exchange rate back onto the TT curve, depending on the flexibility of that exchange rate regime.

Now, the framework can be rewritten to model the domestic demand components that explicitly describe a three-way trade-off among the net trade, aggregate demand, and output/unemployment positions (Carlin and Soskice 2005; Chamberlin and Yueh 2006; see also Bean 2009). Restating the trade balance or BT schedule as follows:

$$\frac{x_{Y^*}(\theta)Y^*}{\theta m_Y(\theta)} = Y_{TB}, \tag{8}$$

where x_{Y^*} is the propensity to consume domestic goods, which is positively related to the real exchange rate, $\theta = \frac{EP^*}{P}$, derived as earlier as the ratio of foreign to domestic prices P, where P is a weighted combination of domestic (P_D) and imported prices (P_M) and the respective weights ϕ and $(1 - \phi)$ reflect the portion of domestic and foreign goods sold in the home market: $P = \phi P_D + (1 - \phi)P_M$. Y^* is the overseas level of income, and the propensity to import $\left(m_Y(\theta)\right)$ is a negative function of the real exchange rate. The level of income where the trade balance is in equilibrium is Y_{TB} when $BT = 0$, where exports are equal to imports: $x_{Y^*}(\theta)Y^* = \theta m_Y(\theta)Y$.

The effect of the real exchange rate on the level of income when the trade balance is in equilibrium will depend on the relative strengths of the competitiveness and terms of trade effects. The substitution effect will dominate when the Marshall Lerner condition holds; that is, the price elasticity of exports and imports sum to greater than 1. Provided that the Marshall Lerner condition is satisfied, an improvement in competitiveness enables the trade balance to remain in equilibrium at higher levels of domestic income. Therefore, the BT curve will slope upwards as seen in Figure 8.14. In other words, when income rises, imports will increase. Therefore, to keep the trade balance in equilibrium at this higher level of income depends on substitution toward domestic goods through an improvement in competitiveness. This requires a real depreciation, accounting for the upward sloping BT curve.

The aggregate demand (AD) schedule is given by:

$$Y_{AD} = \frac{a + I(\Theta, r) + \bar{G} - cT + x_{Y^*}(\theta)Y^*}{\left(1 - c + \theta m_{Y^*}(\theta)\right)}, \tag{9}$$

where consumption is a function of autonomous consumption (a), the marginal propensity to consume (c), and personal disposable income ($Y-T$), where T is the level of lump sum taxes: $C = a + c(Y - T)$; investment is a function of autonomous factors (Θ) such as expectations, taxes, credit restrictions, etc., and a negative function of the interest rate (r): $I = I(\Theta, r)$, $\frac{dI}{dr} < 0$; government spending and lump sum taxes are exogenously determined: $G = \bar{G}$, $T = \bar{T}$; and, net exports are calculated as the trade balance: $X - M = x_{Y^*}(\theta)Y^* - \theta m_Y(\theta)Y$.

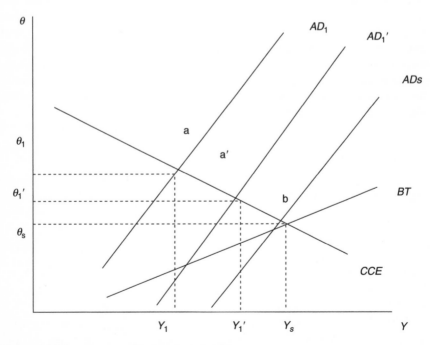

Figure 8.14 Long-run equilibrium in Salter-Swan

Global Integration and Growth: Rebalancing the Economy

If the Marshall Lerner condition holds, the AD schedule will also be upward sloping. The AD schedule incorporates the trade balance, which is also an upward sloping schedule, but it is flatter since most of the domestic components in the AD curve are invariant to changes in the exchange rate.

Finally, the Competing Claims Equilibrium (CCE) is the long run aggregate supply curve in an open economy, determined by the non-accelerating inflation rate of unemployment (NAIRU) and the equilibrium level of output, which completes the framework. The derivation is in the Appendix.

With a trade surplus, China is at point a in Figure 8.14 where potential output is Y_1 which is to the left of the BT schedule. This can be sustained for some time before the economy accumulates an increasing number of assets, which leads to a build-up of liquidity pressures to move the economy onto the BT schedule at point b. Even with capital controls in place, the accumulation of assets due to maintenance of the fixed exchange rate will generate liquidity in the economy, which can be sterilized by the central bank (Riedel, Jin, and Gao 2007). But, leakage through porous borders means that 'hot money' flows will plague China as it does for most open economies (see Blanchard and Giavazzi 2006).

As domestic prices rise as a result of the inflows of liquidity, which generates upward pressure on asset prices in the non-tradable sector (P_N) such as the price of real estate, which has been rising rapidly in major cities, the real exchange rate (θ) will appreciate (P_T/P_N) since the nominal exchange rate (E) is fixed. The economy would shift from a at θ_1 to a point above the CCE line.

As the adjustment in prices continues, the economy will move toward point b, which is the long-run equilibrium of the economy or the sustainable level of output, Y_S, which is at a higher level of output than Y_1. But, it may not reach point b and instead move to a' as the price adjustment is likely to be slow and thus the economy is unlikely to be completely 'rebalanced' because there will still be a trade surplus. But, the gradual revaluation of the RMB will ease some of the price pressures. This is sustainable for a period of time depending on the ability to sterilize the portfolio inflows, which China has been able to achieve to a large extent under a regime of financial repression whereby bills from the People's Bank of China are purchased by state-owned commercial banks (see for example, Riedel, Jin, and Gao 2007).

Even at a', output and aggregate demand (Y'_1) have increased from Y_1. These are wrought through a positive real income effect as the appreciation of the RMB increases the purchasing power of households with respect to imports. The other policy tool in this framework that can be adjusted to reach b is the real interest rate via the AD curve. An expansion of AD with a revaluation of the exchange rate suggests a lower equilibrium interest rate.

At present, there are different lending and deposit rates in China. For households, their consumption decisions are affected by the current 'ceiling' on the deposit rate. Liberalizing the interest rate could lead the deposit rate to rise and therefore household incomes even as the lending rate falls because the equilibrium rate of interest in the economy is likely to be inbetween the 'ceiling' on the low deposit rate and the 'floor' on the lending rate.

291

More apparently for firms, investment is the avenue through which interest rates operate in the Salter-Swan framework. Investment is a function of a variety of policies, but also of the real interest rate: $I = I(\Theta, r)$. Corresponding to the price falls associated with the revaluation of the exchange rate, the liberalization of interest rates through the removal of the 'floor' on the lending rate would lower the cost of borrowing. Although the level of investment is high, the dominance of SOEs and the distortions in the credit system suggest that the allocation of capital can be done in a more efficient and market-based manner. In other words, liberalizing interest rates can improve the mix of investment as between the state-owned and private sectors to increase output. This reform would have the further effect of reducing the savings rate of corporations that has expanded along with household savings with consumption correspondingly falling to a historic low. With more efficient investment, output will increase as the capital expenditure is more productive.

Therefore, over the longer term, a series of price and liquidity pressures will move the Chinese economy toward its equilibrium level of output. Through reforms of two key linked policy instruments, increasing the flexibility of the exchange rate and the interest rate, the adjustment to a future with a smaller trade surplus can be managed in a way that increases the level of income and reduces inflationary pressures, particularly the increases in non-tradable asset prices such as real estate, which can be moderated through an appreciation of the nominal exchange rate. The next section outlines the specific reforms and the challenges lying therein to achieving a more sustainable internal/external balance.

8.4.3 Policy Reforms

The policy reforms needed to increase aggregate demand in this framework centre on reducing the savings rate of households and firms to generate higher output in the context of a smaller trade surplus. Greater government spending can also increase consumption and investment if undertaken to support income and the efficiency of capital markets.

Household savings have averaged 19 per cent of GDP since 1992, after the significant opening of China associated with the decline in consumption (see Figure 8.11). Savings was high, but it increased further by 8 percentage points of GDP from 2000, increasing from 14 per cent to 22 per cent of GDP by 2007 at the onset of the global financial crisis. For firms, the average savings rate was lower at around 15 per cent of GDP from 1992–2007, but grew quickly to reach 22 per cent of GDP by the mid-2000s. The remainder of the savings derives from government, whose savings rate had been around 5 per cent since 1992, but increased dramatically from 5.2 per cent in 2000 to 10.8 per cent in 2007. Taken together, China's savings rate increased from 38 per cent of GDP in the 1990s to peaking at nearly 52 per cent by the late 2000s. Startlingly, the savings rate increased by 17 percentage points during the 2000s (34 per cent in 2000 rising to 51.9 per cent in 2007), which mirrors the fall in consumption as a share of GDP from around 50 per cent of GDP in the early 1990s to 35 per cent by the late 2000s.

Therefore, for households, the issues centre on lagging wage and income growth, while for firms, reforming capital markets is critical. For both sectors, the reforms require adjustments to both the internal and the external balances, consistent with the analysis of the previous section's open economy model.

HOUSEHOLD SAVINGS

For households, income growth and removing the motives for precautionary savings would bring down the savings rate. Industrial output has grown at 14.1 per cent on average per annum for twenty years since 1988 (deflated growth of gross industrial output), but wage growth has not kept pace. Industrial output grew at double the previous pace in the 2000s (23.1 per cent on average per annum) as compared with the two decades before (11.7 per cent). Yet, the average annual real wage growth of urban employees was lower at 11.9 per cent from 1995 to 2008 and only a paltry 5 per cent during the late 1990s. Rural incomes have risen even more slowly. In the 2000s, average wage growth was faster and closer to 15 per cent at 14.9 per cent per annum, but this is against a backdrop of industrial output growth exceeding 23 per cent each year. Thus, because labour income has lagged behind output growth, consumption has fallen as a share of GDP.

Moreover, labour productivity has increased some sevenfold from 1980 to 2005, according to the International Labour Organization (see also Yueh 2008), which suggests that wages do not match the marginal product of labour. Labour productivity has been improving in the 2000s since the significant reform of labour markets at the end of the 1990s and the improvement has been hastened by recent supply-side tightening. The protests in 2009/10 over low wages and a reluctance of rural migrants to return or move to the cities reflect the potential for increased wage growth to match the marginal output of labour. In so doing, there need not be inflationary pressures so long as higher wages prompt growth in labour productivity that outstrips the wage increases and instead can increase incomes that boost consumption.

Other measures that can ease labour market tightness involve removing restrictions on mobility; that is, increase urbanization to allow migrants to settle in urban areas. It would reduce the segmentation in the labour market and increase the mobility of workers to find matches to appropriate jobs and not be barred by geographic or *hukou* (household registration system) barriers. Urbanization is a policy that has been proposed alongside renewed efforts to develop the services sector. As seen in Figure 8.15, the services sector increased steadily as a share of GDP from 23 per cent in 1979 to 40 per cent in the 2000s but has not developed further, leading China to have a lower share of services in GDP than comparable-sized economies where the services sector account more than half of GDP (for example, over 50 per cent in Germany, over 70 per cent in the United Kingdom). Services is a non-tradable sector as it includes items such

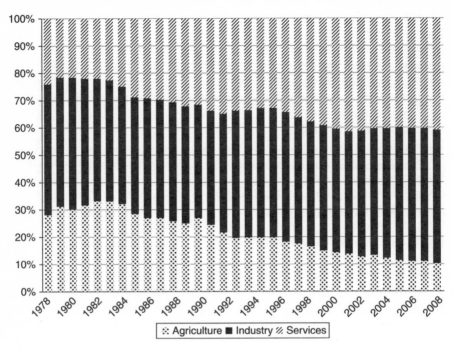

Figure 8.15 Sectoral composition of GDP
Source: China Statistical Yearbook.

as haircuts and government services that would help to increase both domestic demand and reduce savings if such service provision included the delivery of social security. As such, government spending on services can reduce the savings rate of the economy while boosting domestic demand and incomes (see also, Blanchard and Giavazzi 2006). Urbanization further allows the delivery of services to be distributed more efficiently such that there can be greater economies of scale. For instance, health, pensions, unemployment, local services, and schools can all be developed as part of the services sector with the infrastructure needs to support this development, which increases the efficiency of investment and associated industrialization in the urban area.

As such, internal and external sector reforms together would improve the efficiency of the urbanization process by reducing the cost of imported inputs. It would further help on the income side for households since a stronger RMB would reduce the cost of imports, particularly food, and increase disposable income. Removing the 'ceiling' on deposit rates would also increase interest income to households, which has plunged into negative territory with inflation exceeding the deposit rate in the late 2000s. The combination of internal and external rebalancing would thus assist with reducing household savings and increase output.

CORPORATE SAVINGS

Further liberalization of interest rates would improve credit allocation to non-state-sector firms and reduce the savings incentive for firms too. Although interest rates were partially liberalized, including in 2004 when the ceiling on inter-bank lending rates was lifted, there are still limits in terms of the 'floor' on the lending rate. Interest rates reflect the internal rate of return to investment, so such controls distort lending decisions. These restrictions preserve bank margins in the same way that capital controls preserve the deposit base, but they lead to high rates of corporate saving.

The allocation of capital should be more efficient even though the rate of investment may not increase. This suggests greater output for the same amount of invested funds. For instance, the return on assets is high in China, but it is greater for all types of private firms than SOEs and collectives (Figure 8.16). Yet, SOEs continue to receive disproportionate amounts of credit despite being less productive (see for example, Shen et al. 2009; Huang and Wang 2011, for measures of credit distortion and financial repression). Without interest rate liberalization and further reforms of the financial system, the extent of financial repression distorts credit allocation and induces savings by private firms, which has contributed as much as households to the increase in the savings rate in the 2000s. Wages below the marginal product of labour also generate profits, but capital market reform will reduce the distortions to firm savings behaviour, particularly if it is linked to capital account reform.

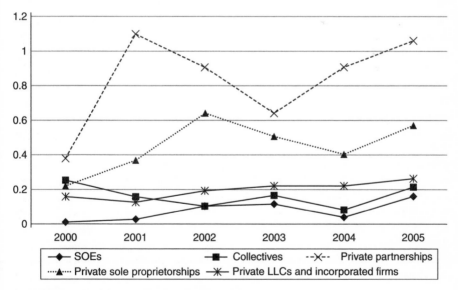

Figure 8.16 Return on assets on Chinese firms
Source: China National Bureau of Statistics and author's calculations

Gradual capital account liberalization, in particular the 'going out' policy that is encouraging Chinese firms to operate as multinational corporations, can reduce savings if firms are permitted to operate in global markets and are allowed to access funding from better-developed overseas credit markets. In other words, firms can raise money on capital markets and not just rely on China's banking system with its controls on credit.

There are also a number of macroeconomic benefits. Capital account reform would not only reduce the motive for corporate savings but also cut the portion of the current account surplus that is funded through the purchase of US Treasuries by allowing capital outflows in the form of investments instead of accumulated in foreign exchange reserves that is discussed further in the next section.

The exchange rate should also become more flexible with greater capital account liberalization since the capital account and the current account will require the RMB for transactions. Recent measures to increase the use of the RMB in trade arrangements already point to the growing internationalization of the Chinese currency. Therefore, exchange rate and interest rate reforms together should produce a better balance between China's internal (savings/investment) and external (balance of payment) positions and help to rebalance the economy.

8.5 Conclusion

Global imbalances have existed for some decades, and their exacerbation in the 2000s formed the backdrop to the worst financial crisis in a century. But, in the short term, the world has already somewhat rebalanced with the US current account deficit falling from 6 per cent to around 3 per cent of GDP in 2010 (some like Bergsten 2009 argue this amount is consistent with the global reserve currency need), and savings have risen in recessionary countries. It further implies that China and other countries will need to rebalance their economies to sustain the rate of growth of the 2000s, which was driven by strong US imports and demand.

For surplus countries like China, US loose monetary policy can be transmitted via fixed exchange rates, which leads capital to flow from low to high interest rate economies. Thus, China should gradually reform its exchange rate to prevent domestic asset bubbles like price increases in the non-tradable real estate sector. Increasing the flexibility of the RMB exchange rate before tightening monetary policy will also be important as an increase in the interest rate in China while the United States maintains a near-zero interest rate (which the Federal Reserve has said that it will keep in place for an extended period of time) will only worsen the capital inflow, eroding the impact of the tightening measures.

Therefore, reforming the exchange rate and the interest rate can induce higher output growth if the switch to higher consumption can be managed while the trade surplus is smaller. The continuation of global imbalances further implies that such liberalization must be carefully regulated to prevent destabilizing capital flows as global liquidity will remain an issue (see also Bernanke 2005). Rebalancing China will not correct global imbalances, but the acute management of the trade surplus along with a recognition that such action will have some effect on rebalancing the global economy will mean a more sustainable growth path for China and perhaps the world economy.

Appendix: Deriving the CCE Curve in the Salter-Swan Model

In an open economy, the long run aggregate supply curve is referred to as the Competing Claims Equilibrium (CCE). The following derives the CCE in an open economy model.

First, in a closed economy, the Non-Accelerating Inflation Rate of Unemployment (NAIRU) and the associated long-run aggregate supply curve are determined by a bargaining equilibrium in the labour market. This is where the price determined real wage (PRW) curve intersects the bargained real wage (BRW) curve, giving equilibrium levels of the real wage and unemployment.

The PRW curve is derived from a firm's price-setting relationship and describes how the price level is determined in the economy. In a closed economy, this was simply a mark up over marginal costs. This can be considered as the price of domestic output (P_D); that is, the price of output produced by domestic firms:

$$P_D = (1 + \mu)\frac{W}{LP}. \tag{A1}$$

The mark up is μ, and marginal costs are simply the ratio of nominal wages (W) and labour productivity (LP). This can be rearranged to give the PRW:

$$PRW: w = \frac{W}{P} = \frac{LP}{(1+\mu)}. \tag{A2}$$

In an open economy, the domestic price level, though, will not be solely determined by the price of domestic goods; it will also consist of the price of goods imported from overseas. The price of imported goods (P_M) will be determined by the foreign price level (P^*) and the nominal exchange rate (E).

$$P_M = EP^*. \tag{A3}$$

The overall price level (P) is then a weighted combination of domestic (P_D) and imported prices (P_M), where the respective weights ϕ and $(1 - \phi)$ reflect the portion of domestic and foreign goods sold in the home market.

$$P = \phi P_D + (1 - \phi)P_M. \tag{A4}$$

By substituting (A2) and (A3) into (A4), the domestic price level can be expressed in terms of all the parameters.

$$P = \phi\left((1+\mu)\frac{W}{LP}\right) + (1-\phi)EP^*. \tag{A5}$$

It is clear from (A5) that in an open economy, the domestic price level will be affected by overseas factors. By altering the price of imported goods, changes in the overseas price level or the nominal exchange rate can feed directly into the domestic price level. As the domestic price level is influenced by external factors, it will follow that the same factors will be a determinant of the NAIRU and long-run aggregate supply. The open economy version of the PRW schedule can be derived from (A5).

First, divide both sides by P,

$$1 = \phi\left((1+\mu)\frac{W}{LP \times P}\right) + (1-\phi)\frac{EP^*}{P}. \tag{A6}$$

Next, substitute in for the real exchange rate, $\theta = \frac{EP^*}{P}$:

$$1 = \phi\left(\frac{(1+\mu)}{LP}\frac{W}{P}\right) + (1-\phi)\theta. \tag{A7}$$

And, finally rearrange,

$$1 - (1-\phi)\theta = \phi\left(\frac{(1+\mu)}{LP}\right)\left(\frac{W}{P}\right). \tag{A8}$$

$$\frac{1 - (1-\phi)\theta}{\phi} = \left(\frac{(1+\mu)}{LP}\right)\left(\frac{W}{P}\right). \tag{A9}$$

$$PRW: w = \frac{W}{P} = \frac{1 - (1-\phi)\theta}{\phi}\left(\frac{LP}{(1+\mu)}\right). \tag{A10}$$

The open economy price determined real wage (PRW) schedule in (A10) is an interesting relationship. The closed economy price-setting relationship will simply result if $\phi = 1$. However, as long as $\phi < 1$, foreign goods will constitute a positive portion of the price level. In this case, the price level will be determined by the real exchange rate, and in particular, the nominal exchange rate and overseas price level. Changes in the real exchange rate will then change domestic prices and the price determined real wage.

If the real exchange rate appreciates (θ falls), then foreign goods become cheaper so overall domestic prices will fall. As a result, the price determined real wage will rise, shifting the PRW schedule upward. Alternatively, real exchange rate depreciation (θ rises) will make foreign goods more expensive and the domestic price level will rise, shifting the PRW schedule downward.

The other side of the bargaining framework is the wage setting relationship, which describes the real wage that workers will push for at each level of unemployment. This is a downward sloping function because workers will moderate wage claims in times of high unemployment. The bargained real wage (BRW) can then be represented in the following way:

$$BRW: \frac{W}{P} = Z - \beta u. \tag{A11}$$

Z represents a set of exogenous factors that determine the real wage, such as trade union power, minimum wage levels, etc., and β the sensitivity of the real wage to the rate of unemployment (u).

The NAIRU is determined by the intersection of the price setting (A10) and wage setting (A11) schedules. In the open economy, though, there is no longer a unique NAIRU. In fact, the NAIRU will be different depending on the level of the real exchange rate.

As the real exchange rate appreciates, the NAIRU falls—meaning that non-accelerating inflation is sustainable at a lower rate of unemployment. As unemployment falls, workers push for higher wages. This will then raise the costs of firms, and lead to an upward pressure on prices. In the closed economy, the increase in prices would then act to reduce the real wage, meaning that it would be impossible to depart from the NAIRU in the long run once wages and prices had fully adjusted.

In an open economy, though, an appreciated exchange rate would give the economy an inflationary subsidy. Falling import prices (P_M) would put downward pressure on the overall price level (P). If unemployment fell, this would put upward pressure on domestic prices (P_D), but this would be offset by the fall in import prices—leaving the overall price level unchanged. Therefore, an exchange rate appreciation enables the economy to move to a lower level of unemployment while maintaining price stability.

Depreciation, of course, would have the opposite effect. Higher import prices means that overall price stability would require a fall in domestic prices and a rise in unemployment. It is clear that in the open economy, the NAIRU will not be uniquely determined, but depend on the real exchange rate θ. The sensitivity of the NAIRU to the real exchange rate will rise as ϕ falls, implying that foreign imported goods are a larger portion of all goods sold in the domestic economy.

In the closed economy, the long-run aggregate supply function was derived from the NAIRU. As there was a unique NAIRU, there was a unique long-run equilibrium level of output where inflation was stable. The long-run aggregate supply curve is simply vertical at this level of output.

The relationship between the NAIRU and the equilibrium level of output is determined in a number of steps. Output is simply a function of employment (N): $Y = F(N)$. The total labour force (L) consists of the total number of employed (N) and unemployed persons (U): $L = N + U$. Dividing both sides by L shows that the relative portions of employed and unemployed workers in the economy add up to one: $1 = \frac{N}{L} + \frac{U}{L}$. So, $1 = \frac{N}{L} + u$, as $u = \frac{U}{L}$ is the unemployment rate.

Rearranging this, employment is a function of unemployment; that is, employment is equal to the portion of the labour force that is not unemployed:

$N = L(1 - u)$. If unemployment $(\hat{u})$ is at the NAIRU, then the long-run aggregate supply level of output $(\hat{Y})$ will be defined as:

$$\hat{Y} = F\big(L(1 - \hat{u})\big). \tag{A12}$$

There is an inverse relationship between the equilibrium level of output and the NAIRU. The CCE is the relationship between the real exchange rate and the equilibrium level of output. From equation (A12), the CCE will be a downward sloping function.

As the exchange rate appreciates, the equilibrium level of output (where inflation is constant) will rise. Note that the slope of the CCE schedule depends on the size of the shifts in the PRW curve for a given change in competitiveness. This is largely determined by the parameter ϕ. If $\phi = 1$, then the foreign price effect on the PRW curve would disappear completely as imports constitute no part of the domestic price level. In this instance, the NAIRU and the equilibrium level of output will once again be uniquely determined.

If this were the case, the CCE schedule would simply be like its closed economy counterpart and would be vertical at the equilibrium level of output. However, as $\phi \to 0$, foreign goods are an increasing portion of the domestic price level. As competitiveness falls, higher levels of output can be sustained without prices rising, so the CCE curve becomes flatter.

The term, Competing Claims Equilibrium, arises because price inflation results from the competing claims of domestic workers and firms—and, also in the open economy, foreign producers. If domestic workers push for higher wages, they are seeking a larger portion of the economy's output. Alternatively, if firms raise prices, they will seek a higher portion of output by limiting the real wage. Therefore, in a closed economy setting, the wage and price demands made by workers and firms respectively represent each party's attempts to gain at the others expense. The NAIRU represents the level of unemployment where these claims are consistent with a stable rate of inflation.

In an open economy, though, these competing claims take on a further dimension. The real exchange rate defines the claim on domestic resources made by the overseas sector. As the real exchange rate appreciates, the relative price of foreign goods falls, so the claims of the foreign sector on domestic output fall. This means that the claims of domestic workers and firms can then be consistent at lower levels of unemployment. Real exchange rate depreciation has the opposite effect. For this reason, a different real exchange rate can sustain a different NAIRU.

9

Conclusion: The Role of the State

9.1 Introduction

Although the state in China is no longer as all-encompassing as it had been during the pre-1979 centrally planned period, it still reaches into numerous areas of the economy. For instance, the state is a competitor through its ownership of state-owned enterprises (SOEs) and banks that can distort the market through exemptions from anti-trust laws or the allocation of credit towards state firms, respectively. These state-owned firms generate revenues and extend loans which in turn help to fund China's continuing development and transition (see for example, Bai et al. 2000, on the multiple roles played by state-owned enterprises including not only profit-maximization but also social welfare provision).

This mixed state–market model is consistent with China's gradual transition where the aim is to support economic growth through partially reforming the existing institutions, but not to wholly privatize or marketize the economy. China sought to avoid the 'transformational recessions' experienced by the former Soviet Union economies of the 1990s and the destabilizing episodes faced by many developing countries when they undertook economic liberalization. As a consequence, the reach of the state is evident in not only overt indicators such as state-owned enterprises continuing to generate some one-third of industrial output, but also more in more subtle ways. The market is increasingly shaped by laws and policies from which state-owned firms are granted exemptions while continuing to benefit from policies such as financial repression in which the rules governing credit favour state firms over others. As such, the economic borders of the Chinese state are broad, but opaque. How stable China's growth will be will depend in large part on the transformation of the state. If government takes on the functions of providing security in land, a level playing field, and social protection, then the final institutional reforms in China will be achieved. For many, both economists and non-economists, this is key to China's continued development.

The chapter will explore the shrinking role of the state in the 1980s and 1990s when market reforms were first adopted, culminating in the late 1990s privatization drive. Then, the slight reversal of this trend in the 2000s when state ownership was retained amongst large industrial firms and the state-owned commercial banks will be examined. The economic data will be supplemented by analysis of major institutional policies and laws which suggest at times a persistent, but less noticed role of the state in the market.

China thus poses a paradox as the state has retained a significant role during the reform period since 1979 that has hampered the development of clearly defined private property rights thought to be necessary to underpin an efficient market economy. However, this approach is consistent with China's gradual transition where the aim is to support economic growth through partially reforming the existing institutions, but not to wholly privatize or marketize the economy, and thus the state continues to have a significant presence in the economy.

Again, China sought to avoid the 'transformational recessions' experienced by the former Soviet Union economies of the 1990s and the destabilizing episodes faced by a number of developing countries when they undertook rapid economic liberalization. As a consequence, the reach of the state is evident in not only overt indicators such as state-owned enterprises (SOEs) continuing to generate some one-third of industrial output, but also in more subtle ways. Namely, the market is increasingly shaped by laws and policies from which state-owned firms are granted exemptions while continuing to benefit from policies such as financial repression in which the rules governing credit favour state firms.

Gradually reforming state-owned enterprises to transition incrementally from central planning was a key part of China's approach. Giving state-owned firms privileged access to high domestic savings helped support economic growth by maintaining employment while reforms were slowly undertaken. Thus, China's high savings rate fuelled investment which in turn drove economic growth, but is increasingly inefficient. There are also less apparent measures such as extending preferential policies and exemptions from otherwise facially neutral laws to favour state-owned enterprises. These are ostensibly to prevent foreign multinational corporations which have achieved economies of scale from dominating the increasingly open domestic market. Following from the initial phase centred on transitioning to a more market-oriented economy, continued economic growth requires productivity improvements that could come into conflict with the lingering role of the state.

A consequence of this more gradual approach is that inefficiencies could have slowed down economic growth by favouring SOEs over the more efficient non-state sector. A counter-argument, though, is that rapid reforms could have resulted in a similarly destabilizing crisis as that experienced by Russia during its transition. In the early stages of reform, the retention of state-owned enterprises helped to maintain stability particularly through minimizing unemployment, but by the 2000s in the third decade of reform, the distortions caused by the state presence have generated inefficiencies that point to a need for the state to become more similar to that found in Western economies; as a provider of social securities rather than as a competitor in industry or for bank loans.

9.2 China's Visible Hand

The neoclassical view of an efficient market requires well-defined property rights and minimal transaction costs. From a theoretical perspective, the 'invisible hand' of the market works efficiently when there exists optimizing agents transacting in a framework of well-defined property rights and sufficiently low or zero transaction costs (see Coase 1937). Law establishes those conditions. A legal system defines the property rights and the costs of transacting and exchange. For instance, ownership recognized by law establishes the security of the private property to be exchanged. A well-functioning legal and regulatory system can ensure that transactions take place efficiently; that is, by providing contracting security. For China, one element of the paradox is the lack of legally protected private property rights (see for example, Jefferson and Rawski 2002). It was not until the Property Law of 2007 that equal protection was granted to both private and public property, and the 2000s marked an era when private firms obtained legal recognition. Indeed, much of China's growth and reform has taken place with the state retaining ownership of enterprises, land, and housing.

From an empirical standpoint, these theoretical insights have been incorporated into the literature advocating the importance of laws and institutions in explaining persistent economic growth (see for example, Rodrik, Subramanian, and Trebbi 2004; Acemoglu and Johnson 2005; Acemoglu, Johnson, and Robinson 2005; Dam 2006). La Porta et al. (1997, 1998) emphasize the importance of legal origin, for example, whether a country had a common or civil law system, in influencing financial sector development and consequently economic development. China did not fit well within this framework, particularly because legal origin was based on the externally imposed legal system of the colonial powers on developing countries. But, for countries such as China which did not adopt a legal system from a particular colonial power, the legal formalism hypothesis would seem to have minimal explanatory power. Studies of other transition economies conclude that the effectiveness of laws is more important than the completeness of the written formal law for economic growth, further reducing the force of the legal origins school. One significant conclusion is that a 'transplanted' legal system into a neophyte transition economy—whereby the wholly formed laws of developed countries which would presumably encompass the necessary elements for a 'rule of law'—does not work (Pistor, Martin, and Gelfer 2000). Glaeser et al. (2004) also emphasize the functional rule of law as relevant for growth. Therefore, the elements of a well-functioning legal system would include an independent judiciary, freedom of executive branch interference, and low risk of expropriation (Pistor and Xu 2005)

Institutional development was therefore considered to be important and the focus has shifted away from legal formalism and legal origin to some extent (see for example, Rodrik, Subramanian, and Trebbi 2004). For instance, Acemoglu and Johnson (2005) emphasize two types of market-supporting institutions which are important for economic growth: property rights institutions which protect against expropriation by government, and contracting institutions which ease contract enforcement. For China, these empirical measures also do not measure up well as compared against its impressive growth rate, giving rise to the 'China paradox'.

Numerous studies have attempted to explain the China paradox (see for example, Allen, Qian, and Qian 2005; Cull and Xu 2005; Lu and Yao 2009) through reference to the importance of informal institutions such as relational contracting that has supported economic growth in the absence of a well-established legal system during the early stages of reform during the 1980s and 1990s. But, there is mounting evidence that by the 2000s, improved legal protection of particularly private firms has contributed to faster economic growth (Long 2010; Li and Yueh 2011). The next section delves into the still ongoing reforms of the state-owned enterprises.

9.3 Reforming State-owned Enterprises

At the end of 1978, China embarked on market-oriented reforms to transform the economy from a centrally planned system to one that is driven by market forces. The motivation for reform was, and is, economic necessity, but not dire need because China did not experience the same dramatic declines experienced in other transition economies on the eve of reform (Naughton 1995). Accordingly, the maintenance of stability—societal and political—has long been a paramount requirement as the reforms went forward (Fan 1994; Lau, Qian, and Roland 2001). The gradualist approach requires sufficient control over the process of liberalization itself so that the marketized segments do not overwhelm the pre-existing state segment (see Murphy, Shleifer, and Vishny 1992). The continuing involvement of the state was therefore a corollary to preserve stability, particularly in preserving employment in state-owned enterprises, as economic reforms progressed.

These themes of stability and economic necessity pervaded first the reforms of the state-owned sector and the subsequent development of the corporate, including non-state, sector. Both policy and legal measures were used to instigate reforms and also to maintain stability. The quickly evolving legal system provides the needed institutional basis to govern market behaviour, contract enforcement, and dispute resolution for an increasingly marketized economy. For instance, township and village enterprises (TVEs) arose due to the need for light industrial goods after decades of heavy industry-biased central planning and as an avenue to absorb surplus labour in the agricultural sector, one of the key challenges for a developing country like China. Permitting the institutional form of TVEs pursuant to laws and regulations governing 'collectively owned' enterprises allowed the economy to generate economic growth without incurring instability since TVEs also served the dual purpose of reallocating labour. Similarly, the need for foreign direct investment and technology meant that

China experimented with opening to the global economy at the very start of reforms in 1979 (Lardy 1998). Realizing that foreign investors needed investment vehicles, various joint venture laws were adopted to facilitate economic growth via opening to international trade/investment, and all the while limiting the reach of FDI to specially designed export-oriented areas known as Special Economic Zones (SEZs). These new institutional forms were kept out of the reach of private Chinese businesses for a time (Huang 2003). This was intended to limit the pace of reforms by controlling the development of the private sector in the name of stability. Starting in the early and mid-1980s, reforms of state-owned enterprises were also undertaken, but the process was gradual (Naughton 1995) and the state presence in the economy remained.

In 1978, state-owned enterprises and collectively owned enterprises were essentially the only firms in China, with SOEs accounting for 77.6 per cent of industrial output and collectives the remaining 22.4 per cent (see Table 9.1). SOEs were state-owned at the national and local levels, whilst collectives were predominantly smaller, communally owned urban enterprises that are the sister firms to the township and village enterprises in rural areas. The dominance of state-owned enterprises undoubtedly reflected the 'urban bias' that had industrialized China (Riskin 1987; Naughton 1995). China was industrialized in 1978 on the eve of market-oriented reforms with industry constituting around half of GDP, a share that has been maintained throughout the subsequent thirty years. In 2007, industry accounted for 48.6 per cent of GDP, a very slight increase from 47.9 per cent in 1978. In other words, China started its reform period with an industrial sector, but one that was devoid of privately owned firms as is characteristic of administered economies under central planning.

However, gradually, with market-oriented reforms introduced at the end of 1978 by Deng Xiaoping, the industrial sector experienced changes that began to diversify the enterprise sector. The process, though, as evident from Table 9.2 and Figure 9.1, was slow in that SOEs continued to dominate both output and employment until the late 1980s and early 1990s when losses at SOEs compelled greater liberalization (Fan 1994). By contrast, urban collectives, unlike TVEs which had a niche in the absence of dominant SOEs in rural areas, quickly lost their economic clout during the reform period and contributed less than 5 per cent of urban employment by 2007, falling from their peak at the start of reforms in 1978 when they had accounted for about 30 per cent.

This 'dual track'—whereby the administrative track exists alongside a new market track consisting of non-state firms—became the model adopted in 1984, known as the 'Dual Track (Plan and Market) System' that was applied to SOEs to incentivize their output. The Third Plenum of the 12th Party Congress implemented the dual track pricing system and gave SOEs autonomy to sell above quota output at market prices and retain the proceeds for profit. A profit tax was introduced to replace the remittance of profit to the state. This Contract Responsibility System (CRS) relied on managerial responses to the link between pay and firm output and gave SOEs some leverage over managers, including the payment of bonuses. Interestingly, not only was the 'dual-track' system modelled on the

Table 9.1 Share of total industrial output by enterprise type

	1978	1979	1980	1981	1982	1983	1984	1985	1986	1987	1988	1989	1990	1991	1992	1993
SOE	77.6%	78.5%	75.7%	74.8%	74.4%	73.4%	69.1%	64.9%	62.3%	59.7%	56.8%	56.1%	54.6%	56.2%	51.5%	47.0%
Collective	22.4%	21.5%	23.8%	24.6%	24.8%	25.7%	29.7%	32.1%	33.5%	34.6%	36.1%	35.7%	35.6%	33.0%	35.1%	34.0%
Getihu	0.0%	0.0%	0.0%	0.0%	0.1%	0.1%	0.2%	1.9%	2.8%	3.6%	4.3%	4.8%	5.4%	4.8%	5.8%	8.0%
Other	0.0%	0.0%	0.5%	0.6%	0.7%	0.8%	1.0%	1.2%	1.5%	2.0%	2.7%	3.4%	4.4%	6.0%	7.6%	11.1%

	1994	1995	1996	1997	1998	1999	2000	2001	2002	2003	2004	2005
SOE	37.3%	34.0%	33.7%	29.8%	26.5%	26.1%	38.2%	35.1%	32.6%	30.1%	28.3%	27.2%
Collective	37.7%	36.6%	36.5%	35.9%	36.0%	32.8%	11.2%	8.3%	6.9%	5.3%	3.2%	2.8%
Getihu	10.1%	12.9%	14.4%	16.9%	16.0%	16.9%	0.0%	0.0%	0.0%	0.0%	0.0%	0.0%
Other	14.9%	16.6%	15.4%	17.4%	21.5%	24.2%	50.5%	56.5%	60.5%	64.5%	68.6%	70.0%

Source: China Yearbook of Industrial Economy.

Table 9.2 Number of state-owned enterprises

1978	1979	1980	1981	1982	1983	1984	1985	1986	1987	1988	1989	1990	1991
348,400	355,000	446,300	494,500	566,600	712,500	869,200	5,185,300	6,706,700	7,474,100	8,105,600	7,980,700	7,957,800	8,079,600

1992	1993	1994	1995	1996	1997	1998	1999	2000	2001	2002	2003	2004	2005	2006
8,612,100	9,911,600	10,017,100	7,341,500	7,986,500	7,922,900	165,080	162,033	162,885	171,256	181,557	196,222	276,474	271,835	301,961

Source: China Statistical Yearbook.

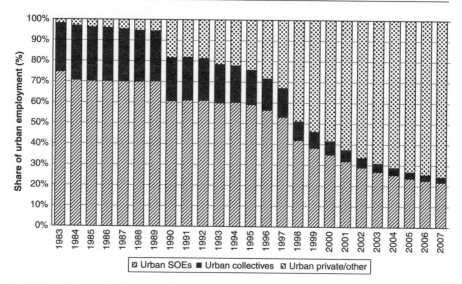

Figure 9.1 Share of urban employment by enterprise type
Source: *China Statistical Yearbook*.
Note: The 1987 and 1990 data were both affected by a census in that year.

rural reforms, the managerial responsibility system adopted in 1985 and 1988 in urban areas was also trialled in rural areas. In 1982, the Ministry of Commerce issued regulations allowing farmers to participate in the selection of cooperative managers and to receive dividends from profits.

Urban reforms thus began in the mid-1980s and were initially considered to be successful in creating a profit incentive in SOEs that were otherwise used to producing to a plan (see for example, Groves et al. 1995). The late 1980s also witnessed a trend of liberalization geared at supporting the partially reformed market. In 1985, direct banking was permitted. Bank loans replaced central government grants to SOEs to make investment decisions more responsive to market signals. Previously, SOEs would ask for funds with a tendency toward over-investment as the true cost of the capital was never realized (see for example, Kornai 1992).

These reforms were thus accompanied by the reforms of the state-owned banking system. At the start of the reform period, China's banking and financial system under central planning was essentially an arm of the state. The People's Bank of China (PBOC) was the sole bank since 1949 until the 1980s reforms with responsibilities for both central and commercial banking operations. Cooperative banks existed to serve rural areas, but there was little else in terms of a financial system. The PBOC was the central bank in charge of monetary policy in the administered economy and oversaw all banking needs, which was primarily to serve as cashier for the state. However, with market reforms occurring successfully in the early 1980s, the banking system itself was reformed to be more market-oriented and be capable of serving a marketizing economy in need of commercial banking services. Nevertheless, China's banking sector is still state-dominated with an estimated 60 per cent of credit issued by the SCBs even in 2009 (Shen et al. 2009).

Thus, the SOE reform process was focused but undertaken gradually and motivated largely by economic necessity. Following from the corporatization policy of 1992 (share issue privatization) and 1993 (restructuring into limited liability companies or LLCs and joint stock companies), the *zhuada fanxiao* ('save the large, let go of the small') policy was enacted in 1994 which effectively privatized the small- and medium-sized SOEs (see Garnaut et al. 2001). Notable fiscal reform in the same year centralized finances such that the support offered by local governments and local state-owned banks toward local SOEs was diluted and aided the reforms.

From over 10 million SOEs in 1994, the total fell by a quarter a year later, as seen in Table 9.2. By 1997, SOE reform was truly underway when the state allowed redundancies to occur. From 1997 to 2001, a quarter of the urban labour force was laid-off, although the figures did not appear in the official urban unemployment rate due to the status of *xiagang* given to such workers, which designated them as nominally laid-off but still registered with their work unit and receiving small amounts of payment while they looked for work (Knight and Yueh 2004).

This significant reform meant that SOEs could be privatized once their employment role was diminished. In 1998, the number of SOEs had shrunk from 7.9 million in the previous year to 165,000. But, the share of total industrial output did not register a similarly dramatic decline. SOE share of output fell from 33.7 per cent to 29.8 per cent, on account of the remaining SOEs which are large companies, in areas such as energy, commodities, utilities, and the four big, state-owned commercial banks.

Far from disappearing such that China would become a fully private economy, SOEs were consolidated and national (state-owned) champions like the National Oil Companies (NOCs) were promoted. In 1999, the NOCs were reorganized into three firms each responsible for a specific segment of the oil market, such as CNOOC geared at offshore exploration. In 2001, the same occurred with the steel industry. The state-owned banks were reformed by a 1995 law and readied for IPOs even whilst the state retained a majority share (Lardy 2002).

Thus, the SOE share of output hovered at around 30 per cent of GDP throughout the late 1990s and 2000s, rather than falling further. However, as some of these are largely capital-intensive industries and non-state firms were granted greater recognition from the late 1990s, the share of urban employment of SOEs declined continuously until they accounted for less than 10 per cent, a far cry from the days when SOEs were maintained despite their losses to meet the government's goal of full employment (Lin, Cai, and Zhou 2003).

Finally, this period of intense marketization included China's industrial policies 'going global'. China's 'going out' policy was also launched in 2000 with the aim of establishing Chinese firms as global players, including SOEs like the

NOCs and the state-owned commercial banks. Chinese firms could learn by operating in more developed economies and benefit from the competitive pressures of selling in global markets. The benefits of economies of scale could also be realized as well as international specialization as Chinese firms locate their production and distribution chains worldwide in the same way that foreign multinationals have in China as part of global supply chains. The policy resulted in international initial public offerings (IPOs) of large companies such as the state-owned bank ICBC and also the flagship carrier, Air China, on the New York and London stock exchanges. It also generated the first overseas commercial acquisition by a Chinese company in 2004, which was enabled by the Mergers and Acquisitions (M&A) Law passed the previous year that set the legal parameters of such deals. China's TCL purchased the Thomson brand of France. A year later, and the largest deal at the time for a Chinese firm, a much better known company, Lenovo (formerly Legend), bought IBM's PC business. These deals were unlike the SOE-led overseas investments in energy and commodities which continued to take place. These were, in effect, the first overtures of domestic firms seeking to expand overseas and a maturation of Chinese corporations aiming to become multinational firms.

In short, the period of the mid- to late 1990s was characterized by the historic downsizing of SOEs and required the development of the non-state sector to sustain economic growth which laid the foundation for rapid market development and legal changes of the 2000s. Notable reforms were undertaken to both restructure SOEs and bolster the institutional foundations of non-state firms. The predominate corporate form that emerged was joint stock companies, through which small- and medium-sized SOEs were 'let go', the more profitable parts of SOEs were spun off, and the large SOEs were consolidated and transformed into shareholding companies. At the same time, the needs of an increasingly decentralized market called for greater legal reforms that led to laws that enabled further market development such as M&As, as opposed to simply legitimizing the economic policies of the government. Nevertheless, the state sector remained a significant part of the corporate sector, evident in the establishment of SASAC (State-owned Assets Supervision and Administration Commission) in 2006 to manage SOEs and the effective exclusion of SOEs from some provisions of the Anti-Monopoly Law.

9.4 The Non-level Playing Field

The gradual transition meant growth of the non-state sector and greater marketization of the economy, which led to the need for more legal and institutional measures to support an increasingly decentralized market in the mid- to late 1990s. The large-scale move to corporatize or *gongsihua* all firms, including the *getihu* or the self-employed and SOEs which had undertaken significant restructuring as part of the 9th Five Year Plan that was completed towards the end of the 1990s. The need for a legal framework to govern these corporatized firms was apparent. The playing field, though, was far from level.

First, the impetus for improved protection of property rights stemmed not only from the state as part of its marketization strategy, but also those who now owned shares in firms, stocks, and housing. As stakeholders, they formed an interested constituency to push for better protection of their property, which is a common phenomenon in the development of other corporate law jurisdictions such as the US and Europe (see Coffee 2001). This was most evident in the area of securities where a series of frauds led to public outrage and the subsequent establishment of a regulator some eight years after the opening of the stock market (see Chen 2003). As such, the laws of the late 1990s and the 2000s were unlike those passed during the early part of the reform period. These statutes and regulations were not the sole instruments of the state in legitimizing the government's economic policies, but were also reflections of the demand for legal reform by interested constituents to increase the security and protection of their property.

In 1999, the Constitution was amended to recognize the rule of law as a necessary part of governance. In 1999, a unified Contract Law was passed, as was a law that established private businesses as sole proprietorships. By 2001, President Zhang Zemin welcomed entrepreneurs into the Communist Party. None of these measures established an effective rule of law and protection of private property overnight, but these enactments reflected the demands of society for better legal protection now that they had property to protect, and also mark a stage where laws are used to further develop markets by offering the necessary institutional support through improving contracting security and legitimacy of corporate forms of ownership. Thus, in 2007, the Property Law granted formal legal protection to private property, a struggle that dates to an attempt twenty years earlier to do so in the General Principles of Civil Law. By the 2000s, China was on its way to having a modern corporate law system. The Company Law was fundamentally revised as the original statute was intended to provide a legal basis for the corporatization of SOEs, but subsequently was revamped to govern the emerged diverse set of firms.

The 2000s witnessed two competing forces. On the one hand, foreign competition and the growth of the non-state sector cried out for effective corporate laws. On the other hand, the state-owned enterprises remained the privileged vestibules for China's industrial growth strategy to underpin its continuing economic development. This meant that significant and much-needed laws were passed in the areas of mergers and acquisitions, corporate governance, bankruptcy, and anti-trust, but SOEs were often privileged and active industrial policies were undertaken to ensure the continuing reach of the state.

For instance, SASAC, a State Council body, took the role of beneficial owner of all state assets and is responsible for the supervision of the very largest SOEs. Exercising direct control over about 180 large SOEs from Beijing, it has branches throughout the country. SASAC was given a remit, and the promise of considerable public funds, to ensure that these SOEs became 'globally competitive' businesses. This led to some tensions. The foundation of these acts and the creation of SASAC showed the 'two-tier' strategy utilized by the Chinese government. The first part in this strategy was the encouragement of greater utilization of the stock market by Chinese enterprises. The second tier was the promotion of the 'national champion' strategy, and the cementing of the status of SOEs in the Chinese economy. In 2004, the SASAC noted that of the fourteen mainland Chinese enterprises listed in the Fortune 500, eight were under its direct supervision, mainly in the heavy industry and telecommunications sectors. The year 2006 saw the first mention of an overt policy to lift this number. SASAC announced that it would maintain controlling positions in key SOEs (the so-called 'national champions'). These sectors included armaments, power generation/distribution, oil/petrochemicals, telecommunications, coal, aviation, and shipping. SASAC's goal is to maintain 'between 30 and 50 internationally competitive conglomerates with intellectual property and famous brand names'.

Alongside this retrenchment of state control, governance by corporate laws and not just policies was gathering pace of an increasingly decentralized and commercial enterprise sector. The aims of the state, though, continued to be manifested in the laws. In 2002 after further WTO-related opening, the China Securities Regulatory Commission (CSRC) announced the guidelines for take-overs and mergers of listed companies, including a 10 per cent limit on the stake that a group of foreign investors can hold in a Chinese company. This was later raised to 25 per cent. Nevertheless, increasing quantities of state-owned shares were sold to non-state entities, including, since 2002, qualified foreign-based institutional investors such as Goldman Sachs, Deutsche Bank, and Merrill Lynch. Accordingly, China's first M&A law was passed in 2003 to provide guidelines. The restriction on foreign control, limiting foreign shareholding, would be enacted through the M&A law for non-listed firms, just as the CSRC rules govern listed ones. They would, in effect, protect SOEs from hostile take-overs whilst promoting the policy of learning from foreign firms but not allowing them to dominate the Chinese market.

The government was often deliberate in targeting these well-known institutional investors, noting that they were 'strategic partners' designed to bring knowledge of corporate governance techniques with them. Many of the larger investors were given seats on the board, such as Goldman Sachs with the float of ICBC, the biggest of the four state-owned commercial banks. Bringing in foreign investors highlighted the need to improve laws to govern the increasingly competitive corporate sector, especially after greater opening with China's WTO accession in December 2001.

The 2006 Enterprise Bankruptcy Law perhaps best illustrates China's two-tier strategy. Its promulgation means that for the first time bankruptcy of all legal persons in China is governed by one uniform bankruptcy law. Previously, the 1986 Interim Enterprise Bankruptcy Law applied only to SOEs, and the bankruptcy of private enterprises and foreign-invested enterprises was governed by a different body of often contradictory or inconsistent laws (Clarke 2003c). This law finally provided an exit strategy for foreign investors. Notably, the Chinese government exempted approximately 2,100 SOEs from the new law, forcing them to close following policy-arranged bankruptcy procedures instead. Law, in this sense, reflected market developments but it also embodied policy by exempting SOEs once again.

The same can be said for the 2007 Anti-Monopoly Law, another pillar of the corporate legal system. It is facially neutral and follows general competition policy principles found in the European Union and the United States in limiting the exercise of undue monopoly power, limiting market concentration, and promoting competition. However, as with the other statutes, it exempts SOEs on the basis of public interest, a clause usually applied to so-called strategic industries crucial for economic security or development.

Therefore, the dual purposes of preserving SOEs and governing a competitive, corporate sector are evident in the laws passed in the 2000s. The various laws are designed to govern a market economy but have carve-outs for SOEs so that China can simultaneously maintain its industrial policies geared at achieving economic growth. Laws, as instrumentation to legitimize policy, have morphed into laws as the indicators of policy mandates. In essence, laws that have been enacted alongside SOE reform are not only significant but also reveal telling signs of where reforms are headed and the limits of market development at each stage of China's transition. It seems as true in the 2000s as it was in the 1980s and 1990s for SOEs even as the laws and regulations are evolving into a more effective set of laws for the non-state sector.

9.5 High Savings and Labour Misallocation

One consequence is the existence of financial repression, which has funnelled China's high savings rate into capital accumulation that has been the most important component of growth (see for example, Zheng, Bigsten, and Hu 2009). The financial system is characterized by financial repression due to the significant diversion of credit to state-owned enterprises via the state-owned banking system which affects non-state firms negatively (see for example, Allen, Qian, and Qian 2005). It is one way in which the high savings rate has supported state-owned enterprises as well, but raises questions over the efficiency of such a system of capital allocation.

The converse of high savings is low consumption, which has been fallen dramatically since the early 1990s. Household savings have averaged 19 per cent of GDP since 1992, after the significant opening of China associated with the decline in consumption. Savings were high, but increased further by 8 percentage points of GDP from 2000, increasing from 14 per cent to 22 per cent of GDP by 2007 at the onset of the global financial crisis. A similar picture exists for firms, where the average savings rate was around 15 per cent of GDP from 1992–2007, but grew quickly to reach 22 per cent of GDP by the mid-2000s. The remainder of the savings derives from government, whose savings rate had been around 5 per cent since 1992, but more than doubled from 5.2 per cent in 2000 to 10.8 per cent in 2007. Taken together, China's savings rate increased from 38 per cent of GDP in the 1990s to peaking at nearly 52 per cent by the late 2000s. Thus, the savings rate increased by 17 percentage points during the 2000s (34 per cent in 2000 rising to 51.9 per cent in 2007), which mirrors the fall in consumption as a share of GDP from around 50 per cent of GDP in the early 1990s to 35 per cent by the late 2000s.

For households, income growth and removing the motives for precautionary savings would reduce the savings rate. Industrial output has grown at 14.1 per cent on average per annum for twenty years since 1988 (deflated growth of gross industrial output), but wage growth has not kept pace. Industrial output grew at double the previous pace in the 2000s (23.1 per cent on average per annum) as compared with the two decades before (11.7 per cent). Yet, the average annual real wage growth of urban employees was 11.9 per cent from 1995 to 2008 and only a paltry 5 per cent during the late 1990s. Rural incomes have risen even more slowly. In the 2000s, average wage growth was faster and closer to 15 per cent at 14.9 per cent per annum, but this is against a backdrop of industrial output growth exceeding 23 per cent each year. Thus, because labour income has lagged behind output growth, consumption has fallen as a share of GDP.

Moreover, labour productivity has increased some sevenfold from 1980 to 2005, according to the International Labour Organization (see also Yueh 2008), which suggests that wages do not match the marginal product of labour. Labour productivity has been improving in the 2000s since the significant reform of labour markets at the end of the 1990s and the improvement has been hastened by recent supply side tightening. The protests in 2009/10 over low wages and a reluctance shown by rural migrants to return to the cities after the global downturn reflect the potential for faster wage growth. So long as higher wages prompt growth in labour productivity, there need not be inflationary pressures. Instead, an increase in income can boost consumption.

Measures that can ease labour market tightness involve removing restrictions on mobility; that is, increase urbanization to allow migrants to settle in urban areas. It would reduce the segmentation in the labour market and increase the mobility of workers to find matches to appropriate jobs and not be barred by geographic or *hukou* (household registration system) barriers. Urbanization is a policy that has been proposed alongside renewed efforts to develop the services sector which will be discussed in the next section.

And, capital market, specifically interest rate, reforms would help. Removing the 'ceiling' on deposit rates would increase interest income to households, which has plunged into negative territory with inflation exceeding the deposit rate in the late 2000s. More investment vehicles such as private health insurance would also reduce the savings motives.

Further liberalization of interest rates would improve credit allocation to non-state sector firms and reduce the savings incentive for firms too. Although interest rates were partially liberalized, including in 2004 when the ceiling on inter-bank lending rates was lifted, there are still limits in terms of the 'floor' on the lending rate. Interest rates reflect the internal rate of return to investment, so such controls distort lending decisions. Private firms save as a result, while state-owned enterprises are taxed lightly and pay few dividends, which together increase the firm saving rate (see Bayoumi, Tong, and Wei 2010, for the argument that Chinese firm savings are high but internationally comparable). These restrictions preserve bank margins in the same way that capital controls preserve the deposit base, but they contribute to high rates of corporate saving.

If there were greater liberalization, then the allocation of capital could be more efficient. For instance, the return on assets is high in China, but it is greater for all types of private firms than SOEs and collectives. Yet, SOEs continue to receive disproportionate amounts of credit despite being less productive (see for example, Shen et al. 2009; Huang and Wang 2011, for measures of credit distortion and financial repression). Without interest rate liberalization and further reforms of the financial system, the extent of financial repression distorts credit allocation and induces savings by private firms, which has contributed as much as households to the increase in the savings rate in the 2000s. Capital market reform could reduce the distortions to firm savings behaviour, particularly if it is linked to capital account reform. Therefore, to achieve a better balance between China's internal (savings/investment) and external (balance of payment) positions, addressing the savings motive and the role of the state would help to rebalance the economy.

9.6 Costs of Distortions

The costs to economic growth of such factor market distortions are difficult to estimate. Greater liberalization of capital/labour markets and faster reform of state-owned enterprises could have resulted in a repeat of the disastrous Russian experience. However, there is nevertheless an efficiency cost. Roubini and Sala-i-Martin (1992) show that financial repression reduces long-term economic growth, while Pagano (1993) argues that such policies like interest rate controls and reserve requirements reduce the capacity for financial intermediation to develop which leads to underdeveloped financial markets. For China, Lardy (2008) estimates that financial repression, mainly through negative real interest rates, has cost Chinese households about 255 billion yuan (US$36 billion) or 4 per cent of GDP, in addition to lowering economic efficiency.

But, at least in the early stages, Huang and Wang (2011) estimate that repressive policies helped economic growth, as a result of a prudent and incremental liberalization approach. But, the impact turned from positive in the 1980s and 1990s to negative in the 2000s, suggesting rising efficiency losses in recent years (see also Li 2001). In terms of economic growth, Lu and Yao (2009) paint a similarly nuanced picture in that better financial development through an improvement in the legal system could have reduced provincial growth by 0.7 percentage points during the 1990s through stemming the positive leakage of funds that was going to the more efficient private investment, but these authors all concur that the picture seemed to change in the 2000s.

In Chapter 3, the impact of such distortions on productivity and growth in the 2000s were estimated. Recall that instead of 23 per cent growth per annum, industrial output growth would have risen by an average of between 15–17 per cent in the 2000s. Improved protection of private property rights, therefore, appears to have contributed to the strong industrial output that boosted the GDP growth rate of the 2000s, which at 10 per cent was stronger than during the previous two decades. If these distortions had been addressed and the legal system and property rights improved during the previous decade, then GDP growth in the 1990s could have been closer to 10 per cent rather than 9 per cent.

9.7 The Next Phase of Growth

After over thirty years of marketization and reform, China remains a mixed picture of state-led policies and a growing number of facially neutral laws with some exemptions for state-owned enterprises. In addition, the state-owned commercial banks continue to benefit from official 'financial repression' policies, such as the preservation of a spread between lending rates (6.31 per cent in June 2012) and deposit rates (3.25 per cent in June 2012). This three percentage point (or 306 basis point) differential helps to generate margins for banks and facilitate their recapitalization (see for example, Riedel, Jin, and Jin 2007). Banks are able to lend at a rate set by the central bank that is higher than the rate at which they are directed to lend, which affords them a profitable trade in taking in deposits and paying low interest while lending at higher rates. This policy also enables the state-owned commercial banks to continue to support government policies ranging from fiscal stimulus to supporting state-owned enterprises, although not without cost to overall economic growth, discussed in the last section.

With the political economy of state ownership at issue, state-owned commercial banks as well as SOEs are managed by Party cadres and are unlikely to become completely privatized. The establishment of SASAC further suggests the retention of SOEs in the economy. However, the problems with doing so are evident, no less in the banking sector. State-owned/publicly run companies can exist in a market economy without causing instability, but the legacy issues of the command economy such as Kornai's 'soft budget constraints' means that for Chinese SOEs, the past and future problems of policy-directed operations must not overwhelm the commercial motive.

Finally, the implication of such a lack of movement towards a completely private economy and policies that show preference to the state-owned sector implies challenges for Chinese growth. The high levels of capital formation (some 40 per cent of GDP) in the past two decades and the inefficient allocation of capital away from more productive private firms are worrying (see for example, Bai, Hsieh, and Qian 2006). The 12th Five Year Plan (2011–15) plans to rebalance the economy towards greater domestic demand and less of a reliance on exports.

A key part of the plan is to increase consumption and other parts such as more urbanization and services development would support investment in developing larger urban areas where migrants can settle and government services can be dispersed more efficiently.

This plan has a thirty-year time-horizon as these policies of migration, urban development, and boosting consumption cannot be achieved in a short time period. Unless China can reorient its growth model including towards more efficient investments by private firms, then it could find it difficult to sustain a strong growth rate. Part of this challenge will include creating a more secure welfare state.

9.8 Optimal Size and Scope of the Chinese State

Curiously, the Chinese state comprises a comparatively small proportion of GDP as these figures only measure government expenditure and not its ownership of state-owned enterprises. Therefore, although the state owned nearly all of the modes of production in 1978, Table 9.3 shows that government spending has averaged 14 per cent of GDP since then. It had not exceeded 17 per cent until the global recession of 2008/9 when government spending increased by over four percentage points of GDP to make up for the collapse in exports. Even then, government's share of GDP was only around 23 per cent.

For China, government expenditure is a comparatively smaller share of GDP than other major and developing countries, as seen in Table 9.3. China has the lowest average share of government as a percentage of GDP than all major country groupings, including other parts of developing Asia, Africa, and comes in at half that of Eastern Europe.

There is a large literature on the optimal size of government which tends to find an inverted-U relationship between the share of government spending and GDP growth (see for example, Barro 1990). It is, though, the efficiency and the

Table 9.3 Government expenditure as share of GDP, 2000–10

	Average government expenditure (% GDP)
China	19.4
Developing Asia	21.4
ASEAN-5	22.5
Sub-Saharan Africa	27.0
Emerging economies	27.7
Latin America	29.9
Middle East/North Africa	31.5
United States	37.8
Central and Eastern Europe	39.8
European Union	46.5

Source: IMF, World Economic Outlook, April 2011.
Note: ASEAN-5 refers to Malaysia, Indonesia, Thailand, the Philippines, and Singapore.

nature of the government spending that matters more for growth than size. From 1960–92, Levine and Renelt (1992) find that government consumption as a share of GDP averaged 16 per cent for fast-growing economies while it was 12 per cent for lagging economies, but they did not find a significant impact on economic growth from an increase in government consumption. Rather, government spending that facilitates productive investment, which can include education and health, seems to have a more significant impact. Tanzi and Schuknecht (1997) find that social spending has increased significantly in the OECD since 1960, but the positive growth effects diminish after government spending reached between 30–40 per cent of GDP.

There is no stated goal to increase the government's share of GDP in China, despite the efforts in the 12th Five Year Plan to support domestic consumption through reducing the savings motive through increasing social service provision, but there is an aim to increase the share of the services sector, which would encompass greater government delivery of services. The service sector comprises about 40 per cent of GDP and held that share throughout the 2000s, which meant that the goal of raising it to 43 per cent by the end of the 11th Five Year Plan in 2010 was missed.

The services sector increased steadily as a share of GDP from 23 per cent in 1979 to 40 per cent in the 2000s but has not developed further, leading China to have a lower share of services in GDP than comparable-sized economies where the services sector account more than half of GDP (for example, over 70 per cent in the United Kingdom). Services is a non-tradable sector as it includes items such as haircuts and government services that would help to increase both domestic demand and reduce savings if such service provision included the delivery of social security. As such, government spending on services can reduce the savings rate of the economy while boosting domestic demand and incomes (see Blanchard and Giavazzi 2006). Urbanization further allows the delivery of services to be distributed more efficiently such that there can be greater economies of scale. For instance, health, pensions, unemployment, local services, and schools can all be developed as part of the services sector with the infrastructure needs to support this development, which increases the efficiency of investment and associated industrialization in the urban area. And, government spending on services could reduce the precautionary motives for household savings.

Therefore, there is a need for the state to retain its presence in the economy, but it is the nature and scope of its activities that need to change. In particular, increasing social spending and public investment that can aid productive private investment to establish more of a social welfare system can aid growth. There is no particular inclination in the 12th Five Year Plan or any other previous plans to move towards a more Western model of a welfare state as found in Europe, but there is a recognition that domestic consumption must be increased which requires addressing the savings motive of households that is related to the inadequate social welfare system. As with all Chinese reforms, there is no explicit goal, but the state acts on the pragmatic need to address a high savings rate that is hampering the rebalancing of the economy.

9.9 Conclusion

The state-owned structure remains in a less prominent form after more than three decades of economic transition, setting China apart from many of the other centrally planned and administered economies in the former Soviet Union that had embraced the market system wholly. China achieved paradoxical strong growth without well-defined property rights by slowly adopting institutional reforms and permitting market-oriented incentives to take hold whilst gradually whittling away the state's presence in the economy.

But, thirty years later, China retains the single Party state and a strong state-led development path. This is not to deny that regional experimentation and marketization happens to a large extent outside and sometimes in conflict with the dictates of the central government, but rather that China's markets are still influenced by the aims of the state's industrial strategy. For instance, capital account liberalization may well be undertaken to relieve the build-up of excess liquidity (money growth over real GDP gains) in the economy but it can also serve to the support the 'going out' policy. Of course, too much capital outflow would not be permitted because the partially reformed system still carries a large degree of bad debts in its banking system, so keeping savings in the country will be a competing priority.

Furthermore, China is not developing in a vacuum. Instead, it is integrated into a world system increasingly characterized by global rules and norms. After the global financial crisis, the pace of global reform accelerated since the crisis exposed the inadequate governance of linked international capital markets. It propelled a new push for better global regulations of financial markets. The G20 group of major economies, including China, entrusted a reconstituted Financial Stability Board based in the Bank for International Settlements or BIS (the central banks' bank) in Basel with the task of fashioning regulations for global capital markets, including greater capital and liquidity requirements. This will reflect back onto China and other economies to harmonize their domestic regulations with global guidelines.

For China, it feeds into the trend of growing laws and regulations to govern its markets. Although imperfect in many respects, the rule of law is being pursued in China to instil confidence and in some ways substitute for the lack of political reform that has not progressed significantly during the reform period. Courts and regulators serve as avenues for redress and consultation in a way that the government does not. Laws provide the veneer of certainty to reassure investors and shareholders. For many reasons including building up a nascent legal system, though, the rule of law is unlikely to be effective in the manner expected in the United States or Europe for some time.

The continued presence of the state further casts doubt on the objectivity of the judiciary which is not independent and is manned by a generation of judges with minimal legal training. It has not deterred foreign investors thus far, and Chinese firms are accustomed to the system. Nevertheless, the further development of the market will require more robust laws and regulations. China is headed down that path but it will take some years yet before the legal system is better developed. Even then, with a one-Party state, the extent of effectiveness of the law may be stymied by the dictates of policy.

Nowhere is this more apparent than in capital markets. Financial repression has contributed to a high corporate savings rate, and in turn, such policies have diverted China's large pool of savings to state-owned enterprises. Investment and capital accumulation have been the most important component of China's growth. But, the result of these policies is that there is inefficiency and doubts over whether capital formation of 45 per cent of GDP can or should continue, raising questions about the sustainability of continued growth. Policies adopted in the latest Five Year Plan aim to rebalance the economy, but a series of internal and external reforms are needed to normalize interest rates and capital markets. If this can be achieved, then China has the potential of sustaining its growth even under an economy where the state has not completely withdrawn even as its GDP makes it the world's second largest economy.

A further paradox is that government spending as a share of GDP is comparatively low for China; indeed, it is the lower than both developing and developed economies. A change is required in the scope of spending to address social welfare concerns which could both reduce the inefficiency of the current level of state involvement while helping the economy rebalance towards domestic consumption as a growth driver.

In conclusion, the reach of the state in China has receded in overt ways, but remains pervasive in other respects. State dominance has faded with the privatization reforms of the 1980s and 1990s, but the cessation of that trend in the 2000s points to a state that will remain active in the market. For instance, the retention of large state-owned enterprises and the continued control of state-owned commercial banks point to continued state ownership. Moreover, it is not in terms of explicit state ownership that defines the borders of the Chinese state. In less overt ways, laws and policies to further the development of the market have not always created a level playing field. The 'financial repression' in the banking sector of directing China's large pool of savings towards state-owned enterprises and government policies and the use of foreign exchange reserves to fund Chinese state-owned enterprises 'going global' are all implicit ways of maintaining state influence in the market. These policies are geared at supporting China's continued economic development and transition, but would still generate distortions and are not without some economic cost to the private sector and to the economy as a whole.

Being less apparent than the obvious restrictions placed on private and foreign businesses in the 1980s and 1990s when laws clearly prohibited certain activities, the reach of the state is now more like a Chinese box. The first box does not delineate the entire border of the state. There are other, larger boxes that encompass it which are less clearly defined, but nevertheless expand the boundaries of the Chinese state in the market. After more than three decades of reform, the Chinese state remains a notable presence in the economy. Its borders, though, may be broader than thought, but also more opaque than before.

For China to grow well for another thirty years will, though, require further reforms to improve the playing field for both its own and foreign firms. Continued reforms of factor markets (capital, labour) as well as rebalancing its economy are also necessary. The impressive track record of the first thirty years of nearly 10 per cent growth every year will not be repeated. But China can grow on a more sustainable basis and continue to increase the standard of living of its people. It will need to focus on the growth drivers for the next stage of its development, which include not just the restructuring of the economy, but pursuit of technological progress and innovation. The evidence looks promising on many fronts, but challenges also lie ahead. If China can pursue both structural and productivity-driven reforms, the future of the world's most populous nation will continue to be bright and it will continue to contribute to global growth as the world's second-largest economy and emerging superpower.

Bibliography

Abraham, K. and Medoff, J. (1982). 'Length of Service and the Operation of Internal Labor Markets'. Proceedings of the 35th Annual Meeting, 28–30 December 1982, Industrial Relations Research Association, pp. 208–18.

Acemoglu, D. and Johnson, S. (2005). 'Unbundling Institutions'. *Journal of Political Economy*, 113/5: 949–95.

Acemoglu, D., Johnson, S., and Robinson, J. (2005). 'Institutions as the Fundamental Cause of Long-Run Economic Growth', in P. Aghion and S. Durlauf (eds.), *Handbook of Economic Growth*. Amsterdam: Elsevier, 385–472.

Adam, C., Cavendish, W., and Mistry, P. S. (1992). *Adjusting Privatization: Case Studies from Developing Countries*. London: James Curry.

Adrian, T. and Shin, H. S. (2009.) 'Money, Liquidity, and Monetary Policy'. *American Economic Review*, 99/2: 600–5.

Aitken, B. J. and Harrison, A. E. (1999). 'Do Domestic Firms Benefit from Direct Foreign Investment? Evidence from Venezuela'. *American Economic Review*, 89/3: 605–18.

Aivazian, V. A., Ge, Y., and Qiu, J. (2005). 'Can Corporatization Improve the Performance of State-owned Enterprises even Without Privatization?' *Journal of Corporate Finance*, 11/1–2: 791–808.

Akerlof, G. A. (1982). 'Labor Contracts as Partial Gift Exchange'. *Quarterly Journal of Economics*, 97: 543–69.

Alford, W. (2000). 'The More Law, the More . . . ? Measuring Legal Reform in the People's Republic of China'. Stanford University, Stanford Center for International Development Working Paper No. 59.

Allen, F., Qian, J., and Qian, M. (2005). 'Law, Finance and Economic Growth in China'. *Journal of Financial Economics*, 77/1: 57–116.

Anderson, T. W. (1986.) *Introduction to Multivariate Statistical Analysis*, second edition. New York: John Wiley & Sons.

Appleton, S., Knight, J., Song, L., and Xia, Q. (2002). 'Labor retrenchment in China: Determinants and Consequences'. *China Economic Review*, 13/2–3: 252–75.

Appleton, S., Song, L., and Xia, Q. (2005). 'Has China Crossed the River? The Evolution of Wage Structure in Urban China During Reform and Retrenchment'. *Journal of Comparative Economics, Symposium: Poverty and Labour Markets in China*, 33/4: 644–63.

Arayama, Y. and Miyoshi, K. (2004). 'Regional Diversity and Sources of Economic Growth in China'. *World Economy*, 27/10: 1583–607.

Arellano, M. and Bond, S. R. (1991). 'Some Tests of Specification for Panel Data: Monte Carlo Evidence and an Application to Employment Equations'. *Review of Economic Studies*, 58: 277–97.

Arrow, K. A. (2000). 'Observations on Social Capital', in P. Dasgupta and I. Serageldin, (eds.), *Social Capital: A Multifaceted Perspective*. Washington, DC: The World Bank.

Ashenfelter, O. and Krueger, A. B. (1994). 'Estimating the Returns to Schooling Using a New Sample of Twins'. *American Economic Review*, 84: 1157–73.

Ashenfelter, O. and Rouse, C. (1998). 'Income, Schooling and Ability: Evidence From a New Sample of Identical Twins'. *Quarterly Journal of Economics*, 113: 253–84.

Aziz, J. and Duenwald, C. K. (2002). 'Growth-Financial Intermediation Nexus in China'. IMF Working Paper, 02/194.

Bai, C., Hsieh, C., and Qian, Y. (2006). 'The Return to Capital in China'. *Brookings Papers on Economic Activity*, 37/2: 61–102.

Bai, C., Li, D. D., Tao, Z., and Wang, Y. (2000). 'A Multitask Theory of State Enterprise Reform'. *Journal of Comparative Economics*, 28/4: 716–38.

Bai, C. and Qian, Z. (2009). 'Who is Squeezing out Household Income: An Analysis of the National Income Distribution in China'. *Social Sciences in China*, 5: 99–115 (in Chinese).

Baker, G., Gibbons, R., and Murphy, K. J. (2002). 'Relational Contracts and the Theory of the Firm'. *Quarterly Journal of Economics*, 117/1: 39–84.

Banerjee, A. and Duflo, E. (2007). 'What is Middle Class about the Middle Classes Around the World?' Centre for Economic Policy Research (CEPR) Discussion Paper No. 6613.

Banerjee, A. and Newman, A. (1993). 'Occupational Choice and the Process of Development'. *Journal of Political Economy*, 101/2: 274–98.

Banner, S. (1997). 'What Causes New Securities Regulations? 300 Years of Evidence'. *Washington University Law Review*, 75: 849–55.

Barro, R. J. (1990). 'Government Spending in a Simple Model of Economic Growth'. *Journal of Political Economy*, 98/5: S103–25.

Barro, R. J. (1991). 'Economic Growth in a Cross Section of Countries'. *Quarterly Journal of Economics*, 106/2: 407–43.

Barro, R. J. (2001). 'Human Capital and Growth'. *American Economic Review*, 91/2: 12–17.

Bartlett, R. L. and Miller, T. I. (1985). 'Executive Compensation: Female Executives and Networking'. *American Economic Review*, 72: 266–70.

Bayoumi, T., Tong, H., and Wei, S. (2010). 'The Chinese Corporate Savings Puzzle: A Firm-level Cross-country Perspective'. IMF Working Paper 10/275.

Bean, C. (2009). ' "The Meaning of Internal Balance" Thirty Years On'. *Economic Journal*, 119/541: F442–60.

Becker, G. S. (1981). *A Treatise on the Family*. Cambridge, Massachusetts: Harvard University Press.

Becker, G. S. (1993 [1964]). *Human Capital*. Chicago: University of Chicago Press.

Benhabib, J. and Spiegel, M. M. (1994). 'The Role of Human Capital in Economic Development: Evidence from Aggregate Cross-country Data'. *Journal of Monetary Economics*, 34/2: 143–73.

Bergsten, C. F. (2009). 'The Dollar and the Deficits'. *Foreign Affairs*, 88/6: 20–38.

Berkowitz, D., Pistor, K., and Richard, J. (2003). 'Economic Development, Legality, and the Transplant Effect'. *European Economic Review*, 47/1: 165–95.

Bernanke, B. (2004). *Essays on the Great Depression*. Princeton: Princeton University Press.

Bernanke, B. (2005). 'The Global Saving Glut and the U.S. Current Account Deficit'. Sandridge Lecture, Virginia Association of Economics, Richmond, Virginia, Federal Reserve Board, March 2005.

Bernard, H. R., Shelley, G. H., and Killworth, P. D. (1987). 'How Much of a Network does the GSS and RSW Dredge Up?' *Social Networks*, 9/1: 49–63.

Berthelemy, J. C. and Demurger, S. (2000). 'Foreign Direct Investment and Economic Growth: Theory and Applications to China'. *Review of Development Economics*, 4/2: 140–55.

Bian, Y. (1994a). *Work and Inequality in Urban China*. Albany: State University of New York.

Bian, Y. (1994b). '*Guanxi* and the Allocation of Urban Jobs in China'. *China Quarterly*, 140: 971–99.

Bian, Y., Shu, X., and Logan, J. (2001). 'Communist Party Membership and Regime Dynamics in China'. *Social Forces*, 79: 805–41.

Biggeri, M. (2003). 'Key Factors of Recent Chinese Provincial Economic Growth'. *Journal of Chinese Economic and Business Studies*, 1/2: 159–83.

Bils, M. and Klenow, P. J. (2000). 'Does Schooling Cause Growth'. *American Economic Review*, 90/5: 1160–83.

Bishop, M. and Thompson, D. (1993). 'Privatization in the UK: Deregulatory Reform and Public Enterprise Performance', in V. V. Ramanadhan (ed.), *Privatization: A Global Perspective*. London: Routledge.

Blanchard, O. and Giavazzi, F. (2006). 'Rebalancing Growth in China: A Three-handed Approach'. *China & World Economy*, 14/4: 1–20.

Blanchflower, D. G. and Oswald, A. J. (1998). 'What Makes an Entrepreneur?' *Journal of Labor Economics*, 16/1: 26–60.

Blomström, M. (2006). 'Foreign Investment and Productive Efficiency: The Case of Mexico'. *Journal of Industrial Economics*, 35/1: 97–110.

Blomström, M. and Kokko, A. (1998). 'Multinational Corporations and Spillovers'. *Journal of Economic Surveys*, 12/3: 247–77.

Blomström, M. and Sjöholm, F. (1999). 'Technology Transfer and Spillovers: Does Local Participation with Multinationals Matter?' *European Economic Review*, 43/4–6: 915–23.

Bloom, N., Griffith, R., and Van Reenen, J. (2002). 'Do R&D Tax Credits Work?' *Journal of Public Economics*, 85/1: 1–31

Bloom, N. and Van Reenen, J. (2007). 'Measuring and Explaining Management Practices Across Firms and Countries'. *Quarterly Journal of Economics*, 122/4: 1351–408.

Blundell, R. W. and Bond, S. R. (1998). 'Initial Conditions and Moment Restrictions in Dynamic Panel Data Models'. *Journal of Econometrics*, 87: 115–43.

Blundell, R. W. and Bond, S. R. (2000). 'GMM Estimation with Persistent Panel Data: An Application to Production Functions'. *Econometric Reviews*, 19: 321–240.

Borensztein, E., De Gregorio, J., and Lee, J. W. (1998). 'How Does Foreign Direct Investment Affect Economic Growth'. *Journal of International Economics*, 45/1: 115–35.

Borensztein, E. and Ostry, J. D. (1996). 'Accounting for China's Growth Performance'. *American Economic Review*, 86/2: 225–8.

Bosworth, B. and Collins, S. (2008). 'Accounting for Growth: Comparing China and India'. *Journal of Economic Perspectives*, 22/1: 45–66.

Bosworth, D. and Yang, D. (2000). 'Intellectual Property Law, Technology Flow and Licensing Opportunities in the People's Republic of China'. *International Business Review*, 9/4: 453–77.

Boyreau-Debray, G. (2003). 'Financial Intermediation and Growth: Chinese Style'. World Bank Policy Research Working Paper No. 3027.

Brandt, L. and Zhu, X. (2010). 'Accounting for China's Growth'. Institute for the Study of Labor (IZA), IZA Discussion Papers 4764. Bonn, Germany, pp. 1–59.

Brock, G. J. (1998). 'Foreign Direct Investment in Russia's Regions 1993–95. Why so Little and Where has it Gone?' *Economics of Transition*, 6/2: 349–60.

Brun, J. F., Combes, J. L., and Renard, M. F. (2002). 'Are There Spillover Effects Between Coastal and Noncoastal Regions in China'. *China Economic Review*, 13/2–3: 161–9.

Bull, C. (1987). 'The Existence of Self-enforcing Implicit Contracts'. *Quarterly Journal of Economics*, 102/1: 147–59.

Burt, R. S. (1992). *Structural Holes: The Social Structure of Competition*. Cambridge, Massachusetts: Harvard University Press.

Cabellero, R. J., Farhi, E., and Gourinchas, P.-O. (2008a). 'An Equilibrium Model of "Global Imbalances" and Low Interest Rates'. *American Economic Review*, 98/1: 358–93.

Cabellero, R. J., Farhi, E., and Gourinchas, P.-O. (2008b). 'Financial Crash, Commodity Prices, and Global Imbalances'. *Brookings Papers on Economic Activity*, 2: 1–55.

Cai, F., Du, Y., and Wang, M. (2001). '*Hukou* System and Labour Market Protection'. *Jingji Yanjiu*, 12: 41–9 (in Chinese).

Cain, G. G. (1976). 'The Challenge of Segmented Labor Market Theories to Orthodox Theory: A Survey'. *Journal of Economic Literature*, 14/4: 1215–57.

Carlin, W. and Soskice, D. (2005). *Macroeconomics*. Oxford: Oxford University Press.

Chamberlin, G. and Yueh, L. (2006). *Macroeconomics*, London: Cengage.

Chang, X. (1999). '"Fat pigs" and Women's Gifts: Agnatic and Non-agnatic Social Support in Kaixiangong Village', in J. West, M. Zhao, X. Chang, and Y. Cheng (eds.), W*omen of China: Economic and Social Transformation*. Basingstoke: Macmillan.

Chen, B., and Feng, Y. (2000). 'Determinants of Economic Growth in China: Private Enterprises, Education, and Openness'. *China Economic Review*, 11/1: 1–15.

Chen, C., Chang, L., and Zhang, Y. M. (1995). 'The Role of Foreign Direct Investment in China Post-1978 Economic Development'. *World Development*, 23/4: 691–703.

Chen, Z. (2003). 'Capital Markets and Legal Development: The China Case'. *China Economic Review*, 14/4: 451–72.

Cheung, K. and Lin, P. (2004). 'Spillover Effects of FDI on Innovation in China: Evidence from Provincial Data'. *China Economic Review*, 15/1: 25–44.

Chi, W. (2007). 'The Role of Human Capital in China's Economic Development: Review and New Evidence'. *China Economic Review*, 19/3: 421–36.

Chinn, M. D. and Ito, H. (2007). 'Current Account Balances, Financial Development and Institutions: Assaying the World "Saving Glut"'. *Journal of International Money and Finance*, 26/4: 546–69.

Chinn, M. D. and Ito, H. (2008). 'Global Current Account Imbalances: American Fiscal Policy Versus East Asian Savings'. *Review of International Economics*, 16/3: 479–98.

Choo, C. and Yin, X. (2000). 'Contract Management Responsibility System and Profit Incentives in China's State-owned Enterprises'. *China Economic Review*, 11/1: 98–112.

Chow, G. C. (1993). 'Capital Formation and Economic Growth in China'. *Quarterly Journal of Economics*, 108/3: 809–42.

Chow, G. C. and Lin, A. (2002). 'Accounting for Economic Growth in Taiwan and Mainland China: A Comparative Analysis'. *Journal of Comparative Economics*, 30/3: 507–30.

Chuang, Y. and Hsu, P. (2004). 'FDI, Trade, and Spillover Efficiency: Evidence from China's Manufacturing Sector'. *Applied Economics*, 36/10: 1103–15.

Clarke, D. C. (2003a). 'Economic Development and the Rights Hypothesis: The China Problem'. *American Journal of Comparative Law*, 51/1: 89–111.

Clarke, D. C. (2003b). 'China's Legal System and the WTO: Prospects for Compliance'. *Washington University Global Studies Law Review*, 2/1: 97–118.

Clarke, D. C. (2003c). 'Corporate Governance in China: An Overview'. *China Economic Review*, 14/4: 494–507.

Clarke, D. C. (2007). 'China: Creating a Legal System for a Market Economy'. The George Washington University Law School Legal Studies Research Paper No. 396, pp. 1–32.

Coase, R. (1937). 'The Nature of the Firm'. *Economica*, 4/16: 386–405.

Coe, D. and Helpman, E. (1995). 'International R&D Spillover'. *European Economic Review*, 39/5: 859–87.

Coffee, Jr., J. C. (2001). 'The Rise of Dispersed Ownership: The Roles of Law and the States in the Separation of Ownership and Control'. *Yale Law Journal*, 111/1: 1–82.

Collier, P. and Knight, J. (1985). 'Seniority Payments, Quit Rates and Internal Labour Markets in Britain and Japan'. *Oxford Bulletin of Economics and Statistics*, 47: 19–32.

Cordell, D. D., Gregory, J. W., and Piche, V. (1998). *Hoe and Wage: A Social History of a Circular Migration System in West Africa*. Boulder, Colorado: Westview Press.

Cragg, J. G. and Donald, S. G. (1993). 'Testing Identifiability and Specification in Instrumental Variable Models'. *Econometric Theory*, 9: 222–40.

Cull, R. and Xu, L. C. (2005). 'Institutions, Ownership, and Finance: The Determinants of Profit Reinvestment among Chinese Firms'. *Journal of Financial Economics*, 77/1: 117–46.

Dam, K. W. (2006). *The Law-Growth Nexus—The Rule of Law and Economic Development*. Washington, DC: The Brookings Institution.

Dasgupta, P. (2000). 'Economic Progress and the Idea of Social Capital', in P. Dasgupta and I. Serageldin (eds.), *Social Capital: A Multifaceted Perspective*. Washington, DC: The World Bank.

Dasgupta, P. and Serageldin, I. (eds.). (2000). *Social Capital: A Multifaceted Perspective*. Washington, DC: The World Bank.

Deaton, A. (1989). 'Looking for Boy-Girl Discrimination in Household Expenditure Data'. *World Bank Economic Review*, 3/1: 1–15.

Dees, S. (1998). 'Foreign Direct Investment in China: Determinants and Effects'. *Economics Planning*, 31/2–3: 175–94.

Demsetz, H. and Villalonga, B. (2001). 'Ownership Structure and Corporate Perform-ance'. *Journal of Corporate Finance*, 7: 209–33.

Démurger, S. (2001). 'Infrastructure Development and Economic Growth: An Explan-ation for Regional Disparities in China'. *Journal of Comparative Economics*, 29/1: 95–117.

Dickens, W. T. and Lang, K. (1988). 'The Re-emergence of Segmented Labour Market Theory'. *American Economic Review*, 78/2: 129–34.

Djankov, A. and Hoekman, B. M. (2000). 'Foreign Investment and Productivity Growth in Czech Enterprises'. *World Bank Economic Review*, 14/1: 49–64.

Djankov, S. and Murrell, P. (2000). *The Determinants of Enterprise Restructuring in Transi-tion: An Assessment of the Evidence*. Washington, DC: World Bank.

Djankov, S., Qian, Y., Roland, G., and Zhuravskaya, E. (2006). 'Who are China's Entrepreneurs?' *American Economic Review Paper and Proceedings*, 96/2: 348–52.

Dobson, W. and Safarian, A. E. (2008). 'The Transition from Imitation to Innovation: An Enquiry into China's Evolving Institutions and Firm Capabilities'. *Journal of Asian Economics*, 19/3: 301–11.

Dong, X., Putterman, L., and Unel, B. (2006). 'Privatization and Firm Performance: A Comparison Between Rural and Urban Enterprises in China'. *Journal of Comparative Economics*, 34/3: 608–33.

Dornbusch, R. (1980). *Open Economy Macroeconomics*. New York: Basic Books.

Dougherty, S., Herd, R., and He, P. (2007). 'Has a Private Sector Emerged in China's Industry? Evidence From a Quarter of a Million Chinese Firms'. *China Economic Review*, 18/3: 309–34.

Du, J. and Xu, C. (2009). 'Which Firms went Public in China? A Study of Financial Market Regulation'. *World Development* (Special Issue on Law, Finance, and Economic Growth in China), 37/4: 812–24.

Durlauf, S. N. (2002). 'On the Empirics of Social Capital'. *Economic Journal*, 112/483: F459–79.

Earl, J. and Estrin, S. (2003). 'Privatization, Competition, and Budget Constraints: Disciplining Enterprises in Russia'. *Economics of Planning*, 36: 1–22.

Eaton, J. and Kortum, S. (1996). 'Trade in Idea: Patenting and Productivity in the OECD'. *Journal of International Economics*, 40/3–4: 251–78.

Estrin, S. (2002). 'Competition and Corporate Governance in Transition'. *Journal of Economic Perspectives*, 16/1: 101–24.

Evans, D. and Leighton, L. (1989). 'Some Empirical Aspects of Entrepreneurship'. *American Economic Review*, 79: 519–35.

Fafchamps, M. and Minten, B. (2002). 'Returns to Social Network Capital Among Traders'. *Oxford Economic Papers*, 54/2: 173–206.

Fan, G. (1994). 'Incremental Change and Dual-track Transition: Understanding the Case of China'. *Economic Policy*, 19/Supp: 99–122.

Fan, J. P. H., Morck, R., Xu, L. C., and Yeung, B. (2009). 'Institutions and Foreign Direct Investment: China versus the Rest of the World'. *World Development*, 37/4: 852–65.

Farber, H. S. (1999). 'Mobility and Stability: The Dynamics of Job Change in Labor Markets', in O. Ashenfelter and D. Card (eds.), *Handbook of Labor Economics*, vol. 3B, ch 37. Amsterdam: Elsevier.

Felmingham, B. S. and Zhang, Q. (2002). 'The Role of FDI, Exports and Spillover Effects in the Regional Development of China'. *Journal of Development Studies*, 38/4: 157–78.

Fleisher, B. and Chen, J. (1997). 'The Coast–Noncoast Income Gap, Productivity, and Regional Economic Policy in China'. *Journal of Comparative Economics*, 25/2: 220–36.

Fleisher, B., Li, H., and Zhao, M. Q. (2010). 'Human Capital, Economic Growth, and Regional Inequality in China'. *Journal of Development Economics*, 92/2: 215–31.

Fleisher, B., and Wang, X. J. (2001). 'Efficiency Wages and Work Incentives in Urban and Rural China'. *Journal of Comparative Economics*, 29/4: 645–62.

Fleisher, B., and Wang, X. J. (2004). 'Skill Differentials, Return to Schooling, and Market Segmentation in a Transition Economy: The Case of Mainland China'. *Journal of Development Economics*, 73/1: 315–28.

Franks, J. R., Mayer, C., and Rossi, S. (2009). 'Ownership: Evolution and Control'. *Review of Financial Studies*, 22/10: 4009–56.

Frye, T. and Zhuravskaya, E. (2000). 'Rackets, Regulation and the Rule of Law'. *Journal of Law, Economics and Organization*, 16/2: 478–502.

Fujita, M., Krugman, P., and Venables, A. J. (1999). *The Spatial Economy: Cities, Regions, and International Trade*. Cambridge, Massachusetts: MIT Press.

Gaetano, A. R. and Jacka, T. (2004). *On The Move: Women and Rural-to-Urban Migration in Contemporary China*. New York: Columbia University Press.

Garnaut, R., Song, L. G., Yao, Y., and Wang, X. L. (2001). *The Emerging Private Enterprise in China*. Canberra: National University of Australia Press.

Gedajlovic, E. R. and Shapiro, D. M. (1998). 'Management and Ownership Effects: Evidence from Five Countries'. *Strategic Management Journal*, 19: 533–53.

Gemmell, N. (1996). 'Evaluating the Impacts of Human Capital Stocks and Accumulation on Economic Growth: Some New Evidence'. *Oxford Bulletin of Economics and Statistics*, 58/1: 9–28.

Giles, J., Park, A., and Zhang, J. (2005). 'What is China's True Unemployment Rate?' *China Economic Review*, 16/2: 149–70.

Glaeser, E., La Porta, R., Lopez-de-Silanes, F., and Shleifer, A. (2004). 'Do Institutions Cause Growth?' *Journal of Economic Growth*, 9/3: 271–303.

Glaeser, E. L., Laibson, D., and Sacerdote, B. (2002). 'The Economic Approach to Social Capital'. *Economic Journal*, 112/483: F437–58.

Gompers, P., Lerner, J., and Scharfstein, D. (2005). 'Entrepreneurial Spawning: Public Corporations and the Genesis of New Ventures, 1986–1999'. *Journal of Finance*, 60/2: 577–614.

Graham, E. M. and Wada, E. (2001). 'Foreign Direct Investment in China: Effects on Growth and Economic Performance'. *Institute for International Economics Working Paper No. 01–03*.

Granovetter, M. (1995 [1974]). *Getting a Job: A Study of Contacts and Careers*. Chicago: University of Chicago Press.

Greif, A. (1993). 'Contract Enforceability and Economic Institutions in Early Trade: The Maghribi Traders' Coalition'. *American Economic Review*, 83/3: 525–48.

Greene, W. H. (2003). *Econometric Analysis*. New Jersey: Pearson.

Greenwald, B. and Stiglitz, J. (1988). 'Pareto Inefficiency of Market Economies: Search and Efficiency Wage Models'. *American Economic Review*, 78: 351–5.

Grossman, G. M. and Helpman, E. (1991). *Innovation and Growth in the Global Economy*. Cambridge, Massachusetts: MIT Press.

Groves, T., Hong, Y., McMillan, J., and Naughton, B. (1995). 'China's Evolving Managerial Market'. *Journal of Political Economy*, 103/4: 873–92.

Guiso, L., Sapienza, P., and Zingales, L. (2004). 'Does Local Financial Development Matter'. *Quarterly Journal of Economics*, 119/3: 929–69.

Gylfason, T. (1999). 'Exports, Inflation and Growth'. *World Development*, 27/6: 1031–57.

Haddad, L., Hoddinott, J., and Alderman, H. (eds.) (1997). *Intrahousehold Resource Allocation in Developing Countries: Models, Methods and Policy*. Baltimore: Johns Hopkins University Press.

Haddad, M. and Harrison, A. E. (1993). 'Are There Positive Spillovers from Direct Foreign Investment? Evidence from Panel Data for Morocco'. *Journal of Development Economics*, 42: 51–74.

Hamermesh, L. A. (2006). 'The Policy Foundations of Delaware Corporate Law'. *Columbia Law Review*, 106/7: 1749–92.

Hansen, L. P. (1982), 'Large Sample Properties of Generalized Methods of Moments Estimators'. *Econometrica*, 50/4: 1029—54

Hansmann, H. and Kraakman, R. (2001). 'The End of History for Corporate Law?' *Georgetown Law Journal*, 89/2: 439–68.

Hao, C. (2006). 'Development of Financial Intermediation and Economic Growth: The Chinese Experience'. *China Economic Review*, 17/4: 347–62.

Hare, D. (1999). 'Push Versus Pull Factors in Migration Outflows and Returns: Determinants of Migration Status and Spell Duration among China's Rural Population'. *Journal of Development Studies*, 35/3: 45–72.

Harrold, P. (1995). 'China: Foreign Trade Reform: Now for the Hard Part'. *Oxford Review of Economic Policy*, 11/4: 133–46.

Hasan, I., Wachtel, P., and Zhou, M. (2009). 'Institutional Development, Financial Deepening and Economic Growth: Evidence from China'. *Journal of Banking & Finance*, 33/1: 157–70.

Hashimoto, M. and Raisian, J. (1985). 'Employment Tenure and Earnings Profiles in Japan and the United States'. *American Economic Review*, 75: 721–35.

Hay, D., Morris, D., Liu, G., and Yao, S. (1994). *Economic Reform and State-Owned Enterprises in China 1979–87*. Oxford: Oxford University Press.

Himmelberg, C. P., Hubbard, R. G., and Palia, D. (1999). 'Understanding the Determinants of Managerial Ownership and the Link Between Ownership and Performance'. *Journal of Financial Economics*, 53: 353–84.

Ho, P. (2006). *Institutions in Transition: Land Ownership, Property Rights and Social Conflict in China*. Oxford: Oxford University Press.

Hoff, K. and Stiglitz, J. E. (2004). 'After the Big Bang? Obstacles to the Emergence of the Rule of Law in Post-Communist Societies'. *American Economic Review*, 94/3: 753–63.

Holtz-Eakin, D., Joulfaian, D., and Rosen, H. S. (1994). 'Entrepreneurial Decisions and Liquidity Constraints'. *Rand Journal of Economics*, 25/2: 334–47.

Horwitz, M. J. (1992). *The Transformation of American Law, 1870–1960: The Crisis of Legal Orthodoxy*. Oxford: Oxford University Press.

Hosios, A. J. (1990). 'On the Efficiency of Matching and Related Models of Search and Unemployment'. *Review of Economic Studies*, 57: 279–98.

Howitt, P. and Aghion, P. (1998). 'Capital Accumulation and Innovation as Complementary Factors in Long-Run Growth'. *Journal of Economic Growth*, 3/2: 111–30.

Hu, A. G. Z. and Jefferson, G. H. (2009). 'A Great Wall of Patents: What is Behind China's Recent Patent Explosion'. *Journal of Development Economics*, 90/1: 57–68.

Hu, A. G. Z., Jefferson, G. H., and Qian, J. (2005). 'R&D and Technology Transfer: Firm Level Evidence from Chinese Industry'. *Review of Economics and Statistics*, 87/4: 780–6.

Hu, Y. and Zhou, X. (2006). 'Managerial Ownership Matters for Firm Performance: Evidence from China'. *Journal of Banking and Finance*, 32/10: 2099–110.

Hu, Z. L. and Khan, M. S. (1997). 'Why Is China Growing So Fast'. IMF Staff papers, 44/1: 103–31.

Hua, J., Miesing, P., and Li, M. (2006). 'An Empirical Taxonomy of SOE Governance in Transitional China'. *Journal of Management Governance*, 10: 401–33.

Huang, J. and Rozelle, S. (1996). 'Technological Change: The Re-discovery of the Engine of Productivity Growth in China's Rural Economy'. *Journal of Development Economics*, 49/2: 337–69.

Huang, L. and Yao, Y. (2010). 'Impacts of Privatization on Employment: Evidence from China'. *Journal of Chinese Economic and Business Studies*, 8/2: 133–56.

Huang, Y. (2003). 'One Country, Two Systems: Foreign-invested Enterprises and Domestic Firms in China'. *China Economic Review*, 14/4: 404–16.

Huang, Y. (2006). *Selling China*. Cambridge: Cambridge University Press.

Huang, Y. and Wang, X. (2011). 'Does Financial Repression Inhibit or Facilitate Economic Growth? A Case Study of Chinese Reform Experience'. *Oxford Bulletin of Economics and Statistics*, 73/6: 833–55.

Hugo, G. (1982). 'Circular Migration in Indonesia'. *Population and Development Review*, 8/1: 59–84.

Imbens, G. W. (2004). 'Nonparametric Estimation of Average Treatment Effects Under Exogeneity: A Review'. *Review of Economics and Statistics*, 86/1: 4–29.

International Monetary Fund (IMF) (2009). *Global Stability Report*. Washington, DC: IMF.

Islam, N. (1995). 'Growth Empirics: A Panel Data Approach'. *Quarterly Journal of Economics*, 110/4: 1127–70.

Islam, N., Dai, E., and Sakamoto, H. (2006). 'Role of TFP in China's Growth'. *Asian Economic Journal*, 20/2: 127–59.

Javorick, B. (2004). 'Does Foreign Direct Investment Increase the Productivity of Domestic Firms? In Search of Spillovers Through Backward Linkages'. *American Economic Review*, 94/3: 605–27.

Jefferson, G. H., Hu, A. G. Z., and Su, J. (2006). 'The Sources and Sustainability of China's Economic Growth'. *Brookings Papers on Economic Activity*, 37/2: 1–60.

Jefferson, G. H. and Rawski, T. G. (1994). 'Enterprise Reform in Chinese Industry'. *Journal of Economic Perspectives*, 8/2: 47–70

Jefferson, G. H. and Rawski, T. G. (2002). 'China's Emerging Market for Property Rights'. *Economics of Transition*, 10/3: 58–617.

Jefferson, G. H., Rawski, T. G., Li, W., and Zheng, Y. (2000). 'Ownership, Productivity Change, and Financial Performance in Chinese Industry'. *Journal of Comparative Economics*, 28/4: 786–813.

Jefferson, G. H., Rawski, T. G., and Zheng, Y. (1992). 'Growth, Efficiency, and Convergence in China's State and Collective Industry'. *Journal of Comparative Economics*, 40/2: 239–66.

Jefferson, G. H. and Su, J. (2006). 'Privatization and Restructuring in China: Evidence from Shareholding Ownership, 1995–2001'. *Journal of Comparative Economics*, 34/1: 146–66.

Jones, C. I. (1995). 'R&D-Based Models of Economic Growth'. *Journal of Political Economy*, 103: 759–84.

Jones, W. C. (2003). 'Trying to Understand the Current Chinese Legal System', in C. S. Hsu (ed.), *Understanding China's Legal System: Essays in Honor of Jerome A. Cohen*. New York and London: New York University Press.

Kaplinsky, R. (2006). 'Revisiting the Terms of Trade Revisited: What Difference does China Make?' *World Development*, 34/6: 981–95.

Kaufmann, D., Kraay, A., and Mastruzzi, M. (2007). 'Governance Matters VI: Governance Indicators for 1996–2006'. World Bank Policy Research Working Paper No. 4280.

Keith, K. (1993). 'Reputation, Voluntary Mobility and Wages'. *Review of Economics and Statistics*, 75: 559–63.

Keller, W. (2000). 'Do Trade Patterns and Technology Flows Affect Productivity Growth'. *World Bank Economic Review*, 14/1: 17–47.

Kim, K. S. (1981). 'Enterprise Performance in the Public and Private Sector: Tanzanian Experience, 1970–75'. *Journal of Developing Areas*, 15: 471–84.

King, A. G. (1974). 'Occupational Choice, Risk Aversion, and Wealth'. *Industrial and Labor Relations Review*, 27/4: 586–96.

Kipnis, A. B. (1997). *Producing Guanxi*. Durham, North Carolina: Duke University Press.

Knack, S. and Keefer P. (1997). 'Does Social Capital have an Economic Payoff? A Cross-country Investigation'. *Quarterly Journal of Economics*, 112/4: 1251–88.

Knight, J. and Li, S. (2006). 'Unemployment Duration and Earnings of Re-employed Workers in Urban China'. *China Economic Review*, 17/2: 103–19.

Knight, J. and Song, L. (1995). 'Towards a Labour Market in China'. *Oxford Review of Economic Policy*, 11: 97–117.

Knight, J. and Song, L. (1999). *The Rural-Urban Divide: Economic Disparities and Interactions in China*. Oxford: Oxford University Press.

Knight, J. and Song, L. (2003). 'Chinese Peasant Choices: Migration, Rural Industry or Farming'. *Oxford Development Studies*, 31/2: 123–47.

Knight, J., Song, L., and Jia, H. (1999). 'Chinese Rural Migrants in Urban Enterprises: Three Perspectives'. *Journal of Development Studies*, 35/3: 73–104.

Knight, J. and Xue, J. (2006). 'How High is Urban Unemployment in China?' *Journal of Chinese Economic and Business Studies*, 4/2: 91–107.

Knight, J. and Yueh, L. (2004). 'Job Mobility of Residents and Migrants in Urban China'. *Journal of Comparative Economics*, 32/4: 637–60.

Kokko, A. (1996). 'Productivity Spillovers from Competition Between Local Firms and Foreign Affiliates'. *Journal of International Development*, 8: 517–30.

Komter, A. (2005). *Social Solidarity and the Gift*. Cambridge: Cambridge University Press.

Konings, J. (2001). 'The Effects of Foreign Direct Investment on Domestic Firms—Evidence from Firm-level Panel Data in Emerging Economies'. *Economics of Transition*, 9/3: 619–33.

Kornai, J. (1992). *The Socialist System*. Oxford: Clarendon Press.

Koo, A. Y. C. (1990). 'The Contract Responsibility System: Transition from a Planned to a Market Economy'. *Economic Development and Cultural Change*, 38/4: 797–820.

Kraay, A. (2006). 'Exports and Economic Performance: Evidence from a Panel of Chinese Enterprises', in B. M. Hoekman and B. Javorcik (eds.), *Global Integration and Technology Transfer*. Washington, DC: The World Bank, pp. 139–60.

Krueger, A. B. and Lindahl, M. (2001). 'Education for Growth: Why and For Whom'. *Journal of Economic Literature*, 39/4: 1101–36.

Kuo, C. C. and Yang, C. H. (2008). 'Knowledge Capital and Spillover on Regional Economic Growth: Evidence from China'. *China Economic Review*, 19/4: 594–604.

La Porta, R., Lopez-de-Silanes, F., Shleifer, A., and Vishny, R. (1997). 'Legal Determinants of External Finance'. *Journal of Finance*, 54/20: 1131–50.

La Porta, R., Lopez-de-Silanes, F., Shleifer, A., and Vishny, R. W. (1998). 'Law and Finance'. *Journal of Political Economy*, 106/6: 1113–55.

La Porta, R., Lopez-de-Silanes, F., Shleifer, A., and Vishny, R. W. (2000). 'Investor Protection and Corporate Governance'. *Journal of Financial Economics*, 58/1–2: 3–27.

Lai, M., Peng, S., and Bao, Q. (2006). 'Technology Spillovers, Absorptive Capacity and Economic Growth'. *China Economic Review*, 17/3: 300–20.

Lall, S. (1978). 'Transnationals, Domestic Enterprises, and Industrial Structure in Host LDCs: A Survey'. *Oxford Economic Papers*, 30/2: 217–48.

Lall, S. and Albaladejo, M. (2004). 'China's Competitive Performance: A Threat to East Asian Manufactured Exports?' *World Development*, 32/9: 1441–66.

Lall S. and Weiss, J. (2005). 'China's Competitive Threat to Latin America: An Analysis for 1990–2002'. University of Oxford, Queen Elizabeth House Working Paper No. 120.

Lam, K. J. (2003). 'Earnings Advantages of Party Members in Urban China'. Business Research Centre Working Paper, Department of Economics, Hong Kong Baptist University, Hong Kong, China.

Lardy, N. R. (1998). *China's Unfinished Economic Revolution*. Washington, DC: Brookings Institution Press.

Lardy, N. R. (2002). *Integrating China into the Global Economy*. Washington DC: Brookings Institution Press.

Lardy, N. R. (2008). 'Financial Repression in China'. Peterson Institute of International Economics, Washington DC, Policy Brief No. 8.

Lau, L.J., Qian, Y., and Roland, G. (2001). 'Reform Without Losers: An Interpretation of China's Dual-track Approach to Transition'. *Journal of Political Economy*, 108/1: 120–43.

Lee, C. K. (1998). *Gender and the South China Miracle: Two Worlds of Factory Women*. Berkeley: University of California Press.

Lemoine, F. (2000). 'FDI and the Opening up of China's Economy'. *CEPII Working Paper*, 2000–11.

Levine, R. (1997). 'Financial Development and Economic Growth: Views and Agenda'. *Journal of Economic Literature*, 35/June: 688–726.

Levine, R. (1998). 'The Legal Environment, Banks, and Long-run Economic Growth'. *Journal of Money, Credit, and Banking*, 30/3 (Part 2): 596–613.

Levine R. and Renelt, D. (1992). 'A Sensitivity Analysis of Cross-country Growth Regressions'. *American Economic Review*, 82/4: 942–63.

Levinsohn, J. and Petrin, A. (2003). 'Estimating Production Functions Using Inputs to Control for Unobservables'. *Review of Economic Studies*, 70/2: 317–41.

Li, B. (2005). 'Urban Social Change in Transitional China: A Perspective of Social Exclusion and Vulnerability'. *Journal of Contingencies and Crisis Management*, 13/2: 54–65.

Li, D. (2001). 'Beating the Trap of Financial Repression in China'. *Cato Journal*, 21/1: 77–90.

Li, H. and Huang, L. (2009). 'Health, Education, and Economic Growth in China: Empirical Findings and Implications'. *China Economic Review*, 20/3: 374–87.

Li, H., Liu, P., Zhang, J., and Ma, N. (2007). 'Economic Returns to Communist Party Membership: Evidence from Chinese Twins'. *Economic Journal*, 117/523: 1504–20.

Li, H. and Rozelle, S. (2003). 'Privatizing Rural China: Insider Privatization, Innovative Contracts and the Performance of Township Enterprises'. *China Quarterly*, 176: 981–1005.

Li, S. and Sato, H. (eds). (2006). *Unemployment, Inequality and Poverty in Urban China*. London and New York: Routledge.

Li, X. and Liu, X. (2005). 'Foreign Direct Investment and Economic Growth: An Increasingly Endogenous Relationship'. *World Development*, 33/3: 393–407.

Li, X. and Yueh, L. (2011). 'Does Incorporation Improve Firm Performance?' *Oxford Bulletin of Economics and Statistics*, 73/6: 753–70.

Liang, Z. (2005). 'Financial Development, Marekt Deregulation and Growth: Evidence from China'. *Journal of Chinese Economic and Business Studies*, 3/3: 247–62.

Lin, C. (2001). 'Corporatisation and Corporate Governance in China's Economic Transition'. *Economics of Planning*, 34: 5–35.

Lin, J. Y. F. (1992). 'Rural Reforms and Agricultural Growth in China'. *American Economic Review*, 82/1: 34–51.

Lin, J. Y. F. (2007). 'Developing Small and Medium Banks to Improve Financial Structure'. China Centre for Economic Research, Peking University, Working Paper (in Chinese).

Lin, J. Y. F., Cai, F., and Zhou, L. (2003). *The China Miracle: Development Strategy and Economic Reform*. Hong Kong: Chinese University Press.

Liu, T. and Li, K. (2001). 'Impact of Liberalization of Financial Resources in China's Economic Growth: Evidence from the Provinces'. *Journal of Asian Economics*, 12/2: 245–62.

Liu, X., Burridge, P., and Sinclair, P. J. N. (2002). 'Relationship between Economic Growth, Foreign Direct Investment and Trade: Evidence from China'. *Applied Economics*, 34/11: 1433–40.

Liu, Z. (2003). 'The Economic Impact and Determinants of Investment in Human and Political Capital in China'. *Economic Development and Cultural Change*, 51/4: 823–49.

Liu, Z. (2009a). 'The External Returns to Education: Evidence from Chinese Cities'. *Journal of Urban Economics*, 61/3: 542–64.

Liu, Z. (2009b). 'Human Capital Externalities and Rural–Urban Migration: Evidence from Rural China'. *China Economic Review*, 19/3: 521–35.

Liu, Z. (2009c). 'Foreign Direct Investment and Technology Spillovers: Theory and Evidence'. *Journal of Development Economics*, 85/1–2: 176–93.

Long, C. (2010). 'Does the Rights Hypothesis Apply to China?' *Journal of Law and Economics*, 53/4: 629–50.

Lu, F. S. and Yao, Y. (2009). 'The Effectiveness of the Law, Financial Development, and Economic Growth in an Economy of Financial Repression: Evidence from China'. *World Development* (Special Issue on Law, Finance, and Economic Growth in China), 37/4: 736–77.

Lucas, R. E. (1988). 'On the Mechanics of Economic Development'. *Journal of Monetary Economics*, 22/1: 3–42.

McConnell, J. J. and Servaes, H. (1990). 'Additional Evidence on Equity Ownership and Corporate Value'. *Journal of Financial Economics*, 27: 595–612.

McKibbin, W. and Stoeckel, A. (2010). 'The Global Financial Crisis: Causes and Consequences'. *Asian Economic Papers*, 9/1: 54–86.

McMillan, J. (1997). 'Markets in Transition', in D. M. Kreps and K. F. Wallis (eds.), *Advances in Economics and Econometrics* vol. 2. Cambridge: Cambridge University Press.

Maddison, A. (2001). *The World Economy: A Millennial Perspective*. Paris: OECD.

Mankiw, N. G., Romer, D., and Weil, D. (1992). 'A Contribution to the Empirics of Economic Growth'. *Quarterly Journal of Economics*, 107/2: 407–37.

Markusen, J. R. and Venables, A. J. (1999). 'Foreign Direct Investment as a Catalyst for Economic Development'. *European Economic Review*, 43/2: 335–56.

Meng, X. and Zhang, J. (2001). 'The Two-tier Labor Market in Urban China'. *Journal of Comparative Economics*, 29/3: 485–504.

Mincer, J. (1974). *Schooling, Experience, and Earnings*. New York: Columbia University Press.

Mincer, J. and Higuchi, Y. (1988). 'Wage Structures and Labor Turnover in the United States and Japan'. *Journal of the Japanese and International Economies*, 2: 97–133.

Mohapatra, S., Rozelle, S., and Goodhue, R. (2007). 'The Rise of Self-employment in Rural China: Development or Distress?' *World Development*, 35/1: 163–81.

Montgomery, J. D. (1991). 'Social Networks and Labor-Market Outcomes: Toward an Economic Analysis'. *American Economic Review*, 81: 1408–18.

Mortensen, D. T. and Vishwanath, T. (1994). 'Personal Contacts and Earnings: It's Who You Know!' *Labour Economics*, 1: 187–201.

Murphy, K. M., Shleifer, A., and Vishny, R. W. (1992). 'The Transition to a Market Economy: Pitfalls of Partial Reform'. *Quarterly Journal of Economics*, 107/3: 889–906.

Narayan, D. and Pritchett, L. (1999). 'Cents and Sociability: Household Income and Social Capital in Rural Tanzania.' *Economic Development and Cultural Change*, 47/4: 871–97.

Naughton, B. (1995). *Growing Out of the Plan: Chinese Economic Reform, 1978–1993.* Cambridge: Cambridge University Press.

Nee, V. (1989). 'A Theory of Market Transition: From Redistribution to Market in State Socialism'. *American Sociological Review*, 54: 663–81.

Nee, V. (1996). 'The Emergence of a Market Society: Changing Mechanisms of Stratification in China'. *American Journal of Sociology*, 101: 908–49.

North, D. (1990). *Institutions, Institutional Change and Economic Performance.* Cambridge: Cambridge University Press.

OECD (2002). *China in the World Economy: The Domestic Policy Challenges.* Paris: OECD.

OECD (2004). *OECD Principles of Corporate Governance.* Paris: OECD.

OECD (2005). *OECD Economic Surveys of China.* Paris: OECD.

Oi, J. C. (1989). *State and Peasant in Contemporary China: The Political Economy of Village Government.* Berkeley: University of California Press.

Oi, J. C. (1999). *Rural China Takes Off: Institutional Foundations of Economic Reform.* Berkeley: University of California Press.

Pagano, M. (1993). 'Financial Markets and Growth: An Overview'. *European Economic Review*, 37/2–3: 613–22.

Pei, M. X. (2001). 'Does Legal Reform Protect Economic Transactions? Commercial Disputes in China', in P. Murrell (ed.), *Assessing the Value of Law in Transition Countries.* Ann Arbor: University of Michigan Press, 180–210.

Persson, T. and Tabellini, G. (2006). 'Democracy and Development'. *American Economic Review*, 96/2: 319–24.

Pissarides, C. A. (1994). 'Search Unemployment with On-the-job Search'. *Review of Economic Studies*, 61: 457–75.

Pistor, K. (2002). 'The Standardization of Law and its Effect on Developing Economies'. *American Journal of Comparative Law*, 1/Winter: 97–130.

Pistor, K., Keinan, Y., Kleinheisterkamp, J., and West, M. D. (2003). 'The Evolution of Corporate Law: A Cross-country Comparison'. *University of Pennsylvania Journal of International Economic Law*, 23/4: 791–871.

Pistor, K., Martin R., and Gelfer S. (2000). 'Law and Finance in Transition Economies'. *Economics of Transition*, 8/2: 325–68.

Pistor, K. and Xu, C. (2005). 'Governing Stock Markets in Transition Economies: Lessons from China'. *American Law and Economics Review*, 7/1: 1–27.

Pivovarsky, A. (2003). 'Ownership Concentration and Performance in Ukraine's Privatised Enterprises'. IMF Staff Papers, 50: 1–42.

Pomfret, R. (1997). 'Growth and Transition: Why Has China's Performance Been so Different'. *Journal of Comparative Economics*, 25/3: 422–40.

Portes, A. (1998). 'Social Capital: Its Origins and Applications in Modern Sociology'. *Annual Review of Sociology*, 24: 1–24.

Prasad, E. S. and Rajan, R. G. (2006). 'Modernizing China's Growth Program'. *American Economic Review*, 92/2: 331–6.

Pritchett, L. (2001). 'Where Has All the Education Gone'. *World Bank Economic Review*, 15/3: 367–91.

Putnam, R. D., Leonardi, R., and Nanetti, R. Y. (1993). *Making Democracy Work*. Princeton: Princeton University Press.

Qian, X. and Smyth, R. (2006). 'Growth Accounting for the Chinese Provinces 1990–2000: Incorporating Human Capital Accumulation'. *Journal of Chinese Economic and Business Studies*, 4/1: 21–37.

Qian, Y. and Xu, C. (1993). 'The M-form Hierarchy and China's Economic Reform'. *European Economic Review*, 37: 541–8.

Rajan, R. G. (2010). *Fault Lines*. Princeton and Oxford: Princeton University Press.

Rajan, R. G. and Zingales, L. (1998). 'Financial Dependence and Growth'. *American Economic Review*, 88/3: 559–86.

Ran, J., Voon, J. P., and Li, G. (2007). 'How Does FDI Affect China? Evidence from Industries and Provinces'. *Journal of Comparative Economics*, 35/4: 744–99.

Rebick, M. E. (2000). 'The Importance of Networks in the Market for University Graduates in Japan: A Longitudinal Analysis of Hiring Patterns'. *Oxford Economic Papers*, 52/3: 471–96.

Rees, H. and Shah, A. (1986). 'An Empirical Analysis of Self-employment in the UK'. *Journal of Applied Econometrics*, 1/1: 95–108.

Riedel, J., Jin, J., and Gao, J. (2007). *How China Grows: Investment, Finance, and Reform*. Princeton and Oxford: Princeton University Press.

Riskin, C. (1987). *China's Political Economy: The Quest for Development Since 1949*. Oxford: Oxford University Press.

Rodríguez-Clare, A. (1996). 'Multinationals, Linkages, and Economic Development'. *American Economic Review*, 86/4: 852–73.

Rodrik, D. (1999). 'The New Global Economy and Developing Countries: Making Openness Work'. Overseas Development Council (Baltimore, Maryland) Policy Essay No. 24.

Rodrik, D., Subramanian, A., and Trebbi, F. (2004). 'Institutions Rule: The Primacy of Institutions over Geography and Integration in Economic Development'. *Journal of Economic Growth*, 9/2: 139–65.

Rogoff, K. (2006). 'Impact of Globalization on Monetary Policy', paper presented at the symposium sponsored by the Federal Reserve Bank of Kansas City on 'The New Economic Geography: Effects and Policy Implications', Jackson Hole, Wyoming, August 2006.

Romer, P. M. (1986). 'Increasing Returns and Long-run Growth'. *Journal of Political Economy*, 94/5: 1002–37.

Romer, P. M. (1990). 'Endogenous Technological Change'. *Journal of Political Economy*, 98/5: S71–102.

Roubini, N. and Sala-i-Martin, X. (1992). 'Financial Repression and Economic Growth'. *Journal of Development Economics*, 39/1: 5–30.

Rousseau, P. L. and Wachtel, P. (2000). 'Equity Markets and Growth: Cross Country Evidence on Timing and Outcomes, 1980–95'. *Journal of Banking and Finance*, 24/12: 1933–57.

Rousseau, P. L., and Xiao, S. (2007). 'Banks, Stock Markets and China's Great Leap Forward'. *Emerging Markets Review*, 8/3: 206–11.

Shan, J. (2002). 'A VAR Approach to the Economies of FDI in China'. *Applied Economics*, 34/7: 885–93.

Shen, Y., Shen, M., Xu, Z., and Bai, Y. (2009). 'Bank Size and Small and Medium-sized Enterprise (SME) Lending: Evidence from China'. *World Development* (Special Issue on Law, Finance, and Economic Growth in China), 37/4: 800–11.

Shirley, M. M. (1999). 'Bureaucrats in Business: The Roles of Privatization Versus Corporatization in State-owned Enterprise Reform'. *World Development*, 27/1: 115–36.

Smith, R. J. and Blundell, R. W. (1986). 'An Exogeneity Test for a Simultaneous Equation Tobit Model with an Application to Labor Supply'. *Econometrica*, 54/3: 679–86.

Solinger, D. J. (1999). *Contesting Citizenship in Urban China: Peasant Migrants, the State, and the Logic of the Market*. Berkeley: University of California Press.

Solinger, D. (2004). 'Policy Consistency in the Midst of Crisis: Managing the Furloughed and the Farmers in Three Cities', in B. Naughton and D. Yang (eds.), *Holding China Together: Diversity and National Integration in the Post-Deng Era*. Cambridge: Cambridge University Press.

Solow, R. (1956). 'A Contribution to the Theory of Economic Growth'. *Quarterly Journal of Economics*, 70: 65–94.

Song, L. and Yao, Y. (2004). 'Impacts of Privatization on Firm Performance in China'. Peking University, China Centre for Economic Research (CCER), Working Paper Series, No. E2004005.

Sonobe, T., Hu, D., and Otsuka, K. (2004). 'From Inferior to Superior Products: An Inquiry into the Wenzhou Model of Industrial Development in China'. *Journal of Comparative Economics*, 32/3: 542–63.

Staiger, D. and Stock, J. H. (1997). 'Instrumental Variable Regression with Weak Instruments'. *Econometrica*, 65/3: 557–86.

Stock, J. H. and Yogo, M. (2005). 'Testing for Weak Instruments in Linear IV Regression', in D. W. K. Andrews and J. H. Stock (eds.), *Identification and Inference for Econometric Models: Essays in Honor of Thomas Rothenberg*. Cambridge: Cambridge University Press, 80–108.

Sun, H. S. and Parikh, A. (2001). 'Exports, Inward Foreign Direct Investment and Regional Economic Growth in China'. *Regional Studies*, 35/3, 187–96.

Sun, L. and Tobin, D. (2009). 'International Listing as a Means to Mobilize the Benefits of Financial Globalization: Micro-level Evidence from China'. *World Development* (Special Issue on Law, Finance, and Economic Growth in China), 37/4: 825–38.

Sun, Q. and Tong, W. H. (2003). 'China Share Issue Privatization: The Extent of its Success'. *Journal of Financial Economics*, 70/2: 183–222.

Tanzi, V. and Schuknecht, L. (1997). 'Reconsidering the Fiscal Role of Government: The International Perspective'. *American Economic Review*, 87/2: 164–8.

Temple, J. (1999). 'A Positive Effect of Human Capital on Growth'. *Economics Letters*, 65/1: 131–4.

Temple, J. (2001). 'Generalizations that Aren't? Evidence on Education and Growth'. *European Economic Review*, 45/4–6: 905–18.

Tian, L. and Estrin, S. (2008). 'Retained State Shareholding in Chinese PLCs: Does Government Ownership Always Reduce Corporate Value?' *Journal of Comparative Economics*, 36/1: 74–89.

Tseng, W. and Zebregs, H. (2002). 'Foreign Direct Investment in China: Some Lessons for other Countries'. IMF Policy Discussion Paper, 02/3.

United Nations Conference on Trade and Development (UNCTAD) (2006). *World Investment Report*. Washington, DC: United Nations Publications.

Van Reenen, J. and Yueh, L. (2012). 'Why has China Grown so Fast? The Role of International Technology Transfers'. London School of Economics and Political Science, Centre for Economic Performance, Discussion Paper No. DP1121, pp. 1–24.

Vining, A. and Boardman, A. E. (1992). 'Ownership Versus Competition: Efficiency in Public Enterprise'. *Public Choice*, 73: 205–39.

Walder, A. G. (1986). *Communist Neo-Traditionalism: Work and Authority in Chinese Industry*. Berkeley: University of California Press.

Waldinger, R. (1996). *Still the Promised City: African-Americans and New Immigration in Postindustrial New York*. Cambridge, Massachusetts: Harvard University Press.

Wang, T., Maruyam, A., and Kikuchi, M. (2000). 'Rural-urban Migration and Labour Markets in China: A Case Study in a North East Province'. *Developing Economies*, 38/1: 80–104.

Wang, Y. and Yao, Y. (2003). 'Sources of China's Economic Growth: 1952–99: Incorporating Human Capital Accumulation'. *China Economic Review*, 14/1: 32–52.

Wank, D. L. (1995). 'Bureaucratic Patronage and Private Business: Changing Networks of Power in Urban China', in A. G. Walder (ed.), *The Waning of the Communist State: Economic Origins of Political Decline in China and Hungary*. Berkeley: University of California Press.

Wasserman, S. and Faust, K. (1994). *Social Network Analysis: Methods and Applications*. Cambridge: Cambridge University Press.

Wei, S. J. (1993). 'The Open Door Policy and China's Rapid Growth: Evidence from City-level Data'. NBER Working Paper, 4602.

Wei, Y. Q., Liu, X. M., Parker, D., and Vaidya, K. (1999). 'The Regional Distribution of Foreign Direct Investment in China'. *Regional Studies*, 33/9: 857–67.

Wen, M. (2007). 'A Panel Study on China—Foreign Direct Investment, Regional Market Conditions, and Regional Development: A Panel Study on China'. *Economics of Transition*, 15/1: 125–51.

Whalley, J., and Xin, X. (2010). 'China's FDI and Non-FDI Economies and the Sustainability of Future High Chinese Growth'. *China Economic Review*, 21/1: 123–35.

Windmeijer, F. (2005). 'A Finite Sample Correction for the Variance of Linear Efficient Two-step GMM Estimators'. *Journal of Econometrics*, 126/1: 25–51.

Wolf, M. (2009). *Fixing Global Finance*. New Haven: Yale University Press.

Woo, W. T. (1995). 'Comments on Wei's (1995) Foreign Direct Investment in China: Sources and Consequences', in A. Krueger (ed.), *Financial Deregulation and Integration in East Asia*. Chicago: University of Chicago Press, 166–89.

Woo, W. T. (2008). 'Understanding the Sources of Friction in U.S.-China Trade Relations: The Exchange Rate Debate Diverts Attention from Optimum Adjustment'. *Asian Economic Papers*, 7/3: 61–95.

World Bank (1997). *China 2020*. Washington, DC: World Bank.

Wu, H. X. (2001). 'China's Comparative Labor Productivity Performance in Manufacturing, 1952–1997: Catching up or Falling Behind?' *China Economic Review*, 12/2–3: 172–89.

Wu, X. (2002). 'Embracing the Market: Entry into Self-Employment in Transitional China, 1978–1996'. William Davidson Working Paper No. 512.

Wu, Y. (2003). 'Has Productivity Contributed to China's Growth'. *Pacific Economic Review*, 8/1: 15–30.

Xia, J., Li, S., and Long, C. (2009). 'The Transformation of Collectively Owned Enterprises and its Outcomes in China, 2000–05'. *World Development*, 37/10: 1651–62.

Yan, Y. (1996). *The Flow of Gifts: Reciprocity and Social Networks in a Chinese Village*. Palo Alto, California: Stanford University Press.

Yang, H. (2001). 'Banking Reform: The Continuing Challenge of Creating Sound Commercial Banks', in O. K. Tam (ed.), *Financial Reform in China*. London: Routledge.

Yang, M. M. (1994). *Gifts, Favors and Banquets: The Art of Social Relationships in China*. Ithaca, New York: Cornell University Press.

Yang, Y. and Xin, X. (1999). 'A Report on Laid-Offs and Re-Employment' [*Xiagang Zhiyuan Jiben Shenhuo Baozhang he Zaijiuye de Diaocha*], in X. Ru, S. Y. Liu, and T. L. Dan (eds.), *1999 Analyses and Forecasts Regarding Chinese Society [1999 Zhongguo Sehuai Xinxiang Fenxi Yu Yuzhe]*. Beijing: Sociological Literature Publishing House (in Chinese).

Yao, Y. (2001). 'Social Exclusion and Economic Discrimination: The Status of Migration in China's Coastal Rural Area'. Peking University, China Centre for Economic Research (CCER) Working Paper No. E2001005.

Yao, Y. and Yueh, L. (2009). 'Law, Finance and Economic Growth in China: An Introduction'. *World Development* (Special Issue on Law, Finance, and Economic Growth in China), 37/4: 753–62.

Young, A. (2003). 'Gold into Base Metals: Productivity Growth in the People's Republic of China during the Reform Period'. *Journal of Political Economy*, 111/6: 1220–61.

Young, S., and Lan, P. (1997). 'Technology Transfer to China through Foreign Direct Investment'. *Regional Studies*, 31/7: 669–79.

Yueh, L. (2004). 'Wage Reforms in China During the 1990s'. *Asian Economic Journal*, 18/2: 149–64.

Yueh, L. (2006). 'Social Capital, Unemployment and Women's Labour Market Outcomes in Urban China', in S. Li and H. Sato (eds.), *Unemployment, Inequality and Poverty in Urban China*. London: RoutledgeCurzon.

Yueh, L. (2007). 'Global Intellectual Property Rights and Economic Growth'. *Northwestern Journal of Technology and Intellectual Property*, 5/3: 436–48.

Yueh, L. (2008). 'How Productive is Chinese Labour? The Contributions of Labour Market Reform, Globalisation and Competition'. University of Oxford Department of Economics Discussion Paper No. 418.

Yueh, L. (2009). 'Patent Laws and Innovation in China'. *International Review of Law and Economics,* 29/4: 304–13.

Yueh, L. (2010a). *The Economy of China.* Cheltenham: Edward Elgar.

Yueh, L. (2010b). 'The U.S., China and Global Imbalances'. *China Economic Journal,* 3/1: 33–48.

Yueh, L. (2010c). 'Accounting for Labour Productivity Growth in China in the 2000s'. University of Oxford, St Edmund Hall, China Growth Centre (CGC) Discussion Paper No. 1, pp. 1–65.

Yueh, L. (2011). *Enterprising China: Business, Economic, and Legal Developments Since 1979.* Oxford: Oxford University Press.

Yusuf, S. (1994). 'China's Macroeconomic Performance and Management during Transition'. *Journal of Economic Perspective,* 8/2: 71–92.

Zhang, J., Wan, G., and Jin, Y. (2007). 'The Financial Deepening-productivity Nexus in China: 1987–2001'. *Journal of Chinese Economic and Business Studies,* 5/1: 37–49.

Zhang, J., Zhang, L., Rozelle, S., and Boucher, S. (2006). 'Self-employment with Chinese Characteristics: The Forgotten Engine of Rural China's Growth'. *Contemporary Economic Policy,* 24/3: 446–58.

Zhao, Y. (1997). 'Rural Labour Migration and the Role of Education'. *Jingji Yanjiu,* 2: 37–42 (in Chinese).

Zhao, Y. (1999). 'Labor Migration and Earnings Differences: The Case of Rural China'. *Economic Development and Cultural Change,* 47/4: 767–82.

Zheng, J., Bigsten, A., and Hu, A. (2009). 'Can China's Growth be Sustained? A Productivity Perspective'. *World Development* (Special Issue on Law, Finance, and Economic Growth in China), 37/4: 874–88.

Zheng, J. and Hu, A. (2006). 'An Empirical Analysis of Provincial Productivity in China 1979–2001'. *Journal of Chinese Economic and Business Studies,* 4/3: 221–39.

Zheng, J., Liu, X., and Bigsten, A. (2003). 'Efficiency, Technical Progress, and Best Practice in Chinese State Enterprises 1980–1994'. *Journal of Comparative Economics,* 31/1: 134–52.

Zheng, Z. and Zhao, Y. (2002). 'China's Terms of Trade in Manufactures'. UNCTAD Discussion Paper No. 161.

Zhong, Z. (2005). 'Migration, Labor Market Flexibility, and Wage Determination in China: A Review'. Institute for the Study of Labor (IZA) EconWPA 0507009.

Index

Abraham, K. 185
Acemoglu, D. 4, 7, 19, 32, 33, 35, 41, 52, 56, 303
Adam, C. 90
Adrian, T. 269, 281
Aghion, P. 11
Aitken, B, J. 156
adverse selection 185
Aivazian, V, A. 95
Akerlof, G. A. 185
Albaladejo, M. 173, 259
Alderman, H. 113, 118
Alford, W. 40
Allen, F. 4, 32, 35, 91, 231, 304, 312
allocative efficiency 87–90
alternative dispute resolution (ADR) 54–5
Anderson, T. W. 215
Anti-Monopoly Law 31, 42–3, 260, 309, 312
Appleton, S. 145, 150–1, 192
Arayama, Y. 11
arbitration 54–5
Arellano, M. 78
Arrow, K. A. 184
Ashenfelter, O. 192
Aziz, J. 8

Bai, C. 286
Bai, Y. 295, 308, 314
Baker, G. 232
Banerjee, A. 204, 231, 236
Bank for International Settlements (BIS), Financial Stability Board (FSB) 44, 55, 318
banks:
  central 275–7, 307
  commercial 22, 315
  credit 237
  loans 26
  losses 277
  reforms 307–8
Banner, S. 41
Bartlett, R. L. 185
Bao, Q. 14
Barro, R. J. 11

Basel accords 55
Bean, C. 276, 289
Bayoumi, T. 314
Becker, G. S. 113–14, 115
Benhabib, J. 11
Bergsten, C. F. 269, 283, 296
Berkowitz, D. 41
Bernanke, B. 269
Bernard, H. R. 212
Berthelemy, J. C. 13
Bian, Y. 185, 186, 232
Biggeri, M. 8
Bigsten, A. 10, 15, 167, 312
Bils, M. 11
Bishop, M. 90
Blanchard, O. 291, 294, 317
Blundell, R. W. 78
Blomström, M. 67, 86, 156, 172
Bloom, N. 100
Blundell, R. W. 215
Boardman, A. E. 94
Bond, S. R. 78
Borensztein, E. 9, 14
Bosworth, B. 16, 55, 167, 283
Boucher, S. 204, 216, 232
Boyreau-Debray, G. 8
Brandt, L. 10, 63, 88
Brock, G. J. 34
Brun, J. F. 14
Budgetary Contracting System 22, 26
Budgetary Responsibility system 22
Burt, R. S. 185, 187

Caballero, R. J. 269, 279, 283
Cai, F. 145, 308
Cain, G. G. 146
capital account 3
  liberalization 280, 283, 296
capital accumulation 10, 15, 16, 167–8
  see also human capital
capital market 8, 20–1, 91–2, 292
Carlin, W. 289
Cavendish, W. 90
Chamberlin 289

Chang, L. 13,
Chang, X. 186
Chen, B. 8, 12
Chen, C. 13
Chen, Z. 33, 45, 49, 50, 51, 56, 206
Cheung, K. 172
Chi, W. 12
China:
    compared to US 41–52
    a competitive threat 262
    economic structure 284–6
    rebalancing 281–96
China Banking Regulatory Commission
    (CBRC) 22, 31
China effect 261–7
China Insurance Regulatory Commission
    (CIRC) 31
China International Economic and Trade
    Arbitration Commission (CIETAC) 29, 55
China Paradox 32–9, 304
China Securities Regulatory Commission
    (CSRC) 31, 44, 49–51, 311
Chinese-foreign Equity Joint Venture
    Law 42, 54
Chinese-foreign joint ventures (JVs) 15–16,
    27, 29
Chinn, M. D. 269, 283
Choo, C. 26
Chow, G. C. 9, 11
Chuang, Y. 156
civil law 32–3, 40, 49, 310
Clarke, D. C. 28, 41, 55
Clarke, D. C. 47, 54, 206, 311
Coase, R. 32, 34, 303
Coe, D. 15
Coffee, Jr. J. C. 33, 40–1, 45, 49, 310
collectively-owned enterprises (COEs) 90, 95
Collier, P. 124
Collins, S. 16, 167, 283
Combes, K. L. 14
commodity prices 261–2, 268, 272
common law 32–3, 40
Communist Party 41, 129, 310
    12th Congress 305
    entrepreneurs 232, 242, 246
    membership 186–7, 189–90, 192, 198, 203,
        209, 226
Communist revolution 111
Company Law 29, 30, 31, 47, 48, 93
Competing Claims Equilibrium (CCE) 291,
    297–300
competition 262
    from China 262
    factor market 64
    and firm performance 94–5

foreign 310
    from multinationals 155
    labour market 65
    product market 64, 66
Constitution 310
consumption 264, 285, 317
contract enforcement 36, 232
    informal 22–3, 28–30, 52–3
Contract Law 42, 48, 91, 310
Contract Responsibility system (CRS) 22, 24–6,
    29, 34, 305
contracting:
    institutions 35
    relational 237
    security 303, 304
copyright law 170
Cordell, D. D. 143
corporate governance 92
corporate law 47–8
corporatization 90–2, 109, 308, 309–10
    see also incorporation
corruption 37
Cragg, J. G. 215
credit networks 206
Cull, R. 32, 35, 304

Dai, E. 9
Dam, K. W. 35, 303
Dasgupta, P. 184, 185
De Gregorio, J. 14
Deaton, A. 113
Dees, S. 13
demand:
    aggregate 292–6
    domestic 256, 263, 281–5, 289–91, 317
    function 290–1
Démurger, S. 11, 13
Deng Xiaoping 24, 173, 257, 305
dispute resolution mechanism (DSU) 55
Dickens, W. T. 146
Djankov, A. 156, 205, 232
Djankov, S. 207, 216, 233, 237, 245
Dobson, W. 15
Donald, S. G. 215
Dong, X. 92, 95
Dougherty, S. 69, 71, 88, 96, 157
Du, Y. 29, 50, 145
Dual Track (Plan and Market) System 305
dual track policies 4
Duenwald, C. K. 8
Duflo, E. 236
Durlauf, S. N. 187

Eaton, J. 15
Earl, J. 66

Economic and Trade Development Zones
(ETDZ) 176, 258
see also Special Economic Zones
education 205, 209, 212, 226, 232–4, 245,
248, 253
and economic growth 10–12
entrepreneurs 232–3, 238, 242, 245–6
household head 117–18, 192
household spending on 113–20
and mobility 141
and personal ability 150
returns to 2, 61, 110, 194, 203
higher 160, 164
years of 129, 133, 150–1, 188–90, 208,
224–5, 242–3, 246
see also human capital
efficiency 292, 294, 312, 314, 316–17
allocative versus technical 63–5, 87–90, 108
and technology 10, 15, 67, 79, 86
employment:
private sector 65
SOEs 65, 66
see also job mobility; job tenure; labour;
self-employment
Enterprise Bankruptcy Law 311
entrepreneurs 41
by province 253–5
Communist Party membership 232,
242, 246
education 232–3, 242, 245
income 243
legal constraints 248–53
migrants 233–4, 242, 246
motivation 236–48
rural 233
social networks 241–2, 245–6
source of capital 232
traits 239, 241
urban 233, 245
wealth 243, 245
see also private firms
entrepreneurship model 238–40
Estrin, S. 66, 91
European Union (EU) 263, 272, 273
Evans, D. 245
exchange rates 3, 289
fixed 277
flexible 280, 283, 296
pegged to US dollar 260–1
exports 3, 14, 63, 283
by firm type 76
collapse of 262–3, 280, 316
shares in global markets 84, 253, 256,
284, 286
technical make-up 173, 177–8, 180

factor market:
competition 64
distortions 314–15
factor reallocation 2, 60, 61
Fafchamps, M. 184
Fan, G. 35, 47, 206, 233, 305
Farber, H. S. 131
Farhi, E. 269, 279, 283
Faust, K. 187
Felmingham, B. S. 156
Feng, Y. 8, 12
financial crisis:
Asian 272, 279
global 263, 266, 268, 275–9, 318
financial repression 232, 237, 241, 248–53,
295, 312, 314–15, 319
financial system 260
deregulation 276, 279
and growth 8–9
liberalization 266
firm performance:
drivers of 98–106
and incorporation 101–3, 104–6
firms:
by ownership type 73–5, 160–1, 187
expectations of foreign firms 54–5
private 231–55, 266
savings 280, 286, 295–6
Five Year Plans:
9th 93, 113, 309
12th 317
Fleisher, B. 12, 14
foreign direct investment (FDI)
China 19, 68
controlled 3, 30, 259, 304–5, 305
outward 256, 265–6
spillovers 13–16, 154, 155–7, 180
foreign exchange reserves 257, 273–5
foreign invested enterprises (FIEs) 14, 91,
93, 257
Franks, J. R. 21, 52
Free Trade Zones (FTZs) 24, 258
see also Special Economic Zones
Frye, T. 204

G7 20
G20 281, 318
Gaetano, A. R. 143
Gao, J. 291
Garnaut, R. 237, 308
Ge, Y. 95
Gedajlovic, E. R. 90
Gelfer, S. 35, 41, 53
Gemmell, N. 11
General Principles of Civil Law 310

Germany 41, 275, 282, 284, 285
Giavazzi, F. 291, 294, 317
Gibbons, R. 232
gifts 214
  see also social capital
Giles, J. 111
Glaeser, E. 35, 186, 204, 303
global economy 271–5
  imbalances 267–81, 272–3, 275, 278,
    279, 296
  rebalancing 280–1
global labour force 271
global trade 282
globalization 67–8, 256–300
going out policy 48, 266, 280, 308, 318
  going global 265–7, 319
  going out bringing in policy 256
Goodhue, R. 205
Gompers, P. 233
Gourinchas, P.-O. 269, 279, 283
government:
  optimal size 316–18
  permissions 231–2
  role of 301–20
  savings 292
  spending 294, 316–18, 319
  see also state sector
Graham, E. M. 13
Granovetter, M. 184, 185, 203
Great Moderation 268, 269, 271,
    272, 276
Great Recession 263
Greenwald, B. 124
Gregory, J. W. 143
Greif, A. 28
Grossman, G. M. 15
growth 19, 20, 265
  catch-up 12–16, 154–83, 259, 284
  drivers of 1–2, 16–17
  endogenous 10–12, 110–53
  and FDI 171–2
  and financial sector 8–9
  from private firms 231–55, 266
  and human capital 10–12, 110–53
  and JVs 168
  and patent laws 45–7
  provincial differences 8
  and technology 12–16, 154–83
growth theories:
  and institutions 4, 7–9, 19–59
  neoclassical 9–10, 60–109
  standard 2–5
Guangdong 24, 69, 77, 84, 96, 146, 157, 173,
    174–5, 180, 257–8
guanxi 5, 184–92, 203–5
  see also social capital, social network

Guiso, L. 9
Gylfason, T. 13

Haddad, L. 113, 118,
Haddad, M. 156
Haier 265
Hammermesh, L. A. 47
Hansen, L. P. 78
Hao, C. 8
Hare, D. 145
Harrison, A. E. 156
Harrold, P. 13
Hasan, I. 7
Hashimoto, M. 124
Hausmann, H. 44
Hay, D. 90
He, P. 69, 71, 88, 96, 157
Helpman, E. 15
Herd, R. 69, 71, 88, 96, 157
High-Technology Development Zones
    (HTDZs) 24, 177, 258
  see also Special Economic Zones
Higuchi, Y. 125
Himmelberg, C. P. 91
Ho, P. 28, 34
Hoddinott, J. 113, 118
Hoekman, B. M. 156
Hoff, K. 7
Holtz-Eakin, D. 233
Hosios, A. J. 124
Household Responsibility System (HRS) 22, 23,
    25, 29, 173
household savings 280, 292, 293–4
Howitt, P. 11
Hsu, P. 156
Hu, A. 9, 65, 67, 312
Hu, A. G. Z. 10, 63, 156, 167, 172
Hu, D. 12
Hu, Y. 95
Hu, Z. L. 9, 11
Hua, J. 92
Huang, J. 11, 95, 314
Huang, Y. 27, 54, 295, 305, 314
Hubbard, R. G. 91
Hugo, G. 143
hukou system 142–4, 146, 149–52, 293, 313
human capital 16, 178, 203
  by gender 114, 115–20
  and growth 10–12
  investment model 113–21
  see also education

ICBC 311
Imbens, G. W. 100, 101
income:
  determinants of 136–8

entrepreneurs 243
  gender differences 211, 226, 227
  and social capital 192–204
incorporation 90–2
  by ownership type 92–5
  definition 97
  and firm characteristics 101–3
  and firm performance 104–6
  and output 103, 106–8
  and value-added 103
  see also corporatization
India 61, 63, 168, 268, 271, 272
industrial output 76, 106–8, 308, 313
industrialization 2, 42, 44, 305
initial public offerings (IPOs) 309
innovation 155, 169–71
  by region 178, 183
  determinants of 177–82
  production function 172
Institute of Economics, Chinese Academy of
    Social Sciences (CASS) 127, 148, 187, 207
institutions:
  contracting 35, 59
  and growth 4, 7–9
  informal 5, 33
  property rights 35
institutional innovation 4, 19, 22, 23–7,
intellectual property rights (IPRs) 155, 169–71
  and the WTO 12–13, 21, 31–2, 55, 57–8
interest rates 291–2, 295, 296
  liberalization 313–14
international financial institutions (IFI) 44
International Monetary Fund (IMF) 281
  COFER 275
investment 171–3, 264, 319
  see also foreign direct investment; human
    capital; R&D
iron rice bowl 2, 60, 64, 110, 125, 133, 242
Islam, N. 9, 11
Ito, H. 269, 283

Jacka, T. 143
Japan 275, 282
  civil law 40
  consumption 264, 285
  domestic demand 263
  economic structure 284
  job tenure 123, 124
Javorick, B. 156, 172
Jefferson, G. H. 9–10, 19, 34, 63, 65, 67, 71, 95,
    156, 172, 303
Jia, H. 143, 145, 146, 151
Jin, Y. 9, 291
job mobility 122–42
  costs of 124, 141–2
  involuntary 122, 123–4, 131, 136, 139–40

and labour reforms 131–42
  latent 133–6
  measurement of 127–31
  migrants 140–2
  model 125–7
  urban residents 129–30
  voluntary 123–4, 131, 133, 139–40
  see also employment; labour; migrants
job tenure 123, 128–9
Johnson, S. 4, 7, 19, 32, 33, 35, 41, 52, 56, 303
joint ventures (JVs) 54, 259
  dataset 157–61
  and growth 168
  and productivity 168
  technology transfers 68–9, 76–7, 79, 154
Jones, C. L. 172, 177
Jones, W. C. 32, 40
judiciary 40

Khan, H. 9
Kikuchi, M. 145
Killworth, P. D. 212
Klenow, P. J. 11
Knight, J. 124, 143, 145, 186
knowledge production function 3–4
Kornai, J. 315
Kuo, C. C. 14

La Porta, R. 7, 33, 35, 40, 45, 303
labour:
  allocated 186
  global 271
  migrant 145–6
  misallocation 312–14
  reallocation 30, 63–4
  reforms 110–11
  sectoral shifts 88–90
  turnover 123
  see also employment; job mobility; migrants
labour market:
  age cohorts 187, 198, 224, 226
  competition 65, 147–52
  flexibility 65, 131
  insider-outside model 146
  ownership sector 187, 198, 200–1
  reforms 61, 64–9, 131–42
  segmented 146
  and social capital 185, 203–4
labour productivity 60–4, 77–86, 293, 313
  by ownership type 71–3, 79, 83
  comparative 61, 62, 63
  estimation 78–9, 80–2
  growth 71, 79, 81–3, 108
  see also productivity
Lai, M. 14
Laibson, D. 186

Lam, K. J. 192
land tenure 29
Lardy, N. R. 314
law 40–1
  Anti-Monopoly Law 31, 309, 312
  bankruptcy 29, 31, 311
  Chinese-foreign Equity Joint Venture
    Law 42, 54
  Company Law 29, 30, 31, 47–8, 93
  Contract Law 42, 48, 91, 310
  copyright 179
  effectiveness of 35
  enforcement 171
  General Principles of Civil Law 310
  Individual Wholly-owned Enterprises 42, 47
  and markets 34–7, 51–2
  Mergers and Acquisitions (M&A) Law 29, 31,
    48, 309, 311
  partnership 47
  patent 12, 29, 45–7, 169, 170, 183
  Property Law 27, 34, 37, 303, 310
  rule of 35, 318–19
  Securities Investment Fund Law 48
  Securities Law 33, 50
  SOE Law 30
  see also legal system
lawyers 240
lay-off policy 63, 65, 111, 144, 145, 236, 242, 308
Lee, C. K. 186
legal system:
  civil and common 32–3, 40, 49, 303
  development measure 240
  effectiveness 303
  German 41
  Japan 40
  measures of 248–53
  provincial 253–5
  reform 20–1, 30–2, 260
  self-employment 206–7
  transplanted 35
  weak 91, 169, 237
Lehman Brothers 263, 277
Lenovo 31, 48, 265, 309
Levine, R. 317
Li, G. 14
Li, H. 11, 12, 192
Li, S. 95, 234
Liang, Z. 8
licensing 180
limited liability companies (LLCs) 91
Lin, A. 9
liquidity effect 267
Liu, X. 15
Liu, Z. 192
Long, C. 95
Lu, F. S. 314

manufacturing GDP per worker 61–3
marital status 212, 246
markets:
  domestic 266–7
  and law 34–7, 51–2
  product 64, 66
  state involvement 40
  see also labour market
Markusen, J. R. 156
Maruyam, A. 145
Meng, X. 145
Mergers and Acquisitions (M&A) Law 31,
    309, 311
migrant labour:
  demand for 146
  gender and region 145–6
migrants:
  and discrimination 142–52
  entrepreneurs 233–4, 242, 246
  job tenure 128–9
  see also job mobility
migration 125
  temporary 143
Mincer, J. 125
Ministry of Commerce 170, 307
Ministry of Labour (MOL) 112–13, 148
Miyoshi, K. 11
Mohapatra, S. 205, 232
Montgomery, J. D. 185
multinational companies (MNCs) 27, 32
  vertical linkages 155

National Bureau of Statistics of China
    (NBS) 69, 95, 127, 148, 154, 157, 187,
    207–8, 234
national champion strategy 311
National Copyright Administration 170
National Economic Research Institute (NERI),
    Marketization Index 84, 86
national oil companies (NOCs) 308
nationalization 112
network externalities 173
New York Stock Exchange (NYSE) 49
New Zealand 275
Non-Accelerating Inflation Rate of
    Unemployment (NAIRU) 291, 297–300

OECD 155, 156
Oi, J. C. 186
oil 261, 268, 272, 308
Open Port cities (OPC) 258
  see also Special Economic Zones
open-door policy 24, 54, 61, 173, 176, 256,
    257, 271, 281, 284
  see also exports; foreign direct
    investment (FDI)

openness 2–3, 178
  by province 84, 86
  provincial variation 161–2
Otsuka, K. 12
ownership:
  forms 96–8
  reforms 61

Pagano, M. 314
Parikh, A. 13
Park, A. 111
patent laws 12, 29, 45–7, 169,
    170, 183
  effectiveness 173–7
patents 57, 58, 155, 169–71
  by province 174–5, 180
  determinants of 169
  growth in 174–5
  production function 173, 177–82
  success rate 170, 174–5
Peng, S. 14
People's Bank of China (PBOC) 291, 307
Pissarides, C. A. 126
Pistor, K. 41, 47
political pluralism 7–8
population 261
price effect 268–70
  see also terms of trade
prices:
  commodity 261–2, 268, 272
  world 272
private firms 231–55, 266
  see also entrepreneurs
private property 315
privatization 90, 92–3
  share issue privatization (SIP) 93
production function 77–8
  innovation 172
  patents 173, 177–82
  value-added 164–5
productivity:
  and factor reallocation 2
  and firm ownership 160–1
  and JVs 168
  see also labour productivity; total factor
    productivity (TFP)
profit incentive 22, 112–13, 307
profit tax 305
Property Law 22, 27, 34, 37, 303, 310
property rights 33, 303
  contractually defined 27–8
  creation of 25–30, 310
  institutions of 35, 304
  measure of 36–7
  uncertain 19
Putterman, L. 95

Qian, J. 7, 8, 33, 156
Qian, M. 7, 8, 33
Qian, Y. 11
Qiu, J. 95

R&D 67
  regional 180, 181
  spending on 155, 170, 171, 172, 183
  studies of 14–15
Raisian, J. 124
Rajan, R. G. 8
Ran, J. 14
real estate 27, 237
redundancy programme 147
  see also xiangang
reform:
  dual track 23–4
  gradual 7–8, 15, 19, 32, 39
  policy milestones 21–2
  regulatory 49–51
  urban 307
regulatory quality 35–6
regulatory system, rules-based and
    principle-based 49
relational contracting 237
Renard, M. F. 14
Renelt, D. 317
reserve currency 273, 275, 279–81
  holdings 277–8
  price effect 267, 268–70
risk 204–5, 207, 213, 224–7
Rodríguez-Clare, A. 156
Rodrik, D. 14
Roubini, N. 314
Rousseau, P. L. 9
Rozelle, S. 205
Russia 66

Sacerdote, B. 186, 212
Shanghai 22, 33, 49, 71, 93, 113, 173, 174, 158,
Safarian, A. E. 15
Sala-i-Martin, X. 314
Salter-Swan model 286–92, 297–300
Sapienza, P. 9
Sato, H. 234
savings 273, 278
  corporate 295–6
  firms 264, 280, 286
  government 292
  high 312–14
  household 280, 292, 293–4
  motive 263–4
  precautionary 285, 293
Schuknecht, L. 317
Securities Investment Fund Law 48
Securities Law 33, 50

self-employment 30, 93
  by gender 208–9, 224, 230
  choice of 206, 207–27
  determinants of 205, 206, 216–25
  earnings 211
  legal system impact 206–7
  as second job 208, 225, 230
  and social networks 204–7, 213, 216,
    227, 230
  and unemployment 214, 224, 255–7
service sector 260, 285, 293–4
Shanghai 22, 33, 49, 71, 93, 113, 173, 174, 258
share issue privatization (SIP) 93
Shelley, G. H. 212
Shenzhen 22, 33, 49, 71, 93, 113, 146, 257, 278
Smyth, R. 11
social capital 52–3, 184–92
  endogenous 193
gifts 214
guanxi 5, 184–92, 203–5
  and income 192–204
  instrumental variables 192–4
  and labour market 185, 203–4
social networks 5, 129, 184–5
  and entrepreneurship 241, 245
  guanxi 5, 184–92, 203–5
  and self-employment 204–7, 213, 216,
    227, 230
  size of 187–8, 211–12, 241–2
social norms 184–5
sole proprietorships 91, 93, 310
Solinger, D. J. 143
Song, L. 95, 143, 145, 186, 192
Sonobe, T. 12
Sovereign Wealth Funds (SWF) 56
Soviet Union 301, 302
Special Economic Zones (SEZs) 3, 24, 146, 155,
    171, 176, 257, 305
Spiegel, M. M. 11
spillovers 13–16, 154, 155–7, 180
  see also foreign direct investment (FDI);
    technology transfers
stability 24, 30, 31, 304–5
Staiger, D. 214
State Asset Supervision and Administration
    Commission (SASAC) 50–1, 309,
    310–11, 315
State Intellectual Property Office (SIPO) 170
State Owned Enterprises Law 30
State Owned Enterprises (SOEs) 26, 34, 301
  employment 65, 66
  incorporation 90
  privatization 27–8, 308
  reform 302, 304–9
state sector:
  decentralization 26

restructuring 65
scope and size 316–18
see also government
Stiglitz, J. 124
Stock, J. H. 214
stock exchanges 8, 27, 29, 40, 49, 78, 160, 309
  listing 73, 76
  Shanghai and Shenzhen 22, 33, 71, 93,
    95, 113
Su, J. 10, 63, 95
Sun, H. S. 13
Sun, L. 56
Sun, Q. 95
supply networks 206
  see also foreign direct investment

Tanzi, V. 317
TCL 31, 48, 265, 309
technical efficiency 10, 87–90, 108
technology 61, 304–5
  and efficiency 67
  and growth 12–16, 154–83
technology transfers 108
  JVs 68–9, 76–7, 79
  model 161–7
  spillovers 13–16, 171–2
  and TFP 167
  terms of trade 262, 267–8
  see also price effect
Tobin, D. 56
Tong, W. H. 95
total factor productivity (TFP) 2
  by industry 85
  by ownership 83–4
  slowdown 9–10
  and technology 61, 167
  see also productivity
Township and Village Enterprises (TVEs) 23,
    25–6, 29, 93, 304
Trademark Office 170

Unel, B. 95
unemployment:
  disguised 144
  forms of 111
  migrants 263
  and self-employment 214, 224, 255–7
  urban 145
United Kingdom 33, 49, 261
United States 4, 33, 61
  budget deficit 273
  compared to China 23, 41–52
  consumption 264, 285
  corporate law 47–8
  Delaware General Corporation Law 44, 51
  dollar 260–1, 267, 268–70, 273, 275, 279–81

domestic demand 263
economic structure 284
entrepreneurs 233
Federal Reserve 277
Glass-Steagall Act 276–7
Gramm-Leach-Bliley Act 276
incorporation 90, 94
job tenure 123, 124
monetary policy 269–70, 277, 296
patent laws 45–7
savings rate 278, 280
Securities and Exchange Commission
(SEC) 44, 49–51
social networks 212
urbanization 293, 313, 317

Van Reenen, J. 15, 17
Venables, A. J. 156
Voon, J. P. 14

Wachtel, P. 7
Wage Adjustment Tax 112–13
wage bill 73–5, 165
wage-employed 208, 210–11, 216, 241–3, 245
wages 127, 133, 136, 141, 146–7
centrally determined 60, 122, 185, 187, 203
growth 293, 313
of Communist Party members 192
reforms 24, 61, 64, 111–13, 122
and social capital 193–4
Wan, G. 9
Wang, J. 145
Wang, X. J. 12, 314
Wang, Y. 11
wealth:
entrepreneurs 243, 245
urban 240
Wei, S. J. 13
Wen, M. 14

Whalley, J. 14
wholly foreign-owned enterprises
(WFOEs) 54, 93
Windmeijer, F. 79
World Bank 9, 69, 157
Worldwide Governance Indicators 35
World Trade Organisation (WTO) 22, 39, 41,
50, 61, 64, 162, 270, 272, 282
Dispute Settlement Mechanism 170–1
intellectual property rights (IPR) 12–13, 21,
31–2, 169
Most Favoured Nation 259
Multi-Fibre Agreement 262
TRIPS 46, 55, 57–8, 170, 183
Wu, H. X. 63
Wu, X. 205, 232

Xia, J. 95
Xia, Q. 192
xiagang 111, 144, 145, 149, 206, 308
see also unemployment
Xiao, S. 9
Xin, X. 14

Yang, C. H. 14
Yao, Y. 11, 95, 145, 314
Young, A. 9, 168
Yueh, L. 15, 17

Zhang, J. 9, 111, 145, 205
Zhang, Q. 156
Zhang Zemin 310
Zhao, M. Q. 12, 14
Zheng, J. 9, 10, 15, 167
Zhong, Z. 145
Zhou, M. 7
Zhou, X. 95
Zhu, X. 10, 63
Zingales, L. 8, 9